Critical Research in Sport, Health and Physical Education

Within the overlapping fields of the sociology of sport, physical education and health education, the use of critical theories and the critical research paradigm has grown in scope. Yet what social impact has this research had?

This book considers the capacity of critical research and associated social theory to play an active role in challenging social injustices or at least in 'making a difference' within health and physical education (HPE) and sporting contexts. It also examines how the use of different social theories impacts sport policies, national curricula and health promotion activities, as well as the practices of HPE teaching and sport training and competition.

Critical Research in Sport, Health and Physical Education is a valuable resource for academics and students working in the fields of research methods, sociology of sport, physical education and health.

Richard Pringle is Professor of Sport and Physical Education at Monash University, Australia, and is on the editorial boards of the *International Review for the Sociology of Sport* and *Curriculum Studies in Health and Physical Education*. He is a critical qualitative researcher who examines diverse socio-cultural and pedagogical issues associated with sport, exercise, health, physical education, bodies and gender relations.

Håkan Larsson is Professor of Physical Education and Sport Pedagogy at The Swedish School of Sport and Health Sciences, Sweden, where he heads the research group for physical education and sport pedagogy. His main interests concern sport, gender and sexuality, and teaching and learning in physical education. In 2015 he held the honorary scholar lecture at the British Educational Research Association's Physical Education and Sport Pedagogy Invisible College.

Göran Gerdin is Senior Lecturer of Physical Education and Sport at Linnaeus University, Sweden, and is on the editorial board of the journal *Curriculum Studies in Health and Physical Education*. His research focuses on how issues of gender, bodies, spaces and (dis)pleasures shape students' participation, enjoyment and identities in school health and physical education.

Routledge Research in Sport, Culture and Society

For more information about this series, please visit: https://www.routledge.com/sport/series/RRSCS

Critical Research in Sport, Health and Physical Education

How to Make a Difference

Edited by
Richard Pringle, Håkan Larsson
and Göran Gerdin

Routledge
Taylor & Francis Group

LONDON AND NEW YORK

First published 2019
by Routledge
2 Park Square, Milton Park, Abingdon, Oxon OX14 4RN

and by Routledge
711 Third Avenue, New York, NY 10017

Routledge is an imprint of the Taylor & Francis Group, an Informa business

© 2019 selection and editorial matter, Richard Pringle, Håkan Larsson and
Göran Gerdin; individual chapters, the contributors

British Library Cataloguing-in-Publication Data
A catalogue record for this book is available from the British Library

Library of Congress Cataloging-in-Publication Data
A catalog record has been requested for this book

ISBN: 978-1-138-57167-9 (hbk)
ISBN: 978-0-203-70259-8 (ebk)

Typeset in Goudy Std
by Cenveo® Publisher Services

MIX
Paper from
responsible sources
FSC
www.fsc.org   FSC™ C013985

Printed in the United Kingdom
by Henry Ling Limited

Contents

Figures

Contributors

Janice Atkin, The University of Queensland, Australia

Lisette Burrows, University of Waikato, New Zealand

Jayne Caudwell, University of Bournemouth, UK

Simon C. Darnell, University of Toronto, Canada

Jim Denison, University of Alberta, Canada

Michael Gard, University of Queensland, Australia

Billy Hawkins, University of Houston, USA

Chris Hickey, Deakin University, Australia

Brendan Hokowhitu, University of Waikato, New Zealand

David Kirk, University of Strathclyde, UK and University of Queensland, Australia

Deana Leahy, Monash University, Australia

Doune Macdonald, The University of Queensland, Australia

Pirkko Markula, University of Alberta, Canada

Roy McCree, The University of the West Indies, Trinidad and Tobago

Louise McCuaig, The University of Queensland, Australia

J. P. Mills, University of Alberta, Canada

Amanda Mooney, Deakin University, Australia

Rod Philpot, University of Auckland, New Zealand

Carolyn Pluim, Northern Illinois University, USA

Mikael Quennerstedt, Örebro Universitet, Sweden

Wayne Smith, University of Auckland, New Zealand

Graham Spacey, University of Brighton, UK

Richard Tinning, University of Queensland, Australia and University of Southern Denmark, Denmark

Jan Wright, University of Wollongong, Australia

Chapter 1

Introduction: Are we making a difference?

Richard Pringle, Håkan Larsson and Göran Gerdin

Introduction: Are we making a difference?

In this co-edited text, *Critical Research in Sport, Health and Physical Education: How to Make a Difference*, we consider the capacity of critical research within the fields of sport, health and physical education to challenge injustices and produce social transformation. In examining these key issues, we are interested in understanding how the use of different research approaches and social theories shape the research process and influence sport policies, national curricula and health promotion activities as well as the practices of school health and physical education (HPE) teaching and sporting practices. Although there are relatively clear distinctions between critical thinking, critical pedagogy, critical theory and critical research (see Kincheloe, McLaren, Steinberg and Monzó, 2018), within this text we are primarily concerned with researchers who accept that the social world is fundamentally unfair and correspondingly use research as a tool to challenge inequities, inequalities and injustices.

At the outset of this text, we wish to dismiss the view that if critical research aims to make a real difference then the focus should be specifically on overtly political issues such as neoliberal capitalism or the growth of the precariat class. We clearly do not dismiss the importance of such critical research, yet we acknowledge that sport and HPE can have significant impact, both positively and negatively, on a range of social issues and injustices. Nelson Mandela (cited in Hansard, 2002) quixotically asserted that: "We can reach far more people through sport than we can through political or educational programmes." Mandela subsequently alleged that sporting practices are "more powerful than politics." Although a debatable claim, we acknowledge that sport and HPE play important roles in shaping concepts and practices concerning embodiment (e.g. obesity, dis/ability, beauty), subjectivities (e.g. sexualities, genders, ethnicities, nationalities, religious affiliations) and health (e.g. fit, youthful, physically active, lean). Sport and HPE can therefore have significant impact on relations of power between different individuals and groups of people and are worthy of critical attention.

We are particularly interested in understanding the various research strategies and processes employed for producing social change. This is not to suggest that we are looking for select solutions on strategies of resistance or transformation, but believe there is value in examining 'ethical practices', which is how we conceive the processes of doing critical research. In drawing from Richard Bernstein's (2011) deliberations on 'going beyond objectivism and relativism', we note:

> In ethical know-how there can be no prior knowledge of the right means by which we realize the end in a particular situation. For the end itself is only concretely specified in deliberating about the means appropriate to a particular situation. (p. 147)

"For the times they are a changing ..." (?)

We are writing this introductory chapter in a given historic moment within which we have witnessed tremendous growth in critical research and various forms of social activism. The protest movements that emerged and proliferated in the 1950, 1960s and 1970s—such as focused on women's 'liberation', civil, indigenous and gay rights—have been accompanied, *typically afterwards*, by a proliferation of critical research projects and publications. This combination of activism, critical research and associated public debate has undoubtedly had impact on policy and social practice. Within post-industrial nations we have observed associated changes in a number of specific areas, such as, the legality of same-sex marriage (now in over 26 countries) and a trend towards equal pay for males and females. More broadly, we acknowledge that there has been a growing acceptance of the tenets of liberal feminism in many western democracies and various attempts, in different countries, to challenge the problems associated with racism and colonisation. Bob Dylan's (1964) anthemic proclamation "that the times are a changing" appears correct.

Yet with hindsight we do not think that it is time for celebration, as we have less confidence in Dylan's secondary assertions that: "the order is rapidly fading and the first one now will later be last." By contrast, we suggest that the existing social order and associated sets of power relations appear somewhat unchanged. Richard Edwards and Tara Fenwick (2015), in a more categorical manner, asserted that despite the best of intentions, critical researchers have "more or less successfully avoided changing the existing reproductions of power and inequalities" (p. 1385). Although such a bold assertion is open to critique, we do at times still question, 'what substantive power-relation changes have been made'?

We could draw on numerous cases to illustrate our concerns but three global political examples suffice: These are the times, we suggest, within which the *hope* that underpinned the election of Barack Obama, has seemingly dissolved and 'white privilege' appears, once again, entrenched via Trump politics and disparaging talk of 'shithole countries' (with particular reference to El Salvador, Haiti and African nations) and 'Mexican rapists' (see Davis, Stolberg and Kaplan, 2018). Although it is 150 years after the end of slavery and five decades after the civil rights movements, the wealth gap between African American and white families in the United States has tripled since 1984 (Shapiro, Meschede and Osoro, 2013). These are also the times within which the assumed set of emancipatory changes associated with feminism and popular culture have been repositioned via the global revelations of sexual abuse, thus indicating that feminist scholarship and activism, such as the #MeToo campaign, are still needed in the contemporary post-feminist context. Lastly, these are the times when the global occupy movement, which raged against socio-economic inequalities in 2011–12, appear to be a distant memory with revelations that the cumulative wealth of the world's billionaires has increased by 18 per cent over the last year (Dolan and Kroll, 2018).

We use the above three examples to indicate that although some specific social justice 'wins' have occurred in recent years that the broad pattern of power relations, that tend to stabilise patterns of privilege and disadvantage, remain seemingly intact. Some might feel that our view concerning the apparent lack of substantive power-relation changes is pessimistic. Yet we concur with George Sage (1990) who argued that criticism, even if it might seem unduly negative, "is actually a form of commitment, a way of saying: There are problems here and unwarranted abuses; let's identify them and work to make things better for everyone" (p. 4).

The rise and impact of critical research in sport, health and physical education

Within the overlapping fields of HPE and the sociology of sport we acknowledge the concomitant growth in the use of critical research and qualitative methods over the last three decades (see Donnelly, 2015; Leahy, Wright and Penney, 2017; Sage, 2015). In fact, qualitative/critical research approaches now dominate research publications in select journals within these fields (e.g. *Critical Public Health; International Review for the Sociology of Sport; Quest; Sport, Education and Society; Sociology of Sport Journal*). We further acknowledge that although the related critical research findings tend to circulate narrowly (see Atkinson, 2011; Zirin, 2008), they are at times drawn upon to inform debate, policy and practice. Donnelly and Atkinson (2015) illustrate, as an example, how Loy and McElvogue's (1970) formative research on racial segregation in sport 'filtered down' and encouraged further research that has contributed to making a social difference. We are also confident that pressure from feminist activists/scholars (e.g. Donnelly and Donnelly, 2013; Kane et al., 2007) has played a role in contributing to the seemingly revolutionary growth in female sport participation and the associated trend towards an equal number of events for female and male competitors at the Olympics. In similar respect, we acknowledge that research efforts have contributed to produce an assortment of specific transformations, such as, the development of 'socio-critical curriculums' in HPE in Australia and New Zealand.[1]

Despite these gains we are concerned that many of the prime socio-cultural issues that were critically examined in the 1980s remain firmly on the contemporary research agenda: indicating that these social problems and associated power relation issues are still in need of attention.[2] Although we recognize that it is complex, perhaps impossible, to ascertain with any certainty the influence of critical research, the following three examples suggest that our ability to orchestrate change in our own fields has been somewhat underwhelming.

Firstly, Toni Bruce (2015) laments that if we exclude the unique and nationalistic coverage devoted to the Olympics that "30 years of activism and pressure on sports media to increase both the quality and quantity of coverage" (p. 383) devoted to sportswomen has produced nominal change in the majority of western countries. She adds, "sportswomen languish at about 10 per cent of everyday coverage" (p. 383) and "the default settings of mediasport—such as marginalization, ambivalence and sexualization" remain (p. 382). In a similar manner of concern, Sheila Scraton (2018) concludes via her reflection on 25 years of feminist research within physical education: "Sadly, even though we do have new powerful understandings, a strong network of feminist researchers and some committed feminist teachers, the final sentence to my (1992) book holds true today" (p. 11). Of which, Scraton's (1992) final sentence states:

> For the future it is important that critical work in physical education is maintained and extended to ensure that not only girls and young women but also boys and young men receive a physical education that is sensitive to, aware of and prepared to challenge gender inequalities. (p. 136)

Secondly, revelations via activist journalists and critical researchers about corruption, doping and abuse of power within the Olympic movement contributed to seemingly radical reforms in the late 1990s (Cashman and Hughes, 1999; Hoberman, 1992; Jennings, 1992; Lenskyj, 1996, 2000). Yet two decades later, and despite ongoing 'reforms' within the International Olympic Committee and a stream of critical publications, the same issues continue to plague the Olympic movement (Bairner and Molnar, 2010; Bale and Christensen, 2004; Georgieff, 2014).

Thirdly, Richard Tinning (1985) raised concerns with what he originally called 'the cult of slenderness' and the related pressures of treating body shape as a signifier of moral worthiness. His attendant realization was that some of the responsibility for this problem "can be attributed to physical educators, who have little tolerance for the varying degrees of fatness associated with different body types" (Tinning, 1985, p. 10). Notwithstanding three decades of critical writings concerned with HPE and the body,[3] we speculate that Tinning's (1985) conclusion that "physical education is itself implicated by both its actions and non-actions" (p. 10) holds contemporary relevance.

The recognition that some of the prime critical research topics have been repeatedly examined within our respective fields and with little evidence in shifts of power was an inspiration for co-editing this text.

Calls and approaches to make more of a difference

We are not alone in raising questions about the impact of our critical research endeavours. In recent years, a growing number of scholars have raised similar concerns and made calls for researchers to make more of a difference (see Atkinson, 2011; Bairner, 2009, 2012; Carrington, 2007; Donnelly and Atkinson, 2015; Giardina and Laurendeau, 2013; hunter, emerald and Martin, 2013; Newman, 2013; Ovens, 2016; Pringle and Falcous, 2018; Silk, Bush and Andrews, 2010). Critical physical education scholar, Juan-Miguel Fernández-Balboa (2017), for example, referred to what he called the "socio-cultural agenda's stalemate" (p. 658) and questioned: "Why, despite the estimable efforts made by many critical scholars and pedagogues in the last decades, are HPE practices still dominated by a neoliberal agenda?" (p. 659). Within sport sociology an increased sense of urgency about the assumed 'stalemate' has also become apparent with recent publication titles proclaiming: "'We cannot stand idly by': A necessary call for a public sociology of sport" (Cooky, 2017, p. 1). and "'Something has got to be done about this': transforming sport, selves, and scholarship" (Carter, Doidge and Burdsey, 2018, p. 1). Sport journalist-critic David Zirin (2008) further issued an appeal to call critical researchers "off the bench" by encouraging them to become more publically engaged. His prime concern was that the critical research messages are not filtering into the public realm.

Post-structural research approaches (e.g. Deleuze, Baudrillard, Foucault) have also been critiqued for being too focused on the textual/discursive and removed from the real world (e.g. Liljeström and Paasonen, 2010). Further, we know from experience that this research is frequently regarded with skepticism by some practitioners (as well as by students of various sport, health and PE programs) since it is seen as difficult, flimsy or even irrelevant. Thus, despite its ambitions to spearhead change, post-structural theorising, at least when it is conducted in a conventional manner, may have a tendency to increase the theory-practice gap.

Others have suggested that it is easy to criticise various sport or educational practices but it is difficult to offer solutions to complex problems. Jürgen Habermas (1982) for example, labelled Michel Foucault a neo-conservative because he asserted that Foucault failed to provide a strategy for political intervention. Yet Foucault countered by raising the issue of whether he had the right to tell others what to do. Foucault (1997) was particularly critical of some of the prophecies and programs promoted by critical scholars and their disciples and the associated social influence (e.g. Marxist revolutionaries).

Internationally esteemed critical theorists/researchers have also raised concerns about the recent trajectory of social theory, the adoption of particular research methods or disconnect between (e.g. St. Pierre, 2014) and associated lack of research impact. Brian Massumi (2002) lamented, as an example, that critical theory has become repetitive and uninventive to the point that the insights drawn lack substance as they primarily reflect the theoretical framework they were interpreted through. Eve Sedgwick (2003) similarly suggested that critical researchers appear uninventive, even paranoid, in their desire to use the 'correct' social theory and their related focus on (re)discovering various social prohibitions rather than experimenting with new ideas and paving new ways forward. Whereas, Bruno Latour (2004) bemoaned that in such troubling times, critical research has seemingly lost its relevance. Latour's concern with the appearance of critique 'running out of steam' rests, in part, on what he views as the somewhat futile attempt of critical researchers to reveal the "social construction of scientific facts" (p. 227). In other words, Latour was concerned that a predominant focus on deconstruction has distracted researchers from having an ability to have 'real' influence. He suggested a way forward by arguing for a return to materialist thinking:

> that if the critical mind, if it is to renew itself and be relevant again, is to be found in the cultivation of a *stubbornly realist attitude* ... a realism dealing with what I will call *matters of concern*, not *matters of fact*. (p. 231)

A number of scholars within the HPE and sport fields have similarly detailed a variety of strategies—pragmatic, theoretical and methodological—to encourage critical researchers to make more of a difference. Peter Donnelly (2015), for example, encouraged researchers to be relevant and engaged by drawing "connections between their work and the larger debates and problems, and by seeking ways to engage various publics when disseminating that research" (p. 422). Relatedly, Kimberly Oliver and David Kirk (2016) have urged critical HPE scholars "to move beyond paradigmatic approaches to adopt a more pragmatic position" (p. 315). John Sugden (2015) has similarly urged critical researchers to leave the 'safety' of academia and get more directly involved in organizing "forms of social and political activism" (p. 609). Indeed, Douglas Booth (2015) has noted that it is primarily *scholar activists* who have had a more direct influence in shaping policy and the public consciousness, thus echoing Friedrich Engels's maxim that 'an ounce of action is worth a ton of theory'. Yet as Ian McDonald (2002) noted, "achieving the balance between researcher, political intervention and activism is not easy" (p. 114), particularly given how specific research outputs are valued within neoliberal universities (see Atkinson, 2011).

The importance of social theory has also gained attention from critical researchers, with various suggestions that the use of specific sophisticated theoretical lenses could make more of a difference. Laurence Chalip (2015), for example, advocated for greater use of action research approaches within sport studies as, he surmised, that this will focus attention on addressing specific problems. In recent years, activist research, critical action research and practitioner research has also grown within the field of HPE. This research has developed much due to a perceived lack of influence on practice that is related to conventional research conducted from a 'bird's-eye-view' (Casey, 2012; Oliver and Kirk, 2016; Ovens and Fletcher, 2014). lisahunter, elke emerald and Gregory Martin (2013) similarly advocated for greater use of action research but as coupled with an activist approach for encouraging broader social change. A similar approach, where school teachers, rather than academics, use action research approaches in order to spearhead change within HPE practices has been promoted by Casey and Larsson (2018) in order to challenge physical education's own version of the movie *Groundhog Day*.

Agnes Elling (2015), in turn, called for greater use of quantitative and mixed method research as she was concerned that within sport and gender research, the overt dominance of qualitative approaches and the limited diversity in theoretical approaches has possibly stalled transformative efforts. Richard Pringle and Mark Falcous (2018) similarly suggested that it is timely to reflect on the epistemological orthodoxies within the sociology of sport and to encourage methodological border crossings (amongst disciplines and methodologies) as strategies worthy of consideration for promoting political change.

Despite the *apparent* recent increase in calls for transformative action, we acknowledge that such requests have, in fact, been made over many years. A perusal of the North American Society for the Sociology of Sport (NASSS) annual conference themes since NASSS's inception in 1980, for instance, reveals ongoing concern for issues of social injustice and desire to promote social change (https://nasss.org/conference/#past). Similarly, José Devís-Devís (2006) acknowledged that critical physical educators have made transformative requests since the 1970s with such calls gaining momentum in the 1980s. In a comparable manner, the recent calls for a *public sociology*, a form that aims to expand the boundaries of sociology and engages the public in conversation and debate, can be traced back to the actions and writings of Howard Becker (1967), C. Wright Mills (1959) and W. E. B. Du Bois (1903). Comparably, Sandlin, O'Malley and Burdick (2011) traced the development of the concept of *public pedagogy* back to the 1890s. And, of course, all of these critical scholars have been influenced by the founding figures in sociology who acknowledged that their underpinning aims were to use research for encouraging social change for the betterment of society.[4]

The calls for research to make a critical difference clearly have a long history. The recent reinvigoration of these calls, at least in mainstream sociology, can be linked in part to the efforts of Michael Burawoy. Burawoy (2004), as President of the American Sociological Association, steered the annual conference in 2004 towards an examination and promotion of public sociologies. He declared that sociology was a "mirror and conscience of society" and should act to define, promote and inform public debate about "class and racial inequalities, new gender regimes, environmental degradation, multiculturalism, technological revolutions, market fundamentalism, and state and non-state violence" (p. 1). He further suggested:

> More than ever the world needs public sociologies—sociologies that transcend the academy and engage wider audiences. Our potential publics are multiple, ranging from media audiences to policy makers, from think tanks to NGOs, from silenced minorities to social movements. Teaching is central to public sociology: students are our first public for they carry sociology into all walks of life. Academic sociology also needs the world. In stimulating debate about issues of the day, public sociologies inspire and revitalize our own discipline as it also connects us to other disciplines. While public sociologies charge the academy with mission and zeal, our professional competencies in theory and research give legitimacy, direction and substance to public sociologies. (Burawoy, 2004, p. 1)

Although one might think that a call for a publicly engaged, socially responsible form of critical research would be uncontroversial, this has not been the case. Burawoy's (2004) call for public sociology provoked major debate about the tasks and nature of the discipline, so much so, that he was soon writing about the public sociology 'wars' (see Burawoy, 2011). Concerns, for example, were raised about the lack of concrete proposals for the practice of public sociology, the difficulty of measuring success, the problems associated with competing critical goals (e.g. whose ideas should we trust?), the lack of incentives for professional sociologists to become public ones, the risk to sociology as an academic subject and methodological arguments about researcher objectivity and value neutrality (Brady, 2004; Burawoy, 2011; Donnelly, Atkinson, Boyle and Szto, 2011). Although we acknowledge that theoretical debate amongst critical researchers is important, the public sociology wars remind us of Eve Sedgwick's (2003) comments about the apparent 'paranoia' of critical researchers to use the correct social theory.

Is widespread social transformation possible via critical research?

In relation to the issue of whether researchers can create widespread social change, we acknowledge that a public pedagogue/sociologist can enter into public debate (e.g. via writing for newspapers, interacting with students, presenting public seminars) and, if successful, steer the public conversation in a particular direction and even shape some people's views or understandings. These possible outcomes may not produce widespread social change but can be considered as 'micro victories' (see Leahy, Wright and Penney, 2017).

On the other hand, we accept that the desire to use research to successfully orchestrate *widespread* social transformation for the public good is somewhat utopian or idealistic. In drawing from Michel Foucault's (1977, 1980) genealogical studies of social transformation, we understand that social change occurs in relation to dynamic and ubiquitous webs of knowledge/power/material relationships: webs that remain outside of individual or researcher control. The prime lesson from Foucault's genealogical examinations is that dominant contemporary social practices are not the result of rational, linear and progressive developments but have evolved from mundane beginnings and been shaped over time by contingencies, accidents, desires, irrationalities and even mistakes. It is in this manner that we view the ability to engineer social change, via critical research, as idealistic. The upside of this seemingly negative view is recognition that current relationships of power do not need to be accepted as 'natural' and are not secure and can be subject to change. Thus, the recognition of the complexities associated with attempting to engineer social change should not necessarily stall critical research endeavours but perhaps temper one's view of success (see Tinning, 2002).

Jennifer Todd (2005) further argued that political transformation is connected to the complexities associated with 'identity change' and that this recognition has become a prime focus amongst a number of critically oriented researchers. She drew from Bourdieu's theory of social reproduction and a case study of political change in Northern Ireland to conclude that transformation occurs slowly in relation to a *collective identity transformation* amongst a population. In drawing from Todd, we understand that the production of new subjectivities—such as the production of 'feminists' or 'environmentalists'—can be linked to alternative ways of performing and interacting which, over time, result in social change. Yet recognition that political transformation is potentially connected to the complexities of identity formations and associated performances does not make the task of inducing social change any easier. Indeed, many parents are well aware of the challenges of attempting to craft the identities of their own children.

Critical researchers often aim to produce a logical argument or coherent body of knowledge (or set of narrative/discursive resources) that can work to challenge how people think and what they consider normal and/or moral. Richard Tinning (2002) noted, however, that success in such critical endeavours requires an ability to induce an "emotional commitment" in individuals, "lest the contingencies of traditional practice take charge to reproduce the existing reality" (p. 236). In support of a Foucauldian stance, he correspondingly argued that there is a need to recognise the "limits of rationality as a catalyst for change" (p. 236).

In this broad light, we acknowledge that the challenges of undertaking critical research to produce social change can be potentially disheartening. After 20 years of feminist activist research, Leslie Bloom and Patricia Sawin (2009), for example, reflected that "attempting to achieve the research ideals can lead to intractable dilemmas or exhausted cynicism, even despair, about the possibility of living up to our expectations for improving the social conditions of those we study" (p. 333). In a similar manner, we have at times wondered whether we might be considered 'cruel optimists' in continuing to desire social transformation via our critical research endeavours?[5] Yet, as Michael Burawoy (2005) commented, despite such frustrations and the "normalizing pressures of careers" our originating "passion for social justice, economic equality, human rights, sustainable environment, political freedom or simply a better world" (p. 5) can continue to sustain our critical research zeal. Indeed, we keep doing critical research!

Introducing the text

We (Richard Pringle, Håkan Larsson and Göran Gerdin) have been impelled to co-write/edit this text in relation to the existing debates and discussions surrounding the state of critical research and critical theory within the overlapping fields of the sociology of sport and HPE. Over the last decade we have become aware of growing concerns that select research topics have been repeatedly examined within our fields but with seemingly little influence. Although we acknowledge that the impact is difficult to measure and that there are differing views of the research outcomes (e.g. see Donnelly, 2015) we have also noted an increased number of calls, some with a sense of urgency, that our critical research must make more of a difference. Yet there is debate about the ways forward. We have been encouraged, as examples, to be more pragmatic and relevant in our research endeavours but at the same time search for more sophisticated theoretical or methodological perspectives; spread our messages more widely but be wary of the risks of being activist/scholars; cross boundaries and undertake interdisciplinary and mixed method research yet maintain paradigmatic coherence, and, attempt to make more of a difference yet be more modest in our aspirational outlook. At the same time, the publish or perish mantra has increased in universities, with academic job descriptions and performance standards increasingly linked to publication and research grant metrics (but not with strategies adopted by public sociologists and pedagogues).

The ideas for this book started developing when Göran visited Håkan in Stockholm to present some of his doctoral work and ended up having a lengthy conversation about the uncertainties of the impact post-structural research has on PE practice. Håkan at this point in time talked about considering "moving on" from doing work/research through a Foucauldian post-structural lens since he had started doubting what kind of impact his research was having. The focus and scope of the book further developed when Richard and Göran, while being involved in teaching on the same course about sport in society in New Zealand, frequently discussed how and why sport and HPE practices seemed to remain much the same despite decades of critical research and policy and curricular changes (for a discussion of this in relation to PE practice, see Gerdin and Pringle, 2017).

It was within this broad context and with concern about our own critical research impact, that we initially met to discuss how we could make more of a difference in our research projects. We had originally connected through some shared research interests (e.g. gender and sexuality) and theoretical approaches (e.g. Foucauldian/post-structural). Yet we typically researched in different contexts, attended different conferences and published in different journals. These points of difference made our conversations more interesting and encouraged our belief that there was research value in crossing disciplinary boundaries. Our first meeting occurred at the 2014 AIESEP (Association Internationale des Écoles Supérieures d'Éducation Physique) conference held in Auckland, New Zealand.

At the outset we were concerned, as Foucauldian scholars, that post-structuralism had been subject to recent critique as it was allegedly too focused on the discursive and removed from the material world (e.g. Liljeström and Paasonen, 2010). An implication of this critique was that Foucauldian inspired research would fail to make a difference in the 'real' world. An argument we did not fully support given our stance that Foucault was a materialist (see Gerdin and Larsson, 2018; Larsson, 2014; Pringle, Kay and Jenkins, 2011). Through discussing these concerns, we wondered what impact differing theoretical or research approaches have with respect to making a pragmatic difference?

We noted that a broad trend amongst sociology of sport and critical HPE research has occurred: from predominantly quantitative approaches in the 1980s through to the contemporary dominance of qualitative research.[6] We also noted a trend towards conflating qualitative research with critical theorizing and transformative intent. A critical framework, as Norman Denzin and Yvonna Lincoln (2018) asserted, is now embedded within qualitative research. They reported that qualitative research: "speaks for and with those who are on the margins. As a liberationist philosophy, it is committed to examining the consequences of racism, poverty, and sexism on the lives of interacting individuals" (p. x). More specifically, Denzin and Lincoln noted that when co-editing the 2018 edition of *The Sage handbook of qualitative research* they desired that the "new edition should advance a democratic project committed to social justice in an age of uncertainty" (p. xi).

It was in relation to these broad discussions that we decided to work together in co-editing this book. We thought it advantageous to invite contributors from overlapping interdisciplinary fields as we recognised that academics often operate in distinct disciplines with risk of suffering the silo effect and associated problems of academic isolation and specialization (Tett, 2015). Through reading across the disciplines, we hoped that this would encourage new questions and modes of analysis. Henry Giroux's (1992, 2004) conceptualisation of border pedagogies and transdisciplinary work was a source of inspiration. His critical concept of border pedagogy was underpinned by a desire to have students' cross borders of meaning in order to destabilise dominant ways of knowing and encourage critical reflection on accepted values and social understandings. In a similar manner, he encouraged transdisciplinary research "because it provides a rationale for challenging how knowledge has been historically produced, hierarchically ordered, and used within disciplines to sanction particular forms of authority and exclusion" (Giroux, 2004, p. 66). We correspondingly invited researchers from our overlapping disciplines to contribute chapters to this book with a desire to encourage "new linkages, meanings and possibilities" (Giroux, 2004, p. 67).

We also wanted to understand how researchers in different fields were meeting the challenges to undertake research that aims to make a pragmatic difference: were they drawing on differing approaches or theoretical tools and what impact were they having? Subsequently we invited researchers from the sociology of sport field, from physical education, and researchers who critically examine 'health' issues within education and broader socio-cultural contexts.

To help provide coherence across the differing chapters—and in recognition that critical researchers in differing contexts have differing goals—we encouraged our contributors to structure their chapters via three broad aims of critical research. We drew from Pirkko Markula and Michael Silk's (2011) ideas to suggest that three pertinent aims of critical research relate to *mapping, critiquing and social change*. *Mapping* refers to a research project that aims to provide a general overview or 'topography' of what is known about a phenomenon, practice or research topic. Mapping, as akin to critical reviews of literature, provide the groundwork for an ability to provide a pertinent critique. *Critiquing* refers to projects that provide a critical or novel insight into the workings of power associated with a phenomenon, practice or field. It is from such critical work that strategies of *social change* can be designed and enacted. *Social change*, therefore, refers to research projects that provide strategies or praxis for creating or encouraging social transformation.

We encouraged our contributors to use this tripartite framework to examine and reflect upon the impact that critical research has had with respect to *select* social issues or injustices. We recognised the importance of examining the workings of power within select cases, as we were aware that wide-sweeping changes tend not to occur but transformation can occur in specialized areas and at differing rates of change. Hence, the need for specialized areas of focus.

We suggested to our contributors that with respect to *mapping* a particular research topic or field we were interested in understanding how the field had developed, what issues have been examined, what theoretical and methodological approaches have been used and what knowledges have been constructed. We were also interested in understanding what critiques have been offered in relation to these mapping exercises and how these critiques have articulated with the development and enactment of strategies or policies for social change. In cases where critical research appears to have had pragmatic influence, we were interested in attempting to understand the various reasons why this might have occurred and how the critical ideas have been used.

The text structure

The first part of this book on critical socio-cultural examinations of sport acknowledges that 'sport' (in a broad sense of the word) "has never been more popular among the general public, nation-states and scholars" (Pike, Jackson and Wenner, 2015, p. 358) and, as such, produces considerable social, political, economic and academic influence. Jay Coakley (2015) contended that the widespread popularity of sport rests, in part, on the perpetuation of what he calls the "great sport myth" (p. 403), that is, the belief that "sport is inherently good and pure" (p. 404). This mythical belief underpins popular ideas that sport builds good character, brings communities together and is a healthy endeavour that all should pursue. These quixotic beliefs counter the need for critical examination of sport and perpetuate a range of social issues connected to sport. Moreover, these beliefs make it easier for governments to invest billions of dollars into the production of sporting infrastructures, the promotion of nationalistic sport tournaments and the associated circulation of problematic sporting discourses (e.g. concerning genders, sexualities, bodies, ethnicities, nationalities, physical abilities) within the global sport media. The sociology of sport field, however, has been active for over 50 years in the production of counter discourses designed to encourage greater concern about sport and social justice issues. Part one correspondingly examines key social issues related to sport (e.g. peace and development, homophobia, corruption, racism, coaching and the production of elite sporting bodies) to provide insight into how these topics are examined and the associated challenge of how to make a transformative difference.

In chapter two, Simon C. Darnell explores 'Exploring the place of critical research in Sport for Development and Peace' (SDP). He considers the extent to which research specifically in the field of SDP has made significant change at a social, cultural and/or political scale. Darnell concludes by stating that what SDP research can offer to the pursuit of social change is to stand as a critical bulwark against the politics, economics and ideologies that tend to keep the sector working primarily in the service of social reproduction.

The third chapter, titled 'Football 4 Peace v Homophobia: A critical exploration of the links between theory, practice and intervention,' by Jayne Caudwell and Graham Spacey examines how the popularity of football can be drawn upon, via a select intervention strategy, to subvert homophobia. Through this chapter, the authors consider the potential to make a difference by using public sociology to change footballing practices. Caudwell and Spacey argue that this project offers an example of intervention that seeks social transformation of attitudes and behaviours towards marginalised sexualities.

Roy McCree in chapter four, 'Autoethnography and public sociology of sport in Caribbean: Engagement, disengagement and despair,' draws on his experiences of the formation and functioning of the Veteran Footballers Foundation of Trinidad and Tobago organization. Through this auto-ethnographic approach McCree discusses the extent to which sport sociologists can become publicly engaged to challenge corruption within influential sporting associations such as FIFA. The chapter also draws on the Gramscian notion of "organic intellectuals" in order to problematize this process of public engagement in trying "to make a difference" in sport and society.

Billy Hawkins in the fifth chapter, 'Critical research on Black sporting experiences in the United States: Athletic activism and the appeal for social justice', examines how the prevalence of racism in the United States shape the sporting experiences of African Americans and other ethnic groups. He argues that the efforts of critical research scholars in giving a voice to the previously voiceless provide the counter-narratives that are necessary for programmatic development to enhance the sporting experiences of all. Hawkins concludes by saying that recovering from the resurgence and radicalization of white supremacy's ideals will take a concerted effort from those seeking to make sure that the racial inequalities and inequities are challenged so that they do not threaten racial justice.

Chapter six, 'Problematizing practice: Coach development with Foucault,' describes how the authors, Jim Denison and Joe Mills, employed Foucauldian thinking in their work as coach-developers. More specifically, they discuss how they have used Foucault's specific analysis of power as their overarching theoretical and conceptual premise to transform coaching from a technocratic and mechanistic process into a highly complex, contextual, social and political process. Denison and Mills argue that it is only with a theory-driven understanding of power that coaches will be able to practice more effectively and ethically, and truly 'make a difference' both to sport and to society through the work they do with their athletes.

Despite the broad growth of the sociology of sport, this field has not typically examined issues related to physical education and school sport experiences. Yet schooling provides an indelible influence on individuals subjectivities and belief systems that can shape a lifetime. Hence, within part two, we turn our attention to 'Physical education: Critical perspectives and social change'. We understand that critical pedagogy and other critical perspectives have had a firm place in physical education research for several decades (e.g. Fernandez-Balboa, 1995; Kirk, 1986; Oliver and Lalik, 2004). This body of research has contributed important insights into the social dimensions of physical education teaching, socialization and learning relating to class, gender, sexuality, ethnicity, (dis)ability, and more. We note, however, that it has been debated to what extent the research has actually changed the physical education practice, and improved the situation for marginalised groups of students as well as physical education as a whole (Tinning, 2004; see also Probyn, 2004). We acknowledge, though, that the success of critical research cannot only be judged by itself (i.e., how it has been implemented in the research and the results it has produced) but that the success must also be judged in relation to the broader social situation where the research is located. This includes, for example, new forms of governance as well as other—and competing—research agendas.

Critical researchers typically approach governance which emphasises marketisation, commercialisation, individualisation with scepticism. Such forms of governance are frequently implicit in much contemporary physical activity and (public) health research, that is, research that exploits the contemporary concern regarding sedentariness and obesity among children and young people (e.g. Evans, Davies and Wright, 2004; Gard and Wright, 2005; Wright and

Harwood, 2012). Such research can also conflate physical education with physical activity. Nevertheless, a situation seems to have occurred where proponents for critical perspectives within the physical education research have started to re-evaluate their research, and to look for possible adjustments in order to be able to meet the challenges with an apparent difficulty to 'reach out' to practitioners and politicians.

The chapters of part two can be read as different ways of approaching the task of re-evaluating critical research within the school subject HPE as well as within physical education teacher education (PETE). In chapter seven, 'Critical pedagogy in physical education as advocacy and action: A reflective account', Richard Tinning reflects on his long career as an advocate for critical pedagogy within HPE, and the extent to which this approach has managed to 'make a difference'. Although to some extent uncertain about the impact of critical pedagogy within HPE, Tinning concludes that contemporary HPE is probably 'more sensitive to the needs of many kids who were previously alienated and/or marginalized by participation in PE classes'. However, he cautions, 'the actual lived experience of some (many?) kids in class still requires attention. In chapter eight, 'A new critical pedagogy for physical education in "turbulent times": What are the possibilities?', David Kirk offers a critique of the thesis that critical pedagogy is suffering from a 'backlash'. There is little 'substantive critique', he argues, and few 'examples of neo-liberal appropriation of critical pedagogy and of deficit scholarship' within the HPE research. Instead, Kirk's chapter serves to 'explore the possibilities for a new critical pedagogy for physical education that is fit for purpose in turbulent times', in particular through using the concept of precarity.

In chapter nine, 'In pursuit of a critically oriented Physical Education: Curriculum contests and troublesome knowledge', Louise McCuaig, Janice Atkin and Doune Macdonald offer an account of the construction and reception of a critically oriented Australian Curriculum: Health and Physical Education (AC: HPE). The chapter is based on their own insights from working with designing the curriculum. They contend that 'socio-critical perspectives pose a source of troublesome knowledge and, as a result, are particularly sensitive to the principled positions that stakeholders adopt in their efforts to influence the intent, knowledges and practices of HPE in schools.

From HPE, we move on to physical education teacher education (PETE). In chapter ten, 'Socially critical PE: The influence of critical research on the social justice agenda in PETE and PE practice', Rod Philpot, Göran Gerdin and Wayne Smith discuss and critique the advocacy and impact of critical scholarship that address social justice in PETE and PE. They acknowledge the ongoing challenges and need for further critical research and change in the name of social justice. In chapter eleven, 'Critical scholarship in physical education teacher education: A journey, not a destination', Chris Hickey and Amanda Mooney further consider the impact of critical scholarship in PETE.

They contend that there may be a need for new approaches to critical scholarship, and they present post-humanism as way of opening up 'new spaces to contemplate possible futures of PETE'.

Finally, in chapter twelve, 'Gender in Physical Education: A case for performative pedagogy?', Håkan Larsson suggests that critical performative pedagogy could be one way for researchers to engage with HPE students and practitioners in an attempt to challenge dominating norms, in this case about gender and sexuality. Performative pedagogy, briefly 'less talk and more action' in educational practice, constitutes an attempt to refrain from persuading the students that they need a critical approach to teaching PE, and instead aims to evoke affect and deliberation among students based on lessons including different movement activities.

Physical education and sporting practices are often legitimated in relation to the belief that they can produce good health. Yet the scholarly examination of health has been overwhelmingly examined via a biomedical lens: a lens that can be prone to underestimating the importance of socio-cultural-material factors in the production of broadly 'healthy' subjectivities and associated lifestyles. The third part, correspondingly, is concerned with holistic notions of health and wellbeing in contexts of education, exercise and fitness. Health Education has emerged as a topic of interest for critical scholars particularly in the last decades as this subject area has been incorporated into the school curriculum either as a separate subject or the merged curriculum area of Health and Physical Education (e.g. in Australia and New Zealand). Critical scholarship in this area has focused on critiquing the way dominant discourses of neoliberalism, healthism, risk and the body (re)construct narrow/limited identities which simultaneously privileges and marginalizes ways of being 'healthy'. In their edited book *Health Education: Critical Perspectives*, Katie Fitzpatrick and Richard Tinning (2014), argue that current approaches to health education can promote a fear of ill health and the need for self-surveillance and individual responsibility, as such risk becomes a form of health fascism and, therefore, there is a need to be cognisant of this potential and its consequences for young people. Other leading critical scholars in the field of health education have attempted to further broaden the socially critical health education agenda by claiming that it should involve 'learning about health not only to save lives as an end point, but also to interrogate health in the present as messy, complicated, difficult, dependent and formed in a context broader than the individual' (Wright, O'Flynn and Welch 2018, p. 127). The chapters in part three extend this critique but also offer ideas about alternative ways of thinking about health, exercise and fitness with respect to broader socio-cultural concerns.

Chapter thirteen, titled 'Schools and health: An argument against the tide' and authored by Carolyn Pluim and Michael Gard, problematizes the idea that the schools are the most appropriate and effective places in which to prosecute health policy goals. The authors argue that school health interventions operate as political and ideological tools which at time are underpinned by calculated cultural, political, financial and ideological motivations that serve to undermine issues of equity, democracy and social justice.

Mikael Quennerstedt and Louise McCuaig discuss the impact of critical research using salutogenic approaches to health in chapter fourteen, titled 'Is asking salutogenic questions a way of being critical?'. They specifically draw on the recent inclusions of salutogenic re-orientations in the Australian HPE curriculum to demonstrate social change, at least on the policy level.

In chapter fifteen, 'Cruel optimism? Socially critical perspectives on the obesity assemblage', Jan Wright, Lisette Burrows and Deana Leahy examine how socially critical obesity work, and post-structural work, in particular, can contribute to new understandings of the 'obesity assemblage' by addressing the ethical, moral and social consequences of charging schools with the burden of ameliorating obesity. They critically review their own advocacy and action when it comes to disrupting dominant obesity discourses by discussing whether this can be seen as exemplars of 'cruel optimism' or if they have made a difference both for young people in the context of health and physical education and for cultural understandings more widely.

Pirkko Markula's chapter sixteen, 'Critical research in exercise and fitness', discusses how as the fitness industry has developed into a globally popular enterprise the interest in studying exercise as a social, cultural and political issue has increased. Through evaluation and comparison of critical and post-structural research, Markula suggests how social change might be produced through exercise and fitness.

In chapter seventeen, 'Un-charting the course: Critical indigenous research into Sport, Health and Physical Education', Brendan Hokowhitu discusses how the increased focus on Indigenous health, and the integration of Indigenous peoples into society through sport and physical education resembles the continued production of discourses centred on savagery. He argues that indigenous critical physical research requires a genealogical approach that comprehends the 'breath of physicality', which inhabits the discourses surrounding Indigenous people. Hokowhitu concludes that the project of Indigenous critical physical research must be at once 'deconstructory' and 'existential'.

In the concluding chapter, we reflect on our contributors' critical reflections and offer comment on the utility of research to make a critical difference and suggestions for future directions.

Notes

1. The HPE fields' definition and understanding of what it means to be 'physically active' and 'healthy' has for some time now been negotiated and renegotiated. In some parts of the world, over the past two decades, this renegotiation has seen HPE curricula move from a predominance of scientific/physiological explanations of physical activity and health, to more critical explanations.

2. The following social justice issues, as illustrations, were critically examined in the 1980s and remain on the contemporary research agenda: homophobia and heterosexism in sport and physical education (e.g. Bennett et al., 1989; Bulken, 1980; Cooper, 1989); healthism, the body and HPE (Kirk and Colquhoun, 1989; Pfister, 1980); racism, discrimination and sport (Birrell, 1989; Edwards, 1979; Lapchick, 1975); and the possibilities for critical health education to act as a tool for social transformation (Labonte, 1986; McLeroy, Bibeau, Steckler and Glanz, 1988; Wallerstein and Bernstein, 1988).

3. The following publications reflect some of the research outputs concerned with the cult of the body and HPE: Evans, Davies, and Wright, 2004; Gard and Wright, 2005; Kirk, 2006; Petersen and Lupton, 1996; Powell and Fitzpatrick, 2015, Pringle and Pringle, 2010.

4. A lineage of the desire to use critical writings to encourage social change can be traced back to the founding figures of modern sociology—Emile Durkheim (1958–1917) and Karl Marx (1818–1883)—who were in agreement concerning the need for sociological research to make a social difference. Emile Durkheim (1958–1917), for example, aspired to ensure that sociology would be accepted as a legitimate science, yet his underpinning motive was to *enhance* the lives of the people he was 'objectively' studying. Karl Marx was much more upfront about his transformative desires, so much so, that the words inscribed on his grave proclaim: "The philosophers have only *interpreted* the world, in various ways. The point, however, is to *change* it."

5. Lauren Berlant (2011) in her affective history of the present, used the concept of *cruel optimism* to offer an explanation for why transformative changes have not taken place in response to the crisis of neoliberalism. She argued that the optimism that many retain for upward mobility and a better future, works to cruelly maintain the neoliberal socio-economic status quo. In a loosely similar manner to Berlant, we have questioned whether we are 'cruel optimists' in believing that our critical research tools and theories will result in the social transformation we desire? To be blunt: does our faith in existing critical qualitative research approaches or our search for better theoretical tools, somehow preclude our efforts to promote social change via other, possibly more viable, approaches?

6. Patti Lather (2013) has noted, relatedly, that qualitative research has come under increased pressure to "provide better evidentiary warrants" (p. 636), yet this pressure has been critiqued as related to attempts to transform qualitative inquiry into tools of neoliberal policy. We now sense that there is mounting pressure amongst critical qualitative researchers to refocus the evidentiary warrants to issues of political and social impact. As such, we might question, what likely impact will a shift to post-qualitative inquiry have on issues of injustices in relation to global inequalities?

References

Atkinson, M., 2011. Physical cultural studies (redux). *Sociology of Sport Journal* 28, 135–144.

Bairner, A., 2009. Sport, intellectuals and public sociology: Obstacles and opportunities. *International Review for the Sociology of Sport*, 44(2–3), 115–130.

Bairner, A., 2012. For the sociology of sport. *Sociology of Sport Journal*, 29, 102–117.

Bairner, A., and Molnar, G., eds., 2010. *The politics of the Olympics: A survey*. London: Routledge.

Bale, J., and Christensen, M., 2004. Introduction: Post Olympism? In: J. Bale and M. Christensen, ed. *Post-Olympism? Questioning sport in the twenty-first century.* Oxford: Berg, 1–12.

Becker, H. S., 1967. Whose side are we on? *Social problems, 14*(3), 239–247.

Bennett, R. S., Duffy, A., Kalliam, D., Martin, M., Woolley, S. N. J., West, E. L., and Whitaker, K. G., 1989. Homophobia and heterosexism in sport and physical education: Why must we act now. *CAHPERD Journal/Times, 51*(8), 16–18.

Berlant, L. G., 2011. *Cruel optimism.* Durham, NC: Duke University Press.

Bernstein, R. J., 2011. *Beyond objectivism and relativism: Science, hermeneutics, and praxis.* Philadelphia: University of Pennsylvania Press.

Biesta, G. J., 1998. Say you want a revolution … Suggestions for the impossible future of critical pedagogy. *Educational theory, 48*(4), 499–510.

Birrell, S., 1989. Racial relations theories and sport: Suggestions for a more critical analysis. *Sociology of sport journal, 6*(3), 212–227.

Bloom, R. L., and Sawin, P., 2009. Ethical responsibility in feminist research: challenging ourselves to do activist research with women in poverty. *International Journal of Qualitative Studies in Education, 22*(3), 333–351.

Booth, D., 2015. Bruce Kidd, sport history and social emancipation. In: R. Field, ed. *Playing for change: The continuing struggle for sport and recreation.* Toronto: University of Toronto Press, 407–436.

Brady, D., 2004. Why public sociology may fail. *Social Forces, 82*(4), 1629–1638.

Bruce, T., 2015. Assessing the sociology of sport: On media and representations of sportswomen. *International Review for the Sociology of Sport, 50*(4–5), 380–384.

Bulkin, E., 1980. Heterosexism and women's studies. *The Radical Teacher,* November 17, 25–31.

Burawoy, M., 2004. Public sociologies: American Sociological Association Annual Conference Final program. Available from: www.asanet.org/sites/default/files/2004_annual_meeting_program.pdf. (accessed 15 March 2018)

Burawoy, M., 2005. For public sociology. *American Sociological Review, 70*(1), 4–28.

Burawoy, M., 2009. The public sociology wars. In: V. Jeffries, ed. *Handbook of public sociology.* Plymouth, UK: Rowman & Littlefield, 449–473.

Carrington, B., 2007. Merely identity: Cultural identity and the politics of sport. *Sociology of Sport Journal, 24*(1), 49.

Carter, T. F., Doidge, M., and Burdsey, D., 2018. 'Something has got to be done about this': Transforming sport, selves, and scholarship. In: T. F. Carter, D. Burdsey, and M. Doidge, eds. *Transforming Sport: Knowledges, Practices, Structures.* London: Routledge, 1–20.

Casey, A., 2012. A self-study using action research: Changing site expectations and practice stereotypes. *Educational Action Research, 20*(2), 219–232.

Casey, A., and Larsson, H., 2018. "It's groundhog day": Foucault's governmentality and crisis discourses in physical education. *Quest,* iFirst, doi: 10.1080/00336297.2018.1451347.

Cashman, R., and Hughes, A., eds., 1999. *Staging the Olympics: The event and its impact.* Sydney: University of New South Wales.

Chalip, L., 2015. Assessing the sociology of sport: On theory relevance and action research. *International Review for the Sociology of Sport, 50*(4–5), 397–401.

Coakley, J., 2015. On cultural sensibilities and the great sport myth. *International Review for the Sociology of Sport Journal, 50*(4–5), 402–406.

Cooky, C., 2017. "We cannot stand idly by": A necessary call for a public sociology of sport. *Sociology of Sport Journal*, 34(1), 1–11.

Cooper, C., 1989. Social oppressions experienced by gays and lesbians. In *Strategies for addressing homophobia in physical education, sports, and dance. Workshop presented at the annual convention of the American Alliance for Health, Physical Education, Recreation, and Dance*, Boston, MA.

Davis J., Stolberg. S., and Kaplan, T., 2018. Trump alarms lawmakers with disparaging words for Haiti and Africa. *New York Times*. Available from:/www.nytimes.com/2018/01/11/us/politics/trump-shithole-countries.html (accessed 10 January 2018).

Denzin, N. K. and Lincoln, L., 2018. Preface. In: N. Denzin and Y. Lincoln, eds. *The Sage Handbook of Qualitative Research*. Thousand Oaks, CA: Sage, ix-xx.

Devís-Devís, J., 2006. Socially critical research perspectives in physical education. *The Handbook of Physical Education*, 37–58.

Dolan, K., and Kroll, L., 2018. Forbes billionaires 2018: Meet the richest people on the planet. Available from: https://www.forbes.com/sites/luisakroll/2018/03/06/forbes-billionaires-2018-meet-the-richest-people-on-the-planet/#69217b556523 (accessed 6 March 2018).

Donnelly, P., 2015. Assessing the sociology of sport: On public sociology of sport and research that makes a difference. *International Review for the Sociology of Sport*, 50(4–5), 419–423.

Donnelly, P., and Atkinson, M., 2015. Where history meets biography: Towards a public sociology of sport. In: R. Field, ed. *Playing for change: the continuing struggle for sport and recreation*. Toronto: University of Toronto Press, 365–388.

Donnelly, P., Atkinson, M., Boyle, S., and Szto, C., 2011. Sport for development and peace: A public sociology perspective. *Third World Quarterly*, 32(3), 589–601.

Donnelly, P., and Donnelly, M. K., 2013. The London 2012 Olympics: A gender equality audit. *Centre for Sport Policy Studies Research Report*. Toronto: Centre for Sport Policy Studies, Faculty of Kinesiology and Physical Education, University of Toronto.

Du Bois, W. E. B., 1903. *The talented tenth*. New York, NY: James Pott and Company.

Dylan, B., 1964. *The times they are a changing*. New York: Columbia Studios.

Edwards, H., 1979. Sport within the veil: The triumphs, tragedies and challenges of Afro-American involvement. *The Annals of the American Academy of Political and Social Science*, 445(1), 116–127.

Edwards, R., and Fenwick, T., 2015. Critique and politics: A sociomaterialist intervention. *Educational Philosophy and Theory*, 47(13–14), 1385–1404.

Elling, A., 2015. Assessing the sociology of sport: On reintegrating quantitative methods and gender research. *International Review for the Sociology of Sport*, 50(4–5), 430–436.

Enright, E., Hill, J., Sandford, R., and Gard, M., 2014. Looking beyond what's broken: towards an appreciative research agenda for physical education and sport pedagogy. *Sport, Education and Society*, 19(7), 912–926.

Evans, J., Davies, B., and Wright, J., eds. 2004. *Body knowledge and control: Studies in the sociology of physical education and health*. London: Routledge.

Fernández-Balboa, J. M., 1995. Reclaiming physical education in higher education through critical pedagogy. *Quest*, 47(1), 91–114.

Fernández-Balboa, J. M., 2017. A contrasting analysis of the neo-liberal and socio-critical structural strategies in health and physical education: reflections on the emancipatory agenda within and beyond the limits of HPE. *Sport, Education and Society*, 22(5), 658–668.

Fitzpatrick, K., and Tinning, R., 2014. *Health Education: Critical Perspectives*. Abingdon, United Kingdom: Routledge.

Foucault, M., 1977. *Discipline and punish* (A. Sheridan, trans.). New York: Pantheon.

Foucault, M., 1980. *The history of sexuality*. Volume 1: *An introduction*. New York: Pantheon.

Foucault, M., 1997. Michel Foucault: An interview by Stephen Riggins. In: P. Rabinow, ed. *Michel Foucault: Ethics, subjectivity and truth*, Volume 1. London: Penguin Books.

Gard, M., and Wright, J., 2005. *The obesity epidemic: Science, morality and ideology*. London: Routledge.

Georgieff, A., 2014. Behind the 2014 winter Olympic was a major Russian Mafia turf war. Available from: https://mic.com/articles/82943/behind-the-2014-winter-olympics-was-a-major-russian-mafia-turf-war#.jc5WX9Sxg (accessed 24 February, 2014).

Gerdin, G., and Larsson, H., 2018. The productive effect of power: (dis)pleasurable bodies materialising in and through the discursive practices of boys' physical education. *Physical Education and Sport Pedagogy*, 23(1), 66–83. DOI: 10.1080/17408989.2017.1294669.

Gerdin, G., and Pringle, R., 2017. The politics of pleasure: An ethnographic examination exploring the dominance of the multi-activity sport-based physical education model. *Sport, Education and Society*, 22(2), 194–213. DOI: 10.1080/13573322.2015.1019448.

Giardina, M. D., and Laurendeau, J., 2013. Truth untold? Evidence, knowledge, and research practice(s). *Sociology of Sport Journal*, 30(3), 237–255.

Giroux, H. A., 1992. *Border crossings: Cultural workers and the politics of education*. London: Routledge.

Giroux, H. A., 2004. Cultural studies, public pedagogy, and the responsibility of intellectuals. *Communication and Critical/Cultural Studies*, 1(1), 59–79.

Habermas, J., 1982. A reply to my critics. In: J. B. Thompson and D. Held, eds. *Habermas: Contemporary social theory*. London: Palgrave, London, 219–283.

Hansard, 2002. *House of Commons Commission Reports*, 13 February, 2002. London: United Kingdom Parliament.

Hoberman, J., 1992. *Mortal engines: The science of performance and the dehumanization of sport*. New York: Free Press.

hunter, l., emerald, e., and Martin, G., 2013. *Participatory activist research in the globalised world*. New York: Springer.

Jennings, A., 1992. *The lords of the rings: Power, money and drugs in the modern Olympics*. Toronto: Stoddart.

Kane, M. J., LaVoi, N., Wiese-Bjornstal, D., Duncan, M., Nichols, J., Pettee, K., and Ainsworth, B. 2007. The 2007 Tucker Center research report: Developing physically active girls: An evidence-based multidisciplinary approach. http://www.cehd.umn.edu/tuckercenter/library/docs/research/2007-Tucker-Center-Research-Report.pdf

Kirk, D., 1986. A critical pedagogy for teacher education: Toward an inquiry-oriented approach. *Journal of Teaching in Physical Education*, 5(4), 230–246.

Kirk, D., 2006. The 'obesity crisis' and school physical education. *Sport, Education and Society*, 11(2), 121–133.

Kirk, D., and Colquhoun, D., 1989. Healthism and physical education. *British Journal of Sociology of Education*, 10(4), 417–434.

Kincheloe, J. L., McLaren, P., and Steinberg, S. R., 2011. Critical pedagogy and qualitative research. In N. Denzin and Y. Lincoln, eds. *The SAGE handbook of qualitative research*. Thousand Oaks, CA: Sage, 163–177.

Labonte, R., 1986. Social inequality and healthy public policy. *Health Promotion International*, 1(3), 341–351.

Lapchick, R. E., 1975. *The politics of race and international sport: The case of South Africa* (No. 1). Westport, Conn: Greenwood Pub Group.

Larsson, H., 2014. Materialising bodies: There is nothing more material than a socially constructed body. *Sport, Education and Society, 19*(5), 637–651.

Lather, P., 2013. Methodology: What do we do in the afterward? *International Journal of Qualitative Studies in Education, 26*(6), 634–645.

Latour, B., 2004. Why has critique run out of steam? From matters of fact to matters of concern. *Critical Inquiry, 30*(2), 225–248.

Leahy, D., Wright, J., and Penney, D., 2017. The political is critical: explorations of the contemporary politics of knowledge in health and physical education. *Sport, Education and Society, 22*(5), 547–551, DOI: 10.1080/13573322.2017.1329141

Lenskyj, H. J., 1996. When winners are losers: Toronto and Sydney bids for the Summer Olympics. *Journal of Sport and Social Issues, 20*(4), 392–410.

Lenskyj, H. J., 2000. *Inside the Olympic industry: Power, politics, and activism*. Albany: State University of New York Press.

Liljeström, M., and Paasonen, S., 2010. Introduction: Feeling differences–affect and feminist reading. In M. Liljeström and S. Paasonen (Eds.), *Working with affect in feminist readings: Disturbing differences*, 1–7. London: Routledge.

Loy, J. W., and McElvogue, J. F., 1970. Racial segregation in American sport. *International Review of Sport Sociology, 5*, 5–24.

Markula, P., and Silk, M. L., 2011. *Qualitative research for physical culture*. Basingstoke: Palgrave Macmillan.

Marx, K., 1848/1994. The victory of the counter-revolution in Vienna (Marx-Engels Institute, trans.). *Neue Rheinische Zeitung, 136*, 7.

Massumi, B., 2002. *Parables for the virtual: Movement, affect, sensation*. Durham and London: Duke University Press.

McDonald, I., 2002. Critical social research and political intervention. In: J. Sugden and A. Tomlinson, eds. *Power Games: A critical sociology of sport*, 100–116.

McLeroy, K. R., Bibeau, D., Steckler, A., and Glanz, K., 1988. An ecological perspective on health promotion programs. *Health education quarterly, 15*(4), 351–377.

Mills, C. W., 1959. *The sociological imagination*. Oxford: Oxford University Press.

Newman, J., 2013. Arousing a [post-]enlightenment active body praxis. *Sociology of Sport Journal, 30*, 380–407.

Oliver, K., and Kirk, D., 2016. *Transformative pedagogies for challenging body culture in physical education*. In: C. Ennis, ed. *Routledge handbook of physical education pedagogies*. Abingdon: Routledge, 307–318.

Ovens, A., 2016. A quest for a pedagogy of critical theorising in physical education teacher education: One physical educator's journey. In: J. Williams and M. Hayler, eds. *Professional learning through transitions and transformations*, Volume 15. Champaign, IL: Springer, 123–135.

Ovens, A., and Fletcher, T., 2014. Doing self-study: The art of turning inquiry on yourself. In *Self-study in physical education teacher education*. Champaign, IL: Springer, 3–14.

Pearce, M., 2015. 'Modern civil rights movement expands on classic methods', *LA Times*, 5 March. Available at: www.latimes.com/nation/la-na-selma-civil-rights-movement-20150306-story.html (accessed 19 March 2018).

Petersen, A., and Lupton, D., 1996. *The new public health: Health and self in the age of risk*. Thousand Oaks, CA: Sage Publications.

Pfister, G., 1980. Gender and sport—empirical data and theoretical considerations. *Health*, 10(3), 365–388.

Pike, E., Jackson, S., and Wenner, L., 2015. On the trajectory, challenges, and future of the field. *International Review for the Sociology of Sport*, 50(4–5), 357–362.

Powell, D., and Fitzpatrick, K., 2015. 'Getting fit basically just means, like, nonfat': children's lessons in fitness and fatness. *Sport, Education and Society*, 20(4), 463–484.

Pringle, R., and Falcous, M., 2018. Transformative research and epistemological hierarchies: Ruminating on how the sociology of sport field could make more of a difference. *International Review for the Sociology of Sport*, 53(3) 261–277. DOI: 10.1177/1012690216654297.

Pringle, R., Kay, T., and Jenkins, J., 2011. Masculinities, gender relations and leisure. *Annals of Leisure Research*, 14(2–3), 107–119.

Pringle, R., and Pringle, D., 2012. Competing obesity discourses and critical challenges for health and physical educators. *Sport, Education and Society*, 17(2), 143–161.

Sage, G. H., 1990. *Power and ideology in American sport: A critical perspective*. Champaign, IL: Human Kinetics Publishers.

Sage, G. H., 2015. Assessing the sociology of sport: On social consciousness and social movements. *International Review for the Sociology of Sport*, 50(4–5), 585–590.

Sandlin, J. A., O'Malley, M. P., and Burdick, J., 2011. Mapping the complexity of public pedagogy scholarship. *Review of Educational Research*, 81(3), 338–375.

Scraton, S., 1992. *Shaping up to womanhood: Gender and girls' physical education*. Buckingham: Open University Press.

Scraton, S., 2018. Feminism(s) and PE: 25 years of shaping up to womanhood. *Sport, Education and Society*, Published online: 5 March 2018. DOI: 10.1080/13573322.2018.1448263.

Sedgwick, E. K., 2003. *Touching feeling: Affect, pedagogy, performativity*. Durham: Duke University Press.

Shapiro, T., Meschede, T., and Osoro, S., 2013. *The roots of the widening racial wealth gap: Explaining the black-white economic divide*. Institute on Assets and Social Policy Research and Policy Brief. Brandeis University, Waltham, MA.

Silk, M., Bush, A., and Andrews, D., 2010. Contingent intellectual amateurism, or, the problem with evidence-based research. *Journal of Sport & Social Issues*, 34(1), 105–128.

St Pierre, E. A., 2014. A brief and personal history of post qualitative research: Toward post inquiry. *Journal of Curriculum Theorizing*, 30(2), 2–19.

Sugden, J., 2015. Assessing the sociology of sport: On the capacities and limits of using sport to promote social change. *International Review for the Sociology of Sport*, 50(4–5), 606–611.

Tett, G., 2015. *The silo effect: Why putting everything in its place isn't such a bright idea*. London: Little, Brown.

Tinning, R., 1985. Physical education and the cult of slenderness: a critique. *ACHPER National Journal*, (108), 10–13.

Tinning, R., 2002. Toward a "modest pedagogy": Reflections on the problematics of critical pedagogy. *Quest*, 54(3), 224–240.

Tinning, R., 2004. Rethinking the preparation of HPE teachers: ruminations on knowledge, identity, and ways of thinking. *Asia-Pacific Journal of Teacher Education*, 32(3), 241–253.

Todd, J., 2005. Social transformation, collective categories, and identity change. *Theory and Society*, 34(4), 429–463.

Wallerstein, N., and Bernstein, E., 1988. Empowerment education: Freire's ideas adapted to health education. *Health education quarterly*, 15(4), 379–394.

Wright, J., and Harwood, V. (eds.), 2012. *Biopolitics and the 'obesity epidemic'. Governing bodies*. London: Routledge.

Wright, J., O'Flynn, G., and Welch, R., 2018. In search of the socially critical in health education: Exploring the views of health and physical education preservice teachers in Australia. *Health Education*, 118(2), 117–130.

Zirin, D., 2008. Calling sports sociology off the bench. *Contexts* (summer), 27–31.

Part I

Critical socio-cultural examinations of sport

Chapter 2

Exploring the place of critical research in Sport for Development and Peace

Simon C. Darnell

Mapping Sport for Development and Peace

Sport for Development and Peace is a term now commonly used to refer to the organization and mobilization of sport and sport programs to meet the goals of international development and peace building. These goals include (but are not limited to): gender empowerment, health promotion, the securing of human rights, economic development, and post-conflict reconciliation. Some of the historical roots of SDP lie in 19th century ideologies and social formations such as rational recreation and muscular Christianity (Kidd 2008), in which participation in sport and structured physical activity was understood to contribute to the personal and character-based development of individuals. Such ways of thinking influenced, among others, Pierre de Coubertin as he revived the notion of Olympism and the modern Olympic Games in the late 1800s, in part to support the development of French youth after losing the Franco-Prussian war (Chatziefstathiou and Henry 2012). By the late 20th century, as sport was being used for programs of social control like Midnight Basketball in the United States (Hartmann 2016), sport was increasingly included within larger practices of international development and foreign aid, particularly as relatively rich, donor nations, such as Canada and those from Scandinavia, provided resources and expertise to support capacity building and the improvement of sport systems in so-called developing countries. This international sport-based outreach began to morph in the face of massive social and health challenges, such as the HIV/AIDS pandemic in Africa that peaked in the 1990s, and sports aid shifted to the use of sport to meet broader social goals like reducing the spread of HIV/AIDS. As more and more intergovernmental and non-governmental organizations (United Nations and Right to Play, respectively) joined the field, the Sport for Development and Peace sector emerged, characterized by its focus more on *plus sport* approaches (programs where development is paramount, and sport organized in its service) than on *sport plus* (which principally organizes sport, and from which development might follow) (Coalter 2007).

Some important milestones were necessary for this shift to SDP to take place and for the sector to cohere on an international scale; many of these had to do with the integration of SDP within the United Nations system. In 2001, then UN Secretary-General Kofi Annan appointed former Swiss President Adolf Ogi to the newly created position of Special Advisor on Sport for Development and Peace. This was followed by the creation of the United Nations Office on Sport for Development and Peace (UNOSDP) and the formation of the UN Interagency Task Force on Sport for Development and Peace. The Task Force, convened during the Salt Lake City Olympics in 2002, was comprised of stakeholders from across the United Nations system, including UNESCO and the International Labour Organization, with support from organizations like Right to Play. The Task Force released a major report in 2003 entitled *Sport as a Tool for Development and Peace: Towards Achieving the United Nations Millennium Development Goals*, in which it concluded that sport offered a practical and affordable framework through which the UN could pursue development and support its existing efforts (UN Inter-agency Task Force 2003). At the 2004 summer Olympics in Athens, a new major SDP group was formed, the Sport for Development and Peace International Working Group, with the aim of advocating for SDP and working towards its integration within the policies and strategies of national governments.

A subsequent milestone was the UN's granting of Permanent Observer status to the International Olympic Committee in 2009, a move that signaled the increased recognition of SDP within the highest levels of international sport. Permanent Observer status allows the IOC to take the floor at the UN General Assembly and advocate for international sport. In 2014, former IOC President Jacques Rogge was also appointed as the Special Envoy of the Secretary-General for Youth, Refugees and Sport, further solidifying the relationships between the two organizations. On May 4, 2017 UN Secretary General Antonio Guterres announced the closing of the United Nations Office on Sport for Development and Peace, and the establishment of a new direct partnership between the UN and International Olympic Committee in order to avoid "parallel work" between the two organizations (Wickstrom 2017).

The institutionalization of SDP was further fomented by the specific inclusion of sport within the Sustainable Development Goals (SDGs), the UN's development agenda through 2030. Article 37 of the SDGs references sport as an important enabler of sustainable development, claiming that sport can contribute to "the empowerment of women and of young people, individuals and communities as well as to health, education and social inclusion objectives" (United Nations 2016). Accompanying the SDGs is the assertion that sport "can contribute to combatting climate change" by raising awareness, encouraging action and supporting relief and reconstruction in affected areas (UNOSDP 2016).

Thus, SDP has achieved significant institutionalization and recognition over the past two decades, and hundreds of SDP organizations are now in operation, accompanied by coordinating organizations like the International Platform on Sport & Development (see sportanddev.org) and streetfootballworld, which advocate for the sector. That said, some key stakeholders, particularly national governments and intergovernmental organizations who were key drivers of the SDP concept and its institutionalization, have changed tack somewhat. Some governments—such as Canada, the United Kingdom and Australia—have shifted sport policy priorities back to the delivery of sport programs primarily, and to international outreach based on sporting pathways, in a *sport plus* model. Examples include UK Sport, who divested itself of International Inspiration, a major legacy project of the 2012 London Olympics that reached more than 25 million children around the world through its programs focused on gender equality, healthy choices, child protection, disability sport, and financial empowerment. International Inspiration was initially delivered through a partnership between the British Council, UNICEF and UK Sport, with funding from the London Organizing Committee for the Olympic Games and support from various celebrity endorsers. After the London Olympics, however, International Inspiration became an independent charity housed under UK Sport before splitting from UK Sport to become its own organization. Similarly, the closing of the UNOSDP, and the transfer of this portfolio to the IOC, an organization whose mandate is still more sport focused on elite sport than the challenges of international development, signals that the SDP sector may be experiencing something of a return to *sport plus* programming.

These shifts and trends have contributed to the recognition of SDP as a significant sub-set of the global sport landscape, and of the international development sector more broadly. In the next section, some trends in SDP research are discussed, particularly the somewhat uneasy tension between monitoring and evaluation (M&E) and critique.

Trends in SDP research—from M&E to critique

Accompanying the growth and shifts in SDP policy and practice over the past several decades has been research into its effects and impact, as well as its structures, politics and meanings. The most traditional and recognizable, and often the most politically palatable, approach to SDP research has been M&E, meaning research that is designed to assess the outcomes of SDP programs, to monitor their progress, and to measure what impact (if any) involvement in SDP has on participants. Clearly, such information is important to SDP organizations, particularly those who exist within a competitive funding structure and must prove that their efforts are having an impact in order to justify their continued income. Pre- and post-tests are often the preferred methodology in this kind of research, and Randomized Control Trials (RCTS) have even been used recently (McFarlane et al. 2017), suggesting a space for normative research practices within the sector.

M&E is no doubt useful for researchers and SDP organizations when they wish to understand and document the effects that SDP programs have upon participants. Given that the goal of SDP is often to produce some kind of behavior change and/or social benefit, understanding the 'before and after' of SDP programs is of interest. And for organizations who may be implementing projects over time, a monitoring process that tracks quality assurance is also necessary. With that said, there are several limitations to the traditional approach to M&E.

One is that such research tends to lack appreciation of, or fails to provide insight into, the contextual factors that shape SDP. This notion of context has several dimensions. It refers to the social, historical and political context to which SDP programs attend and in which they operate. For example, the spread of the HIV/ AIDS pandemic was exacerbated by structural adjustment programs implemented by the World Bank in the 1980s that reduced public spending on health care, as well as by international aid programs, like the President's Emergency Plan for AIDS Relief (PEPFAR) that made abstinence-only education the preferred response to the spread of the virus (Santelli et al. 2013). Context also speaks to the cultural norms, values and structures in which SDP programs operate. For example, if gender empowerment is a focus of an SDP program, this would encourage an appreciation of the ways that gender is understood, practiced and performed in that particular cultural context. Overall, the objectivity embedded in much M&E activity does little to account for such context and its significance.

A second limiting factor of M&E in relation to SDP is that it may do little to speak to or illuminate the specific role that sport plays in development and peace building processes. In other words, while it may be possible to evaluate behavior change using a pre- and post-test methodology, such results may say little about the role that sport played (or did *not* play) in affecting such change. In such cases, sport is often presumed to be the catalytic factor, but without empirical support, such claims are often based on mythopoeic notions of sport's social positivity and transformative abilities (Coalter 2007).

Third, and given the importance of context as well as the need to account for the specific role of sport, there is a need for theories of change when researching and assessing SDP (Coalter 2007). This approach would move the assessment of SDP from the results of particular programs to an appreciation of the mechanisms of change (if any) that occur through SDP. Theories of change help to explain how/why development and/or peace outcomes proceed from sport, and make such results more applicable—and increase the chance of them being replicable—in other cultural and geographic settings.

Overall, then, there are limits—epistemological, methodological, and political—of conventional approaches to SDP research. Coalter (2013) has also shown that the assessment of SDP's outcomes has tended to skew knowledge production within the SDP sector. He draws attention to 'incestuous amplification' in SDP, which refers to the process by which positive outcomes of sport programs are selectively highlighted and celebrated, and then used to form the basis of future and ongoing claims about SDP's efficacy. Similarly, 'displacement of scope' occurs when micro or individual level changes supported by and through SDP are presumed or claimed to have macro or social level effects without data or evidence to support such declarations (Coalter 2013). This is a particularly pernicious process in SDP given that M&E of SDP programs tends to focus on individual experiences and behavior change, rather than structures and/or change at the community, regional and/or cultural levels. As Guest (2013, p. 173) notes of SDP, "while intending to promote both individual and community development, the logistical complications of working at the community level leave most programs focusing primarily (if not exclusively) on individuals."

Taken together, these critical perspectives highlight the need for caution and reflection upon the politics and economics of SDP, particularly the ways in which the organizational context in which SDP programs operate often encourages results that 'prove' the development benefits of sport. It is within this milieu that critical research into SDP has emerged, emanating from the relatively disparate fields of sociology, post-colonial studies, political science, international relations, development studies, social psychology, and sport management, among others. While a full recap and overview of these disciplinary approaches to SDP research is beyond the scope of this chapter, some trends and themes can be identified.

Sociology, notably including feminist and post-colonial theorizing and analysis, has tended to examine the extent to which SDP policies and programs challenge and/or confirm social hierarchies of race, class and gender, particularly within the historical structures and practices of imperialism and colonialism. Scholars working in this framework have found that SDP may offer marginalized groups important opportunities to assert agency (Kay 2009, Hayhurst 2014) but that SDP can also confirm the normativity of Whiteness (Darnell 2007) and traditional gender norms, while privileging First World knowledge production (Nicholls et al. 2010).

Meanwhile, scholars working in a development studies framework, meaning the inter-disciplinary field of study concerned with the history, practice and politics of international development, have tended to examine SDP within the broader development landscape. This has led to discussions about whether SDP constitutes a form of top-down development, in which it is imposed on relatively powerless actors, subjects and locales—often in the global South—by relatively powerful institutions and forces, and/or whether SDP affords bottom-up development by and through which local actors are able to take some control over development (see Black 2010, 2017). Some notable research in SDP has found evidence of both within a single SDP program (see Hayhurst 2014), supporting Black's argument that SDP is actually characterized by significant inter-dependency between top-down and bottom-up actors, and so what calls for attention in SDP practice and research is less the absence of such interdependence and more "the *form* and *effects* of these connections" (2017, p. 8, italics in original).

Scholars from social psychology have also made important contributions to SDP research in recent years. Social psychology has been used as a lens through which to conceive, and even measure or account for, behavior change that may or may not occur through SDP programs and interventions. As Guest (2013, p. 170) concludes, many SDP programs are focused on "broad non-psychological objectives such as community development or social change, but in their actual goals, practices, and evaluation the focus goes disproportionately to individual and psychological characteristics." At the same time, social psychology may offer SDP researchers something of a toolkit through which to conduct research that is sensitive and receptive to participants, particularly through an appreciation of the importance of listening, collaborating and theorizing (Guest 2013).

Finally, the discipline of sport management has also made important contributions to SDP research in recent years. This approach has tended to focus on the organizational structures and partnerships, as well as leadership practices, that are required to optimize the implementation and realization of successful SDP programming (e.g., Welty Peachey et al. in press). Sport management scholars have also offered frameworks for program design that may be informative across contexts (e.g., Schulenkorf 2012). More recently, some SDP research has emerged that blends management questions with sociologically informed analyses, by focusing on, for example, the experiences of international and trans-migrant women who work as staff members for global SDP organizations (see Thorpe and Chawansky 2017). This type of work shows that the organization of SDP programs can itself be a gendered practice, and calls for recognition of "womens' lived experiences as a valid and valuable form of knowledge that could be used to inform management approaches adopted by sport for development (SfD) organizations" (Thorpe and Chawansky 2017, p. 546).

Taken as a whole, then, the field of SDP research is firmly multi-disciplinary. This is not to say that individual or particular SDP studies are themselves *inter-*disciplinary, but the field does include work from a range of theoretical and methodological perspectives. In turn, there are several important critical questions that have emerged.

One is whether, at a conceptual, ideological and/or practical level, SDP constitutes an imperial and/or neo-colonial practice. There is an argument to be made that SDP—like the traditional approach to international development more broadly—is primarily a process by which powerful institutions assert their influence and their preferred version of the social and political economy upon the relatively marginal members of the global South (Darnell 2012). Following from this have been Orientalist arguments, in which SDP is seen to construct and secure an understanding of the preferred third world subject that serves to confirm the sanctity of northern benevolence and munificence (Darnell 2014).

Related to this, and second, is the question of whether—or at least to what extent—SDP is socially challenging versus reproductive. At issue is that SDP may align with, but do little to challenge, the dominant political and cultural framework of neo-liberalism that tends to privilege individual responsibility and regulation. Following this logic, Hartmann and Kwauk (2011) have argued that the dominant form of sport for development is designed primarily to teach marginalized people the skills and tools to survive amidst structures of inequality, a process that is fundamentally different than challenging such structures themselves. This thesis is corroborated by studies that show that even if individual participants in SDP programs learn important life skills—such as how to be an entrepreneur—this still often leaves the logic and structure of neo-liberalism in place, and may even secure it further (Hayhurst 2014).

Taken to its logical conclusion, a third critical question emerges: if the point of SDP is to pursue a more just and egalitarian society, is it reasonable to expect that

SDP programs can ever achieve their goals? There are important constraining factors that need to be acknowledged and even accounted for when assessing this question. In the case of the SDGs for example, the environmental track record of sport is so poor that it behooves critical scholars to think carefully about whether sport can in fact make a positive contribution to the challenges of global climate change and environmental sustainability (see Miller 2017). Similarly, the efficacy of sport programs in achieving non-sport goals is consistently complicated by the cultural norms and expectations attached to competitive sport itself. For example, the Football for Peace (F4P) program in Israel, which has worked for years to position football (soccer) as a medium for understanding and reconciliation between ethnic communities, has had to navigate the desires of many of its participants who often wish, first and foremost, to become elite football players, which can trump the intended goals of the F4P program (Schulenkorf et al. 2014). In this sense, simply stating that a program will follow a *plus sport* framework is no guarantee that such an ethos will be readily accepted or interpreted. All of this highlights the difficulty and contestability of actually organizing sport and SDP in such a way that it might make a positive contribution to meeting development goals.

SDP research and the question of social change

The penultimate section of this chapter considers the extent to which research specifically in the field of SDP has made significant change at a social, cultural and/or political scale. The question of what a more transformative approach to SDP research might look like is then considered.

Overall, and despite the growth and institutionalization of SDP in recent years, it would be presumptuous or even naïve to suggest that the relatively small amount of SDP research—coupled with SDP's moderate significance within the broader structures of international sport and international development respectively—has had a major effect and led to social change. However, with the notion of reasonable expectations in mind, there are some examples to suggest that SDP research has contributed to change, particularly by shifting SDP practice and policy.

One example is the growing series of literature reviews that have been conducted by SDP scholars in recent years (e.g., Langer 2015, Schulenkorf et al. 2016, Svensson and Woods 2017) some of which have been commissioned by SDP non-governmental organizations, inter-governmental bodies, and funders. In 2007, for example, Right to Play commissioned literature reviews from researchers at the University of Toronto, to assess the current state of the research evidence regarding sport's applicability and utility in meeting development goals (Kidd and Donnelly 2007). Similarly, in 2017, the Laureus Sport for Good Foundation and Commonwealth Secretariat—both important global stakeholders in the SDP sector—commissioned a team of researchers to conduct a systematic review of evidence regarding the outcomes of sport for development literature, and compare it to the extant literature in youth development more broadly (Whitley et al. 2017). Literature reviews such as these have offered scholars the opportunity to conduct rigorous, yet critically cautious, assessments of the research literature and present these findings to stakeholders who may be in a position to make or adjust SDP policy accordingly. This is not to suggest that such relationships are free of politics—privately commissioned research can indeed come with significant strings attached—but such opportunities do offer scholars a conduit through which to make their research available to SDP stakeholders.

In addition, two other possible forms of influence emerge from these kind of activities. One is that it opens up possibilities for SDP researchers to work with partners, such as the Commonwealth Secretariat and Laureus, who are generally keen to learn about the insights and opportunities available through the academic sector. While navigating these partnerships is invariably tricky, it does offer scholars access and opportunity to see their work lead to change. Two, policy reports—which include recommendations about how to improve SDP policy—are increasingly welcome by key SDP stakeholders, particularly in organizations (governmental and non) that are new to SDP. This, too, suggests a willingness on the part of SDP stakeholders to learn from research, an opportunity on which critical scholars might continue to capitalize.

In addition, there is a sense (though one that is hard to quantify or confirm) that the post- and/or neo-colonial critiques of SDP put forth by critical scholars have led to greater awareness of the importance of history, context and power within the organizations and practices of the SDP sector. A few examples of this are pertinent: The argument that international internships in SDP largely confirmed the benevolence of First World subjects while reifying the passivity of the developing world seems to have contributed to a general move in the SDP sector to scale back the use of international volunteers and instead work more with professional staff and local partners. Similarly, the argument that local knowledge in SDP is often subjugated in relation to objective data, or only considered significant when corroborated by outside actors, has led to important discussions within the sector about how to integrate different types of data—or even expanded notions of what counts as evidence—within the M&E of SDP activities.

Overall, however, there is unquestionably more to be done to make critical SDP research more significant in its impact, or even to re-organize it in such a way that it could make a contribution to social change. In this respect, it is worth restating Hartmann and Kwauk's (2011) argument that SDP—at least in its dominant form—is not designed or intended to pursue social change as much as it is to prepare marginalized persons for the challenges of trying to survive in the current social formation. If this is correct, then SDP scholars have to think beyond simply assessing the outcomes of SDP programs, and move towards research that sets out to make a difference. So, what might SDP research look like if the goal was to support social change? The final section of the chapter offers several ideas.

SDP research and the pursuit of social change

First, and in the broadest sense, SDP research that seeks to contribute to social change should start from a position that research does not equal, and cannot be reduced to, a process of M&E. The context and significance (historical, cultural, political, etc.) of SDP is such that critical scholars need to keep asking questions about SDP's impact and effects in the most holistic sense, while resisting the tendency to reduce their research to an assessment of individual experiences, pre- and post-programming.

To that end, it clearly behooves SDP research—even in its most critical form—to recognize and respect the context and structural constraints in which the sector operates. This is something of an appeal to *realpolitik* in critical SDP research, whereby scholars would ground their research in appreciation of the lived experiences and quotidian struggles of SDP stakeholders. Guest's (2009) analysis of the differing needs, goals and desires between SDP programmers and program recipients in Angola is a good example of these experiences. Another is Jeanes and Lindsey's (2014) insights into the pressures placed on local employees of SDP NGOs, who are often faced with significant incentives to conclude that SDP programs yield positive benefits because their livelihoods depend on it. This work within the 'reality' of SDP might require critical scholars and researchers to consider the productive possibilities of working with more traditional or conventional researchers, rather than (only) developing critiques from qualitative, post-structuralist or discursive perspectives. As Pringle and Falcous (2016) have discussed, the field of critical sport sociology is likely to remain limited in its scope and impact if it refuses to engage with the theories, methods and means of empiricism that are hallmarks of more traditional, conventional research paradigms. The overall point here is that for critical SDP research to make a difference, its proponents may have to develop an appreciation for the situations and structures in which it occurs and which constrain its practice.

With that in mind, there is a clear trend in SDP research to move from simply researching its outcomes and effects, to working *with* participants, partners, and stakeholders in ways that support the agency of local people and even help to push and frame critical issues. Several means of praxis are available. One is Participatory Action Research, and Feminist Participatory Action Research, which has been advocated for a number of years by SDP scholars as a way to challenge relations of dominance in SDP (see Darnell and Hayhurst 2014, Hayhurst 2017). There have been important successes derived from SDP, notably the relationships built with co-researchers whose experiences and insights have traditionally been marginalized in international development and SDP. That said, PAR and FPAR are by no means a panacea or a guarantee of successfully pursuing social change. Issues such as the exposure of co-researchers to violence have been noted (Thorpe et al. in press), as have the difficulties in researchers actually relinquishing control and authority over the research (Spaaij et al. in press). Still, the sense that the presumed beneficiaries of SDP research should be passive research subjects has largely passed, and SDP researchers need therefore to continue to think about how their work might engage with all manner of research stakeholders in a spirit of collegiality.

Similarly, critical pedagogy has been explored as a possible framework for SDP praxis. In the tradition of liberation theology, and pedagogues like Paulo Freire, SDP could be repositioned and pursued (in both research and practice) as something other than the integration of marginalized subjects into the structures of competitive capitalism (Spaaij and Jeanes 2013, Spaaij et al. 2016). Instead, it may be possible to pursue SDP as reflection upon, and the exposing of and resistance to, structures and relations that secure development inequalities and the need for SDP interventions in the first place (Darnell 2012). This explicitly political and transformative approach to SDP is unlikely to be entirely popular, but it remains available to SDP scholars, particularly given the rich history of critical pedagogy as a sub-discipline within the social sciences.

Further, the time may be right for pursuing an ethics of SDP, which would see critical scholars move past critique and towards proposing a vision and framework for how best to pursue equitable and sustainable development through sport. Recently, the Capabilities Approach has been discussed by researchers as a possible conceptual basis for SDP, one that privileges the freedoms of individuals to pursue development on their own terms (Darnell and Dao 2017, Suzuki 2017, Svensson and Levine 2017). The point here is not that any one framework can or should become the correct way in and through which to organize SDP, but rather that in order to make a positive contribution and to pursue change, critical scholars may need to offer frameworks and approaches, and even a political vision, for what SDP *should* look like.

To conclude, then, it is reasonable to suggest that what SDP research can offer to the pursuit of social change is to stand as a critical bulwark against the politics, economics and ideologies that tend to keep the sector working primarily in the service of social reproduction, and often do so through the limited research framework of M&E. In this sense, when SDP advocates or champions put forth grandiose claims about SDP's role as an agent of change, it will likely continue to be up to critical scholars to hold the sector to account, through assessments of SDP that are grounded in the values of empiricism, specificity and honesty.

References

Black, D. R., 2017. The challenges of articulating 'top down' and 'bottom up' development through sport. *Third World Thematics: A TWQ Journal*, 2 (1), 7–22.

Black, D. R., 2010. The ambiguities of development: Implications for 'development through sport'. *Sport in Society*, 13 (1), 121–129.

Chatziefstathiou, D., and Henry, I., 2012. *Discourses of Olympism: From the Sorbonne 1894 to London 2012*. Basingstoke: Palgrave Macmillan.

Coalter, F., 2013. *Sport for development: What game are we playing?* London: Routledge.

Coalter, F., 2007. *A wider social role for sport: Who's keeping the score?* London: Taylor & Francis.

Darnell, S. C., 2014. Orientalism through sport: Towards a Said-ian analysis of imperialism and 'Sport for Development and Peace'. *Sport in Society*, 17 (8), 1000–1014.

Darnell, S. C., 2012. *Sport for development and peace: A critical sociology*. London: Bloomsbury Academic.

Darnell, S. C., 2007. Playing with race: Right to play and the production of whiteness in 'development through sport. *Sport in Society*, 10 (4), 560–579.

Darnell, S. C., and Dao, M., 2017. Considering sport for development and peace through the capabilities approach. *Third World Thematics: A TWQ Journal*, 2 (1), 1–14.

Darnell, S. C., and Hayhurst, L. M., 2014. De-colonising the politics and practice of sport-for-development: Critical insights from post-colonial feminist theory and methods. In: N. Schulenkorf and D. Adair, eds. *Global Sport-for-Development: Critical perspectives*. Basingstoke: Palgrave Macmillan, 33–61.

Guest, A. M., 2013. Sport psychology for development and peace? Critical reflections and constructive suggestions. *Journal of Sport Psychology in Action*, 4 (3), 169–180.

Guest, A. M., 2009. The diffusion of development-through-sport: Analysing the history and practice of the Olympic Movement's grassroots outreach to Africa. *Sport in Society*, 12 (10), 1336–1352.

Hartmann, D., 2016. *Midnight basketball: Race, sports, and neoliberal social policy*. Chicago: University of Chicago Press.

Hartmann, D., and Kwauk, C., 2011. Sport and development: An overview, critique, and reconstruction. *Journal of Sport & Social Issues*, 35 (3), 284–305.

Hayhurst, L. M., 2017. Image-ining resistance: using participatory action research and visual methods in sport for development and peace. *Third World Thematics: A TWQ Journal*, 2 (1), 117–140.

Hayhurst, L. M., 2014. The 'Girl Effect' and martial arts: social entrepreneurship and sport, gender and development in Uganda. *Gender, Place & Culture*, 21 (3), 297–315.

Jeanes, R., and Lindsey, I., 2014. Where's the "evidence"? Reflecting on monitoring and evaluation within Sport-for-Development. In: K. Young and C. Okada, eds. *Sport, social development and peace*. Bingley: Emerald Group Publishing, 197–217.

Kay, T., 2009. Developing through sport: Evidencing sport impacts on young people. *Sport in Society*, 12 (9), 1177–1191.

Kidd, B., 2008. A new social movement: Sport for development and peace. *Sport in Society*, 11 (4), 370–380.

Kidd, B., and Donnelly, P., 2007. *Literature reviews on Sport for Development and Peace*. http://www.righttoplay.com/moreinfo/aboutus/Documents/Literature%20Reviews%20SDP.pdf

Langer, L., 2015. Sport for development—a systematic map of evidence from Africa. *South African Review of Sociology*, 46 (1), 66–86.

McFarlane, J., et al., 2017. Preventing peer violence against children: Methods and baseline data of a cluster randomized controlled trial in Pakistan. *Global Health, Science and Practice*, 5 (1), 115–137.

Miller, T., 2017. *Greenwashing sport*. London: Taylor & Francis.

Nicholls, S., Giles, A. R., and Sethna, C., 2010. Perpetuating the 'lack of evidence' discourse in sport for development: Privileged voices, unheard stories and subjugated knowledge. *International Review for the Sociology of Sport*, 46 (3), 249–264.

Pringle, R., and Falcous, M., 2016. Transformative research and epistemological hierarchies: Ruminating on how the sociology of the sport field could make more of a difference. *International Review for the Sociology of Sport*, 1012690216654297.

Santelli, J. S., Speizer, I. S., and Edelstein, Z. R., 2013. Abstinence promotion under PEPFAR: The shifting focus of HIV prevention for youth. *Global Public Health*, 8 (1), 1–12.

Schulenkorf, N., 2012. Sustainable community development through sport and events: A conceptual framework for Sport-for-Development projects. *Sport Management Review*, 15 (1), 1–12.

Schulenkorf, N., Sherry, E., and Rowe, K., 2016. Sport for development: an integrated literature review. *Journal of Sport Management*, 30 (1), 22–39.

Schulenkorf, N., Sugden, J., and Burdsey, D., 2014. Sport for development and peace as contested terrain: place, community, ownership. *International Journal of Sport Policy and Politics*, 6 (3), 371–387.

Spaaij, R., and Jeanes, R., 2013. Education for social change? A Freirean critique of sport for development and peace. *Physical Education and Sport Pedagogy*, 18 (4), 442–457.

Spaaij, R., Oxford, S., and Jeanes, R., 2016. Transforming communities through sport? Critical pedagogy and sport for development. *Sport, Education and Society*, 21 (4), 570–587.

Spaaij, R. et al., In press. Participatory research in sport-for-development: Complexities, experiences and (missed) opportunities. *Sport Management Review*.

Suzuki, N., 2017. A capability approach to understanding sport for social inclusion: Agency, structure and organisations. *Social Inclusion*, 5 (2), 150–158.

Svensson, P. G., and Levine, J., 2017. Rethinking Sport for Development and Peace: the Capability Approach. *Sport in Society*, 20 (7), 905–923.

Svensson, P., and Woods, H., 2017. A systematic overview of sport for development and peace organisations. *Journal of Sport for Development*, 5 (9), 36–48.

Thorpe, H., and Chawansky, M., 2017. The gendered experiences of women staff and volunteers in Sport for Development organizations: The case of transmigrant workers of Skateistan. *Journal of Sport Management*, 31 (6), 546–561.

Thorpe, H., Hayhurst, L. M., and Chawansky, M., In press. 'Once my relatives see me on social media … it will be something very bad for my family': The ethics and risks of organizational representations of sporting girls from the global south. *Sociology of Sport Journal*.

UN Inter-Agency Task Force on Sport for Development and Peace, 2003. *Sport as a tool for development and peace: Towards achieving the United Nations Millennium Development Goals*. https://www.un.org/sport2005/resources/task_force.pdf

United Nations, 2016. *Transforming our world: The 2030 agenda for sustainable development*. https://sustainabledevelopment.un.org/post2015/transformingourworld

UNOSDP, 2016. *Sport and sustainable development goals*. https://www.un.org/sport/content/why-sport/sport-and-sustainable-development-goals

Welty Peachey, J. W. et al., In press. Challenges and strategies of building and sustaining inter-organizational partnerships in sport for development and peace. *Sport Management Review*.

Whitley, M. et al., 2017. *Sport for development: A systematic review and comparative analysis—final report*. Laureus Sport for Good Foundation & Commonwealth Advisory Board on Sport.

Wickstrom, M., 2017, UN Secretary-General closes UNOSDP. http://www.playthegame.org/news/news-articles/2017/0309_un-secretary-general-closes-unosdp/

Football 4 Peace v Homophobia: A critical exploration of the links between theory, practice and intervention

Jayne Caudwell and Graham Spacey

Introduction

In this chapter, we draw on our different biographies to explore the links between theories of sexualities and genders, and anti-homophobic, anti-transphobic and anti-biphobic intervention within UK University footballing contexts. Our critical discussion includes long-term involvement with scholarship and campaigning surrounding gender and sexuality in football (Caudwell) and long-term project development of the Football 4 Peace (F4P) International reconciliation initiative (Spacey). We seek to plot the ways sociological and pedagogical scholarship, especially related to discrimination, equity, gender and sexualities, informs grassroots provision and praxis at the level of student sport. We focus on the aim to make a difference when it comes to challenging social divisions and inequalities vis-à-vis Sexual Orientation and Gender Identity (SOGI). During our discussions we draw from observations and interviews to demonstrate the ways participation in an annual football event can support anti-discriminatory practice and policy.

The chapter starts with a depiction of the project: Football 4 Peace (F4P) v Homophobia, and the connections between the initiative, the authors and student involvement. This includes a description of the research that underpins the empirical material presented in the two main sections of the chapter. The first main section considers the potential to 'make a difference'. In other words, the possibilities to interpolate a public sociology/pedagogy of anti-discrimination into student sporting/footballing practice. The second main section appraises levels of intervention to gain a view of how the project contests heteronormativity.

Football 4 Peace v Homophobia

On 2 and 3 May 2012 the inaugural F4P v Homophobia event took place at the University of Brighton, UK. The event and associated project represented a tribute to professional footballer Justin Fashanu (19 February 1961–2 May 1998); he was the first and only professional male footballer in the UK to publicly come out as gay. Tragically he took his own life on 2 May 1998. The inaugural event involved a football festival (Justin Student Football Festival) and a symposium (Justin Campaign

Symposium: Campaigning for Change) as well as a weeklong art exhibition located in the main entrance to the University sport centre. The project entitled *Taking a Stand: Sexualities and Sport Participation*, was funded by the University of Brighton Community University Partnership Project (CUPP). Jayne Caudwell applied for the funding and organised the art exhibition and symposium. Graham Spacey led the running of the football festival, including managing student volunteers.

The Community University Partnership brought together volunteers for, and followers of, The Justin Campaign (no longer active), the Football for Peace (F4P) reconciliation initiative, the Football v Homophobia initiative (now with Pride Sports), East Sussex Youth project: Tackle Homophobia, a number of County Football Associations (FA), The Rugby Football League, University of Brighton Sport Brighton (student sport provider), undergraduate and postgraduate students, and University staff.

The two days were a success in terms of participation and knowledge exchange. For instance, 30 people attended the symposium and roughly 130 people participated in the football festival (12 teams of 7 players, 24 student volunteers, and 30 plus spectators). Of the 24 student volunteers 20 were from BA (hons) Physical Education and 4 from BA (hons) Sport Journalism courses. The journalist students sent out two press releases to local papers, posted tweets and photographed/recorded the events. They produced two short video clips, which continue to be used today. A number of emails were received after this inaugural event, including the following:

> I just wanted to say how much I enjoyed the Football versus Homophobia Festival. I thought the atmosphere was fantastic. You put on a fantastic afternoon where everyone seemed to enjoy themselves and most importantly, from what I could see, you got the message through to some people who had never thought about sexuality and football before. (from a University student participant)

> I am having an evening of introspection after fielding a string of innocent questions from my daughter. 'Why was Justin gay?', 'Why were people unkind to him', 'Is it wrong to be gay', 'Why was the football table pink?' It is so difficult to gauge readiness of children to grapple with some big life questions. Interestingly race and disability have never been questioned and I can only assume that in her world there is greater acceptance and equality than in ours. (from a member of University staff)

Since its inception in 2012, the F4P v Homophobia football festival at the University of Brighton has taken place every year at the beginning of May. It has included high profile supporters and participants, including Sophie Cook, the first trans woman Labour Party candidate (in 2017). Managed by Spacey and sustained through student volunteering, in particular F4P student volunteers, the project has had a reach beyond the University of Brighton. For example, a football festival led by University of Brighton student volunteers took place at Sussex Downs College of Further Education; the Office for Standards in Education (Ofsted), Children's

Services and Skills identified it as good practice. Although Ofsted represents the emergence of an education audit culture in the UK, their recognition of this anti-discrimination campaign reflects positive institutional attitudes towards LGBT and sport. Importantly, the recognition documents student engagement:

> to promote tolerance and understanding of lesbian, gay, bisexual, and transgender (LGBT) issues, the college established a successful learner-led project called 'Football 4 Peace', which resulted in a heightened level of understanding of

> Level 2 business learners organised a successful college-wide football competition to challenge stereotypes and misconceptions around homophobia in sport. (Ofsted Inspection Report, 12 June 2014, p. 11)

More recently, in February 2017, Spacey and University of Brighton students helped deliver a similar project at Bournemouth University. It involved a football festival and a symposium for students (BSc and MSc Sport Management), staff and community groups. The timing of this event coincided with LGBT History Month and Football v Homophobia (a Pride Sports campaign) Month of Action. The initiative Football v Homophobia was originally devised by The Justin Campaign and involved a day of action—19 February, Justin Fashanu's birth date. The Bournemouth University 2017 event entitled *LGBT Young People and Their Sport and Leisure*, was badged as a partnership between Bournemouth University and University of Brighton. Speakers from Student Union, Pride Sports and Space (Dorset's LGBT+ Youth Project) attended.

In February 2018, another football festival and symposium (jointly entitled *LGBT+, Sport, Leisure and Wellbeing*) took place at Bournemouth University. Speakers included Commui-T (a local transgender group), Dorset police, and Dorset and Wiltshire Fire and Rescue. The University of Brighton organised their seventh annual F4P v Homophobia football festival on 2 May 2018 accompanied by a *Teaching Social Justice* symposium. All events aim to: further develop university–community connections; promote student awareness of abuse, discrimination, and prejudice; and build teaching and policy agendas vis-à-vis justice and equity.

Unique to the F4P initiative is the values-based pedagogy that underpins the delivery of football participation for co-existence. University student volunteers embed the values of equity, inclusion, respect, responsibility and trust into their coaching and officiating practice. This means participation is not based on traditional notions of sporting competition and winning through scoring goals. Instead participants are awarded points for on-field behaviours that reflect the five values. Behaviours such as players greeting each other with handshakes before and after games, collecting the ball for the opposing team, helping an opposition player to their feet, and admitting foul play are awarded points. These values have been carried over into the F4P v Homophobia projects, and in addition to player conduct, participants play under the banners of Football v Homophobia, Biphobia

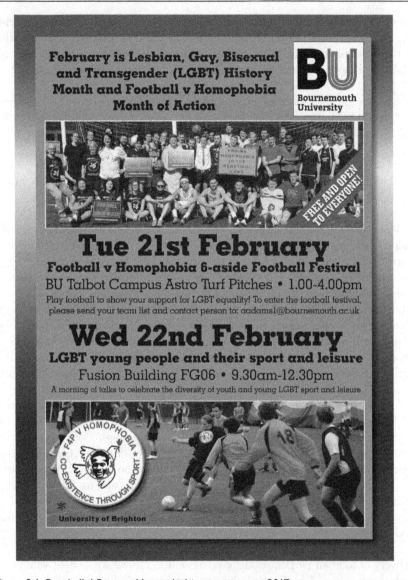

Figure 3.1   Football 4 Peace v Homophobia event poster 2017

Source: Designed and produced by Alan Wares. Commissioned by Jayne Caudwell

and Transphobia (see figure 3.1). In this way, the values are not only displayed via gesture, they are visible through signs and symbols of equity, inclusion and respect.

It is this core pedagogy as well as the network of partnerships and community groups that provide the foundations for linking theory, practice and intervention. As a sustained and considered successful initiative the F4P v Homophobia football festivals and symposiums might be viewed through current UK Higher Education discourse under 'impact'. Indeed the F4P initiative was graded at the highest level of 4* Impact Case Study in UK Research Excellence Framework (REF) 2014. Clearly this grading is given through a ratcheted-up auditing of Higher Education Institutions (HEIs) in the UK. Regardless, an important point is that academics cannot take sole credit for the achievement of impact. It is often students, research assistants and project officers (e.g., Spacey) that deliver university-based education initiatives into communities of the public.

In this chapter, we offer a critical reflection on the possibilities of the project and initiatives described above in relation to the aspiration to 'make a difference'. We draw from previous scrutiny of F4P v Homophobia (e.g., Burdsey and Caudwell 2014; Spacey and Caudwell, 2012), including existing empirical research material from interviews with student participants, participant observation and observation. Spacey has attended all F4P v Homophobia events to date. Caudwell attended in 2012, 2013, 2016, 2017 and 2018; she played in the staff football team on all five occasions. Additionally, we rely on a recent interview dialogue between the authors that occurred on 22 September 2017. The interview dialogue lasted about one and a half hours and followed a format that positioned Caudwell as the interviewer and Spacey as the interviewee. Although we have spoken about the projects previously, and asked ourselves a number of critical questions regarding the worth of F4P v Homophobia, we have not focused our dialogue and reflection in the way an interview affords.

Public sociology/pedagogy: Anti-discrimination through student football

JC: I've come to it from a background of activism and politics as opposed to pedagogy. And so, when I got involved with F4P in Israel (2005 and 2009) it was my politics around Palestine … and it was very male, you know boy participation … so I withdrew [from F4P]. But when this opportunity came up to do v Homophobia for me it was a political activist agenda: "let's raise issues around homophobia and discrimination and Justin Fashanu". It fitted in with my work for the Justin Campaign at the time (2011–2013). I didn't necessarily see it as training coaches. How do you see it?

GS: I'm from a teaching background, and actually I found it a male-dominated space: F4P especially in Israel despite trying certain things. It was a bunch of men including myself trying to do the right thing. Trying to retain females has always been an issue. … it's something I think we need to look at. But, I see F4P v Homophobia as another opportunity. In terms of those students that get involved that are political activists like you, it's a chance for them to see and learn a different way of activism [through football]. From the pedagogical side, it's students like the teacher-training student or PE student, or the sport-coaching student. It's an opportunity to get them thinking about activism and politics. So many of them think it has nothing to do with them as the "social sciences teacher" would do it, or the "English teacher", and "I'm PE". And then they suddenly realise that there are links. It may not manifest itself at university, but it does when they go into school and they realise "ah"! If you look at our alumni that have done F4P in Israel or done F4P v Homophobia, a lot of them are becoming heads of departments or head teachers—especially the ones from the early days. It may not be quite clear ... It's sort of "you're a political activist you're left wing", you know, whereas "I'm not right wing and I'm not left wing I'm a teacher and I'm going to teach the kids how to throw a ball and run round a field". And then it becomes "I'm going to teach values and life skills and try and teach them about issues that go on around the world, through sport, ... because now I understand those issues and why they happen I understand why there are political activists, and I'm becoming more of a political activist myself."

Anti-discrimination activism and protesting homophobic, transphobic and biphobic discrimination are complex activities. Students that study sport and physical education at undergraduate and postgraduate levels often learn the nature and theories of inequality, discrimination and equality in the classroom. As such, the process of learning—gaining knowledge and developing critical response—is often separate from their active involvement with physical activity. Participating in sporting events that carry anti-discriminatory messages changes this dynamic of separation. In this section we discuss anti-discrimination activism (through student-led football festivals), and the scope of public sociology and public pedagogy. First, it is important to get a sense of what is meant by public sociology and public pedagogy.

Public sociology

Donnelly (2015) links public sociology with sociological work that 'makes a difference' (p. 419). He charts the development of the sociology of sport, discusses the production of sociological knowledge for its own sake and/or 'for the sake of humanity' (p. 420), and draws from Burawoy's four dimensions of sociological work: professional, policy, critical and public. Donnelly cites a specific sociological study of sport—Loy and McElvogue's (1970) account of racial segregation in men's sport in the United States and the concept of staking—that entered the public domain, albeit over a period of time, and changed the tone of public debate. According to Donnelly (2015), the original study, and subsequent replicated studies, provided meaningful research findings to incite change.

Cooky (2017) identifies the shift from studying inequality and injustice in sport to impacting the sporting domain as public engagement. She acknowledges the value of translational research in supplying evidenced-based findings, and extends the notion of public sociology to community-led activism and advocacy. She provides current examples (e.g., #BlackLivesMatter) of US athletes adopting visible forms of advocacy and activism, and argues that their activities offer a platform for sociologists of sport to launch a unique, contemporary public sociology. Moreover, that sport academics engage with communities in ways that avoid being framed by University neoliberal impact measurements.

The idea that sport allows opportunity for social justice (Maguire, 2004), and that athletes can be activists (Kaufman and Wolff, 2010), is not a new phenomenon. There are a number of historical examples of a range of protests instigated by athletes. In this way, sport can be viewed as a field of play and protest (Kaufman and Wolff, 2010). Sport sociologists have worked with some of these athletes and/ or made visible their actions to the academy (Kaufman, 2008). This work continues. Similarly, examples of the use of sport sociological research to inform sporting practices and cultures of equality and justice are apparent and ongoing (e.g., Women's Sport Foundations in the United States and UK). Critical dialogues are taking place, to varying degrees, between sport sociologist, athletes, investigative journalists and the myriad of governors of sport. This suggests that a public sociology of sport exists. Calls to action for a more influential public engagement might benefit from a consideration of the intricacies of public pedagogy.

Public pedagogy

Commentators from the fields of sport studies (King-White, 2012), physical education (Kirk, 2006; Timing 2002) and health studies (Mansfield and Rich, 2013; Rich, 2011) sometimes refer to the work of Giroux (2000, 2001, 2004) when they explain public pedagogy. In turn, Giroux (2000) draws from Stuart Hall, as well as Antonio Gramsci, to emphasise how an in-depth understanding of culture, power and cultural power can serve social and political transformation. Giroux supports Hall's point of view that 'culture is central to understanding struggles over meaning, identity and power' (p. 342) as well as struggles over subjectivity and ideology. From this cultural studies perspective, the focus is the public and popular domain. It follows that if we learn and teach how culture functions in formulating and defining our ideological and material conditions, we can also learn and teach how to re-make counter configurations to contest these conditions. Thus, the work of public pedagogy:

> as a struggle over identifications is crucial to raising broader questions about how notions of difference, civic responsibility, community, and belonging are produced 'in specific historical and institutional sites within specific discursive formations and practices, by specific enunciative strategies'. (Hall, 1996: 4; cited in Giroux, 2000, p. 352)

The details of when, how and where cultural power, and public pedagogy operate are varied, and this presents a challenge to defining public pedagogy. In simple terms, Sandlin et al. (2011) suggest public pedagogy is present at sites where teaching and learning processes occur outside of 'formal schooling' (p. 338). They go on to offer a coherent appraisal of public pedagogy through a useful review of existing literatures arranged under five conceptual themes: '(a) citizenship within and beyond schools, (b) popular culture and everyday life, (c) informal institutions and public spaces, (d) dominant cultural discourses, and (e) public intellectualism and social activism' (p. 338).

Making public Football 4 Peace v Homophobia

F4P v Homophobia can be viewed as both public sociology and public pedagogy. Caudwell's research (1999, 2007, 2011, 2014) with LGBT community members together with similar academic research findings (e.g., Anderson, 2005; Griffin, 1998; Sykes, 2011; Travers and Deri, 2011) provides evidence of the extent and nature of homophobia and transphobia in sport and physical activity. Academics who study social inequalities often disseminate their work to non-academic communities. During 2011–2013 Caudwell was a volunteer with The Justin Campaign[1]; she presented findings gleaned from academic research at public lectures (e.g., during LGBT History Month), and in schools, colleges and two men's prisons (Winchester and Lewes). Volunteers for The Justin Campaign identified as LGBT activists.

Spacey's physical education related work with F4P International (Spacey, 2016; Spacey and Sugden, 2015) draws from and informs on-going critical engagement with values-based coaching embedded within projects in The Gambia, South Korea, South Africa, Jordan, Israel, Ireland, Northern Ireland and in England. Working mostly with children participants, student-volunteers, local youth workers, teachers and coaches teach the values of equity, inclusion, respect, responsibility and trust. A number of partners, associations and ambassadors have adopted the approach to build and develop further opportunities for co-existence. Football 4 Peace has a significant reach in terms of advocacy, and the notion of 'public good' (Sandlin et al., 2011, p. 340).

The foreground of the project F4P v Homophobia reflects a combination of activism (e.g., Caudwell) and advocacy (e.g., Spacey). In this way, it can be considered public sociology. However, public pedagogy might be a more apt descriptor following the terms set out by Sandlin et al. (2001); more specifically, public pedagogy that involves 'informal, yet institutionalized sites as spaces of learning' (p. 348). In essence football as a sport is institutionalised and the football playing fields are public spaces. The F4P v Homophobia football festivals rely on players and participants performing contestation of homophobia, biphobia and transphobia through adopting embodied behaviours, and symbolic representations, of equity, inclusion, respect, responsibility and trust.

Giroux (2001)—citing Grossberg's (1969) notion of 'the act of doing'—brings together concepts of public and of performance in his term performative pedagogy. For him, performing public pedagogy 'represents a moral and political practice rather than merely a technical procedure. ... projects designed to further racial, economic, and political democracy'; he argues that public pedagogy involves a 'socially engaged citizenship' (p. 9). It is this premise that can be applied to evaluate F4P v Homophobia as public sociology/pedagogy. Clearly there is potential to make a difference, but does this happen?

Contesting LGBT discrimination: Subverting sporting heteronormativity?

Notably, the v Homophobia initiative developed from the infrastructures of Football 4 Peace. This means that an evaluation of the links between theory and practice involves aspects that do not initially align with discrimination based on gender identity and sexual orientation; for example, Football 4 Peace generates broader discussion that involves complex political/military milieu and co-existence.

JC: Do you think, in terms of students at Brighton and students at Bournemouth, they actually connect the theory and the practice?

GS: I think they begin to; it's a learning process. Again, coming from an educational point of view, I think you've got to experience something to understand it fully. Some people get it [values-based coaching methodology] but the majority of people, especially if they've not been taught that way, don't get it initially. But, we are beginning to have students that did F4P when they were in school and were taught by a F4P coach. I'm beginning to see a difference. More so on the pedagogical [PE and Sport coaching students] side.

JC: When we went out to Israel, I mean the history and the conflict is so complicated and I don't know if we, or the students actually grasp it [co-existence in Israel]?

GS: I know students who went to Israel and had their eyes open, read about Israel, and then didn't want to go the next year because they were like I don't agree with the politics of Israel. I have students who worked on F4P for a few years and then say I want to work in Palestine. There was one female student who was born in Iraq. She understood Arabic but didn't really use it; she fell in love with it in Israel and now speaks fluent Arabic. These are anecdotal conversation I have with students.

As Spacey highlights, student experiences of Football 4 Peace can operate beyond the established set of coaching methodology values (equity, inclusion, respect, responsibility and trust). The various contexts in which students deliver the values-based coaching can impress new parameters of learning. The conditions in Palestine and Israel provide one example of the project's reach to engender personal and political views, which are not directly related to sport participation. We discussed if this was the case for the focus on sexual orientation and gender identity:

JC: How would you say that students engaged with the issue of homophobia?

GS: One of the students, a big footballer, I didn't realise he has two mums and no one realized and he found it [F4P v Homophobia] good because it sort of validated that it was alright. Not that he needed validation.

JC: Do you think it [F4P v Homophobia] touched people more on a personal level than the co-existence stuff?

GS: It's when we get prominent people like Sophie Cook who's like 'yeah I'll come along and play'. When Sophie came, there were students who went: "I know gays, I know lesbians, I live with them I go to Uni with them. I've never met a trans person in my life." It's not that they're transphobic, it's just not in their realm of experience.

This disjuncture between 'knowledge of' and 'experience of' seems to be significant to the processes of public sociology/pedagogy that involve student culture. Students studying sport (coaching, development, management, science) and physical education can learn about LGBT participation through lectures, seminars, and popular culture. Within a classroom context we can discuss abuse, and discrimination, we can deconstruct stereotypes, identify barriers and constraints, and embrace stories of 'coming out' promoted by popular culture as well as critique associated crass backlash. Beyond key terms and issues, students are invited to engage with the complexities of concepts such as heteronormativity and its circulation of power (socio-cultural, economic and political), and the density of theory such as queer theory. A small number of students, through reading intricate journal articles, produce excellent assignments that demonstrate lucid and coherent understanding of, for example, subverting sporting heteronormativity. However, the question remains, how does F4P v Homophobia provide a platform for performative pedagogy that is subversive?

Students who have participated in the football festival and agreed to be interviewed tend to talk about the intervention in terms of raising awareness and demonstrating support:

> If you bring in the value of respect into the realm of football fans, the crowds are going to respect the players that come out as gay. (Athos)

> to build awareness, because, there's not many students who know about homophobia, and about Justin [Fashanu], 'cause I certainly didn't know anything, until I came [to university] … my flatmates as well, … it was nice to teach them, because they didn't learn it either … they didn't know anything about it. (Fran)

> I think it's very important for universities to have these events because, I know it's a bit of a stereotype, but sports students are generally [sports jocks] … of course there are one or two who are completely not like that. But, to have such an event on a sports campus like this is really good. And it was nice to see everyone turn up and support it. (Kris)

Students and staff play under the banner of v Homophobia as well as v Biphobia and v Transphobia. This support is made explicit when teams pose for photographs with visual signifiers such as placards, T-shirts and bibs, and make verbal statements on camera justifying why they participate. Signifying participation in this way can be viewed as performance and/or acts of activism and points to the "politics of advocacy and possibility" (Denzin and Giardina, 2012) within Higher

Education in the UK. The images and messages recorded continue to have currency when circulated on social media, and when they are used to promote subsequent events. For example, the flyer (see figure 3.1) captures aspects of 2013 and 2016 events and was used in 2017.

Raising awareness and signifying support for LGBT participation in sport, specifically football, through F4P v Homophobia becomes a collective endeavor. Homophobia, biphobia and transphobia are often experienced at the level of the individual and frequently manifest as personal and/or private 'troubles' (to borrow from C Wright Mills). Collective action, according to Gane and Back (2012), is a critical response:

> In a neoliberal world which seeks to tear asunder private troubles from public issues, and thereby turn social uncertainty into a personal failure that is divorced from any collective cause or remedy, the linking of biography and history is a vital part of a sociology that is both politically and publicly engaged. (405)

To date, the extent to which participants and on-lookers (both traditional spectators and social media followers) achieve an enduring critique of the structures of normativity, such as the socio-cultural, political and economic underpinnings of heteronormativity, remains elusive.

Detailed analyses familiar to scholars of gender and sexualities (e.g., Butler, 1993; Stein and Plummer, 1994) offer radical and robust debate of inequalities and injustices. Sport and physical education are prime sites for this type of analyses, but it is rare (lisahunter, 2018). Consequently, it is difficult to convey detailed critique to students, and into public sociology/pedagogy. And so, advocacy and activism tend to produce public engagement that serves contestation, but not subversion. Through performative pedagogies of awareness raising and collective support, students and staff can publicly contest homophobia, biphobia and transphobia. This contestation tends to happen at the locale, although social media usage blurs the boundaries of local, national and international. How to subvert sporting heteronormativity is apparent in some academic scholarship (e.g., King, 2008), but to date there is little evidence of public sociology/pedagogy that accomplishes the subversion of sporting heteronormativity.

Conclusion

In this chapter, we have examined the links between theory, practice and intervention through a focus on F4P v Homophobia. The discussion identifies how our individual academic/scholarly biographies (PE pedagogy and sport sociology) have informed the development of the project, including values-based coaching advocacy and anti-discrimination activism. We have considered the ways the project can be viewed as public sociology and/or public pedagogy. In the end, we use the term performative pedagogy to describe participation by students and staff, and the visual signification that marks this particular playing of football. Through performative pedagogy and aspirations to engage students and a broader public, we can argue that F4P v Homophobia successfully contests homophobia, biphobia and transphobia. As such it is an example of intervention that seeks social transformation of attitudes and behaviours towards marginalised sexualities. However, it is impossible to conclude that this performative pedagogy subverts the obdurate structures of heteronormativity.

Note

1. Brighton-based LGBT+ and physical activity advocacy initiative established as a consequence of the circumstances surrounding the death of the professional footballer Justin Fashanu.

References

Anderson, E. (2005) In the game: gay athletes and the cult of masculinity. Albany: State University of New York Press.
Burdsey, D. and Caudwell, J. (2014) Activism, intervention and academic-student collaboration on campus: fighting homophobia, biphobia and transphobia in/through football. Paper presented at The Sporting Arena: Academics, Activists and Activism[s]. North American Society for the Sociology of Sport. November 5–8, Portland, Oregon, United States.
Butler, J. (1993) Critically queer. GLQ: A Journal of Lesbian and Gay Studies 1: 17–32.
Caudwell, J. (2014) [Transgender] young men: Gendered subjectivities and the physically active body. Sport, Education and Society 19(4): 398–414.
Caudwell, J. (2012) Challenging heteronormativity through football and education: Activism and/or Assimilation? Invited paper presented at Faculty of Arts and Education. September 17, Deakin University, Melbourne, Australia.
Caudwell, J. (2011) "Does your boyfriend know you're here?": The spatiality of homophobia in men's football culture in the UK. Leisure Studies, 30(2): 123–138.
Caudwell, J. (2007) Queering the field? The complexities of sexuality within a lesbian-identified football team in England. Gender, Place and Culture, A Journal of Feminist Geography, 14(2): 183–196.
Caudwell, J. (1999) Women's football in the United Kingdom: Theorising gender and unpacking the butch lesbian image. Journal of Sport and Social Issues, 23(4): 390–402.
Cooky, C. (2017) "We cannot stand idly by": A necessary call for a public sociology of sport. Sociology of Sport Journal, 34(1): 1–11.
Donnelly, P. (2015) Assessing the sociology of sport: On public sociology of sport and research that makes a difference. International Review for the Sociology of Sport, 50(4–5): 419–423.
Gane, N. and Back, L. (2012) C. Wright Mills 50 years on: The promise and craft of sociology revisited. Theory, Culture & Society 29(7/8): 399–421.
Giardina, M. D. and Denzin, N. K. (2011) Acts of activism ↔ politics of possibility: Toward a new performative cultural politics. Cultural Studies ↔ Critical Methodologies 11(4): 319–327.
Giroux, H. A. (2004) Cultural studies, public pedagogy, and the responsibility of intellectuals. Communication and Critical/Cultural Studies, 1(1): 59–79.

Giroux, H. A. (2001) Cultural studies as performative politics. *Cultural Studies ↔ Critical Methodologies*, 1(1): 5–23.

Giroux, H. A. (2000) Public pedagogy as cultural politics: Stuart Hall and the crisis of culture. *Cultural Studies*, 14(2): 341–360.

Griffin, P. (1998) *Strong women, deep closets: lesbians and homophobia in sport.* Leeds: Human Kinetics.

Kaufman, P. (2008) Boos, bans, and backlash: The consequences of being an activist athlete. *Humanity and Society*, 32(3): 215–237.

Kaufman, P. and Wolff, E. A. (2010) Playing and protesting: Sport as a vehicle for social change. *Journal of Sport and Social Issues*, 34(2): 154–175.

King, S. (2008) What's queer about (queer) sport sociology now? *Sociology of Sport Journal*, 25(4): 419–442.

King-White, R. (2012) Oh Henry!: Physical cultural studies' critical pedagogical imperative. *Sociology of Sport Journal*, 29(3): 385–408.

Kirk, D. (2006) Sport education, critical pedagogy, and learning theory: Toward an intrinsic justification for physical education and youth sport. *Quest*, 58(2): 255–264.

lisahunter. (2018). HPE: Pedagogy, feminism, sexualities and queer theory, in L. Mansfield, J. Caudwell, B. Wheaton and R. Watson (Eds.). (2018) *Palgrave Handbook of Feminisms and Sport, Leisure and Physical Education.* London: Palgrave, 427–445.

Maguire, J. (2004). Challenging the sports-industrial complex: Human sciences, advocacy and service. *European Physical Education Review*, 10(3): 299–322.

Mansfield, L., and Rich, E. (2013) Public health pedagogy, border crossings and physical activity at every size. *Critical Public Health*, 23(3): 356–370.

Rich, E. (2011) "I see her being obesed!": Public pedagogy, reality media and the obesity crisis. *Health*, 15(1): 3–21.

Rossing, J. P., (2016) Emancipatory racial humor as critical public pedagogy: Subverting hegemonic racism. *Communication, Culture & Critique*, 9(4): 614–632.

Sandlin, J. A., O'Malley, M. P. and Burdick, J. (2011) Mapping the complexity of public pedagogy scholarship. *Review of Educational Research*, 81(3): 338–375.

Spacey, G. (2016) Learning and teaching values through physical education: using the experience of Rugby 4 Peace in schools, in G. Stidder and G. Hayes (Eds.), The Really Useful PE Book (2nd ed.). Routledge, 201–213.

Spacey, G. and Caudwell, J. (2012) Community University Partnership Projects(CUPP): University of Brighton, Football4Peace (F4P) and The Justin Campaign. Paper presented at Contemporary Ethnography Across the Disciplines. November 20–23, University of Waikato, Aoteraoa, New Zealand.

Spacey, G. and Sugden, J. T. (2015) The Football 4 Peace experience, in D. Conrad (Ed.), *Sport Based Health Interventions—Case Studies from Around the World.* London: Springer, 117–128.

Stein, A. and Plummer, K. (1994) "I can't even think straight": "Queer" theory and the missing sexual revolution in sociology. *Sociological Theory*, 12(2): 178–187.

Sykes, H. (2011) *Queer Bodies: Sexualities, Genders and Fatness in Physical Education.* Oxford: Peter Lang.

Tinning, R. (2002) Toward a "modest pedagogy": Reflections on the problematics of critical pedagogy. *Quest*, 54(3): 224–240.

Travers, A. and Deri, J. (2011) Transgender inclusion and the changing face of lesbian softball leagues. *International Review for the Sociology of Sport*, 46(4): 488–507.

Chapter 4

Autoethnography and public sociology of sport in the Caribbean: Engagement, disengagement and despair

Roy McCree

Introduction

In 2008, I was invited to become involved in the formation of a player organization in Trinidad and Tobago, the Veteran Footballers Foundation of Trinidad and Tobago (VFOTT), in a society which has no history of player organizations or unions and where the British legacies of amateurism and voluntarism still dominate over professional sports. The organization was made up largely of ex-soccer players some of whom took part in the North American Soccer League (NASL) from the late 1960s, up to the 1980s. VFOTT had 3 major objectives which were: (i) to see about the welfare of veteran soccer players; (ii) to contribute to the better organization and development of local soccer and (iii) to document the local history of the sport (VFOTT 2009, 2). In this noble attempt to improve the organization of local soccer, a major challenge had to do with confronting the power wielded by Trinidadian, and former controversial FIFA Vice President, Jack Warner, over the game globally and locally. While I have never played either professional soccer or organized soccer beyond high school and community leagues, I remain a strong fan of the game. This invitation and involvement was influenced by two major factors: the research that I conducted on male soccer on the island in the 1990s (McCree 1995, 2000) as well as my familiarity with some of the players who were part of the nascent organization. Interestingly, in that very same year of its formation, I had delivered a conference paper entitled "The Struggle of Player Unions in the Commonwealth Caribbean" at the University of Toronto. The conference was organized by Peter Donnelly to commemorate the anniversary of the famous black power symbol by American sprinters Tommie Smith and John Carlos at the 1968 Olympic Games under the theme, "To Remember Is to Resist: 40 Years of Sport and Social Change, 1968–2008."

Up to 2008, and since 1997, when I first started to teach the sociology of sport (McCree 2017), I would say that I was more of a professional sociologist, borrowing from Burawoy's typology (see below), because my major activities centered around teaching, researching, conferencing and publishing in relation to the sociology of sport and public sport policy. I embraced this opportunity therefore, because I felt that these activities, while extremely valuable and very much necessary, were not sufficient enough to make a difference in the study and development of sport on the island. To make a real difference, I felt that I should be on the ground so to speak, and in the frontline, as part of a process of advocacy and activism in local soccer, the supposed hallmark of the organic intellectual (Bairner 2009). This was the thinking and context that influenced my decision to become a member of the organization and, eventually, Chair of its Committee for Research and Education as I tried to become a more public-oriented sociologist. What follows is a reflection of my 9 year involvement in this organization and its methodological and theoretical significance for issues relating to the autoethnographic study of experience as well as the conversation on being a more publicly engaged sociologist of sport.

Public Sociology

The role of the sociologist and the relevance of sociology to society has been a subject of much controversial discussion in both Europe and North America (Burawoy 2005; Turner 2006; Clawston et al. 2007; Patterson 2014). At the core of the debate, is the extent to which the sociologist should be a "public intellectual" or be "publicly engaged" in various social issues and the broader public policy process in particular. The same discussion has replicated itself in the context of the sociology of sport and its own marginalization within sociology itself (Jarvie 2007; Bairner 2009; Donnelly, Fraga and Aisenstein 2014; Donnelly 2015; Cooky 2017). And so much so, that the main theme of the 2016 conference of the NASSS was: "Publicly Engaged Sociology of Sport" (McCree 2017). This issue would of course hinge on how we define "public intellectual" or "public engagement."

In his now seminal paper, Burawoy (2005) gave a more nuanced understanding of the different types of public intellectuals and sociologists. In this regard, he identified four major related types of sociology or sociologists: the professional, public, critical and policy oriented. Professional sociology is distinguished by a focus on theoretical, conceptual and methodological issues and communicating with one's peers through conferences, research and publications. Public sociology is distinguished by its communication with persons or publics outside of academia, which may include minorities, workers, women and other groups. However, this may assume two forms: (i) an elitist type of engagement where the sociologist remains largely invisible while examining major social issues and (ii) a more participatory or advocacy type of engagement in which the sociologist becomes actually involved with the organization or groups in question. The latter type of public sociologist is more involved in public advocacy and action which may assume a political character. The defining characteristic of public sociology though is that it involves communication with some wider public outside of the narrow sphere of one's professional peers. Policy sociology meanwhile is concerned with providing paid service(s) for some client(s) while critical sociology serves to interrogate the particular assumptions, "biases" and "silences" of professional sociology. Burawoy notes, however, that these categories are neither "water tight" nor "mutually exclusive" since they may overlap and even feed into each other (Burawoy 2005) thus rendering his classificatory scheme a heuristic device within which to locate the possible multiple positioning of the sociologist.

In my estimation, the public intellectual or sociologist can perhaps be seen along a continuum which varies from being directly involved (visible, active participation) to being indirectly involved (behind the scenes/giving advice, donations) or from hardcore (involvement in marches, sit ins and other forms of public protests) to soft core (giving advice/speeches). As far as my involvement was concerned in VFOTT, it assumed more of a direct character though not its more hardcore or radical variant.

Methodology: Autoethnography

While qualitative research on the whole foregrounds the voice and interpretation of the lived experience of its respondents, autoethnography (AET) foregrounds the lived experience of the researcher him or herself and their interpretation of that experience: akin to a type of research selfie although others may also be in the picture. The major problems or experiences which have been the focus of AET have been typically private and personal issues dealing with death, grief, disability, injury, illness, divorce, and strained relationships (Bochner and Ellis 2016). While several strands of AET have emerged such as critical, analytic, queer, performance, and evocative (ibid., pp. 59–61), two of the major variants which have provoked much discussion and controversy relate to "evocative or emotional auto-ethnography" and "analytic autoethnography". This study draws particularly from the latter approach.

As part of his critique of evocative AET, which was distinguished by its literary style of writing and the use of the first person narrative, Anderson introduced the notion of analytic autoethnography, which he defined as follows:

> *analytic autoethnography* refers to ethnographic work in which the researcher is (1) a full member in the research group or setting, (2) visible as such a member in the researcher's published texts, and (3) committed to an analytic research agenda focused on improving theoretical understandings of broader social phenomena. (Anderson 2006, p. 375)

In another definition, he noted that "analytic autoethnography involves complete membership, sustained reflexive attention to one's position in the web of field discourse and relations, and textual visibility of the self in ethnographic narratives" (ibid., p. 385). The architecture of analytical autoethnography therefore, rests on four major related pillars or ingredients: group membership, textual visibility of the author, reflexivity and theoretical relevance, which is what makes it analytical. In the latter regard for instance, he notes that "I use the term *analytic* to point to a broad set of data-transcending practices that are directed toward theoretical development, refinement, and extension" (ibid., p. 387). For Anderson, the aim of autoethnography was not just to represent the experience or situation under study but to use the experience of self and others to provide "theoretical illumination" by gaining "insight into some broader set of social phenomena than those provided by the data themselves" (ibid., p. 386). In the context of my study, autoethnography is being used to interrogate the issues surrounding public sociology and the public sociology of sport based on my experiences as a member of a local player-oriented soccer organization in Trinidad and Tobago.

In discussing the nature of group membership or complete member researcher status (CMR), Anderson (2006) distinguishes between two variants: the opportunistic and the converted. Opportunistic CMR refers to a situation where "group membership precedes the decision to conduct research on the group" while with the converted, the researcher begins "... with a purely data-oriented research interest in the setting but become[s] converted to complete immersion and membership during the course of the research" (ibid., p. 379). In these respects, my membership in VFOTT was more opportunistic in nature because when I became involved in its formation, I never had the faintest idea or intention to undertake research on its structure, workings or problems although one of my functions in the organization was to help document the history of its members and football in general in the country.

Since my involvement in VFOTT was never conceived as a research project, this has resulted in one major drawback: I do not have copious notes or recordings of my many conversations with other members over the years. And, as a further consequence, I do not have their actual words to capture their voice or to illustrate some of my experiences and interactions with them. Fortunately, while it is not necessarily a substitute for this kind of data, I have benefitted from two other sources of information: email correspondence which I received as a member of the organization's listserv and my record of the minutes of one of the inaugural meetings held on Saturday, 17 January 2009. These sources of data have served to provide some evidence of their actual voices, our exchanges, as well as a chronology of events and activities over the years. Unfortunately, another significant limitation stems from the fact that three of the original foundation members have recently passed away who included the founding President with whom I had many interesting and informative discussions.

Sport and Autoethnography

In the context of the study of sport, autoethnography, also referred to as "narratives of self," seems to have first emerged in the 1990s (Richardson 2000; Sparkes 2000) as it started to undergo disciplinary expansion as part of the general growth of qualitative research during this period. This was further evident in a special 2000 issue of the *Sociology of Sport* journal devoted entirely to what the editors called "more evocative ways of writing than standard practice" (Denison and Rinehart 2000, p. 1). Since that time, the approach has been applied to a range of different sports such as the triathlon, running, hockey, rugby, rowing, base jumping as well as sport coaching. Not surprisingly, the major issues which have formed the subject of enquiry include recovery from injury and identity (Collinson 2003, 2005; Hockey 2005; Allen-Collinson 2012; Fisette 2015); elite athlete identity (Tsang 2000; McMahon and McGannon 2017); gender (Dorkan and Giles 2011; Dashper 2013); fat and body image (Zanger and Gard 2008).

Admittedly, while injury has been the dominant subject in the application of autoethnography to sport, the thread that connects the diverse topics relate to the questions of identity formation be it in relation to athletic identity, body identity or gender identity. In this regard, my autoethnography converges and diverges at the same time with this literature for while it is also concerned with identity, this has more to do with my professional or occupational identity as a sport sociologist with an interest in a public sociology of sport. Relatedly, my study is also different because I write or reflect from the standpoint of a researcher and fan, as opposed to an ex-football player, who is reflecting on his experiences in trying to help manage and develop a nascent player-oriented sport organization. The subject of my autoethnography therefore contrasts sharply with previous applications of the approach, which focus heavily on dealing with injury, hurt and grief.

Case of VFOTT

As with all new organizations, one of the first tasks in the formation of VFFOT was to define the goals of the organization and create a constitution to guide its operations. While I had no specialist training in or knowledge of the creation of any kind of constitution, this merely served to encourage my interest even more to become involved. In fact, most of the founding members were in the same situation, three of whom were ex-high school teachers. Together however, we sought examples of constitutions from similar organizations or sport clubs through the internet which were used as a guide to creating our own. I consider this to be one of the most delightful and satisfying experiences for it involved serious and many times prolonged debate over a range of issues that included: the naming of the organization, coming up with our own motto ("Building bridges through football"), defining our own aims, the criteria for membership, setting up various committees, defining the roles of various Officers, the rights of members, the structure of voting and the relationship between the Executive and General Council.

At my behest, one of the Committees that was set up, and for which I served as Chair was Research and Education. This process of organizational formation was a real exercise in participatory democracy, for while everyone had their say, this was often met with critique and counter critique, argument and counter argument until we arrived at a consensus. These debates were often so intense that they lasted hours and sometimes got out of hand until the Chair had to reign us all in by sometimes taking a break and not necessarily for coffee or tea only, but for some spirituous liquor. One such discussion involved agreeing on the Motto of the organization for which there were 3 positions: Building Bridges, Building

Bridges through Sport and Building Bridges through Football. This discussion took over four hours across two separate days. I supported the "Building Bridges through Football" option since "through sport" was too general and "Building Bridges" alone was too vague.

Because of this intensity, it took no less than one year before we had agreed on the first draft of the Constitution (VFOTT 2009b). Following the creation of the constitution and the formal election of officers, VFFOT now had to turn its attention to the other important pressing issues like a membership drive, funding, seeing about the welfare of its ageing membership, the bulk of whom ranged in ages from 60 to 80. In one of the founding meetings in 2009, the late President Gwenwyn Cust stated that "there were veteran players who were financially, socially and physically destitute" (VFOTT 2009a). The other burning matter which they had to confront was the problem of Governance in football which plagued the sport locally and globally, around the time of its formation in 2008.

VFOTT, Warner and governance in soccer

One of the major concerns of the organization was the governance of soccer both locally and globally in relation to the issues of accountability, transparency and particularly, the treatment of players (VFOTT 2009a). A major actor or player in all of this was Trinidadian Jack Warner. Warner who wielded significant power and influence over the sport for over 30 years in his various roles as Secretary of the local soccer association, Presidents of the Confederation of North American, Central American and Caribbean countries (CONCAFAF) and the Caribbean Football Union (CFU), Vice President of FIFA, a one-time close confidant of FIFA President Sepp Blatter and a member of his inner circle (Tomlinson 2007). However, on top of all this, Warner also assumed a powerful position in the politics and Government of Trinidad and Tobago where he served as a Member of Parliament and Minister of Government from 2007 to 2013 and was also Chairman and financier of the party in government (GORTT n.d.)

Warner, however, was generally perceived as an ethically challenged individual who used players and soccer to advance his own personal, political and economic interests (Tomlinson 2007; FIFA 2017). As a result, his relationship with players was generally drenched in conflict and personal animosity (McCree 1995, 2000; Singh 2006; Tomlinson 2007). Not surprisingly therefore, all the former players and members of the organization, including myself, had a very dim view of Warner in relation to his treatment of players over the years and his general organization of the sport locally. They were still visibly disgruntled and dissatisfied with how he treated them as well as others in the sport. I would often hear stories of the difficulty they had in getting their per diems when on national duty or being placed in second rate hotels while the officials stayed in more first class alternatives although Warner would not have been the only one guilty of this practice.

As a result, in view of the power he wielded in and outside of football, Warner was generally perceived as a clear and present danger to the nascent organization (VFOTT 2009a), which was dominated by anti-Warner elements and formed at a time when Warner was still at the height of his ascendancy in sport and politics. But once perched at the apex of soccer's power structure and a key member of FIFA's power elite, Warner was forced to resign all his positions in football in 2011 and local politics in 2013 after a series of reports alleging his involvement in widespread corruption (FIFA 2017). His final coup de grâce (or perhaps disgrace) would come in 2015, when he was indicted by the US Government on multiple counts of "racketeering, wire fraud, money laundering and bribery" and subsequently placed on Interpol's most wanted list (Alexander 2015). He is currently challenging extradition to the United States to face these charges.

Public sociology and VFOTT

So how did the player organization attempt to deal with the all mighty Warner and the problem of Governance in football, before his political meltdown? And how did I as a member and professional sociologist deal with it as well? The organization was divided among those who preferred a confrontational approach (go after him) based on media attacks and calls for his resignation, and those who preferred what I call constructive engagement (more wait and see) which involved the staging of two public seminars to educate the soccer community and the public in general about the problems affecting soccer. Consistent with the more confrontational approach, one email to members in 2012 called for "retaining our focus on the following: (1) Action against the illegal Trinidad and Tobago Football Federation (TTFF) by meeting with the clubs in the East and Tobago; (2) Decision on legal action to put a stop to the fraud that is the TTFF and (3) Communication with President [of Trinidad and Tobago] Maxwell Richards" (VFFOTT 2012). These actions were to form part of a public mobilization campaign to help place the administration of local soccer on a path to good governance and although the email was sent almost a year after Warner's resignation from all forms of football in 2011, it was action that was being contemplated long before his resignation.

But where did I stand on all this, public sociologist wannabe and all that? I sided with those who preferred constructive engagement over belligerence out of one major concern. I feared that the confrontational approach may have jeopardized or compromised my future research on soccer on the island, particularly if I needed to interview officials of the soccer federation who were under his control, interview him directly or even interview current national players on the question of governance in soccer when he still reigned supreme. I saw trying to take on Warner as a very futile endeavour given the influence and resources at his command compared to that of VFFOT, which was next to nought. What I saw therefore was a possible conflict of interest and some tension between my multiple roles as member/officer of the organization, public sociologist and professional sociologist. I therefore had to find some kind of balance between what Norbert Elias called attachment and detachment in order to safeguard my research interests and credibility.

This division and dilemma reminded me of Alvin Gouldner's admonition that "it is to values, not to factions that sociologists must give their most basic commitment" (cited in McDonald 2002, p. 110). Gouldner's admonition might be relevant in another context, but in my situation, I saw the need to be more cautious in dealing with Warner and, as a result, I choose to align myself with the faction for constructive engagement. However, my position of constructive engagement, in no way compromised my commitment to the values of fairness, justice or good governance in soccer in particular and sport in general. Indeed, while in my heart I supported the more confrontational approach when I recall Warner's manipulation of the vote of no confidence against him by many of the same players in 1984 (*Trinidad Guardian*, 23 January 1984, p. 30), his refusal to pay players their bonuses after qualifying for the 2006 World Cup in Germany and black listing them from playing for the national team because they took him to the Court of Arbitration for Sport over the matter which they eventually won, and which he also refused to comply with, I still saw the need for a more controlled or calibrated approach given the realities of Warner's power and VFOTT's collective powerlessness.

Research and education

And what about the formal role I assumed as Chair of the Research and Documentation Committee, a role which I had relished given my background in sport research and teaching coupled with the lack of research on football locally? At best, I can state that my experience has been a rather mixed one. In this regard, I tried to assist the organization in five major ways: i) helping to design a questionnaire to collect biographical data on players as part of the development of a player data bank; (ii) suggesting the creation of a special soccer collection at the University of the West Indies consisting of player photos and other memorabilia in relation to soccer on the island in which the Library had expressed an interest (McCree 2011); (iii) suggesting the interviewing of players to capture their life history; (iv) the creation of a VFOTT column in one of the local newspapers to act as a mouthpiece of the organization on matters concerning players and the sport of football as well as (v) participating in two public fora on the state of local football held in 2011 and 2017 where I examined the history of player struggles locally and the possible educational role of football academies.

Apart from taking part in these public fora and assisting with questionnaire construction, I had no success in realizing any of the other suggestions due in large measure to the absence of funding to carry out the necessary research, hire Research Assistants, pay for transcriptions and the like. In addition, overtime, I formed the view that somehow, I may have been expected to do this research freely given the voluntary nature of the organization, the state of its finances and the amateur sport background of most of its membership. As a professional researcher however, this was never an option given the sheer volume of work that had to be done in relation to player interviews, the collection of relevant documents, newspaper reports, photos and so on. In his work on anti-racism in English cricket, McDonald (2002) was lucky to have received funding in part from the English Cricket Board, but to conceive of the local football association giving VFFOT funding to carry out research on its former players when they were all opposed to their benefactor Warner was to engage in wishful thinking.

As a result, if my involvement in the creation of the constitution was a delight in highlighting the workings of democracy and being a public sociologist of sport, my research and documentation experience was a rather disappointing one. And it was in this context that I did not seek re-nomination as Chair of this committee in 2016 though I remain a financial member of the organization. Even in the post-Warner era therefore, the lack of funding and a research culture in football and sport, continue to undermine the study and documentation of the history of the local game.

Discussion and conclusion

Both autoethnography and the conversation surrounding public sociology speak to the issue of relocating the researcher and intellectual in the study and development of society in order to achieve more mutually positive outcomes for all involved. The challenge is at once therefore, methodological, theoretical, political and developmental. While my involvement in VFOTT was never conceived as a research project, my immersion in the organization for almost a decade served to provide me with insights into various activities, and issues (e.g., making of constitution, tackling issues of governance in local soccer, funding, research) faced by footballers and their various attempts to negotiate them. Relatedly, it also provided me with access to documents and communication about the organization which I would not ordinarily or easily have had access to as an outsider or non-member. Unfortunately, the death of a few key members with whom I worked closely in the making of the organization did not allow me to make them a more visible, vocal and prominent part of the narrative which is one of the central requirements of the autoethnographic approach and qualitative research in general. In this sense therefore, my study lacked a dialogic quality.

On the question of public sociology or being a public sport sociologist, my VFOTT experience was at best a very mixed one. Undeniably, my involvement in the formation of its constitution, and some of its data gathering and public education activities demonstrates the important role that we can play as sport sociologists in the development of sport and making a difference in society however small or minuscule that may seem. However, the limits or constraints of this role were clearly in evidence in relation to my failure to advance the research and documentation agenda and the rather conservative position I adopted in dealing with the problem of governance and more particularly, the Jack Warner question or the juggernaut that was Jack. These constraints, however, direct attention to the material, political and situational limits of trying to practice public sociology, and even more so, its hard core, activist variant. In a recent attempt to advocate and illustrate the importance of a public sociology of sport to deal with issues of racism and sexism in the United States, Cooky (2017) also directed attention to the various institutional challenges (e.g., funding, requirements for tenure and promotion) faced by Faculty in adopting this mode of civic engagement although she still maintains that we should not sit idly by.

Moreover, my adoption of a more conservative approach to dealing with Warner at the historical point in time can serve to demonstrate that however blurred or imaginary it might be, there is still this line between the troika or triumvirate of the personal, professional and political in trying to become more actively involved in either sport development or sport for development. On all fronts, I was experiencing pulls and tugs as a person who supported the players' just cause, as a professional sociologist in a volunteer-oriented sport culture and as a wannabe public sociologist but I resolved my dilemma by taking the line of least resistance. And I did this by deciding to protect my professional interests or identity given the realities of power or powerlessness which confronted the organization in trying to take on Jack and the local football establishment. The deeper irony or contradiction here is that while I had set out to be on the frontline in trying be a public sport sociologist, when the war on Warner was looking to heat up, I beat a hasty retreat, which reminded me of the saying, "Be careful what you wish for."

However, my predicament or dilemma reflects one of the central conundrums in the conversation dealing with activism and the academy. St Louis (2007, p. 120) captures this when, in referencing Adams (2007), he notes that "it is difficult to reconcile the shifting ceaseless formation of subjectivities - what we might consider our identities - with the political projects we might wish to link them to." In an attempt to protect my "vulnerable self" (Bochner and Ellis 2016, p. 65), this reconciliation proved problematic. In another case however, McDonald (2002) did not have this identity dilemma for he was able to reconcile his role as a researcher and political activist against racism in the sport of cricket in England since his research was used to generate evidence to fight against it. It is important to note however, that the funding of his research by the English cricket authorities provided the necessary resources to conduct his research and facilitate inadvertently, his activism.

Consequently, notwithstanding the clarion and fervent call for a public sociology of sport in the academy, in part to help rescue the discipline from continuing marginalization, without the required resources, the right people, the right conditions and the right moment, it would remain a nice, rosy, romantic ideal that has limited impact on the development and transformation of either sport or society. While this might beg the questions as to when right is right, this is best left to the judgment of those working in the trenches for change.

References

Adams, M. I. 2007. Response to Helstein's "Seeing your sporting body: Identity, subjectivity, and misrecognition." *Sociology of Sport Journal* 24, 104–108.

Alexander, G. 2015. Jack on Interpol wanted list. *Trinidad Guardian*, 4 June. Available from www.guardian.co.tt/news/2015-06-03/jack-interpol-wanted-list [Accessed 30 November 2017].

Allen-Collinson, J. 2012. Autoethnography: Situating personal sporting narratives in socio-cultural contexts. *In*: K. Young and M. Atkinson, eds. *Qualitative Research on Sport and Physical Culture*. Bingley, UK: Emerald Press, 191–212.

Anderson, L. 2006. Analytic auto ethnography. *Journal of Contemporary Ethnography*, 35(4), 373–395.

Bairner, A. 2009. Sport, intellectuals and public sociology: Obstacles and opportunities. *International Review for the Sociology of Sport*, 44(2–3), 115–130.

Bochner, A. P. and C. Ellis. 2016. *Evocative Ethnography: Writing Lives and Telling Stories*. New York: Routledge.

Burawoy, M. 2005. For public sociology. *American Sociological Review*, 70, 4–28.

Clawston, D. et al., eds., 2007. *Public Sociology: Fifteen Eminent Sociologists Debate Politics and the Profession in the Twenty-First Century*. Berkeley: University of California Press.

Collinson, J. 2003. Running into injury time: Distance running and temporality. *Sociology of Sport Journal*, 20(4), 331–370.

Collinson, J. 2005. Emotions, interaction and the injured sporting body. *International Review for Sociology of Sport*, 40(2), 221–240.

Cooky, C. 2017. "We cannot stand idly by": A necessary call for a public sociology of sport. *Sociology of Sport Journal* 34(1): 1–11.

Cust, G. gwenwyn@yahoo.com. 24 August 2012. VFOTT activities resume in September 2012. Email to Roy McCree (Roy.McCree@sta.uwi.edu).

Dashper, K. 2013. Getting Better: An auto ethnographic tale of recovery from sporting injury. *Sociology of Sport Journal*, 30(3), 323–339.

Denison, J. and Rinehart, R. 2000. Introduction: Imagining sociological narratives. *Sociology of Sport Journal*, 17(1), 1–4.

Donnelly, P. 2015. Assessing the sociology of sport: On public sociology of sport and research that makes a difference. *International Review for the Sociology of Sport*, 50(4–5), 419–423.

Donnelly, P., Fraga, B. A. and Aisenstein, A. 2014. For a public sociology of sport in the Americas: An editorial call on behalf of a socially engaged scholarship on sport and physical education. *Movimento*, 20, 9–20.

Dorkan, S. and Giles, A. 2011. From ribbon to wrist shot: An auto ethnography of (a) typical feminine sport development. *Women in Sport and Physical Activity Journal*, 20(1), 13–22.

FIFA. 2017. FIFA, *Report on the Inquiry into the 2018/2022 FIFA World Cup Bidding Process*. Zurich: FIFA.

Fisette, J. 2015. The marathon journey of my body-self and performing identity. *Sociology of Sport Journal*, 32(1), 68–88.

Government of Republic of Trinidad and Tobago (GORTT). n.d. Members of past parliaments. www.ttparliament.org/members.php?mid=26&pid=25&id=JWA01 [Accessed 14 December 2017].

Hockey, J. 2005. Injured distance runners: A case of identity work as self-help. *Sociology of Sport Journal*, 22(1), 38–58.

Jarvie, G. 2007. Sport, social change and the public intellectual. *International Review for the Sociology of Sport*, 42(4), 411–424.

McDonald, I. 2002. Critical social research and political intervention: Moralistic versus radical approaches. *In:* J. Sugden and A. Tomlinson, eds. *Power Games: A Critical Sociology of Sport*. London: Routledge, 100–116.

McCree, R. 1995. *Professionalism and the Development of Club Football in Trinidad and Tobago*. MS Thesis, The University of the West Indies, St. Augustine, Trinidad and Tobago.

Mc Cree, R. 2000. Professional soccer in the Caribbean: The case of Trinidad and Tobago, 1969–1983. *International Review for the Sociology of Sport*, 35(2), 199–218.

McCree, R. RoyMcCree@sta.uwi.edu, 28 June 2011. UWI library. Email to Gwenwyn Cust (gwenwyn@yahoo.com).

McCree, R. 2017. Caribbean sport sociology: The ongoing journey. *In:* K. Young, ed. *Research in the Sociology of Sport* (Volume 10). Bingley, United Kingdom: Emerald Group Publishing, 119–133.

McMahon, J. and McGannon, K. 2017. Re-Immersing into elite swimming culture: A meta-auto ethnography by a former elite swimmer. *Sociology of Sport Journal*, 34(3), 223–234.

Patterson, O. 2014. How sociologists made themselves irrelevant. Retrieved from www.chronicle.com/article/How-Sociologists-Made/150249/.

Richardson, L. 2000. New writing practices in Qualitative Research. *Sociology of Sport Journal*, 17(1), 5–20.

Singh, V. 2006. *Jack Warner: Zero to Hero*. Port of Spain: Medianet Ltd.

Sparkes, A. 2000. Auto ethnography and narratives of self: Reflections on criteria in action. *Sociology of Sport Journal*, 17(1), 21–43.

Tomlinson, T. 2007. Lord, don't stop the carnival: Trinidad and Tobago at the 2006 FIFA World Cup. *Journal of Sport and Social Issues*, 31(3), 259–282.

Trinidad Guardian. 1984. Footballers firm on "no confidence". 23 January, 30.

Tsang, T. 2000. Let me tell you a story: A narrative exploration of identity in high-performance sport. *Sociology of Sport Journal*, 17(1), 44–59.

Turner, B. A. 2006. British sociology and public intellectuals: Consumer society and imperial decline. *British Journal of Sociology*, 57(2), 169–188.

VFOTT. 2009a. Minutes from Meeting of Interim Committee, 17 January, San Fernando, Trinidad and Tobago.

VFOTT. 2009b. *Constitution: Veteran Footballers Foundation of Trinidad and Tobago*. Port of Spain: VFOTT.

Zanker, C. and Gard, C. 2008. Fatness, fitness, and the moral universe of sport and physical activity. *Sociology of Sport Journal*, 25(1), 58–65.

Chapter 5

Critical research on Black sporting experiences in the United States: Athletic activism and the appeal for social justice

Billy Hawkins

Introduction

It is impossible to discuss the intersection of race and sport without providing an overview of the current context whereby the discussion of these topics is situated in the United States. In providing a context for this chapter, I am reminded of the song, "The thrill is gone." This song was made famous in 1970 and garnered the late great B.B. King a Grammy Award for Best Male R&B Vocal Performance. The lyrics of this song expresses the woes of being mistreated while caught under the spell of love. Prior to the election of President #45[1], many Blacks[2] I have communicated with entertained a type of thrill, a mild euphoric sensation that stemmed from the symbolic empowerment the former President Barack Obama provided during his two-term tenure in the White House. It was a type of love affair with the prospect of change and in a hope that the United States might be capable of living up to the potential stated in its Declaration of Independence, where it declares that:

> We hold these truths to be self-evident, that *all men are created equal*, that they are endowed by their Creator with certain unalienable Rights, that among these are Life, Liberty and the Pursuit of Happiness.

Though the creators of this document did not factor in women or people of color during its inception we have had to make it work for us, even though the spirit of its content should guarantee provisions for us today. This chapter will seek to provide an overview of the literature on race and sport, explore critical insight about existing knowledge on race and sport, and finally highlight research that is seeking to produce emancipatory structures for racial justice. The limitation of this chapter is that it will favor the Black athletic experience predominantly, with cursory attention to other emerging racial populations; for example, Latin Americans in baseball or Pacific Islanders in American collegiate and professional football.

In the United States, one can conclude that since the creation of this sacred document to the election of President Obama there have been changes in race relations and racial equality, with some efforts toward racial equity in this country. Therefore, upon President Obama's initial election, we were caught under a spell that the prophet of hope preached during his presidential campaign; our expectation for change was high, yet at the close of a chapter in U.S. history in 2016, during the sunset of this nations' first Black President's tenure in the White House, myself and many Blacks I know were left wanting. The celebratory outlook we had during his first election lingered throughout his second term, until the increased racial tension and violence against Blacks caused many to question whether having a 'Black face in high place', according to the late Professor Manning Marable (1998), could make a difference. At a time when this country could have embraced the hope of racial inclusion and progress towards a post-racial society, we have witnessed a rise in racial crimes and lenient or no punishment to the perpetrators of these violent crimes; indeed, several of the perpetrators were those who were charged with the duty to protect and serve.

Furthermore, the thrill is gone because in this age of social media and the preeminence of the visual culture, on display in the highest political office in this nation is a clear definition of "unobstructed" white male privilege. We are consistently receiving images and verbal text from this administration that blatantly defines and clearly demonstrates an unobstructed privilege that white males have enjoyed since they assumed it was their duty to control the world through colonization and imperialism. What has emerged from this revitalization of unobstructed privilege is the fortification of institutional racism and radicalization of individuals who act violently in expressing their flawed racist beliefs.

The world is watching as the president of the most powerful nation in the world demonstrates, and has demonstrated prior to taking office, what it means to have unobstructed white male privilege. It is that ability to say and do whatever you want with little to no repercussions, no moral checks and balances, and no intellectual filters to regulate ones' actions. It is also the ability to censure, fire, discredit, and/or degrade anyone who doesn't agree with you without consequences. It is like having access and opportunity to whatever you want regardless of who owns it or whose feelings you might hurt in taking what you want, saying what you want, and simply doing whatever you want.

To further examine the social context where race matters and racism prevails, we have to critically deconstruct how President #45 is exhibiting actions towards people of color that clearly align themselves with the actions of white supremacists. For example, he and his administration established a travel ban on predominantly Muslim countries, which are, typically people of color; his administration seeks to build a wall to keep Hispanics out (also people of color); his administration initially rescinded DACA (Deferred Action for Childhood Arrivals) policy and unveiled a restrictive reform policy known as the SUCCEED Act; he and his administration treated Puerto Ricans and Puerto Rico, like America's sidepiece, not warranting the full attention or resources to meet their dire needs and jokingly tossing rolls of toilet paper amidst a crowd of Puerto Ricans while blaming them for his administration's budget woes; another example is where he referred to members of the Klu Klux Klan (KKK), one of the most notorious terrorist organizations in American history especially in regards to acts of terrorism against Blacks, as "good people" but referred to Black National Football League (NFL) players who peacefully protested racial injustices in this country by taking a knee during the singing of the national anthem as, "Sons of Bitches"; finally, in a discussion on immigration, he has referred to African immigrants as individuals seeking to migrate from "shithole" nations. The list of racially charged and sexist acts goes on by a leader who arrogantly and boastfully demonstrates unobstructed white male privilege, while simultaneously radicalizing white supremacy.

This unobstructed privilege enables supporters of President #45's tweet about the NFL players to project their slave-master's ideology on people of color, in general, and Blacks, specifically. For example, these supporters have asserted that professional Black male athletes should be grateful for the amount of money they are making, thus, they should just shut up and play ball. These supporters also proclaim that the game should not be politicized. They forget that the entry of the national anthem or the presence of the American flag automatically politicizes these sporting events and venues, because how can you separate the political ideology of a nation from the national symbols that distinguishes it from other nations? These sporting venues have been and continue to be ideological outposts for political propaganda about nationalism. But these supporters are disgruntled because a few NFL players protest. Thus, once again, we have whites seeking to control the Black body, establishing parameters within which it can exist, and determining how the Blacks are supposed to behave.

This behavior, within the broader socio-historical context, continues to entrench a racial divide in a country that has never adequately addressed its race problem. The United States has never truly atoned or provided sufficient reparations for the millions of Native Americans who suffered genocide or for the millions of lives that were displaced because of the Atlantic slave kidnapping and slavery. The United States has never sought to provide Native Americans or Blacks with the equal access to opportunities that the majority of whites assumed from birth. There are a few universities that are acknowledging their connections to and benefits from slavery with token concessions.[3] Yet the racial wounds are deep and have been festering for hundreds of years. The United States has tolerated this illness, ignored it symptoms, while only superficial treatment has been applied with the hope that it will get better. Despite, making some symbolic progress when this nation elected President Barack Obama to two terms, the progress to a post-racist society has been held captive. The momentary destabilization of hopelessness fostered by the prophet of hope has been undermined and dismantled by President #45.

Again, this is the social context in which the intercentricity of race and racism are currently being played out. There is historical precedence in the United States for the current racial climate. Protests and social movements have fostered the ebbs and flows of race relations and racial justices and not the moral development of this nation. Sporting experiences have mirrored this pattern as well. The disease of white supremacy and unobstructed white male privilege continues to undergird the social institutions of this nation and sport is not inoculated against the associated psychosocial damage. It has been and continues to be a contested terrain in which racial ideologies are reflected, reinforced, and at times resisted. Thus, black male and female athletes, specifically, have exhibited both tragedy and triumphs. Sport has provided opportunities on and off the field, while simultaneously reinforcing notions of scientific racism where Blacks are still perceived to be athletically superior but intellectually inferior.

Overview of race and sport literature

Research on Black sporting experiences have mainly addressed issues of representation and discrimination, or it has focused on ideological issues about race and racialized identities and performance. Regarding issues of representation and discrimination, positional segregation or stacking based on race in collegiate and professional sports has been well-documented (e.g., Davis, 1990; Berghorn, Yetman, and Hanna, 1988; Koch and Vander Hill, 1988; Leonard, 1987; McPherson, 1976; Johnson, and Marple, 1973; Loy and McElvogue, 1970). This research is based mainly on Blalock's work on occupational discrimination and his theoretical assumptions about minority group relations (Blalock, 1961 and 1967). It highlights how race has determined the positions Black athletes could or could not occupy. For example, the racialization of these positions classifies them as "thinking" positions, where White athletes are expected to play, and "non-thinking" positions, where Black athletes are expected to play. To further expound, "thinking" positions (e.g., quarterback, pitcher, and center) are the leadership position in which a disproportionate number of White athletes occupied during the 1960s-1990s when the majority of the data for this research was collected. Conversely, Blacks occupied the majority of "non-thinking" positions (e.g., running backs, outfielders, forwards). These categories are used to describe positions mainly in the sports of football, basketball, and baseball, also because the majority of the research has examined these three sports.

The research on positional segregation has expanded beyond binary racial categories of black and white and beyond the traditional sports of basketball, baseball, and football to include, for example, the stacking of Aboriginal hockey players in Canada in the role of enforcers (Valentine, 2012); racial segregation of Black soccer players in the non-central forward position, based on stereotypical beliefs about racial abilities (Maguire, 1988; Melnick, 1988); or Aborigines in Australian Rugby League racially segregated in non-central positions (Hallinan, 1991).

Of importance is that the racialization of positions is not only based on perceived assumptions about racialized performance, but more so on racial ideologies that are rooted in the beliefs from scientific racism which claim to prove that Blacks are genetically physically superior, and Whites are intellectually superior. What is also inherent in the practice of stacking, in regard to Black athletes, is the intercentrality of race and pervasiveness of racism. Even with the increased representation of Black athletes at the quarterback (QB) position in football, the intercentricity of race and racism prevails because expectations for Blacks in this position are to be mobile (i.e., exploit their physicality). Therefore, the Black QB is a multiple threat to the defense, unlike the traditional drop-back or pocket passing White QB. Because of the Black QB's perceived physical abilities, he becomes an additional running back in conjunction with his passing abilities. Once again, reinforcing racialized assumptions about physicality and athleticism and exploiting these assumptions for a competitive advantage.

Racial and athletic identity and the Black athlete

African American racial identity and sport is another popular area of research that has gained traction in examining how the theory of racial identity development can assist in explaining the over-representation of African American in certain sports and the under-representation in others (see, e.g., Harrison, Harrison, and Moore, 2002). Also, how racial and athletic identities can impact sporting and lived experiences for Black athletes in the collegiate context (see, e.g., Steinfeldt, Reed, and Steinfeldt, 2009; Bimper and Harrison, 2011). Researchers in this area consider the relationship between racial identity and athletic identity and are seeking to explain how the socialization processes of race and sport may impact academic performance and outcomes.

Other works regarding issues of representation and Black sporting experiences include the works of Dr. Richard Lapchick and The Institute for Diversity and Ethics in Sport's annual publication of the Racial and Gender Report Card. This work has been instrumental in assessing the representation of people of color in leadership positions in professional and collegiate sports. This Institute also catalogues the National Collegiate Athletic Association (NCAA) graduation rates of major NCAA sporting events (e.g., Division I men's and women's basketball tournament, Bowl-Bound college football teams, and Super Regional Men's baseball teams), as well as the racial and gender representation of the creative directors who are responsible for which advertisement spots are broadcasted during the Super Bowl (TIDE, 2018). And finally, the works of Dr. Shaun Harper and the Center for the Study of Race and Equity in Education. One of this Center's report entitled, *Black Male Student Athletes and Racial Inequities in NCAA Division I College Sports: 2016 Edition*, exposed the racial inequalities in the Power 5 conferences (Harper, 2016).

Both of these efforts have policy implications in terms of increasing diversity and inclusion at the professional and collegiate levels as well as promoting programmatic policies needed to increase the degree attainment of athletes who are in highly commercial time-demanding revenue generating sports. This research on representation also exposes the pervasiveness of race and racism in sport and the discriminatory practices inherent in sporting practices in the United States.

Black women sporting experiences

A growing body of literature has developed on the study of Black women's sporting experiences. This research has emerged as a necessary addition to the literature on race and sport in the U.S. Scholars have engaged this topic by examining the historical and current sporting experiences of Black women (see, e.g., Cahn, 1994; Leonard, 2014; McDowell, and Carter-Francique, 2016; Sloan-Green, Oglesby, Alexander, and Franke, 1981; Smith, 1992, 2000). The research on Black women's collegiate experiences have grown exponentially (e.g., Bruening, Armstrong, and Pastore, 2005; Carter, 2008; Bernhard, 2014; Carter-Francique and Richardson, 2015; Cooper, Cooper, and Baker, 2016). Professional and collegiate sport remain sites of hegemonic masculinity, thus, these scholars are examining how the oppressive structures and culture are contributing to the lack of Black women in administrative positions and their experiences as athletes.

These scholars and many others who are contributing to the examination of Black women sporting experiences are exposing the varying jeopardies Black women encounter as being Black, women, athletes, sexuality, and from a certain socioeconomic group. These scholars are also illustrating how the intersectionality of these jeopardies have impacted the sporting experiences of Black women in unique ways often causing them to triumph in the face of tragedy and be trendsetters in sports previously reserved for upper-class white women; especially in the case of being isolated and denied access to all-white women's division during the early years of women athletic competition in the United States. For the first time in U.S. Open history in 2017, three Black women advanced to the quarterfinals created a counter narrative to the dominant narrative about Black women in country club sports. Similarly, the scholars who are producing research on Black women sporting experiences are challenging stereotypical notions and the dominant narrative about Black women athleticism and femininity.

Critical insight on race and sport

The work of Dr. Harry Edwards has made an indelible imprint in the literature on race and sport. As one of the forerunners and trendsetters for studying race and sport, his work continues to provide critical insight on the subjects of race and sport. His 2016 NASSS keynote address provided critical historical overview of what he calls "the trajectory of the development at the interface of sport, race, and society in America" (Edwards, 2016). He captures the Black sporting experiences using four waves: The first wave involved athletes like Jack Johnson, Major Taylor, Paul Robeson, Jesse Owens, Joe Louis, and others who struggled for legitimacy in expressing their athletic talents at both the national and international levels; the second wave represented the Black athletes who were cautioned to be politically silent on issues of race and discrimination, but who sought to work within the systems of desegregation until they could gain access to white only professional sporting leagues and universities; the third wave produced a politically active and racially conscious Black athlete, such as, Bill Russell, Jim Brown, Muhammad Ali, Curt Flood, John Carlos, Tommie Smith, and others who struggled for dignity and respect, but spoke out and demonstrated publicly against racial injustices; and finally the fourth wave involves athletes in pursuit of power, and they are demonstrating it in the form of athletic activism. For example, athletes like Colin Kaepernick are leveraging their publicity and status as professional athletes to make political statements against social injustices (Edwards, 2016). What is critically insightful about Edwards' lecture is the historical role several Black athletes have played in using their status to address broader social injustices.

It has been and continues to be a reoccurring theme with Black sporting practices where Black athletes have had to convert their publicity and status as professional and collegiate athletes into political power to voice their discontent with racial injustices nationally and internationally. Oftentimes it is because the lived experiences of Black athletes are not compartmentalized from the lived experiences of Blacks, in general; that is, the economic gains many Black professional athletes have received have not quarantined them from the racial injustices members of the larger Black population incur. Thus, the athletes who have chosen the path of activism have not opted for political compartmentalization for the sake of maintaining their market value for commercial gains. Future critical inquiry will hopefully provide a counter-narrative to assure that the activist efforts of these athletes are not converted into meaning something else or co-opted and transformed into meaning something less.

Another seminal work that is providing critical insight on the intersections of race and sport is Dr. Ben Carrington's work, *Race, Sport, and Politics*. He posits that sport contributes to the "making and remaking of western ideas about racial difference" (p. 2). He further asserts that:

> throughout the twentieth century and into the present there has been a continuous struggle over the meaning of 'the black athlete'. It has been contested from within and without. (Carrington, 2010, p. 2)

Thus, what once was "developed out of and from a white masculinist colonial fear of loss and impotence, revealing the commingling of sex, class, race, and power," (Carrington, 2010, p. 3) has evolved to satisfy the needs of the power elite through ultra-commercialized collegiate and professional sports and through the process of once again commodifying the black body.

The evolution in meaning of the Black athlete forever binds him/her to the conventions that defines him/her, thus restricting self-expression and/or activism until it is co-opted into the capitalist machinery and converted into profits. For example, according to Heitner (2016), the selling of Colin Kaepernick's jersey rose from the 20th best seller among San Francisco 49ers, before he protested the national anthem, to becoming the number one selling jersey among all NFL players, after he began protesting the national anthem. The Black body, once again, remains useful as commodity on and off the field, where his/her athletic talent benefit capitalist elite because they not only control the product 'Black body' producing on the field but also they control the revenue that the Black body's likeness and image can generate.

The critical insight these works provide illustrate that there have been evolutionary strides for Blacks in sport since the days of Jack Johnson, which Carrington (2010) suggests was the making of the Black athlete, however, the advancements Blacks have made in sports has been and continues to be tempered by the intercentricity of race and racism. Race and racism continues as a shadow to the accomplishments of Black athletes. Whether it is couched within comments about the hyper-athleticism of Serena Williams, the "kemptness" of Gabby Douglas' hair, or the continuous commentary highlighting the physicality of the black athlete yet emphasizing the intellectual and leadership abilities of the white athlete.

Because sport continues to contribute to racial ideologies, the employment of critical race theory (CRT) has been fruitful in examining sporting experiences, and it has provided critical insight in the intersection of race and sport. CRT was actually a movement that started in the 80s and has given birth to various theoretical movements (e.g., Latino Critical Theory, Critical Race Feminism, Asian American Critical Race Studies, and American Indian Critical Race Studies). Initially, it was a group of scholar-activists who were interested in examining and transforming the relationship among race, racism, and power (Delgado and Stefancic, 2001).

There are several core principles that provide insight into the interworkings of race and race relations (see, e.g., Bell, 1980, 1989; Crenshaw, Gotanda, Peller, and Thomas, 1995; Delgado, 1995; Delgado and Stefancic, 2001; Ladson-Billings and Tate, 1997; and Yasso, 2005). For example, the notion that race matters and is an enduring reality in the American life; especially in the lives of people of color in general, and Black specifically. It is an ordinary reality and consistently prevalent in the daily experiences of many people of color. The social structuring of race and the psychic conditioning it induces often culminate in lives lost at the hands of perpetrators infected by racism's virus; knowingly and unknowingly. The use of counter-narratives to the dominant narratives about current social conditions is another tenet of CRT. Other tenets of CRT seek to challenge dominant ideologies and promote a commitment to social justice.

Building on the foundation of Hylton's book, 'Race' and Sport: Critical Race Theory (2009), Hawkins, Carter-Francique, and Cooper's (2017) volume on CRT and Black sporting experiences in the United States informs of how race and racism are situated in sporting practices of Black collegiate and professional athletes. Several authors contributed chapters in this volume to expose the intercentricity of race and racism, provide a counter-narrative to the dominant narrative about Black athletes, and provide a revolutionary framework that promotes racial justice.

CRT is useful in providing a counter-narrative to the dominant narrative regarding racial progress Blacks have made in sports. The prominent narrative, when examining the representation on the field and in a few coaching positions, is that Blacks have fared well, however, the counter-narrative is that within the sports of intercollegiate football and men's basketball and in the NFL and National Basketball League (NBA), there is a racial imbalance in power and in wealth transfer where whites benefit significantly from the athletic labor of the Black body as owners, administrators, and coaches. Thus, the institutionalization of white supremacy is reinforced in these sporting practices.

Deposing of white supremacy and its social arrangements will take revolutionary measures undergirded by revolutionized theories like CRT, and more specifically interest convergence; where the interests of whites to accumulate capital will converge with Blacks seeking racial justice and a balance in power. Thus, the use of protest has been necessary means throughout the history of this country to make progress towards equity and equality; whether it was voting rights, access to public facilities, and equitable educational resources.

A dominant theme in the sporting practices of Blacks in the United States has been the use of sport as a platform to make a political statement. In a country that has consistently denied Blacks humanity, our very existence has been and continues to be political and politicized. Therefore, as survivors of human degradation and daily microaggressions, just showing up in the arena or running on the field makes a political statement. So, whether it is the Jack Johnson's desire for self-expression, Paul Robeson's fight for political inclusion, Jesse Owens' call for economic inclusion, Althea Gibson's fight for legitimacy, Muhammad Ali's protest for religious expression (like Muhammad Ali), or the raised fists of John Carlos and Tommie Smith in their protest for social and racial justice in the United States, sport has served as a platform for social and racial activism.

This activism continues in our modern era of sport with Venus Williams's call for equity in gender pay for men and women competing in Grand Slam events back in 1998 or the Williams' boycott of Indian Wells because of the racist atmosphere during the 2001 tournament. Furthermore, the racial injustice and police brutality against Blacks produced a tipping point for Colin Kaepernick in 2016, while a player for the San Francisco 49ers. Again, there is a long history of athletes using sporting events as a platform to make a political statement, thus, Mr. Kaepernick simply took up the baton of social activism with his act of kneeling during the playing of national anthem. He has been joined by the women cheerleaders of Howard University and thousands of others at various levels of sport participation who have decided to take a stand by taking a knee.

The significance of protests and the economic impact they engender are debatable. Regarding the "take a knee" protest, Watanabe, Yan, and Soebbing (2017) are examining how the "take a knee" protests are causing market disruption in the NFL. Preliminary data suggests that ticket sales are being impacted, but it is yet to be determined if it is specifically a result of this protest or other market conditions. However, *CBS MoneyWatch* have reported that operators of two of the largest U.S. ticket marketplaces say they are seeing declines in orders for

NFL games amid the controversy of the "take a knee" protests (Berr, 2017a). Papa John's pizza corporation has blamed the "take a knee" protest during the playing of the national anthem for taking a multimillion-dollar slice out of its pizza earnings (Dickey, 2017). Berr (2017b) has also reported that the NFL television ratings are impacted with viewership down 11% during midseason. Additional qualitative and quantitative research is necessary to determine the actual impact this protest has had on the NFL and NFL sponsors. Finally, NBC broadcaster suggest the NFL rating decline may be a result of the comments President #45 made at a rally in Alabama where he insisted that NFL owners should fire the players who protested during the playing of the national anthem. It is suggested by Nielsen data that the week after Trumps that NFL ratings drop 4% from the prior week to his comments (Snider, 2017). Furthermore, besides disrupting the profits of these corporations, will policies be implemented and enforced to address the issue of police brutality against Blacks in the United States? Most important to this initial market disruption is whether the interest of whites in accumulating capital will converge with the interests of Black seeking racial justice? How and will NFL owners, in their respective cities, join with city officials and seek to address issues of police brutality, racial profiling, and other racial injustices?

Conclusion

The prevalence of race and racism in the United States has impacted the sporting experiences of Blacks, specifically, and other people of color, in general. In terms of representation, Blacks continue to be overrepresented in revenue generating intercollegiate sports (Hawkins, 2010) and the sports of professional football and basketball, while an increasing Latin American presence is being witnessed in Major League Baseball. Furthermore, the presence and success of Black women in Olympic swimming (Simone Manuel), boxing (Claressa Chields), Water Polo (Ashleigh Johnson), shot putting (Michelle Carter), and gymnastics (Gabby Douglas and Simone Biles), or in professional tennis with young Black women like Sloane Stevens, Madison Keys, and so on, are continuing the legacy of Althea Gibson, Zina Garrison, the Williams sisters, and other Black women athlete who were vanguards. Based on the representation and the performances of Black women in these sports, the future looks promising for young Black girls in country club sports; sports where they have had limited access, more so due to race and class rather than athletic ability.

Ideologically, however, this racial progress on the field and in the arenas in the United States will further the racist beliefs that are rooted in scientific racism, where the innate physicality of the Black body warrants it superior athletically, but intellectually inferior. Thus, Blacks are more suitable and acceptable in their role as athletes, but lack the intellectual abilities to be leaders, coaches, and administrators. Consequently, the beliefs in the superior physicality and intellectual inferiority of the Black body corroborates the reproduction of the imbalance of power and wealth transfer in sport to benefit whites. The meaning of the Black athlete will continue to serve the needs of white supremacy, until emancipatory structures are created to reduce the imbalance in power and wealth transfer.

Critical research that continually exposes this imbalance in power and wealth is necessary, whether it is the disproportionate amount of Black athletes in revenue generating sports at predominantly white institutions and their low graduate rates or the disproportionate amount of Black players in the NBA and NFL but the small percentage of Blacks in leadership positions or owners of these teams. The efforts of critical research scholars in giving a voice to the previously voiceless provide the counter-narratives that are necessary for programmatic development to enhance the sporting experiences of Black athletes. For example, the work Dr. Akilah Carter-Francique is doing with her Sista to Sista program at Prairie View University, where she has developed a holistic development program for Black female collegiate athletes, which is undergirded with the research she conducts on the experiences of Black female collegiate athletes (Sista to Sista, 2018). Another program that is grounded in critical race methodology is the Collective Uplift program at the University of Connecticut directed by Dr. Joseph Cooper (Collective Uplift, 2018). It is also a holistic development support program designed to assist Black male college athletes matriculate through the challenges they experience at predominantly white institutions. These are examples of efforts that are being developed to convert these once oppressive structures in regards to athletic exploitation into emancipatory structures where Black athletes are matriculating to graduation and transitioning to being leaders in their respective careers.

Furthermore, the critical race methodology of counter-storytelling, where counter-narratives are produced will not only inform policies that impact Blacks participation in sports but also help reshape the dominant public perception regarding the Black sporting experiences. These narratives also challenge dominant ideologies about racialized performance and representation and present alternative perspectives regarding the socialization patterns and cultural norms that influence the Black sporting experience opposed to the scientific racist beliefs in the genetic physical superiority of the Black athlete.

In *And We Are Not Saved: The Elusive Quest for Racial Justice*, Professor Derrick Bell proclaims: "It appears that the worst fears have been realized: we have made progress in everything, yet, nothing has changed" (1989, p. 10). This captures the overall theme for this chapter and it may suggest a hopeless future, in regards to race relations. Recovering from the resurgence and radicalization of white supremacy's ideals will take a concerted effort from those seeking to make sure that the racial inequalities and inequities experienced anywhere are challenged, even in the context of sport, so that they do not threaten the racial justice we have achieved at this point in our human development.

Notes

1. President #45 will be used instead of invoking the name Donald J. Trump.
2. The terms Black and African American are used interchangeably in this chapter.
3. Beyond making public statements regarding their connection to and benefit from slavery, several of these institutions have made public apologized and provide other concessions. For example, in 1838, Georgetown University sold 272 slaves to secure its financial future. Two buildings were renamed to honor theses slaves, and Georgetown granted preferential admission treatment to the descendants of these slaves; similar to admission consideration it offers children of alumni. Other institutions, like Yale University, Harvard University, and University of Virginia, either renamed buildings that were named after advocates of slavery or slave owners, removed monuments associated with their slave history, and/or constructed memorials to recognized enslave people who benefit these institutions.

References

Bell, D. 1989. *And we are not saved: The elusive quest for racial justice*. New York: Basic Books.

Berghorn, F. J., Yetman, N. R., and Hanna, W. E. 1988. Racial participation and integration in men's and women's intercollegiate basketball: Continuity and change, 1959–1985. *Sociology of Sport Journal*, 5(2), 87–106.

Bernhard, L. M. 2014. Nowhere for me to go: Black female student-athlete experiences on a predominantly white campus. *Journal for the Study of Sports and Athletes in Education*, 8, 67–76.

Berr, J. 2017a. NFL national anthem protest denting ticker sales. *CBS MoneyWatch*. Available from www.cbsnews.com/news/nfl-national-anthem-protest-denting-ticket-sales/ [Accessed 1 December 2017].

Berr, J. 2017b. NFL national anthem protest denting ticker sales. *CBS MoneyWatch*. Available from www.cbsnews.com/news/nfl-national-anthem-protest-denting-ticket-sales/ [Accessed 1 December, 2017].

Bimper Jr., A. Y. and Harrison Jr., L. 2011. Meet me at the crossroads: African American athletic and racial identity. *Quest*, 63(3), 275–288.

Blalock, H. M. 1962. Occupational discrimination: Some theoretical propositions. *Social Problems*, 9(3): 240–247.

Blalock, H. M. 1967. *Toward a theory of minority group relations*. New York: John Wiley and Sons.

Bruening, J., Armstrong, K., and Pastore, D. 2005. Listening to the voices: The experiences of African American female student-athletes. *Research Quarterly for Exercise and Sport*, 76(1), 82–100.

Carrington, B. 2010. *Race, sport and politics: The sporting Black diaspora*, Los Angeles, CA: Sage.

Carter, A. F. 2008. *Negotiation identities: Examining African American female collegiate athlete experiences in predominantly white institutions*. Ph.D. dissertation, University of Georgia.

Carter-Francique, A., and Richardson, F. 2015. Black female athlete experiences at historically black colleges and universities. In B. Hawkins, J. Cooper, A. Carter-Francique, and J. K. Cavil, eds. *The athletic experience at historically Black colleges and universities*. Lanham, MD: Rowman & Littlefield, 61–83.

Collective Uplift. 2018. Available from https://wp.uplift.education.uconn.edu/our-goals/ [Accessed 9 February 2018].

Cooper, J. N., Cooper, J. E. and Baker, A. R. 2016. An anti-deficit perspective of Black female scholar-athlete's achievement experiences at a Division I Historical White Institution (HWI). *Journal for the Study of Sports and Athletes in Education*, 10(2), 109–131.

Corbett D., and Johnson W. 1993. The African-American female in collegiate sport: Sexism and racism. In D. Brooks and R. Althouse, eds. *Racism in college athletics: The African American athlete's experience*. Morgantown, WV: Fitness Information Technology, 199–225.

Crenshaw, K., Gotanda, N., Peller, G., and Thomas, K. 1995. *Critical race theory: The key writings that formed the movement*. New York: New Press.

Davis, L. R. 1990. The articulation of difference: White preoccupation with the question of racially linked genetic differences among athletes. *Sociology of Sport Journal*, 7(2), 179–187.

Delgado, R. 1995. *Critical race theory: The cutting edge*. Philadelphia: Temple University Press.

Delgado, R., and Stefancic, J. 2001. *Critical race theory: An introduction*. New York: New York University Press.

Dickey, J. 2017. Papa John's mess reveals drawbacks of NFL's power. Available from www.si.com/nfl/2017/11/06/papa-johns-john-schnatter-nfl-protests-alexander-ovechkin-putin [Accessed 22 January 2018].

Edwards, H. 2016. Harry Edwards keynote address at North American Society for the Sociology of Sport conference. Available from www.youtube.com/watch?v=Oimoyyx0HpE [Accessed 16 January 2018].

Hallinan, C. J. 1991. Aborigines and positional segregation in Australian Rugby League. *International Review for the Sociology of Sport*, 26(2), 69–79.

Harper, S. R. 2016. *Black male student-athletes and racial inequalities in NCAA Division I college sports*. Available from https://equity.gse.upenn.edu/sites/default/files/publications/Harper_Sports_2016.pdf [Accessed 15 January 2018].

Harrison, L., Harrison, C. K., and Moore, L. N. 2002. African American racial identity and sport. *Sport, Education, and Society*, 7(2), 121–133.

Hawkins, B. J. 2010. *The new plantation: Black athletes, college sports, and predominantly White NCAA Division I Institutions*. New York: Palgrave Macmillan.

Hawkins, B. J., Carter-Francique, A. R., and Cooper, J. N. 2017. *Critical race theory and American sport*. New York: Palgrave Macmillan.

Heitner, D. 2016. Colin Kaepernick tops jersey sales in NFL. *Forbes*. Available from www.forbes.com/sites/darrenheitner/2016/09/07/colin-kaepernick-tops-jersey-sales-in-nfl/ [Accessed 29 January 2018].

Hylton, K. 2009. *'Race' and sport: Critical race theory*, New York: Routledge.

Johnson, N. R., and Marple, D. P. 1973. Racial discrimination in professional basketball. *Sociological Focus*, 6(4), 6–18.

Koch, J. V., and Vander Hill, C. W. 1988. Is this discrimination in the Black man's game? *Social Science Quarterly*, 69(1), 83–94.

Ladson-Billings, G., and Tate IV, W. F. 1997. Toward a critical race theory of education. *Teachers College Record*, 97(1), 47–68.

Lee, C. 2007. Cultural convergence: Interest convergence theory meets the cultural defense. *Arizona Law Review*, 49, 912–958.

Leonard, D. J. 2014. Dilemmas and contradictions: Black female athletes. In L. L. Martin, ed., *Out of bounds: Racism and the Black athlete*. Santa Barbara, CA: Praeger, 209–230.

Leonard, W. M. 1987. Stacking in college basketball: A neglected analysis. *Sociology of Sport Journal*, 4(4), 403–409.

Loy, J. W., and McElvogue, J. F. 1970. Racial segregation in American sport. *International Review of Sport Sociology*, 5(1), 5–24.

Maguire, J. A. 1988. Race and position assignment in English soccer: A preliminary analysis of ethnicity and sport in Britain. *Sociology of Sport Journal*, 5(3), 257–269.

Marable, M. 1998. *Speaking truth to power: Essays on race, resistance, and radicalism*. Boulder, CO: Westview Press.

McDowell, J., and Carter-Francique, A. 2016. Experiences of female athletes of color. In E. Staurowsky, ed., *Women and sport: Continuing a journey of liberation to celebration*. Champaign, IL: Human Kinetics, 95–115.

McPherson, B. D. 1976. Minority group involvement in sport: The Black athlete. In A. Yiannakis, T. D. McIntyre, M. J. Melnick, and D. P. Hart, eds. *Sport sociology*. Dubuque, IA: Kendall/Hunt, 153–166.

Melnick, M. J. 1988. Racial segregation by playing in the English football league: Some preliminary observations. *Journal of Sport and Social Issues*, 12(1), 122–130.

Sista to Sista. 2018. Available from http://sistatosista.org/Sista_to_Sista/Welcome_to_Sista_to_Sista.html [Accessed 9 February 2018].

Sloan-Green, T., Oglesby, C., Alexander, A., and Franke, N. 1981. *Black women in sport*. Reston, VA: American Alliance of Health and Physical Education Recreation and Dance Publications.

Smith, Y. 1992. Women of color in society and sport. *Quest*, 44(2), 228–250.

Smith, Y. 2000. Sociohistorical influences of African American elite sportswomen. In D. Brooks and R. Althouse, eds. *Racism in college athletics: The African American Athlete Experience*, 2nd ed. Morgantown, WV: Fitness Information Technology, 173–197.

Snider, M. 2017. Are NFL player protests 'massively, massively' hurting TV ratings? *USA Today*. Available from www.usatoday.com/story/money/business/2017/09/26/nfl-player-protests-hurting-ratings/703619001/ [Accessed 7 February 2018].

Steinfeldt, J. A., Reed, C., and Steinfeldt, M. C. 2009. Racial and athletic identity of African American football players at historically Black colleges and universities and predominantly White institutions. *Journal of Black Psychology*, 36(1) 3–24.

TIDE, 2018. *The institute for diversity and ethics in sport*. Available from www.tidesport.org/reports.html [Accessed 15 January 2018].

Valentine, J. 2012. New racism and old stereotypes in the National Hockey League: The "stacking" of Aboriginal players into the role of enforcer. In J. Joseph, S. Darnell, and Y. Nakamura, eds. *Race and sport in Canada: Intersecting inequalities*. Toronto: Canadian Scholars' Press, 107–138.

Watanabe, N., Yan, G., and Soebbing, B. 2017. The political economy of Kaepernick's protests: An alternative understanding of athlete activism. North American Society for the Sociology of Sport paper presentation.

Yasso, T. J. 2005. Who's culture has capital? A critical race theory discussion of community culture wealth. *Race ethnicity and education*, 8(1), 69–91.

Chapter 6

Problematizing practice: Coach development with Foucault

Jim Denison and J. P. Mills

Introduction

Move through and around any city or town today and you will undoubtedly come across a host of playgrounds, sport fields, courts, pools, parks and gyms. Some of these spaces will be occupied, others will not. Some will be operated commercially or belong to a school; others will be managed by the city or town. And what do we notice when we come across such spaces? More often than not, very little—they fold into the background the way billboards and power lines do. And if these spaces themselves have become invisible, what is even more invisible is what takes place in these spaces. What are people doing, why and with what effects? Yes, of course, they are most probably exercising or playing in some manner or fashion: they are moving. But *how* are they moving? And we do not mean 'how' as in their velocity, energy expenditure or motor coordination. Rather, how have their movements been determined and organized? What explains their rhythms, sequences and gestures? Moreover, *who* has set these ways of moving, these specific programs and for what purpose?

For many who work in the allied fields of human movement studies—exercise physiologists, sport scientists, exercise psychologists—such questions might seem insignificant or trivial. Faced with a so-called obesity crisis, for instance, their thinking might simply be: Isn't all that really matters is that people are *just* moving? And so it is that many of the effects of how we have come to know and understand how to move remain invisible. There is simply no urgency or wider relevance attached to such a concern despite the fact that as human beings we were born to move. As a result, how will we ever understand all that sport, exercise and play do—society's most prevalent expressions of movement, of being human—if we do not put before our eyes and scrutinize the formation and organization of our movement practices?

When Michel Foucault was asked, following the publication of *Discipline and Punish*, about the invisibility of prisons in cities, including the invisibility of what goes on in them, he explained how the study of history only makes visible that which one's instruments can see. In other words, similar to our concern with the invisibility of movement across the fields, parks and gyms of our cities and towns, Foucault (1980, pp. 50–51) recognized that "to make visible the unseen ... mean[s] ... addressing oneself to a layer of material which had hitherto had no pertinence for history and which had not been recognized as having a moral, aesthetic, political, or historical value."

Accordingly, what interests us about human movement are the minute acts people practice, perfect and perform. More specifically, we are interested in the details of coaches' practices as strategies of power and how everything a coach does with his or her athletes—whether it be technical, tactical, physical or instructional—"reaches into the very grain of individuals, touches their bodies and inserts itself into their actions and attitudes, their discourses, learning processes and everyday lives" (Foucault 1980, p. 39). Speaking boldly, we would argue that it is impossible to understand what coaching means and does if one cannot see how power is exercised every day *in practice* on the field, track, court, gym or pool. Thus, when we say, and as *we have said* (e.g., Denison and Mills 2013, Mills and Denison 2014), that our remit as Foucauldian-informed coach developers is to help coaches learn how to coach in less disciplinary or dominating ways, we do not mean that we want to make coaches into more benevolent sovereigns. Rather, we want to help coaches learn how to foster and create more ethical relationships with their athletes by beginning to problematize the many invisible details and myriad relations of power present and active within their existing practices and their daily training environment. In this regard, and in line with the focus of this book, our work as coach developers has concerned, first, mapping and critiquing the research surrounding what it means for a coach to 'be effective' and, second, collaborating with coaches to help them learn how to problematize many of their everyday practices. In what follows, we discuss these two steps and how they align with our Foucauldian-informed research rationale.

Mapping and critiquing effective coaching

The following represents an underlying tenet of our work as Foucauldian-informed coach developers: What coaches say and do with the bodies in front of them can no longer be understood as a coherent or homogenized ensemble of techniques or 'tools of the trade' but as a complex play and coming together of different mechanisms of power each of which all retain their specific character. In this regard, the multiple decisions that a coach makes on an everyday basis ranging from how to structure a practice, to who to put into the starting lineup and how to balance work with recovery, must be seen as the result of an interplay of various knowledges or discourses that do not necessarily consolidate or define what effective coaching is but instead form (read rationalize) what coaches come to believe—and defend—to be the 'right' or 'best' way to coach. And it is through this process that 'being an effective coach' becomes highly political, a condition that most scholarly analyses of coaching have ignored.

In an effort to offset the apolitical position of studying and researching coaching, in particular psychology's individualistic narrative of human nature, knowledge and decision making, we have made it the aim of our coaching scholarship, and our accompanying work with practicing coaches, to understand how various relations of power might be transformed through the articulation and implementation of 'new coaching knowledges' such that power and all that power does begins to be seen as supple, inventive and precarious, not fixed, permanent and hierarchical. In this way, when working with a coach, it is critical for us that he or she become more aware, intentional and strategic concerning the possibilities he or she has for establishing more ethical relationships and coaching with a minimum of domination by recognizing (and responding to) how everything he or she does comes with multiple effects. Otherwise, what is problematic, constraining or limiting the actions and experiences of one's athletes, will likely go unchallenged: they will escape the necessary scrutiny that any set of practices should be subject to if one believes in the promise of critical thinking to promote and foster positive change.

Now, clearly we know—trust us we do—that what we have just outlined is an ambitious, academic-heavy position that is unlikely to speak to coaches. So let's unpack this position a bit; let's see what is at its center—its key assumptions—and what relevance it might hold for practicing coaches.

For sure, we would say, as Foucault did about his work in his debate with Chomsky, that to problematize coaching means, if nothing else, to politicize coaching. "The essence of our life consists, after all, of the political functioning of the society in which we find ourselves" (Chomsky and Foucault 2006, p. 37). But as coaches say to us all the time, "Coaching ... political? It's my passion. I do it because I love it. I just want to help the kids." Despite these protests we have continued to persist with our politicizing of coaching—our mapping and critiquing, our 'problem-identifying.' Not surprisingly, this has led to us inhabiting the fringes of coach development. As 'problem-setters' (Denison and Avner 2011), we have a much harder 'sell' when working with coaches than say 'problem-fixers,' such as physiologists, nutritionists or psychologists (especially psychologists who also analyze experience and behavior) for whom economic forces, logic systems or relations of power do not feature in their interventions. But then there are these words from Foucault that justify why the development of coaches must address such concerns—the politics of coaching.

> It is the custom ... to consider that power is localized in the hands of the government and that it is exercised through a certain number of particular institutions, such as the administration, the police, the army, and the apparatus of the state. One knows that all these institutions are made to elaborate and to transmit a certain number of decisions, in the name of the nation or of the state, to have them applied and to punish those who don't obey. But I believe that political power also exercises itself through the mediation of a certain number of institutions which look as if they have nothing in common with

the political power, and as if they are independent of it, while they are not. One knows this in relation to the family; and one knows that the university, and in a general way, all teaching systems [read coaching], which appear simply to disseminate knowledge, are made to maintain a certain social class in power; and to exclude the instruments of power of another social class. Institutions of knowledge [read coach education], of foresight and care, such as medicine [read sport medicine], also help to support the political power. (Chomsky and Foucault 2006, pp. 39–40)

So then, where and how should we begin our political analysis—our mapping and critiquing—of coaching, especially given our aim to be viewed as relevant? One mapping tact that we have taken is to analyze what coaches know, how they know it and what happens in practice—a coach's daily training environment—as a result. And by extension, we have analyzed how the details of what coaches say and do every day—their instructions and training plans—establish their relations with their athletes and accordingly what the act of coaching actually becomes: what it looks like, what it does and the effects (read results) it produces. And it is the idea of the coach-athlete relationship that we turn to next in our effort to problematize what effective coaching means.

Coach-athlete relations in sport

It should be clear by now that we are not concerned with discovering or reifying what effective coaching *is*. Correspondingly, while the formation and implementation of the details of coaches' practices, and what this might mean for coach-athlete relations, is important to us, it is not trying to discover what the coach-athlete relationship *is* that we think will produce more effective coaches and more successful athletes. Such an aim is to assume that there is this thing called 'the coach-athlete relationship'—an object that can be observed, understood and known definitively. Such an aim is to ignore how the very act of studying coach-athlete relations serves to give it the characteristics around which it should supposedly function or operate.

For example, according to Jowett and Meek (2000), sport psychologists who have written about coach-athlete relations, "the coach-athlete dyad is an interpersonal relationship that is specific and important to sport psychology … [and] crucial to the achievement of a successful performance and interpersonal satisfaction" (p. 157). Following this pronouncement, Jowett and Meek created a sport-specific framework and methodology to study dyadic relationships in sports. This, they stated, would allow them "to develop a model from which distinct coach-athlete relationship types could be examined and subsequently explained in a systematic way" (p. 158). To support their model, Jowett and Meek first operationalized interpersonal relationships in sports. Borrowing from Kelley et al. (1983), they defined an interpersonal relationship as "a situation in which two people's emotions, thoughts, and behaviors are mutually and causally interconnected" (p. 158).

Next, they employed the psychological constructs of closeness, co-orientation, and complementarity—the 3 C's—to examine the nature of coaches' and athletes' interpersonal relationships.

Using the 3 C's to then investigate the coach-athlete relationship, Jowett and Cockerill (2003) concluded that there are a number of specific components to positive personal and relational outcomes in sport-specific settings. These included trust, respect, communication, shared goals and cooperation. Based on these conclusions, they recommended that coach education programs, as part of their curriculum for fostering success, should provide information that will assist coaches to develop effective relationships with their athletes.

But can the development of effective coach-athlete relationships be reduced to the analysis of dyads, systems or models? Following this line of thinking, relationship 'problems' should be able to be understood and controlled (read medicated) in the same way that cardiac output, for example, can be measured and changed: in a direct causal fashion. This suggests that an athlete's confidence can be increased or a coach and athlete's partnership enhanced just by selecting the appropriate intervention—pressing the "this-is-the-right-way-of-talking-in-this-situation" button. There must exist a simple linear logic that runs from problem to diagnosis and treatment—problem-fixing vs. problem-solving. Similarly, once a coach and athlete determine their goals for an upcoming season and plot a path to achieve them they should be able to carry on freely in this direction until they are attained. Thus, all responsibility for change falls upon individuals: the coach and/or athlete. All prospects for a healthy relationship, therefore, are seen to be within us and it is our responsibility (or perhaps in consultation with a sports psychologist) to allow it to emerge and ultimately flourish (Denison and Winslade 2006).

Through our position against the idea of the coach-athlete relationship as something that can be known objectively, we are of course arguing that there is no external position of certainty, no universal understanding that is beyond history and society. Like Foucault, who across the entire span of his work problematized the actual existence of such broad concepts as human nature and studied instead how such concepts come to function the way that they do, we are not interested in producing a universal understanding or model of the coach-athlete relationship. How could we possibly capture every understanding, every moment, every nuance? In this regard, to study the coach-athlete relationship as if it is something real in and of itself instead of "an idea which in effect has been invented and put to work ... as an instrument of a certain political and economic power" (Chomsky and Foucault 2006, p. 187) is to operate as if 'certainty in knowing' was a real possibility. Accordingly, from a Foucauldian point of view, research into any social phenomena such as coach-athlete relations should fundamentally be about altering relations of power (Foucault 2010). For the knowledge of any phenomena, or any practices which constitute our world, can never be above clashes in domination or external to power. Rather, and most interestingly when one thinks about it, this knowledge can simultaneously serve domination and combat it.

And so it is, Foucault argued, that knowledge and power always operate—grapple even—with each other, always forcing the production of so-called truths.

For the purpose of our discussion here concerning the everyday details of coaches' practices, however, and the manner in which those details work to establish coaches' relations with their athletes and what the act of coaching eventually becomes and does, it is important to recognize that, like Foucault, we are not concerned with the study of knowledge and power in and of themselves. Rather, as Foucault stated, "the goal of my work during the last twenty years has not been to analyse the phenomena of power, nor to elaborate the foundations of such an analysis. My objective, instead, has been to create a history of the different modes by which, in our culture, human beings are made subject" (Foucault 2010, p. 7). And without question one mode, or one apparatus, by which coaches and athletes have been made into particular types of subjects, or bodies, who then operate according to a set of specific meanings and norms has been the widespread adoption across all facets of sport of a range of disciplinary practices (for a comprehensive review of this formation, see Shogan 1999). And so normal and out of view are these disciplinary practices that their criticism across any and all coach education curricula has for the most part been non-existent.

Coaches, moreover, believe in these various practices, thus making the scrutiny of all that they do even more unlikely for researchers to take up. And why wouldn't coaches believe in these practices? They have proven their utility; they have been shown to produce subject positions that can lead to all manner of awards, praise and recognition. And because coach education generally only addresses problems that coaches can clearly see or point to (Denison et al. 2015), the problems the disciplines might contribute to (and there are many) due to their presence and activity persist either unacknowledged (read unseen) or worse they get attributed to some unrelated circumstance just because it is more visible or tangible. It is this paradox behind discipline's effects, that is, these techniques and instruments' simultaneous useful and problematic consequences, that has led us to ask such mapping and critique questions in our research as: How and why do the disciplines work the way they do to form particular types of practices and relationships between coaches and athletes? And how and why do they continue to go unchallenged by the majority of researchers working in sport despite producing so many unintended effects? It is these mapping and critique questions that we take up next in an effort to explain why we believe what we are doing as Foucauldian-informed coach developers and researchers, as compared to most other coaching researchers, offers the promise to challenge and change so much of what gets ignored in the understanding and promotion of effective coaching.

Coaching as a disciplining practice

According to Foucault (1980, p. 195), any apparatus of power, such as discipline's techniques and instruments, could be defined as a "system of relations that can be established between [various] elements." Importantly for Foucault, the 'invention' of any apparatus of power and the relations and connections between its various elements always had a dominant strategic function. For example, and as his work has clearly illustrated, there were a number of strategic imperatives at play, mostly economic, that led to the increasing degree of control or subjection over the mad, the neurotic and the delinquent but also the sane and the normal—all in an effort to make every body productive.

However, the recognition that the exercise of discipline, which became clear to see, produced useful bodies that could easily be transformed, also made bodies docile, which was to a degree unexpected. But instead of this consequence—this effect—being seen as a problem that necessitated a readjustment of the relationship between the elements within this apparatus of power, what arose instead was a reinterpretation of this apparatus so that it could continue undisturbed. Take imprisonment as a case in point. There was no question that the exercise of disciplinary power "made measures of detention appear to be the most efficient and rational method that could be applied to the phenomena of criminality" (1980, p. 195). But when this apparatus also produced effects that had nothing to do with its 'original' intention, such as the "constitution of a delinquent milieu very different from the kind of seedbed of illegalist practices and individuals found in eighteenth-century society ... the prison operated as a process of filtering, concentrating, professionalizing and circumscribing a criminal milieu" (pp. 195–196). In other words, what quickly arose within the penal system was "an immediate re-utilization of this unintended, negative effect within a new strategy which came in some sense to occupy this empty space, or transform the negative into a positive" (p. 196).

Thus, with respect to coaching, while docility and its many associated problems, as brought on by the use of discipline's techniques and instruments by coaches has been shown to undermine the development of more effective coaching practices and ethical coach-athlete relations (e.g., Barker-Ruchti and Tinning 2010, Denison 2007), their greater 'benefit'—and why these practices tend to go unchallenged— could very likely be how they might serve to create economically functioning citizens: the obedient, compliant, 'good athlete' who also supports the larger status quo by not speaking or acting against it in any significant or material way. Importantly, this suggestion is not informed by a deductive process that views discipline as a totalizing force. However, the question we think this suggestion raises is, how and why have coaching's many taken-for-granted, or invisible, disciplinary practices ascended to such a position whereby coaches believe they would be unable to relate effectively to their athletes and know how to coach without them?

Like Foucault (1980), therefore, we are not seeking to understand why a coach might want to relate to his or her athletes in a dominant or docile-making fashion, and what his or her strategy would be in this regard. Instead, we want to understand:

> how things work at the level of on-going subjugation, at the level of those continuous and uninterrupted processes which subject our bodies, govern our gestures, dictate our behaviors, etc. In other words, rather than ask

ourselves how the sovereign appears to us in his lofty isolation, we should try to discover how it is that subjects are gradually, progressively, really and materially constituted through a multiplicity of organisms, forces, energies, materials, desires, thoughts, etc. We should try to grasp subjection in its material instance as a constitution of subjects. (p. 97)

Such an aim necessitates a move away from framing effective coaching and the formation of 'positive' or 'adjusted' coach-athlete relations as the act of a single will, a position too often promoted by traditional studies of coaching and performance enhancement in sport. A coach influenced by this idea will never be able to see all that what he or she does every day with his or her athletes *does* and how what he or she does every day with his or her athletes is a result of the effects of power. No better example of this exists than the empty rhetoric so often spouted by coaches concerning athlete empowerment. For as Denison et al. (2015) illustrated, the failure to see how proclamations of empowerment will go unfilled without addressing coaching's disciplinary legacy is to make a false promise to one's athlete's. And it is because of such disconnections between words and action that we have deliberately pursued such a strong change agenda in our work with coaches that we have come to call, learning to problematize.

Learning to problematize

What we believe we have demonstrated up to this point, that is both mapped and in turn critiqued, is the mechanics of the coercive forces within sport whose exercise has led to what Foucault referred to as "a *society of normalization*" (1980, p. 107, italics in original) such that coaches and athletes can only know, understand and experience their relations in a number of specific ways. But more than that, we hope we have begun to demonstrate the manner in which change, or more specifically resistance, against normalization can occur. And as Foucauldians this is not to be done by objecting to the rules of right imposed by the sovereign. To limit in some way the disciplines and all the effects of power and knowledge that are linked to them—to move on from mapping and critique, to change—one must turn towards the possibilities that can arise from less disciplinary practices. That is, one must begin to problematize that which has become normal. Or more specifically, one must become in Foucault's words, "anti-disciplinarian" (1980, p. 108).

Accordingly, we believe strongly in working collaboratively with coaches to create 'ways of coaching' that are not so grounded in discipline and control and normalization if indeed coaches' practices and coach-athlete relations are to be transformed. Of course this is not to say that coaches need to begin to coach outside power relations because such a possibility simply does not exist. Rather, it is to say that coaches need to begin to coach with a greater awareness of power relations, or all that their coaching does (Denison et al. 2015). And such a change, of course, will undoubtedly be seen as subversive. For to coach in ways that challenge sport's modernist logic and its disciplinary legacy others will no doubt take notice; a host of ripple effects and questions will result, many of which we have encountered through our work with coaches. And to illustrate this, we would like to discuss briefly one particular challenge that surfaced while the first author was collaborating with a coach in an effort to help him learn how to problematize.

The coach's eye

As we expect is clear by now, visibility—what can be seen and what remains obscured—has been an important theme for us in this chapter: the visibility of spaces, the invisibility of practices; the visibility of doing, the invisibility of all that one's doing does. Along the same line, as the first author began to help a young and up and coming soccer coach learn how to coach in a less disciplinary way so that he could begin to change his domination of his athletes through a less restrictive pedagogy, their conversations repeatedly touched on the power of the 'coach's eye' as a barrier to change: an invisible power that was by no means benign.

Jim began to work with Ben (a pseudonym) in the fall of 2016 and for six weeks they met twice a week for upwards of an hour so that Ben could begin to learn how to design less controlling passing and shooting drills. More specifically, Ben wanted to become less direct in terms of determining his drills' purpose and design. Therefore, with the support of Jim, he began to ask his players questions about scoring and defending in actual game situations and what kind of drills they thought might help them score more and defend better.

Early in their collaboration, Ben raised the specter of the 'senior soccer coach' watching him implement some of these new drills and judging them as, "odd ... strange ... inefficient and ineffective." Interestingly, no senior soccer coach was ever in attendance at Ben's practices. Ben was the head coach of a Boys' Under-14 team and aside from a couple of casual assistant coaches he largely operated on his own at every practice. But the effects of being observed, of being judged, were real. As Ben said in his second meeting with Jim following his implementation of a drill where he organized a small group activity with minimal instructions, "I can't help imagining Simon [a pseudonym; a senior coach in the community he admires], being on the sideline raising an eyebrow as he watched me coach the boys today."

Ben's interest in learning how to become a less controlling coach arose following his completion of Jim's graduate coaching course where the focus was on learning how to problematize the effects from such Foucauldian-inspired processes as hierarchical observation and normalization. Through this example of the 'coach's eye', Ben was clearly experiencing the power of these two forces and the manner in which they influenced his coaching, especially his efforts to coach differently. This presented Jim with an excellent opportunity to help Ben better understand why that was, as this snippet of conversation from their third meeting indicates.

JIM: Okay, Ben, we know that Simon is not there on the sidelines watching and judging you, but clearly you feel his presence. But do you think it is *his* presence you feel or something else?

BEN: Well, it is *him*, that I feel and sense, but I know, too, that there is something more, like you are suggesting. Something bigger.

JIM: Keep going.

BEN: I mean, Simon's 'eye' that I feel judging me is not his per se. It's soccer's in general.

JIM: And so that means what about how you have come to understand what it means to be a soccer coach?

BEN: It means, I think, that it is not coming from Simon but the history of soccer and the traditions of 'how to coach' that have become established over the years and become normalized in the process.

JIM: Which makes changing them difficult.

BEN: Really difficult. Because I don't want to be seen as ineffective or an ignorant coach, and working with my players to design drills in the way that we have been talking about really marks me as different.

JIM: So, back to the problem you are having with idea of the coach's eye, what is it, really?

BEN: It is not, Simon. I know that now. It's the various relations of power that have established the existence of 'a Simon' whose eyes then serve to regulate and control me. And I guess those eyes regulate and control Simon, too.

Keep in mind, Ben had spent a semester as part of this graduate studies reading Foucault so he had a good working understanding of many of Foucault's main concepts. As a result, moving forward in his collaboration with Jim, it became easier and easier for Ben to ascribe any doubts or insecurities he had about coaching differently to the effects of power and knowledge and history and not the personality of some senior coach or his own inadequacies. Along those lines, he and Jim exchanged this bit of dialogue in their fifth meeting.

BEN: I find it a lot less difficult to change my long-standing practices knowing they are just ideas from the past and so not necessarily 'true' or 'best.' Plus, I can see that my players, after some time trying these different practices, don't care at all that they might be different. These new practices are working for them—they are more confident and independent in games—and I can see that that is what matters most to them.

JIM: What does that tell you, then, about coaching?

BEN: Well for sure one thing it tells me is how contextual coaching is and that if I want to be as effective as possible and best serve the needs of my players, I can't be afraid to challenge and change what might be considered normal or correct to do, as hard as it might be to detect those things.

Conclusion

To close, we would like to pose a question inspired by a recent publication from two of this volume's editors (Gerdin and Pringle 2017), that we believe captures the difficulty of problematizing that which has become normal. It is: How does one challenge or transform a set of knowledges and practices so tightly tied to pleasure, success, reward, esteem, privilege, status and power even though those very same knowledges and practices may also produce a number of problems? Put differently, how does one begin to point out and promote new ways of thinking and doing about something—new knowledges and practices—when what is currently done and practiced is part of an entrenched model of acting that is highly valued and at the same time in discursive symmetry with a broad range of qualities or ways of being that are celebrated and cherished across society as a whole?

As Foucauldian-informed coach developers committed to problematizing what it is that coaches say and do on an everyday basis, this is a situation we find ourselves in regularly. As a result, and as we have already mentioned, getting 'buy in' from coaches can be quite difficult. In other words, to problematize what has been so effectively normalized, and to a degree is working, one risks being seen as an advocate for the other side of the coin: promoting displeasure over pleasure, losing over winning, laziness over discipline and chaos over order. And who could ever stand up and defend that? Moreover, who would want to?

It is here, therefore, where problematizing is often misunderstood. After all, and to paraphrase Foucault, do you think we have really been working as hard as we have the last decade problematizing what coaches say and do just to be annoying or a nuisance? Of course not. We care deeply about athletes succeeding and coaches being effective. In this respect, to problematize coaching is not to think cynically about coaching. It is to be unafraid and willing to question our normal ways of being and doing in an effort to see all that those ways of being and doing are doing. And it is from such a position, we believe, that change for the better can become a real possibility.

References

Barker-Ruchti, N. and Tinning, R., 2010. Foucault in leotards: Corporeal discipline in women's artistic gymnastics. *Sociology of Sport Journal*, 27 (3), 229–250.

Chomsky, N. and Foucault, M., 2006. *The Chomsky-Foucault debate: On human nature.* New York: The New Press.

Denison, J., 2007. Social theory for coaches: A Foucauldian reading of one athlete's poor performance. *International Journal of Sports Science & Coaching*, 2 (4), 369–383.

Denison, J. and Avner, Z., 2011. Positive coaching: Ethical practices for athlete development. *Quest*, 63 (2), 209–227.

Denison, J. and Mills, J. P., 2014. Planning for distance running: Coaching with Foucault. *Sports Coaching Review*, 3 (1), 1–16.

Denison, J., Mills, J. P. and Konoval, T., 2017. Sports' disciplinary legacy and the challenge of 'coaching differently.' *Sport, Education and Society*, 22 (6), 772–783.

Denison, J., Pringle, R., Cassidy, T. and Hessian, P., 2015. Informing coaches' practices: Towards an application of Foucault's ethics. *International Sport Coaching Journal*, 2 (1), 72–76.

Denison, J. and Winslade, J., 2006, Understanding problematic sporting stories: Narrative therapy and applied sport psychology, *Junctures*, 6 (1), 99–105.

Foucault, M., 1980. *Power/Knowledge: Selected interviews and other writings*. New York: Pantheon Books.

Foucault, M., 1995. *Discipline and punish: The birth of the prison*. New York: Vintage Books.

Foucault, M., 2010. *The Foucault Reader*. New York: Vintage Books.

Gerdin, G. and Pringle, R., 2017. The Politics of pleasure: An ethnographic examination exploring the dominance of the multi-activity sport-based physical education model. *Sport, Education and Society*, 22 (2), 194–213.

Jowett, S. and Cockerill, I. M., 2003. Olympic medallists' perspective of the athlete-coach relationship. *Psychology of Sport and Exercise*, 4 (3), 313–331.

Jowett, S. and Meek, G., 2000. Coach-athlete relationships in married couples: An exploratory content analysis. *The Sport Psychologist*, 14 (1), 157–175.

Kelley, H. H., Berscheid, E., Christensen, A. Harvey, H. H., Huston, T. L., Levinger, G., McClintock, E., Peplau, L. A. and Peterson, D. R., eds., 1983. *Close relationships*. New York: Freeman.

Mills, J. P. and Denison, J., 2013. Coach Foucault: Problematizing endurance running coaches' practices. *Sports Coach Review*, 2 (1), 136–150.

Shogan, D., 1999. *The making of high-performance athletes: Discipline, diversity and ethics*. Toronto: University of Toronto Press.

Critical perspectives and social change within school physical education

Part II

Chapter 7

Critical pedagogy in physical education as advocacy and action: A reflective account[1]

Richard Tinning

In this chapter I take the liberty of reflecting on my long career as an advocate for critical pedagogy within HPE (Health & Physical Education). As I think of my career one question dominates my thoughts: what difference did I make? In seeking an answer I can scan my CV and read the titles of the things I have written, the presentations I have made all around the world as I lived out my privileged career. I can even log on to ResearchGate and see how many citations I have received. However, none of this tells me anything about how the ideas I have been prosecuting may have been picked up, or whether they have in any way been influential on the readers.

Now of course, the contemporary neoliberal university requires academics to justify (with evidence) the impact of our work. But beyond (and I would say including) the use of the metric 'impact factor' this is a slippery process. Piecing together bits of information about impact is a certain skill that some develop better (and faster) than others. But regardless of the skill in the process, there remains much that is unknowable about how one's work impacts on the lives, or the thinking, of others. For example, back in 1977 Marilyn French had no idea how her book *The Women's Room* would affect a 30-year-old male PE lecturer living in another continent.

Across the past four decades I have been a vocal advocate for the need for physical education to problematise its own knowledge construction, legitimation and dissemination, and to critically engage its own ideology, power and culture (Tinning, 1991). Moreover, I have also argued that issues relating to gender equity, equality of opportunity, diversity, and challenging unjust practices such as motor elitism, should be an integral part of physical education (e.g., Tinning, 1987a). However, like some others committed to the critical project of education, I have become more cautionary in the claims that I think can be made for the transformative possibilities of schooling in general and HPE in particular (see, for example Hickey, 2001; Philpot, 2015; Curtner-Smith, 2007).

Much of my work would fit under the now popular broad concept of transformative pedagogy (see Tinning, 2017). There are two dimensions of change that are implicit in transformative pedagogy – personal change and social change. There is also an assumption that empowerment at the individual level will lead to a social transformation in the form of a more democratic, equitable and liberal social world (see Ukpokodu, 2009). Transformative pedagogies include, but are not limited to, the discourse communities of critical pedagogy, critical action research, critical teaching, liberatory pedagogy; critical inquiry, and critical reflection. For the purposes of this chapter I will limit my attention to the transformative pedagogies that can be 'grouped' as advocacy *for* and research *on* critical pedagogy.

The assumption that empowerment at the personal level will lead to a social transformation in the form of a more democratic, equitable and liberal social world is, in my view, more aspirational than probable. While I recognize that powerful ideas can transform society (for example, Marxism or neoliberalism), to think that we can, as critical HPE scholars, by means of our writing and our pedagogies, bring about social change is an overreach. Rather, the opposite seems to be the case; critical HPE scholars have not brought about social change, but instead are caught up in its wake. Social changes such as the gender movement, the rise of social media, the increased marketing/advertising of the body, the contemporary focus on identity making, and changes in health policy, have all had significant influence on HPE, and not the other way around. This point is the central orienting theme in this chapter.

Desirable and undesirable bodies

Almost 30 years ago I wrote a paper titled "Physical Education and the cult of slenderness: A critique" (see Tinning, 1985). In that paper I argued that the field of physical education was implicated in what I called the cult of slenderness, that in turn was a manifestation of the discourses of body image and obesity. I claimed that school physical education was failing to educate young people to become critical consumers of physical culture and as a consequence they were less likely to resist the pernicious influence of the cult of slenderness.

Now it is true that the paper received considerable positive feedback from readers who considered that I had indeed exposed a serious problem. But did it really contribute to a heightened consciousness in readers or even some change in practice?

I used the phrase 'cult of slenderness' to name the hegemony of the 'look' (slim, trim, taut) that within contemporary Western cultures works in many ways to reinforce unhealthy body practices such as repetitive dieting, bulimia-nervosa and excessive exercising. Some six years later Kirk (1991: 105) asserted that school physical education programs of the time did little to "address these cultural 'side-effects'". Gard and Wright (2001) also argued that far from providing a critique of the cult of slenderness, the physical education profession is deeply implicated in the reproduction of healthism values through its active and uncritical promotion of obesity as a problem to be attacked through the school curriculum.

Some 17 years later, with colleague Trish Glasby (Tinning and Glasby, 2002: 112), we argued that

> it seems that there are grounds for believing that there is still work to be done in understanding how and why physical education continues to be implicated in the reproduction of values associated with the cult of slenderness. Said another way, we need to understand why HPE continues to be ineffective in helping young people gain some measure of analytic and embodied 'distance' from the problematic aspects of the cult of the body.

And, now, a further 16 years on, I consider that the same statement is relevant. This of course raises the question of "why should the collective efforts of HPE have been so ineffective, so impotent in bringing about desired change in regard to the cult of slenderness?"

Now it's not as if nothing has changed over the three decades since I wrote 'the cult of slenderness' paper. Since the 1990s the field of physical education (more recently known as Kinesiology/Human Movement Studies/Exercise Science) has become increasingly connected to the obesity discourses. Indeed, in many ways the obesity crisis has galvanised PE/Kinesiology with something of a shared mission (Tinning, 2014). This has spawned numerous research projects related to physical activity and health (see for example Sallis, McKenzie et al., 1997), and considerable advocacy for PE as THE site for the amelioration of the obesity crisis (see Sallis and McKenzie, 1991). It has also spawned scholarship that has cautioned such advocacy (see for example, Gard, 2008; Kirk, 2006).

There has also been considerable scholarship in the field of PE/Kinesiology regarding what might be broadly called the sociology of the body (e.g., Fitzclarence, 1990; Kirk, 1993; Oliver and Lalik 2001; Rich et al., 2004; Burrows, 2004; Gard and Wright, 2005; Sykes and McPhail, 2007; Wright and Harwood, 2009; Rich, 2010; Evans and Davies, 2011; Pringle and Pringle, 2012; Rail, 2012; Robinson and Randall, 2016).

There is no denying the fact that we live in a social context that gives unprecedented attention to the body (see Petersen and Lupton, 1996); to sport and physical activity (see Coakley, 2017) and to health (Lupton, 1996). However, as I argued previously (Tinning, 2003), for all our theorising on the body in culture, the practices and discursive productions of meaning that are part of the social processes of postmodern culture have continued to increase the importance of the body in the struggle for cultural capital (Bourdieu, 1991; Baudrillard, 2005). In other words, notwithstanding what we know from our theorising and research about how certain cultural practices contribute to limited, restricted or oppressive bodily practices, we have seen little significant systemic change in such practices.

While acknowledging that some young people have positive and healthful attitudes to their bodies, many young people still graduate from our schools oppressed by the tyranny of the cult of the body[2] (Petersen and Lupton, 1996). Anxiety regarding our bodies (what we put in them, what we do and can do with them, what they look like, what they 'should' look like) continues to be endemic. As Shapiro (2002: 14) argued, "The fears and panics around the body that fill the news, impel a continuous series of fads, diets and exercises". Indeed, according to Bauman (2000), the social production of the body is the primal scene of post-modern ambivalence and neuroticism. Importantly, the field PE/Kinesiology must share some responsibility for this state of affairs since the discourses underpinning its professional missions inform, advocate and reinforce risk avoidance, prudent living and preventative and ameliorative physical activity.

Gard (2004: 76) evocatively suggests that schools "have been drawn into the obesity vortex". In this context, Kirk (2006: 121) claims that 'stopping' obesity has become a major purpose of school physical education and that "there is a need for a critical pedagogy in physical education to provide a morally and educationally defensible form of engagement with obesity discourse". Such a critical pedagogy should, according to Kirk, problematise the obesity discourse and seek to empower young people, of all sizes and shapes, to understand whose interests are served and which bodies are privileged and/or oppressed.

In this regard, we might be pleased to note that in many school HPE curricula, body image is now a key learning focus through which young people are supposed to develop 'body positivity' (Gay, 2017), to learn to be 'critical consumers' of physical culture and as a consequence to be more likely to resist the pernicious influence of the cult of body. But there is a problem in that much of the pedagogical work done regarding the cult of the body is done by 'cultural players' beyond the school gates, by what Kenway and Bullen (2001) call the 'corporate curriculum'. This has huge implications for the field of physical education and health since it limits the possibility for young people to be empowered through HPE.

So, overall, in the thirty years since the "Cult of Slenderness" was published, there have been advances in the sophistication with which the HPE field engages with the issue of body image. Alternative discourses and powerful critiques are available, but their impact has been varied at best (see Tinning et al., 2017). Moreover, the gains made by HPE have been more than checked or countered by the social change created beyond the school gate. As Rose (2000: 1398) argues, "schools have been supplemented and sometimes displaced by an array of other practices for shaping identities and forms of life". For example, we can readily recognise the power of social media shaping attitudes and creating anxieties with regard to the body (see Szto and Gray, 2015; Ward et al., 2018).

Resistant forces to a socio-critical curriculum

In the late 1980s the Ministers of Education in the various Australian states and the Federal government, agreed to commit to some National goals for Australian schools. The school curriculum was to be structured around eight Key Learning Areas (KLAs). HPE was one such KLA. Importantly, although there was no explicit curriculum for each KLA, all learning areas were supposed to be oriented around three key principles: social justice, diversity and supportive environments.

Importantly, these three underpinning principles were not incorporated as a consequence of the work of critical pedagogy advocates in HPE. Rather they were principles that, at the time, had become somewhat *de rigueur* within broader political discourse. It was the Australian Curriculum Corporation (1992) that 'gave voice to' the underlying sociocultural perspective and social justice principles.

Here is how the 1999 Queensland syllabus for Years 1–10 in Health & Physical Education, explained the purpose of these principles:

> The sociocultural perspective and social justice principles underpinning the syllabus encourage students to consider social and cultural developments which may affect themselves and others, now and in the future. (1999: 5)

Macdonald and Kirk (1999) then argued that this official discourse meant that HPE teachers in Australia have a "responsibility to [teach] the socially critical liberal curriculum as defined by the State" (140). However, many teachers found the new curriculum difficult to understand and implement because it rested on a different way of thinking (a sociocultural and critical way). More often than not, as a result of their own undergraduate training they had come to understand the field through a biophysical perspective and an acceptance of the status quo (see Glover and Macdonald, 1997).

The most recent 'national' curriculum for HPE in Australia (2017) has been developed in response to what is considered by the Australian Curriculum body (ACARA) as what is needed to 'make' (prepare) future healthy citizens. The writing of the curriculum went through numerous iterations, each of which responded to community consultations. The chief writer of the new national HPE curriculum was Professor Doune Macdonald who, in addition to working in state-level curriculum development, had also published widely on HPE matters and was advocate for a socio-critical perspective. This new HPE 'national' curriculum is intended to shape teachers' work in the direction of certain essential learnings in both health and physical education. Within the health dimension of HPE, sexuality is now a key focus. However, as the following example reveals, though progressive socio-critical liberal ideals may be embedded in curriculum documents, the translation of such values into practice still met with resistance from powerful 'stakeholders'.

In 2014, as a response to the documented bullying of LGBTIQ students in Australian schools, the Federal government introduced the *Safe Schools* program. This program actually provided some more detail and resources for teachers who were already teaching about sexuality within the schools' HPE curriculum. Within the HPE curriculum focus area of 'relationships and sexuality' is the unambiguous statement that it is "crucial" for schools to "acknowledge and affirm diversity in relation to sexuality and gender".

As part of the *Safe Schools* program funding, a number of resources were developed to help teachers meet their responsibility. One resource was called *All of Us*. This resource, however, came under virulent and vitriolic attack from the Christian right and the *Australian* and other Murdoch News Corps newspapers. One of the criticisms of the *All of Us* resource was that it had been hijacked by queer theorists and Marxists who were trying to "indoctrinate kids with their ideology". Benjamin Law's *Quarterly Essay* titled 'Moral Panic 101: Equality, acceptance and the Safe Schools scandal' (2017) provides an excellent analysis and rebuttal of this attack. While this is not the place to expand on his arguments, the issue of schools' (and more specifically HPE's) involvement in, and responsibility for, sexuality education, and the backlash by certain sectors of the conservative community provides a clear example of the powerful forces that can be unleashed when one (individual teacher, school or curriculum) attempts to disrupt the status quo. Or, more particularly, how the status quo is vigorously defended.

So, in relation to young people's bodies and their sexualit(ies), the good news is that they are both 'in the curriculum' and are meant to be 'approached' by means of a well-researched and thoughtful socio-critical perspective. However, when the status quo (e.g., heteronormativity, see Larsson et al., 2010) is critically challenged, other more powerful forces come into play. These may be stakeholders outside the school and curriculum community, such as corporations that market certain bodies, fitness, fashion and food for commercial purposes. It also includes conservative organisations such as the Christian lobby and some sections of the media that have powerful ways to create 'moral panic' and to undermine the best efforts of schools and their communities to bring about transformative ends.

So, once more we see that the advocates of a socio-critical HPE have not created social change, but instead are caught up in its wake. In saying this I am not denying that there are HPE teachers 'out there' who are making significant differences to the lives of some young people. However, I doubt whether as a field HPE can claim much credit for the achievements of individual teachers who, as I argue below, happen to have a certain disposition that is receptive to the socio-critical perspective.

Reflective practice and a critical disposition

There is no doubt that one of the major trends in teaching, teacher education and PETE over the last few decades has been the rise of reflection as a dominant concept (see Tsangaridou and O'Sullivan, 1997). All across the Western education world it seems that reflective teaching/practice is part of the 'official' text. Notwithstanding concerns over the ubiquitous and sometimes problematic use of the term reflection (e.g., Kincheloe, 1993; Smyth, 1992), PETE undergraduate texts were written that placed reflection at the center of becoming a (good) PE teacher (e.g., Hellison and Templin, 1991). Moreover, there were some PETE programs that were clearly, and explicitly, being oriented around critical reflection (Ovens, 2004).

My commitment to the ideal of *critical* reflection began back in the 1980s and I wrote about my advocacy and experiences in trying to facilitate critical reflection especially through action research (e.g., Tinning, 1987b, 1992, 1993). My ideas were first articulated in a monograph I wrote for students studying an off-campus course at Deakin University. The students in the course were mainly primary school teachers who, by means of off-campus study were upgrading their qualifications. The monograph was titled *Improving Teaching in Physical Education* (1987) and it aimed to disrupt some of the taken-for-granted notions of PE as it is conceived and practiced. It had an explicit aim of encouraging teachers (and student teachers) to become reflective practitioners by addressing, through action research, questions such as: 'What are the implications of what I choose to teach?' and 'What are the implications of how I teach?' The monograph was also intended to problematize certain notions of effective teaching, and to introduce students to Schon's (1993) idea of reflective practice, and Stenhouse's (1975) concept of the extended professional.

As a major course assessment task, students were expected to conduct an action research project on some aspect of their PE teaching. From their course feedback it appeared that the monograph and the action research project did challenge their taken-for-granted notions of PE teaching and *seemed* to help them improve their PE teaching. But beyond this teacher self-report 'evidence', I have no idea if it did *actually* create any meaningful change in teacher dispositions towards PE or any significant change in their practice.

The monograph, however, found its way to Spain via some PETE colleagues who worked at the University of Valencia. Unbeknown to me, the monograph was translated into Spanish and published by the Universitat de Valencia Press. So, in 1993, when I took a sabbatical leave in Spain, PETE colleagues across the country were enthusiastic readers of the book. Moreover, on a number of occasions I witnessed PE teachers in schools using the monograph. All this was both a shock and a compliment. Of course there is no way of telling whether or not the teachers I met were typical, but I do think that the monograph seemed to connect more with those Spanish teachers. And this raises the question "Why did the monograph seem to have more purchase in Spain than in Australia?" In part, I think the answer lies in the fact that teachers and teacher educators in Spain had an affinity with the socio-critical liberal democratic ethic of the book. This ethic embraced a sense of criticality (Rizvi, 2011) that seemed to 'connect with' their broader political dispositions. Remember, it had only been 20 years (one generation) since the death of military dictator General Franco and the memories of his repressive fascist rule were still alive in most families.

Now I don't want to overstate the case, or reduce it to a simplistic answer, but I would like to think that there was something in the Spanish (teacher) culture that encouraged a more receptive disposition to reflective practice. I use the term reflective practice here as a broader concept than the more common reflective teaching or reflection. The distinction is significant. *Reflective practice* can be considered to be a *disposition* which functions like a set of lenses through which to view all educational and cultural practices (both micro and macro). Moreover, these 'ways of seeing' will be taken beyond the classroom and reflective practice will be 'applied to' more than the act of teaching. Reflective practice will also engage issues relating to schooling and education as inherently political and ideological social structures. In this sense it embodies a sense of criticality (Rizvi, 2011) and is at the very foundation of critical pedagogy.

It seems to me that for the ethic of critical pedagogy to 'work' its transformative possibilities, there needs to be a 'receptive' audience. Receptive in the sense that their individual experiences render them open to challenges to the status quo, open to challenges to the taken-for-granted and with an openness to consider matters of social justice, power differentials and abuse, and inequality. I am suggesting that this is a *disposition*. Of course it is possible that a critical HPE teacher who possesses such a disposition might facilitate the conditions in which students develop a more critical disposition. I am thinking here of the work of HPE teacher 'Dan' so thoughtfully portrayed by Fitzpatrick (2013) in her *Critical Pedagogy, Physical Education and Urban Schooling.* The problem is that teachers like Dan are a rare-breed.

However, notwithstanding some exceptions, I think that some (students, teachers) will never connect with such notions, for their personal ideology is one in which the system basically reflects their values, or they see themselves as not interested at all in politics (macro or micro). It seems that unless HPE teachers (or student teachers) have a certain disposition or level of emotional commitment (Giddens, 1991) to engage the values underpinning the socially critical curriculum and critical reflection, then the success of critical pedagogy will be marginal at best.

The receptivity to the idea of reflective practice as a skeptical, constantly questioning worldview, is something I have always tried to develop in my students. It was the ethic that was embedded in *Improving Teaching in Physical Education* all those years ago and later in *Becoming a Physical Education Teacher* (Tinning et al., 2000). The hope was that these texts would sustain those who had a disposition that was open to reflective practice and, perhaps just maybe, help move others towards being more willing to develop such a disposition. Unfortunately, in this case, the gap between hope and happening is difficult to gauge. The advocacy for reflective practice still lacks demonstrable action.

The beneficiaries of critical pedagogy

In what sense is it possible to say that critical pedagogy, and the critical project more broadly, has had success in transforming social practice in HPE in particular and the social world more generally? Have the experiences of kids in school HPE classes improved as a consequence of our work? Has our work led to better, more democratic, equitable and fairer social practices? There are two answers I would offer. First, while HPE discourse (as read in curriculum documents, journals and texts) is more sensitive to the needs of many kids who were previously alienated and/or marginalized by participation in PE classes, the actual lived experience of some (many?) kids in class still requires attention. Second, there is no evidence that advocacy, scholarship or practice for/in HPE critical pedagogy has actually influenced any social transformation. That remains a well-intentioned, but probably unattainable, aspiration. Notwithstanding some individual successes, the impact (I prefer the term influence) of our work in the critical project has been marginal at best. Accordingly, not only should we be modest in our claims for what critical pedagogy *might* achieve, we should also be modest in what we claim it *has* achieved.

When I think of the backlash to the agenda of the liberal left that was manifest in the election of Donald Trump, I am considerably bothered. The backlash to liberal thinking is also is evident in the Christian right's lobby to destroy the Safe Schools project in Australian schools. But I am also bothered when I think of powerful corporate pedagogues who shape the minds of young people for commercial interests that are often in direct conflict or tension with the messages regarding body image and sexuality of the HPE curriculum. Towards such 'trends' that bother me I maintain a 'modest rage'.

I am also bothered by the fact that perhaps the main beneficiaries of our work have been 'we the critical scholars'. Certainly there are those of us who have built, or are building, a career around critical scholarship and no doubt that will continue. The words of Fernandez Balboa (2017: 664) are troubling in this regard:

> many of those who do understand these imbalances and could do something about them tend to be middle-class intellectuals leading quite privileged lives. As such, although there are among them some eager to sacrifice their comfortable position in order to truly engage in radical activism, the vast majority (and, admittedly, I include myself in this group) make do with writing 'critical papers'. While doing so can contribute to the knowledge base of the socio-critical intelligentsia and affords these scholars a position within the system from which to continue to push and raise the profile of counter discourses, they also harvest certain benefits (e.g. institutional prestige, tenure, promotion) within the neoliberal accountability system of 'scholarship'. Could this be something of a contradiction in values?

As I reflect on my career of advocacy and research for/in the critical project I find myself blushing as Fernandez Balboa's words ring in my ear. His general point is a good one. However, I don't think that we all need to engage in radical activism, for sometimes, good work can be done from within the system. Moreover, even the harvesting of "certain benefits (e.g. institutional prestige, tenure, promotion)" can provide a stronger platform from which to advocate for change. But maybe that's just the rationalization of an old, generously rewarded, white, male professor.

Of course my less than sanguine assessment does not mean that there is no place for critical pedagogy advocacy or research. Perhaps paradoxically, I still believe that it is necessary for advocates of critical pedagogy to maintain an optimistic disposition with regard to the *possibility* that this work may, in certain circumstances, create some shifts in thinking, and maybe even in practice, regarding matters relating to the body, physical activity and health. I have managed to keep motivated over my years as a critical scholar, despite the lack of obvious signs of influence, because I remain committed to the ideal of a more just, equitable and peaceful world. There are, however, ever-present dangers that the ideals of equity that drive critical scholarship become mere bureaucratic rhetorical devices that limit the possibilities for change.

Moreover, it is equally important that critical scholars pursue research agendas that endeavour to provide empirical evidence for the impact/influence of their work on thinking and practice. Of course this means continually engaging in epistemological debates regarding the nature of evidence and, equally importantly, taking a rather long-term view of such potential influence. Above all, as critical scholars, we need to maintain a 'modest rage' at injustice and inequity such that our voice is heard and our work is continued.

Notes

1. Thank you to Lindsay Fitzclarence and Bernie Hernon-Tinning for their feedback on early versions of this chapter.
2. I think that this phrase is better than the 'cult of slenderness'.

References

Baudrillard, J. (2005). The finest consumer object: The body. In D. Fraser and M. Greco, eds., *The Body: A Reader*. London: Routledge, 277–283.

Bauman, Z. (2000). *Liquid Modernity*. Cambridge, UK: Polity Press.

Bourdieu, P. (1991). *Language and Symbolic Power*. Oxford: Polity Press.

Burrows, L. (2010). "Kiwi kids are Weet-Bix kids"—body matters in childhood. *Sport, Education & Society* 15(2): 235–253.

Croakley, J. (2017). *Sports in Society: Issues and Controversies*. New York: McGraw-Hill.

Curriculum Corporation. (1992). *National statement on health*. Australian education council curriculum and assessment committee.

Curtner-Smith, M. (2007). The impact of a critically oriented physical education teacher education course on preservice classroom teachers. *Journal of Teaching in Physical Education* 26(1): 35–56.

Davis, C. (1997). Body image, exercise and eating disorders. In K. Fox, ed., *The Physical Self: From Motivation to Well-Being*. Champaign, IL: Human Kinetics, 143–175.

Evans, J. and Davies, B. (1986). Sociology, schooling and physical education. In *Physical Education, Sport and Schooling: Studies in the Sociology of Physical Education*. London: Falmer Press, 35–52.

Evans, J. (1988). Body matters: Towards a socialist physical education. In H. Lauder and P. Brown, eds., *Education in Search of a Future*. Lewes: The Falmer Press: 174–191.

Evans, J. (2003). Physical education and health: A polemic or "let them eat cake". *European Physical Education Review* 9(1): 87–101.

Evans, J. and Davies, B. (2011). New directions, new questions? Social theory, education and embodiment. *Sport, Education & Society* 16(3): 263–279.

Evans, J., et al. (2003). Fat free schooling: The discursive production of ill-health. *International Studies in the Sociology of Education* 12(2): 191–215.

Evans, J., et al. (2004). The emperor's new clothes: Fat, thin, and overweight. The social fabrication of risk and ill-health. *Journal of Teaching in Physical Education* 23: 372–391.

Evans, J., et al., eds. (2004). *Body Knowledge and Control. Studies in the Sociology of Education and Physical Culture*. London: Routledge.

Fernandez-Balboa, J.-M. (2017). A contrasting analysis of the neo-liberal and sociocritical structural strategies in health and physical education: reflections on the emancipatory agenda within and beyond the limits of HPE. *Sport, Education & Society* 22(5): 658–668.

Fitzclarence, L. (1990). The body as commodity. In D. Rowe and G. Lawrence eds., *Sport and leisure: Trends in Australian popular culture*. Sydney: Harcourt Brace Jovanovich, 96–108.

Fitzpatrick, K. (2013). *Critical Pedagogy, Physical Education and Urban Schooling*. New York: Peter Lang.

Gay, R. (2017). *Hunger: A Memoir of (My) Body*. London: Corsair.

Gard, M. (2005). HPE and the "obesity epidemic". In R. Tinning et al., eds., *Teaching Health & Physical Education in Australian Schools*. Frenchs Forest, NSW: Pearson, 78–88.

Gard, M. (2008). Producing little decision-makers and goal-setters in the age of the obesity crisis. *Quest* 60(4): 488–502.

Gard, M. and Wright, J. (2001). Managing uncertainty: Obesity discourses and physical education in a risk society. *Studies in Philosophy and Education* 20(6): 535–549.

Gard, M. and Wright, J. (2005). *The Obesity Epidemic: Science, Morality and Ideology*. London: Routledge.

Giddens, A. (1991). *Modernity and Self-Identity. Self and Society in the Late Modern Age*. Cambridge, UK: Polity Press.

Glover, S. and Macdonald, D. (1997). Working with the Health and Physical Education Statement and Profile in physical education teacher education: Case studies and implications. *ACHPER Healthy Lifestyles Journal* 44(3): 21–26.

Hellison, D. and Templin, T. (1991). *A Reflective Approach to Teaching Physical Education*. Champaign, IL: Human Kinetics.

Hickey, C. (2001). I feel enlightened now, but …: The limits to the pedagogic translation of critical social discourses in physical education. *Journal of Teaching in Physical Education* 20(3): 227–246.

Kenway, J. and Bullen, E. (2001). *Consuming children: Education-entertainment-advertising*. Buckingham: Open University Press.

Kenway, J., et al. (1995). New education in new times. *Journal of Education Policy* 9(4): 317–333.

Kincheloe, J. (1993). *Toward a critical politics of teacher thinking: Mapping the Postmodern*. Westport, CT: Bergin & Garvey.

Kirk, D. (1991). Taggart's reaction to Tinning on health based physical education: A rejoinder. *Unicorn: Journal of the Australian College of Education* 17(2): 104–106.

Kirk, D. (1993). *The body, schooling and culture*. Geelong: Deakin University Press.

Kirk, D. (2006). The "obesity crisis" and physical education. *Sport Education and Society* 11(2): 121–135.

Lather, P. (1998). Critical pedagogy and its complicities: A praxis of stuck places. *Educational Theory* 48(4): 487–497.

Law, B. (2017). Moral panic 101: Equality, acceptance and the Safe Schools scandal. *Quarterly Essay* 67: 1–87.

Larsson, H., Redelius, K. and Fagrell, B. (2010). Moving (in) the heterosexual matrix. On heteronormativity in secondary school physical education. *Physical Education & Sport Pedagogy* 14(1): 1–17.

Lupton, D. (1996). *Food, the Body and the Self*. London: Sage.

Macdonald, D. and Brooker, R. (1999). Articulating a critical pedagogy in physical education teacher education. *Journal of Sport Pedagogy* 5(1): 51–63.

Macdonald, D. and Kirk, D. (1999). Pedagogy, the body and Christian identity. *Sport, Education and Society* 4(2): 131–142.

Oliver, K. and Lalik, R. (2004). "The beauty walk": Interrogating whiteness as the norm for beauty within one school's hidden curriculum. In J. Evans et al., eds., *Body Knowledge and Control: Studies in the Sociology of Physical Education and Health*. London: Routledge, 115–130.

Ovens, A. (2004). The (Im)Possibility of Critical Reflection: The Lived Experience of Reflective Practice in Teacher Education. PhD dissertation, The University of Queensland, Brisbane.

Petersen, A. and Lupton, D. (1996). *The New Public Health: Health and Self in the Age of Risk*. Sydney: Allen & Unwin.

Philpot, R. (2015). Critical pedagogies in PETE: An Antipodean perspective. *Journal of Teaching in Physical Education* 34(2): 316–332.

Pringle, R. and Pringle, D. (2012). Competing obesity discourses and critical challenges for health and physical educators. *Qualitative Research in Sport, Exercise and Health* 17(2): 143–161.

Rail, G. (2012). The birth of the obesity clinic: Confessions of the flesh, biopedagogies and physical culture. *Sociology of Sport Journal* 29, 227–253.

Rich, E. (2010). Body pedagogies, education and health. *Sport Education and Society* 15(2): 147–150.

Rich, E., et al. (2004). "Hungry to be noticed": Young women, anorexia and schooling. In J. Evans et al., eds., *Body Knowledge and Control: Studies in the Sociology of Physical Education and Health*. London: Routledge, 173–191.

Rizvi, F. (2011). Contesting criticality in a scholarship diaspora. In R. Tinning and K. Sirna, eds., *Education, Social Justice and the Legacy of Deakin University*. Rotterdam and Boston: Sense Publishers, 145–157.

Robinson, D. and Randall, L., eds. (2016). *Social Justice in Physical Education: Critical Reflections and Pedagogies for Change*. Toronto: Canadian Scholars' Press, 1–15.

Rose, N. (2000). Community, citizenship, and the third way. *The American Behavioural Scientist* 43(9): 1395–1411.

Sallis, J. and McKenzie, T. (1991). Physical education's role in public health. *Research Quarterly for Exercise and Sport* 62(2): 124–137.

Sallis, J., et al. (1997). The effect of a 2 year physical education program (SPARK) on physical activity and fitness in elementary school students. *American Journal of Public Health* 87: 1328–1334.

Schon, D. (1983). *The Reflective Practitioner. How Professionals Think in Action*. New York: Basic Books.

Shapiro, S. (2002). The life-world, body movements and new forms of emancipatory politics. In S. Shapiro and S. Shapiro, eds., *Body Movements: Pedagogy, Politics and Social Change*. Cresskill, NJ: Hampton Press, 1–25.

Smyth, J. (1992). Teachers' work and the politics of reflection. *American Educational Research Journal* 29(2): 267–300.

Stenhouse, L. (1975). *An Introduction to Curriculum Development & Research*. London: Heinemann.

Sykes, H. and McPhail, D. (2007). Unbearable lessons: Contesting fat phobia in physical education. Special Issue on Social Construction of Fat, *Sociology of Sport Journal* 25, 66–96.

Szto, C. and Gray, S. (2015). Forgive me father for I have thinned: Surveilling the bio-citizen through Twitter. *Qualitative Research in Sport, Exercise and Health* 7(3): 321–337.

Tinning, R (2017). Transformative pedagogies and physical education: Exploring the possibilities for personal change and social change. In C. Ennis, ed., *Handbook of Physical Education Pedagogy*. Routledge: London, 281–295.

Tinning, R. (1987a). *Improving Teaching in Physical Education*. Geelong: Deakin University Press.

Tinning, R. (1987b). Beyond the development of a utilitarian teaching perspective: An Australian case study of action research in teacher preparation, in G. Barrette et al., eds., *Myths, Models and Methods in Sport Pedagogy*. Champaign, IL: Human Kinetics.

Tinning, R. (1992). Reading action research: Notes on knowledge and human interest. *Quest*, 44(1): 1–15.

Tinning, R. (2002). Towards a "modest" pedagogy: Reflections on the problematics of critical pedagogy. *Quest*, 54(3): 224–241.

Tinning, R. (2003). Conclusion: Ruminations on body knowledge and control and the spaces for hope and happening. In J. Evans et al., eds., *Body Knowledge and Control: Studies in the Sociology of Physical Education and Health*. London: Routledge, 218–239.

Tinning, R. (2014). Catching obesity: A memetic analysis of the obesity crisis and the field of Kinesiology. *Quest* 66: 27–38.

Tinning, R. and Glasby, T. (2002). Pedagogical work and the "cult of the body": Considering the role of HPE in the context of the "new public health". *Sport, Education & Society* 7(2): 109–119.

Tinning, R., et al. (2001). *Becoming a Physical Education Teacher: Contemporary and Enduring Issues*. Melbourne: Prentice Hall.

Tinning, R., Philpot, R. and Cameron, E. (2016). Critical pedagogy, physical education, and obesity discourse: More advocacy than pedagogy. In D. Robinson and L. Randall, eds., *Social Justice in Physical Education*. Toronto: Canadian Scholars Press, 297–322.

Tsangaridou, N. and O'Sullivan. M. (1997). The role of reflection in shaping physical education teachers' educational values and practices. *Journal of Teaching in Physical Education* 17: 2–25.

Ukpokodu, O. (2009). "Pedagogies that foster transformative learning in a multicultural education course: A Reflection." *Journal of Praxis in Multicultural Education* 4(1): DOI: 10.9741/2161-2978.1003.

Ward, P., et al. (2018). Embodied display: A critical examination of the biopedagogical experience of wearing health. *Fat Studies* 7: 93–104.

Wright, J., and Harwood, V., eds. (2009). *Biopolitics and the "Obesity Epidemic": Governing Bodies*. New York: Routledge.

Chapter 8

A new critical pedagogy for physical education in 'turbulent times': What are the possibilities?

David Kirk

Introduction

Few of us who read the daily news are likely to disagree with journalist Rafael Behr (*The Guardian*, April 2017) that we live in 'turbulent times'. Financial crises and economic austerity, the growing gap between the ultra-rich and the rest, climate change, the renewed threat of nuclear war, populist right wing politics, terrorism, an epidemic of sexual assault, the mass displacement of whole populations through war: any one of these and other crises contribute to Behr's turbulent times. Nor can we deny Lawson's (2018) reasoning that futures are complicated and uncertain. Within this context, educational workers, including school teachers, teacher educators, and educational researchers, particularly those committed to education for social justice and equity, are having to rethink many of our most basic assumptions about the nature of society and of human wellbeing and happiness. We can no longer continue to use stock notions of social class, for example, in the relatively straightforward way that Paul Willis could in his 1977 classic *Learning to Labour: How Working Class Kids Get Working Class Jobs*. The changing nature of labour-market conditions is just one indicator of the turbulence wrought by neo-liberal free-market ideology over a 60 years period. Without doubt, for many of the world's population, social and economic turbulence is contributing significantly to the uncertainty and precarity of everyday life (Standing, 2016).

What might be the purpose and, indeed, relevance, of school physical education in turbulent times? Since at least the mid-1980s, physical educators have been discussing and practising versions of critical pedagogy as a means of tackling myriad forms of social injustice and inequity. What are the possibilities for critical pedagogy now, when generations of young people are facing the prospect of, or already living in, precarity? The challenge for critical pedagogy is to address the changes that have taken place in society in the past 50 years, since the earliest appearance of this concept inspired by the work of activist scholars such as Paolo Freire among others. Recent social analyses have questioned standard conceptions of political divisions around Left and Right, traditional strategies of resistance to oppression, and critical pedagogy aspirations such as empowerment and emancipation. A particular focus of this work has been social injustice

(Dorling, 2010), inequality (Atkinson, 2015), 'hard times' and economic crises (Clark, 2014), the reshaping of concepts of social class (Savage et al., 2015) and the rise of the 'precariat' (Standing, 2016).

This chapter takes up the challenge of a new critical pedagogy for turbulent times within a broader context of what Lawson (2018) describes as the 'redesign' of school physical education. The focus is how such work might be undertaken through physical education for the benefit of all young people (Standal, 2015). Without doubt, physical education teachers around the world increasingly will be teaching young people whose lives are shaped by precarity. It is important, then, that they have some understanding of the nature of the turbulence caused by membership of this emerging social class. Physical education itself has been repositioned recently in the school curriculum in many countries, most often within larger configurations of school knowledge such as 'health and wellbeing'. This repositioning and the requirement for physical educators to work with new subject matter beyond sports and games has created risk but also opened up new possibilities for critical pedagogy in turbulent and precarious times.

Turbulent and precarious times

A lens through which to focus on social turbulence is the concept of precarity. While this notion is relatively new to scholars in the English-speaking world, it has been part of the lexicon of social researchers in France for at least two decades. In Bourdieu's (1997) early formulation of precarity, he comments:

> It is clearly apparent that precarity is everywhere today. In the private sector, but also in the public sector, which has multiplied temporary and interim positions, in industrial enterprises, but also in the institutions of production and cultural diffusion, education, journalism, media, etc., where it produces effects which are always more or less identical. These effects become particularly visible in the extreme case of the unemployed: the deconstruction of existence, deprived among other things of its temporal structures, and the degradation of the whole relation to the world, time, space, which ensues. Precarity deeply affects those who suffer it; by making the future uncertain, it forbids any rational anticipation and, in particular, that minimum of belief and hope in the future that must be had to revolt, especially collectively, against the present, even the most intolerable. (Bourdieu, 1997, my translation)

Precarity is rooted in the temporary and indeterminate nature of work and is thus influenced by the economic conditions prevalent in society. Bourdieu highlights the psychological and health-related effects of precarious employment. It is these psychological effects, particularly in relation to mental health, that have been emphasised by scholars of precarity. For example, Swedish political scientists Näsström and Kalm (2015) argue that the effects of precarity are felt far beyond the workplace, noting that "precarious work not only affects the material side of life; it also affects the soul ... and character ... of workers, including one's sense of happiness, meaning and ability to develop long-term relationships" (p. 563).

Building on this work, Standing (2016) has argued that a 'new dangerous class' has begun to emerge, becoming more visible following the global economic crisis of 2008, which he calls the precariat. The precariat is highly heterogeneous, consisting not only of those who might traditionally be associated with an underclass such as unskilled workers, undocumented migrant labourers and so on. It contains young and old, men and women, skilled and unskilled, in many countries, across a range of occupations including academe and the cultural industries. He explains:

> The precariat could be described as a neologism that combines an adjective 'precarious' and a related noun 'proletariat' ... We may claim that the precariat is a *class-in-the-making*, if not yet a *class-for-itself*, in the Marxian sense of that term. (Standing, 2016, p. 8)

He, like Bourdieu and Näsström and Kalm, highlights the effects of insecure employment, such as ongoing temporary contracts and so-called zero hours contracts, as well as chronic episodes of unemployment, on self-identity and wellbeing. He writes:

> Another way of looking at the precariat is in terms of the process, the way in which people are 'precariatised'. ... To be precariatised is to be subject to pressures and experiences that lead to a precariat existence, of living in the present, without a secure identity or sense of development achieved though work and lifestyle. (Standing, 2016, p. 19)

In this respect, it is Bourdieu's final point that is of particular interest, the possibility of what Standing calls the precariat as a new social class, a class-*in*-itself, being capable of taking collective action against the ill-effects of precarity, as a class-*for*-itself. The nature of precarity makes this possibility remote, however, and less likely still when we consider the effects of digital technology:

> The precariat shows itself as not yet a class-for-itself partly because those in it are unable to control the technological forces they face. ... The precariat is defined by short-termism, which could evolve into a mass incapacity to think long term. The internet, the browsing habit, text messaging, Facebook, Twitter and other social media are all operating to rewire the brain. (Standing, 2016, p. 21)

Recent research by Goodyear, Armour and Wood (2018) amplifies Standing's concerns about the potential detrimental effects of social media use on the mental health and wellbeing of young people. This work also echoes Postman's (1985) critique of the rise of television to replace print as a primary medium of communication in 1980s America. In his book *Amusing Ourselves to Death*, Postman cites the 'Huxleyan Warning', referring to Aldous Huxley's dystopian novel *Brave New Word* (1932). He writes:

> What Huxley teaches is that in the age of advanced technology, spiritual devastation is more likely to come from an enemy with a smiling face than from one whose countenance exudes suspicion and hate. In the Huxleyan prophecy, Big Brother does not watch us, by his choice. We watch him, by ours ... When a population becomes distracted by trivia, when cultural life is re-defined as a perpetual round of entertainments, when serious public conversation becomes a form of baby-talk, when, in short, a people become an audience and their public business a vaudeville act, then a nation finds itself at risk; culture-death is a clear possibility. (Postman, 1985: 156)

A society distracted and sedated by social media trivia may be unlikely to have the resources to take political action on its own behalf. More contemporaneously, Näsström and Kalm (2015) suggest that precarity and its ill-effects are at odds with democratic forms of government, which rest on the principle of shared responsibility, and the conditions it creates corrupt democracy. This is in part why Standing describes the precariat as 'the dangerous new class'.

According to Wilkinson and Pickett (2009), there is a clear relationship between the level of inequality in a society, a key feature of precarity, and a range of social problems, including health and wellbeing. They show that a wide range of social problems such as obesity, mental illness, incarceration and teen pregnancy are higher in societies that are more unequal. They argue that the effects of income inequality do not just affect the poor. The nature of these problems creates a burden for society as a whole, where only a very few if any remain unaffected.

This conclusion highlights the pervasive and inequitable influence of social turbulence and precarity. Not everyone needs to experience precarity directly to feel its effects. Young school-age people are particularly vulnerable since precarity shapes not only their health and wellbeing but also their life chances.

Precarity, young people and health and wellbeing

In 2018 and an age of rising precarity, young people in their diversity face some similar hazards as they navigate their way to adulthood, including in addition to the usual aches and pains of growing up, obesity, depression, self-harming, body image disturbance, social media abuse, homophobic violence and cyberbullying. In this context, we have seen in the past decade accelerating attention among physical education researchers to enduring issues such as health and wellbeing (McCuaig and Quennerstedt, 2016), and related matters such as motivation (van den Berghe, 2014), resilience and coping (Lang et al., 2017), body image

(Kerner et al., 2017), and perceived physical competence (Bardid et al., 2016). Each of these health-related issues has significant affective dimensions in terms of attitudes, values and emotions.

There is a growing body of recent research highlighting the many intertwined issues around young people and health and wellbeing. Some of this research has analysed data from the 2013/2014 Health Behaviour in School-aged Children (HBSC) data base. HBSC is a cross-national study aimed at gaining insight into young people's wellbeing, health behaviours and their social contexts. This research collaboration with the WHO Regional Office for Europe is conducted every four years in 45 countries and regions across Europe and North America.

In a recent study, Frasquilho et al. (2017) drew on Portuguese data of the wellbeing of adolescents living with unemployed parents. They reported detrimental effects on the wellbeing of both girls and boys, though girls from lower socio-economic families reported more negative emotional wellbeing related to parental unemployment. Also using HBSC data from 40 countries, Elgar et al. (2016 found a strong association between early-life income inequality and reduced health and wellbeing in adolescence, particularly among girls. Moore et al.'s (2017) study of school composition, school culture and socioeconomic inequalities in young people's health drew on HBSC data from Wales to expose an important nuance of the differential health experiences for wealthier and poorer children. Attending schools that were generally affluent, poorer children fared worse in terms of health and wellbeing than they did when they attended schools where the majority of children were also poor. The authors conclude that affluent schools are more inequitable than poorer schools across a range of health behaviours, and that attending a more affluent school lowered young people from poorer families' subjective wellbeing.

This brief overview of recent research is intended to provide a glimpse of the nature of the challenge facing educational workers, where the health and wellbeing of young people is interwoven with poverty, deprivation and precarity in turbulent times. It would appear that, in this context, a critical pedagogy for physical education concerned with social justice and equity would have an important contribution to make to alerting teachers and other educational workers to the detrimental effects of precarity. In increasingly turbulent and uncertain times, critical pedagogy has found itself in a precarious situation within the academy.

The flight from critical pedagogy in physical education?

In the late 1980s and early 1990s there was the beginnings of a backlash against critical pedagogy. In a widely cited paper, Ellsworth (1989) asked 'why doesn't this feel empowering?' and claimed critical pedagogy had taken a "highly abstract and utopian line which does not necessarily sustain the daily workings of the education its supporters advocate' (p. 297). In *The Struggle for Pedagogies*, Gore (1993) argued that critical pedagogy was both gender and race blind, and its advocates failed to locate themselves reflexively within their analyses. In physical education, the backlash began with a paper by O'Sullivan, Siedentop and Locke (1992) who argued that critical pedagogy inappropriately took the moral high ground, that it lacked evidence for its claims, was overzealous, and that it was long on criticism but short of practical solutions to physical education's many shortcomings.

The backlash has continued, with Tinning's (2002) call for a 'modest pedagogy' and more recently Enright et al.'s (2014) advocacy for Appreciative Inquiry (AI). Tinning repeats many of the claims of the earlier critics, and recants his own enthusiasm for critical pedagogy in the 1980s and 1990s. He appears convinced by Biesta's (1998) argument that critical pedagogy has become a grand narrative and its very possibility in practice is doubtful. It has, he claims, been too susceptible to appropriation and mis-use by neo-liberals who use the language of critical pedagogy (e.g. empowerment, emancipation) as a cover for exploitation. Enright et al. take a different tack, claiming that critical pedagogy has been obsessed with what is 'broken' in physical education, in the process failing to see the good things that go on in physical education's name. Critical pedagogy is guilty in their view of 'deficit theories', deficit scholarship', 'grievance narratives' and 'deficit thinking'.

The earlier critiques of critical pedagogy made some telling points about a movement that was in its infancy. There was excitement and energy about critical pedagogy, and some polemic and intentional provocation too (e.g. McKay, Gore and Kirk, 1990). Some physical education scholars in the 1980s and 1990s without doubt felt threatened by what they saw as a confrontational approach. Asking hard questions about received wisdom was interpreted as disloyal and as sowing disunity. This said, I do not recognise the accounts of critical pedagogy provided by either Tinning, who has gone on to repeat many of his 2002 argument in his book *Pedagogy and Human Movement* (2010), or Enright et al. (2014). Neither provide any substantive critique nor examples of neo-liberal appropriation of critical pedagogy and of deficit scholarship. In the next few paragraphs I provide some examples that have shaped my own view of critical pedagogy that do not fit with many of the criticisms just cited.

One of the earliest advocacies for critical pedagogy in the physical education literature was my paper 'A critical pedagogy for teacher education: toward an inquiry-oriented approach' which appeared in the *Journal of Teaching in Physical Education* in 1986. I noted that much of the literature on teacher education focused on teaching as a technical process, where the overriding concern was for 'effectiveness'. This approach, I claimed, underplayed or ignored the political and moral aspects of education. I was writing against a backdrop of an emerging action research movement (e.g. Carr and Kemmis, 1983) and socially critical curriculum theorizing (Apple, 1979). This work formed a basis for a critical pedagogy that understands the school curriculum to be socially constructed and teachers to be potential agents for change.

Some other contributors to the physical education literature around this time were, like critical pedagogues, seeking to question received opinion and taken-for-granted assumptions about physical education as a school subject and physical education teaching, even though they were not necessarily using this specific term (e.g. Lawson, 1984). Macdonald and Brooker (1995), Fernández-Balboa (1997) and others further developed the theorizing around critical pedagogy and social critique more broadly.

By the late 1980s, critical pedagogy was a central pillar of my practice as a teacher educator as much as it was a topic for academic debate and theorizing. My chapter in 2000 on a 'Task-Based Approach to Critical Pedagogy' is an example of this work, where I was concerned to assist students to see beyond surface appearances and to resist simplistic and quick-fix solutions to complex problems (Kirk, 2000). The pathfinding work of Don Hellison (1978) and Kim Oliver (e.g. Oliver and Lalik, 2004) I regard as forms of critical pedagogical praxis *par excellence*, involving theoretically informed practice, working with alienated youth and African-American girls respectively. Both programs of work are concerned with the oppression of young people in different contexts, and both display high levels of critical self-awareness and reflexivity.

More recently, aspects of critical pedagogy have found their way into the school curriculum, most notably in Australia (McCuaig et al., 2016) and New Zealand (Culpan and Bruce, 2007), and continue to challenge teacher educators (e.g. Philpot, 2015) and teachers (e.g. Fitzpatrick, 2013). Social critique has also been underway in relation to the influence of neoliberalism in physical education (e.g. Evans and Davies, 2014) and outsourcing of services (Williams and Macdonald, 2015).

It is difficult to see how any of this valuable and necessary work could be described as 'deficit scholarship'. Far from requiring a 'modest pedagogy', instead we require in my view a re-energised and sharper edged critical pedagogy fit for purpose in turbulent times. The terrain has shifted since the emergence of critical physical education scholarship in the 1980s, and critical pedagogy must also shift to meet new challenges.

Possibilities for a new critical pedagogy for turbulent times

There are at least three priorities for re-energising and taking forward a new critical pedagogy for physical education that I will sketch briefly here, a focus on 'pedagogies of affect', specialised professional learning for teachers, and the development of inclusive networked learning communities. As Antonovsky (1996) argued within his salutogenic theory of health promotion, sense of coherence (SOC) in the lives of individuals and communities is a crucial explanatory factor in how people stay healthy. It is precisely the diminishment or absence of meaningfulness, comprehensibility and manageability, the constitutive features of SOC, that are as Standing (2016) and others argue the psychological and health-related effects of precarity. The three points of focus for the renewal of a critical pedagogy for turbulent times are concerned to address this issue of SOC directly and explicitly.

A first priority in formulating a new critical pedagogy for physical education is to sharpen its focus on pedagogy, that is, the interdependent and interacting components of teaching, learning, curriculum and assessment. The inexorable shift to a health-based rationale for physical education in precarious times requires us to respond to the increasing recognition of mental health issues. The challenge here is to promote and support the health and wellbeing of young people by treating learning aspirations in the affective domain as of central pedagogical concern rather than desirable by-products. We can no longer suppose that by merely engaging in sports and games young people will automatically gain benefits to their health and wellbeing.

When we begin to focus on such issues, in particular on attitudes, perspectives and values, we can put into context the increasingly pervasive notion that 'exercise-is-medicine' (Jette and Vertinsky, 2011) and a high level of moderate to vigorous physical activity (MVPA) is a gold standard for physical education teaching (e.g. McKenzie and Lounsbury, 2009). In a recent pilot project based in Glasgow that sought to develop an activist pedagogical model for working with adolescent girls, Kim Oliver and I (Oliver and Kirk, 2015) adopted as the main idea for the model Siedentop's (1996) notion, that teachers and researchers should support young people to learn to value the physically active life. While participation in MVPA will be part of a process of young people coming to value the physically active life, the pedagogical requirements of facilitating the latter process are light years away from achieving the former. Getting young people to engage in 'sufficient' levels of MVPA in school physical education may be challenging enough, as McKenzie and Lounsbury attest, but the teacher strategies and subject matter for doing this are well known to physical educators. We are in new territory entirely when we come to consider the pedagogical implications for assisting young people to value physical activity to the extent that they will be disposed to engage in physical activity even when there are attractive alternatives.

The Glasgow pilot project, built on 20 years of Kim Oliver's pathfinding work, shows in stark relief the unsuitability of traditional pedagogy for working in the affective domain. A critical element of the activist pedagogical model developed in this project was student-centredness. Listening to girls' voices was crucial, as was responding to them constructively. We sought, in Cook-Sather's (2002) terms, to 'authorise student voice', which involved a shift in the power dynamic between teachers and students towards the students. Our findings show positive and enthusiastic responses from girls as this approach worked explicitly with the students to create learning environments in which they felt safe and comfortable to engage in physical education (Kirk et al., 2018). In many respects, the focus of this work is the girls *being well* (Cassidy, 2018), in the moment of their engagement in physical education (Standal, 2015). In another project, Oliver and I have worked with colleagues to develop a pedagogical model for working with socially vulnerable youth in Brazil (Luguetti et al., 2017).

A second priority is forms of professional learning that equip teachers with the specialised skills to work with young people whose lives are shaped by precarity. Teachers are encountering disenchantment, alienation and disaffection among young people increasingly as precarity becomes more and more pervasive.

Of specific importance for physical educators is young people's increasing uses of social media as sources of health-related information, and its detrimental effects (Goodyear, Armour and Wood 2018). Moreover, teachers' own wellbeing is at risk in such contexts (Bartholomew et al., 2014). Teacher agency then becomes of key importance, where teachers have support for their professional learning and 'spaces for manoeuvre' to work with their pupils to co-create programs that meet young people's needs locally (Kirk et al., 2018; Priestly, Biesta and Robinson, 2015).

Antonovsky argued (1996) that SOC applies to collectives as well as individuals. In the face of precarity and turbulent times, collective local action in response to global challenges may be required. Thus, a third priority is the inclusion of a range of stakeholders in the critical pedagogy project with clear delineation of what each brings to the mix. While teachers may have a degree of agency to lead innovative pedagogical projects in their schools, they cannot do this work alone. Day and Townsend (2009) have advocated for the development of networked learning communities that include teachers and pupils, parents, and other educational workers. Stenhouse's (1975) vision of teacher-as-researcher was of teachers working within what he called a 'scientific community'. Collaboration, then, is of the utmost importance in taking forward this vision. Each member of this community brings complementary skills and expertise to the critical testing of new ideas. For example, Kirk and Macdonald (2001) argued that the specific insights teachers bring to this process are as experts in the local context of implementation. Teachers know their pupils, classrooms, and school-communities in ways that policy-makers and researchers cannot. Similarly, young people can bring their own views, needs and insights to test new ideas (Oliver and Kirk, 2015). Our focus here needs to be pragmatically on what works and what does not, and what is possible.

Conclusion

My purpose in this chapter has been to explore the possibilities for a new critical pedagogy for physical education that is fit for purpose in turbulent times. I argued after Standing (2016) that the rapid emergence of precarity and a 'new dangerous social class', the precariat, is of major importance to physical educators, for several reasons. More and more of their pupils are going to be living in precarious situations as these children's parents are among the working poor, experiencing multiple-deprivation as inequity grows. I sought to show that there is a strong link between precarity and issues of mental health and wellbeing. It may be no coincidence, then, that the rationale for physical education's existence in the core curriculum of schools is shifting increasingly from a sport and leisure focus to a health focus. The evidence has yet to be generated that physical education can make a valuable contribution to young people's health and wellbeing (see e.g. Hastie, 2017) but, nevertheless, governments have shown faith in physical education through the investment of considerable sums of public money in preparing and employing teachers in many public schools around the world.

I noted the need for a new critical pedagogy, for a number of reasons. One has been an ongoing backlash to critical pedagogy. While recent commentaries have, I think, failed to engage in a persuasive critique of actual critical pedagogical practice, nevertheless the changed and changing conditions that exist today compared to the 1980s when the notion of critical pedagogy first appeared in the physical education literature warrants a reconsideration of possibilities. Drawing on Antonovsky's (1996) notion of SOC as a key constituent of why people stay healthy and the detrimental effects of precarity on health and wellbeing, I suggested as a priority the need to focus in particular on pedagogies of affect and to engage in forms of activist pedagogy. I also proposed teacher professional learning to develop specialised skills for working with young people living in precarity, and for the development of inclusive networked learning communities to support teacher learning and agency.

Whether we continue to need the terminology of 'critical pedagogy' is for me an open question as we seek to develop fit for purpose forms of physical education in turbulent and precarious times. It may be sufficient to develop pedagogies that take social justice and inequity and the health and wellbeing of young people as their central concern without labels that appear to provoke concern and criticism from some physical education scholars. To address the detrimental effects of social turbulence and precarity we have little choice, however, but to face the brutal facts of life and to ask hard questions about received wisdom. If we can do this then there may be some continuing educational relevance for school physical education in turbulent times.

References

Antonovsky, A. (1996) The salutogenic model as a theory to guide health promotion. *Health Promotion International*, 11(1), 11–18.

Apple, M.W. (1979) *Ideology and curriculum*. London: RKP.

Atkinson, A.B. (2015) *Inequality: What can be done?* Cambridge, MA: Harvard University Press.

Bardid, F., de Meester, A., Tallir, I., Cardon, G., Lenoir, M. and Herens, L. (2016) Configurations of actual and perceived motor competence among children: Associations with motivation for sports and global self-worth, *Human Movement Science*, 50, 1–9.

Bartholomew, K. and Ntoumanis, N., Cuevas, R. and Lonsdale, C. (2014) Job pressure and ill-health in physical education teachers: The mediating role of psychological need thwarting. *Teaching and Teacher Education*, 37, 101–107.

Biesta, G. (1998) Say you want a revolution … Suggestions for the impossible future of critical pedagogy. *Educational Theory*, 49(4), 499–510.

Bourdieu, P. (1997) *La précarité est aujourd'hui partout. Intervention lors des Rencontres européennes contre la précarité*. Grenoble, 12–13 December. http://natlex.ilo.ch/wcmsp5/groups/public/—ed_dialogue/—actrav/documents/meetingdocument/wcms_161352.pdf.

Carr, W. and Kemmis, S. (1983) *Becoming critical: Knowing through action research*. Geelong: Deakin University Press.

Cassidy, C. (2018) Wellbeing, being well or well becoming: Who or what is it for and how might we get there? pp. 13–28 in M. Thorburn (ed.), *Wellbeing and Contemporary Schooling*. London: Routledge.

Clark, T. (2014) *Hard Times: The divisive toll of the economic slump*. New Haven: Yale University Press.

Cook-Sather, A. (2002) Authorizing students' perspectives: Towards trust, dialogue, and change in education. *Educational Researcher*, 3(4), 3–14.

Culpan, I., and Bruce, J. (2007). New Zealand physical education and critical pedagogy: Refocusing the curriculum. *International Journal of Sport and Health Science*, 5, 1–11.

Day, C. and Townsend, C. (2009) Practitioner action research: building and sustaining success through networked learning communities. pp. 178–189 in Susan E. Noffke and Bridget Somekh (eds.), *Handbook of Educational Action Research*, London: Sage.

Dorling, D. (2010) *Injustice: Why social inequality persists*. Bristol: The Policy Press.

Elgar, F. J., Gariépy, G., Torsheim, T., and Currie, C. (2016). Early-life income inequality and adolescent health and well-being. *Social Science & Medicine*. DOI: 10.1016/j.socscimed.2016.10.014.

Ellsworth, E. (1989) 'Why doesn't this feel empowering?': Working through the repressive myths of critical pedagogy. *Harvard Educational Review*, 59(3), 297–324.

Enright, E., Hill, J., Sandford, R. and Gard, M. (2014) Looking beyond what's broken: Towards an appreciative research agenda for physical education and sport pedagogy, *Sport, Education and Society*, 19(7), 912–926.

Evans, J. and Davies, B. (2014) Physical education PLC: neoliberalism, curriculum and governance. New directions for PESP research. *Sport, Education and Society*, 19(7), 869–884.

Fernández-Balboa, J. M., ed. (1997) *Critical postmodernism in human movement, physical education and sport*. Albany: State University of New York Press.

Fitzpatrick, K. (2013) *Critical pedagogy, physical education and urban schooling*. New York: Peter Lang.

Frasquilho, D., Matos, M. D., Marques, A., Gaspar, T., and Caldas-De-Almeida, J. (2017). Factors affecting the well-being of adolescents living with unemployed parents in times of economic recession: Findings from the Portuguese HBSC study. *Public Health*, 143, 17–24.

Goodyear, V. A., Armour, K. M. and Wood, H. (2018) Young people and their engagement with health-related social media: New perspectives. *Sport, Education and Society*, https://doi.org/10.1080/13573322.2017.1423464.

Gore, J. M. (1993) *The struggle for pedagogies: Critical and feminist discourses as regimes of truth*. New Yor: Routledge.

Hastie, P. A. (2017) Revisiting the National Physical Education content standards: What do we really know about our achievement of the physically educated/literate person? *Journal of Teaching in Physical Education*, 36, 3–19.

Hellison, D. (1978) *Beyond bats and balls: Alienated (and other) youth in the gym*. Washington, DC: AAPHERD.

Jette, S. and Vertinsky, P. (2011) 'Exercise is medicine': Understanding the exercise beliefs and practices of older Chinese women immigrants in British Columbia, Canada. *Journal of Aging Studies*, 25(3), 272–284.

Kerner, C., Haerens, L., and Kirk, D. (2017). Understanding body image in physical education: Current knowledge and future directions. *European Physical Education Review*. Electronic publication ahead of print. DOI: 10.1177/1356336X17692508.

Kirk, D. (1986) A critical pedagogy for teacher education: Towards an inquiry-oriented approach. *Journal of Teaching in Physical Education*, 5(4), 230–246.

Kirk, D. (2000) A task-based approach to critical pedagogy in sport and physical education. pp. 201–219 in Jones, R. and Armour, K.M. (eds.), *Sociology of sport: Theory and practice*. Harlow: Pearson.

Kirk, D., Lamb, CA, Oliver, KL with Ewing-Day, R., Fleming, C., Loch, A. & Smedley, V. (2018) Balancing prescription with teacher and pupil agency: Spaces for manoeuvre within a pedagogical model for working with adolescent girls. *The Curriculum Journal*, 29(2), 219–237.

Kirk, D. and Macdonald, D. (2001) Teacher voice and ownership of curriculum change. *Journal of Curriculum Studies*, 33(5), 551–567.

Lang, C., Feldmeth, A. K., Brand, S., Holsboer-Trachsler, E., Pushe, U. and Gerber, M. (2017) Effects of a physical education-based coping training on adolescents' coping skills, stress perceptions and quality of sleep. *Physical Education and Sport Pedagogy*, 22(3), 213–230.

Lawson, H. A. (1984) Problem-setting for physical education and sport. *Quest*, 36: 48–60.

Lawson, H. A., ed. (2018) *Redesigning physical education: An equity agenda in which every child matters*. London: Routledge.

Luguetti, C., Oliver, K. L., Kirk, D. and Dantas, L. (2017). Exploring an activist approach to working with boys from socially vulnerable backgrounds in a sport context. *Sport, Education and Society*, 17(4), 493–510.

Macdonald, D. and Brooker, R. (1995) Professional education: Tensions in subject design and implementation. *Educational Research and Perspectives*, 22(2), 99–109.

McCuaig, L., Enright, E., Rossi, A., Macdonald, D. and Hansen, S. (2016) An eroding social justice agenda: The case of physical education and health Edu-business in schools. *Research Quarterly for Exercise and Sport*, 87(2), 151–164.

McCuaig, L. and Quennerstdet, M. (2016) Health by stealth—exploring the sociocultural dimensions of salutogenesis for sport, health and physical education research. *Sport, Education and Society*, 23(2), 111–122.

McKay, J., Gore, J. and Kirk, D. (1990) Beyond the limits of technocratic physical education. *Quest* 42 (1), 52–76.

McKenzie, T. L. and Lounsbery, M. A. (2009) School Physical Education: The pill not taken *American Journal of Lifestyle Education*, 3, 219–225.

Moore, G. F., Littlecott, H. J., Evans, R., Murphy, S., Hewitt, G. and Fletcher, A. (2017) School composition, school culture and socioeconomic inequalities in young people's health: Multi-level analysis of the Health Behaviour in School-aged Children (HBSC) survey in Wales. *British Educational Research Journal*, DOI: 10.1002/berj.3265.

Nässtrom, S. and Kalm, S. (2015) A democratic critique of precarity. *Global Discourse*, 5(4), 556–573.

Oliver, K. L. and Kirk, D. (2015). *Girls, gender and physical education: An activist approach*. London: Routledge.

Oliver, K. L. and Lalik, R. (2004) "The beauty walk, this ain't my topic": Learning about critical inquiry with adolescent girls. *Journal of Curriculum Studies*, 36(5), 555–586.

O'Sullivan, M., Siedentop, D. and Locke, L. (1992) Toward collegiality: Competing viewpoints among teacher educators. *Quest*, 44: 266–280.

Philpot, R. (2015) Physical education initial teacher educators' expressions of critical pedagogy(ies): Coherency, complexity or confusion? *European Physical Education Review*, 22(2), 260–275.

Postman, N. (1985) *Amusing ourselves to death: Public discourse in the age of show business.* New York: Penguin.

Priestley, M., Biesta, G. and Robinson, S. (2015) *Teacher agency: An ecological approach.* London: Bloomsbury.

Savage, M. et al. (2015) *Social Class in the 21st Century.* New York: Penguin.

Siedentop, D. (1996) Valuing the physically active life: Contemporary and future directions. *Quest*, 48, 266–274.

Standal, O. F. (2015) *Phenomenology and pedagogy in physical education.* London: Routledge.

Standing, G. (2016) *The precariat: The new dangerous class.* London: Bloomsbury Academic.

Stenhouse, L. (1975) *An introduction to curriculum research and development.* London: Heinemann.

Tinning, R. (2002). Toward a "modest pedagogy": Reflections on the problematics of critical Pedagogy. *Quest*, 54(3), 224–240.

Tinning, R. (2010). *Pedagogy and human movement: Theory, practice and research.* London: Routledge.

Van den Berghe, L., Vansteenkiste, M., Cardon, G., Kirk, D. and Haerens, L. (2014) Research on self-determination in physical education: Key findings and proposals for future research. *Physical Education and Sport Pedagogy*, 19(1), 97–121.

Wilkinson, R. and Pickett, K. (2009) *The Spirit Level: Why more equal societies almost always do better.* London: Allen Lane.

Williams, B. J., and Macdonald, D. (2015) Explaining outsourcing in health, sport and physical education. *Sport, Education and Society*, 20(1), 57–72.

Chapter 9

In pursuit of a critically oriented Physical Education: Curriculum contests and troublesome knowledge

Louise McCuaig, Janice Atkin and Doune Macdonald

Introduction

Australian Health and Physical Education (HPE) curricula in the latter decades of the twentieth century were underpinned by philosophical positions that emphasised a sociocultural perspective, social justice principles and the development of sociocritical skills. Yet, conducting a search for the terms 'sociocritical' or 'socially critical' in the current Australian Curriculum: Health and Physical Education (AC:HPE), results in the Adobe Acrobat notification of "Adobe Acrobat Reader has finished searching the document. No matches were found." In this chapter we seek to explain how and why HPE curriculum reform in the Australian context has resulted in these relatively paradoxical outcomes. In the first section, we undertake a mapping of sociocritical perspectives in the Australian HPE curriculum documents of the 1980s and 1990s and the research of sociocritical scholars informing the design and implementation of these. We then introduce two analytic concepts: principled position and threshold concepts (Cousin 2006; Hunter 1994; Meyer, Land and Baillie 2010), which provide a useful lens through which we can understand and respond to the ambivalent enactment of the most recent iteration of a critically oriented AC:HPE. In so doing, we seek to contribute further understanding to those factors that enable and trouble anticipated social change through HPE curriculum design and implementation.

Mapping the socio-critical orientations to past Australian HPE

In 1989 the Australian Education Council (AEC) established a collaborative initiative with federal and state governments to improve Australian schooling, and "address the areas of common concern embodied in the Ten Common and Agreed National Goals for Schooling in Australia" (Ministerial Council on Education, Employment, Training and Youth Affairs [MCEETYA] 1989, p. 1). One of these national goals called upon Australian schools "to provide for the physical development and personal health and fitness of students, and for the creative use of leisure time" (MCEETYA 1989, p. 1). A further outcome of this national collaboration was the establishment of eight broad areas of compulsory learning, subsequently organized into Key Learning Areas (KLA) (Dinan-Thompson 2006). These national initiatives in curriculum development stimulated much debate and contestation amongst those who had vested interests in the HPE field, some even claiming a crisis of identity for PE (Kirk 1996). Despite these often heated debates, HPE was established as one of eight national KLAs and the AEC set about the construction of the first iteration of a nationally consistent HPE curriculum framework.

The resulting *Statement on health and physical education for Australian schools* (AEC 1994), provided curriculum authorities with a framework for the translation of the national vision into state-based syllabus documents. Key principles and values upon which this statement was purported to have been based are identified as diversity, social justice and supportive environments. Expanding further on each of these, the HPE statement explains that the promotion of social justice involves:

- Concern for the welfare, rights and dignity of all people.
- Understanding how structures and practices affect equity at personal, local and international levels.
- Recognising the disadvantages experienced by some individuals or groups (for example, remote communities or people with disabilities) and actions that can redress them. (AEC 1994, p. 5)

A list of goals for the HPE study area also indicated that learning in this KLA would assist students to: promote their own and others' worth, dignity and rights; evaluate the influence of diverse values, attitudes and beliefs; and, "develop an understanding of how individuals and communities can act to redress disadvantage and inequities" (AEC 1994, p. 7).

This national HPE statement demonstrates an emerging imperative to recognise young people as social actors whose lives are shaped by a complex environment of social, cultural and political forces. An emerging and vibrant intellectual engagement with 'the critical' amongst Australian and international HPE scholarship also informed Australia's curriculum reform activities. Tertiary PE teacher educators, sport historians and sociologists were particularly vocal, given their location within sport and exercise science teaching and research settings. In debates surrounding the place of the critical project in PE of the early 1990s, these scholars argued that it was extremely difficult to engage HPETE students in critical inquiry, as their sporting success typically generated an "understanding of human physical activity as predominantly biological, individualist, elitist, masculine and mesomorphic" (McKay, Gore and Kirk 1990, p. 61). In their identification of the need for a sociocritical agenda within Australian PE teacher education (PETE), these scholars further claimed that:

> Most students are unaware of racial and ethnic inequalities in sport and physical education and when presented with evidence on these topics, invariably

attempt to counter them with biological and individualistic accounts. Trying to explain to them that there are social classes in capitalist societies is a difficult task, let alone suggesting that sport and physical education are shot through with class inequalities. (McKay et al. 1990, p. 61)

During this debate, Kirk (1992) was to caution that in all innocence, physical educators may "well be in the business of reproducing oppressive social conditions in the process of teaching students [and others] how to get fit, how to play games and sports, and how to recreate" (p. 53).

As a consequence of these influences, HPE teachers in the state of Queensland were expected to explicitly model and foster principles relating to a social view of health, social justice, and a dynamic and multi-dimensional model of health. Identity and relationships were to be considered in light of the "impacts of change, media, popular culture, cultural inheritance, and inequities in relationships" (QSCC 1999, p. 26). Engagement in physical activity likewise included a sociocultural perspective, with students expected to explore disability, role models, cultural beliefs, media messages, body image, gender, and their impact on their own and others' participation (QSCC 1999). Yet, the designers of the Queensland HPE curriculum warned that "teacher attitudes and concerns" (QSCO 1996, p. 23) could be an impediment, as British researchers had found that "teachers' attitudes to gender equity and inclusivity [were] one of the stumbling blocks to changing practice in schools" (QSCO 1996, p. 23).

Sociocritical perspectives as threshold concept

Such concerns were to prove well-founded. Reflecting on this era of HPE curriculum reform, McCuaig and colleagues (2014) argued that the "translation of the 'critical vision' from curriculum document to HPE classroom has comprised an ongoing challenge for the field" (p. 219). As Gard and Wright (2014) contend, instead of implementing pedagogical practices that inspire students to "gain a critical self-consciousness and social awareness and take appropriate action against oppressive forces" (p. 113), school-based health interventions and curricula are "heading in a more instrumental, individualistic and even punitive direction" (p. 113). Given the cautions raised by Queensland curriculum writers, researchers not surprisingly found that the implementation of the HPE KLA was a negative experience for teachers, citing challenges to self-identity, ontological security and sense of competence (Tinning 2004). In one of the few interrogations of an American PETE program employing a sociocritical orientation, Curtner-Smith and Sofo (2004) found that an ambitious attempt to inspire a social justice orientation amongst PETE students had "virtually no impact on them at all" (p. 134). By way of explanation, participating teachers in research conducted by Cliff, Wright and Clarke (2009) found the differences between biomedical and sociocritical knowledges in HPE difficult "to reconcile, especially given the fact that

HPE pre-service teacher education programs continue to foreground the rationality and certainty of science" (p. 8).

While claims of certainty may be elusive, scholarship has demonstrated a growing clarity regarding the characteristic features of a socially critical orientation to school HPE. Physical educators adopting this position devise courses that explore and question "the status quo, the dominant constructions of reality and the power relations that produce inequalities, in ways that lead to advocacy and community action" (Swalwell 2013, p. 6). As Cliff (2012) explains, educators who employ a sociocritical perspective consider the social component of 'sociocultural' perspectives to involve interrogation of "power and social relations, political and economic factors", whilst the cultural invites an exploration of "shared ways of thinking and acting" (p. 296). Advocacy of a socially critical tradition emphasises the explicit teaching and modelling (by educators) of social justice principles (Cliff 2012; Penney and Chandler 2000), including in the enactment of assessment in HPE (Hay and Penney 2013). As with education colleagues more broadly, physical educators adopting a sociocritical orientation hope their students "will be aware of injustices, feel a sense of agency to address those injustices and, ultimately, choose to act by participating in social movements and organizing around these issues" (Swalwell 2013, p. 2).

Despite the challenges of engaging teachers with critical perspectives, HPE researchers in Australia, New Zealand and Britain have continued to interrogate the interrelationship between HPE, broader sociocultural practices and the potential for HPE to produce and counter social oppression. There has been a flourishing sociocritical exploration of HPE and its role in the construction of citizens, identity, health and bodies (Beckett 2004; Evans, Davies and Wright 2004; Tinning and Glasby 2002). Australian and international scholarship has likewise argued for a stronger critical dimension in PETE (e.g., Garret and Wrench 2012), curricula (Macdonald 2014) and pedagogies (Hill and Azzarito 2012). Interestingly, the sociocritical position has gained less advocacy within American PE contexts (Curtner-Smith and Sofo 2004) than that of countries such as Australia and New Zealand (Philpot 2015), Britain (Brown and Evans 2004), Scandinavia (Dowling 2006; Larsson and Redelius 2008), and Canada (Melnychuk et al. 2011). Some have argued that this situation has possibly evolved as "more has been written about advocacy for critical pedagogy than on how it might be operationalized" (Philpot 2015, p. 319). Others such as Gard and Pluim (2017) point to the limited American critical scholarship in favour of a more socially conservative and bio-physically oriented research agenda as reflected in the publication patterns of the field's US-based journals.

Reflecting on the HPE profession's varying encounters and engagement with the sociocritical, we consider the analytic potential posed by the combination of Meyer, Land and Baillie's (2010) notion of a threshold concept and Hunter's (1994) idea of principled positions to be particularly useful. As Meyer, Land and Baillie (2010) explain, a threshold concept "builds on the notion that there are certain concepts, or certain learning experiences, which resemble passing through a portal, from which a new perspective opens up" (p. ix). This new perspective represents a "transformed way of understanding, or interpreting, or viewing something, without which the learner cannot progress, and results in a reformulation of the learners' frame of meaning" (p. ix). These concepts have common characteristics: they are transformative, often irreversible, integrative, bounded and troublesome. Threshold concepts are transformative as they demand "an ontological as well as a conceptual shift" (p. 4), but as learners grapple with new perspectives, transformation can involve a "degree of recursiveness, and of oscillation" (p. xi). Of most relevance, is the recognition that transition to understanding is often associated with troublesome knowledge. As argued by the original theorists, knowledge underpinning threshold concepts may be troublesome because "it requires adopting an unfamiliar discourse, or perhaps because the learner remains 'defended' and does not wish to change or let go of their customary way of seeing things" (Meyer et al. 2010, p. x).

More recently, scholars have devised a process of engagement with threshold concepts that involves learners' journeying through three modes. In the preliminal mode, learners first encounter the troublesome knowledge that is inherent within the threshold concept. Such encounters are unsettling and render previous certainties and understandings fluid. As a result, learners enter a state of liminality requiring "an integration of new knowledge" and "reconfiguration of the learner's prior conceptual schema and a letting go or discarding of any earlier conceptual stance" (Meyer et al. 2010, p. xi). During the liminal mode, Meyer and colleagues suggest learners may experience "a state of partial understanding, or 'stuck place' in which understanding approximates to a kind of 'mimicry' or lack of authenticity" (p. x). In contrast, those who acquire new understanding experience a transformation, passing through a portal to a final postliminal mode.

As with Shelley (2018), we argue that sociocritical knowledge in HPE can be likened to a threshold concept. Efforts directed at achieving social change through a sociocritically oriented HPE are often diverted by key stakeholders, such as political, education sector and school leaders whose preferential focus is directed towards outcomes related to national imperatives such as literacy, sport or public health. As a result, the profession more broadly experiences pockets of intertia, an incapacity to move beyond the preliminal or liminal modes of engagement with this threshold concept. Following Hunter (1994), we suggest that this 'stuck place' reflects the interaction between stakeholders' principled positions and sociocritical perspectives. As Hunter (1994) argues, perspectives on the success or otherwise of popular schooling are highly principled as they treat "the existing school system as the (partial or failed) realisation of certain underlying principles" (p. xv). Individuals and organisations assuming critical stances, create and adopt different positions that all "cohere around the notion of an ideal formation of the person" (p. xv). Within the context of Australian HPE curriculum reform, McCuaig and Hay (2013) identified two enduring and dominant principled positions, the healthy citizen and sports performer positions, which have underpinned the advocacy of preferred knowledge, skills and attitudes within HPE programs. These scholars further evidenced pathogenic and salutogenic orientations to the healthy citizen principled position, with the pathogenic orientation seeking to "fix" biophysical and psychosocial disease, while a salutogenic orientation promotes the provision of the individual and community resources that underpin good living.

In the following section we illustrate the troublesome interactions between these dominant HPE principled positions and sociocritical concepts, through the documentation of key moments in Australia's most recent endeavours to implement a sociocritical orientation to HPE. In what follows we consider the various policy, curriculum and consultation documents that emerged during the recent construction of the AC:HPE (2014), which was managed by the Australian Curriculum, Assessment and Reporting Authority (ACARA). Authors of this chapter were intimately involved in this process. Macdonald was the lead writer of the Shape Paper and writers' mentor for the AC:HPE, Atkin lead the development of the AC:HPE in her role as Senior Project Officer at ACARA, and McCuaig was a member of ACARA's HPE Advisory Panel throughout the curriculum development process. In collating data for the writing of this chapter permission was sought from ACARA to publish excerpts from documentation that was not available publicly.[1]

Seeking social change through a sociocritical HPE—troublesome knowledge continues

Following its formation in 2009, ACARA (formerly known as the National Curriculum Board) managed an extensive and collaborative curriculum development process in order to produce an Australian Curriculum covering 14 learning areas (see Figure 9.1). This process was uniform for all subject areas and based on the process outlined in ACARA's *Curriculum Development Process document v6.0* (2012). ACARA's curriculum development process involved four interrelated phases—the curriculum shaping phase, the curriculum writing phase, the preparation for implementation phase and the monitoring and evaluation phase. The process was designed to ensure broad engagement of stakeholders by providing opportunities for discussion and feedback at key points in the development. Here we document the journey of the sociocritical as a threshold concept through the first three phases of this process.

During the curriculum shaping phase, ACARA produced a number of documents for discussion by different parties. The first document was a Position Paper, designed to identify key issues that warrant consideration prior to the commencement of the development of the Draft Shape of the AC:HPE, and presented to the ACARA Board for feedback. The position paper was informed by an

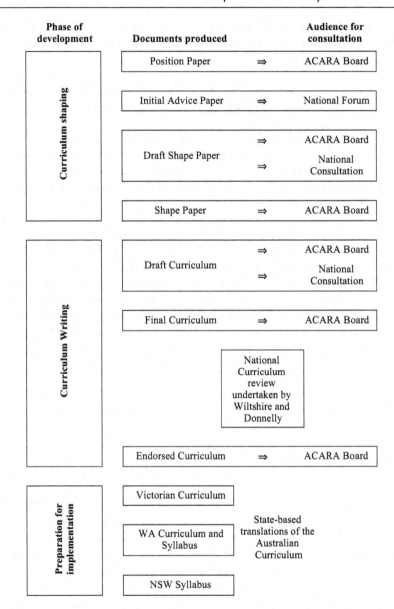

Figure 9.1 ACARA's Curriculum development and consultation process

environmental scan, analysis and review of existing policy and practice nationally and internationally; the collation and consideration of existing state, territory and international examples of curriculum for HPE; and discussions at the HPE preliminary planning workshop held prior to the start of the development process.

It is within this document that we find the beginning of the sociocritical's journey as a threshold concept within the curriculum. The Position Paper taken to the ACARA Board stated:

> Development of the Shape of the Australian Curriculum: Health and Physical Education will reflect the following in relation to the preferred position.
>
> - The curriculum will come from a sociocultural perspective.
> - The importance of developing a sense of responsibility and the skills of critical inquiry through exploration of the social and cultural factors related to physical activity and health behaviours will be clearly articulated. (ACARA 2011, p. 8)

The Position Paper was supported by the ACARA Board and, stemming from this, an Initial Advice Paper was developed to establish a broad outline for the direction, structure and organisation of the HPE curriculum. It was intended to guide the writing of the Shape Paper and was developed to provide a platform for discussion and feedback at the HPE National Forum. The Initial Advice Paper, presented at the National Forum, included five draft "propositions" for the HPE curriculum that were first introduced to the profession and subsequently gained strong support from the vast majority (96%) of participants. A socially critical perspective thus sat alongside four other "big ideas" for HPE, that included: developing health literacy, focusing on educative outcomes; learning in, about and through movement; and taking a strengths-based approach (ACARA 2012b).

The socially critical perspective was initially included as the following proposition:

> (e) Include a socially critical perspective
> 22. The interaction of personal, social, cultural, economic and environmental factors shapes how individuals, groups and communities think about health and their potential to take actions to improve their own and others' health and wellbeing. A socially critical approach requires students to explore a range of critical questions about health and physical activity and encourages them to recognise that a range of factors influence health and physical activity choices and behaviours. When students explore the choices people make about their health and physical activity participation from a socially critical perspective, they will learn to question taken-for-granted assumptions and power inequalities, explore aspects of cultural difference, inclusiveness, diversity and social justice, and develop strategies to achieve change. (ACARA 2011, p. 4)

The final output of the curriculum shaping phase was the development of the *Shape of the Australian Curriculum: Health and Physical Education (Shape Paper)* intended to provide a roadmap for the more detailed curriculum to follow. It was during consultation on the Shape Paper that the inclusion of the fifth proposition became contentious. After much negotiation, the explanatory text of this prop-osition included within the *Draft Shape of the Australian Curriculum: Health and Physical Education* was revised to read:

> (e) Include an inquiry-based approach.
> 20. The Health and Physical Education curriculum will draw on its multi-disciplinary base with students learning to question the social, cultural and political factors that influence health and well-being. In doing so students will explore matters such as inclusiveness, power inequalities, taken-for-granted assumptions, diversity and social justice, and develop strategies to improve their own and others' health and wellbeing.
> 21. Through the study of Health and Physical Education young people will learn that a range of factors influence health and physical activity val-ues, behaviours and actions. These factors include individual, interpersonal, organisational, community, environmental and policy influences. When considering and analysing the influence of these factors on wellbeing, the curriculum should support students to understand that health practices and physical activity participation are, in part, socially constructed. (ACARA, 2012c, page 5)

While the change was relatively superficial as the explanatory text remained very grounded in the sociocritical, it was the heading's reference to an inquiry-based approach that was changed to gain stakeholder approval at the ACARA Board level. Curiously this heading suggested a proposition about *pedagogy* which was not the remit of the larger Australian *curriculum* project. It nevertheless was considered a pragmatic solution in response to some opposition to, what may have been interpreted as, a "paradigmatic" bias. For example, a highly considered submission from Sports Medicine Australia offered:

> We believe there is a lot to like about this document, but in our opinion it needs to be strengthened by including a broader range of evidence-based research to support the promotion of health, movement and physical activity in youth. It is also apparent that the advisory panel has an imbalance of paradigmatic representation that has created the emerging bias and hidden curriculum contained within this document.

While the point was well-taken about the emerging documents' reference list, the criticism expressed in this submission was more about assumptions concern-ing the advisory panel's over-representation of critical pedagogy scholars, and that such scholars drove a 'hidden curriculum' when compared to a 'value free' position of other scholarship communities. This submission was interpreted by some in ACARA as a warning about an over-allegiance with the work of critical ped-agogues, positioning such work as antithetical to evidence-based, rigorous, and socially neutral pedagogical and biophysical work undertaken by others in the field.

Nevertheless, feedback from the public consultation process as described in the *Draft Shape of the Australian Curriculum: Health and Physical Education Consultation Report* (ACARA, 2012c) concerning the fifth proposition, demonstrated there was "overwhelming support across all written submissions for the inclusion of each of the five propositions" (p. 16). The case was made, however, of a "mismatch" between the heading and the text that followed. Further advocacy for "critical" to be included in the heading drew on: the overtly critical dimension to the health literacy approach that was well-accepted as the fourth proposition and, the intent of the Australian Curriculum project itself that clearly foregrounded the General Capabilities of 'critical and creative thinking', 'ethical understanding' and 'personal and social responsibility'.

As a result of feedback received during the public consultation about the change in the fifth proposition from the Initial Advice Paper to the Draft Shape Paper, the heading and description included within the final approved version of the *Shape of the Australian Curriculum: Health and Physical Education* (ACARA 2012b) was changed yet again. The title was modified to become "Include a critical inquiry approach" and the inclusion of an introductory sentence that emphasised pedagogical elements, recognition of learner diversity and alignment with the general capabilities and cross-curriculum priorities shared across all of the Australian Curriculum subject areas. The essence of this proposition was maintained in the final published curriculum, headed as 'Include a critical inquiry approach' and described as:

> The Health and Physical Education curriculum engages students in critical inquiry processes that assist students in researching, analysing, applying and appraising knowledge in health and movement fields. In doing so, students will critically analyse and critically evaluate contextual factors that influence decision making, behaviours and actions, and explore inclusiveness, power inequalities, taken-for-granted assumptions, diversity and social justice.
>
> The Health and Physical Education curriculum recognises that values, behaviours, priorities and actions related to health and physical activity reflect varying contextual factors which influence the ways people live. The curriculum develops an understanding that the meanings and interests individuals and social groups have in relation to health practices and physical activity participation are diverse and therefore require different approaches and strategies. (Version 7.5)

During the early years of Australian Curriculum implementation there was to be a change of government at the national level and, as a result of a review conducted by two appointees of the conservative government, a further revised description of the sociocritical proposition emerged (Donnelly and Wiltshire 2014). In the new statement "taken-for-granted" was deleted to be replaced with "explore inclusiveness, power inequalities, assumptions, diversity and social justice" (AC:HPE version 8.3). As *The Review of the Australian Curriculum* report (Donnelly and Wiltshire 2014) makes no mention of any concerns or issues with this aspect of the curriculum, it was unclear why this change would have been made as part of the final revision of the HPE curriculum.

Despite the title change to *Include a critical inquiry approach* and the subtle modifications of language as demonstrated above, the essence of the proposition's definition was maintained throughout the long development journey. Encouragingly, the detail of the curriculum that guides teachers' planning provides socially critical content descriptions for Year 5 and 6 students as follows:

- Examine how identities are influenced by people and places (ACPPS051)
- Recognise how media and important people in the community influence people's attitudes, beliefs, decisions and behaviours (ACPPS057)
- Participate in physical activities from their own and others' cultures, and examine how involvement creates community connections and intercultural understanding (ACPMP066)
- Identify how valuing diversity positively influences the wellbeing of the community (ACPPS060)

In Year 7 and 8 Australian students or HPE are expected to:

- Investigate the benefits to individuals and communities of valuing diversity and promoting inclusivity (ACPPS079)
- Participate in and investigate cultural and historical significance of a range of physical activities (ACPMP085)

During the evolution of the AC:HPE, two of the authors had the opportunity to trial a unit of work that aligned with the big ideas expressed in the Shape paper (McCuaig et al. 2012). Working with twenty school teachers and approximately 500 school students, the e-health literacy project provided both inspiration and confirmation that the AC:HPE suite of propositions were mutually supportive and provided the foundations for a sociocritical awareness. We were most buoyed by student feedback that indicated their appreciation of the unit's social action and change orientation, as Alexander explains:

> I actually got into doing this work because it was going towards helping others. The other work in other classes - the physical education classes was more about you being healthy and stuff like that. It didn't really tell us about helping others and stuff like that.

At the time of writing, five jurisdictions (ACT, NT, QLD, SA, and TAS) of the eight Australian states and territories are using the Australian Curriculum as published. Additional support for teachers was provided by Education Queensland, which developed the Curriculum to Classroom (C2C) resource, that delivers a comprehensive set of whole-school and classroom planning materials for single-level and multi-level classes, students with disability, and for students who study through the schools of distance education. The remaining three states have incorporated the Australian Curriculum into local frameworks (Western Australia [WA] and Victoria) or syllabus structures (New South Wales [NSW]). In translating the AC:HPE to their local structure, WA has designated all sociocritical content to optional status, reflecting a perception that the sociocritical perspective remains troublesome, unfamiliar and sits outside the principled positions the HPE profession in WA hold in relation to the learning area. NSW and Victoria have replicated the sociocritical content from the AC:HPE without change (NSW Education Standards Authority 2017). Given this variability, there is little evidence available to determine the extent to which the Australian HPE profession has successfully navigated the journey of transformation with the sociocritical dimensions of the AC:HPE.

Conclusion

As Macdonald (2014) reveals, the inclusion of a *critical* dimension within the AC:HPE resulted in questions concerning its *applicability* and what was, for some, its *ideological* appropriateness. Fundamentally, the AC:HPE reform journey is a story of the power and politics of language. "Socially critical" was a trigger for powerful voices, some from the biophysical sciences, who saw the concept as a territorial signifier of division and opposition in the human movement field's theories, methodologies, emphases and career trajectories. In contrast, the majority of teachers and their professional bodies drew predominantly upon their "tacit knowledge" of schools, teaching and students (Hargreaves 1999) to support the inclusion of sociocritical and strengths-based perspectives that resonated with the needs and interests of their students and communities. Stakeholders, whose "customary way of seeing things" (Meyer et al. 2010, p. x) was grounded in a pathogenic-biomedical orientation, clearly adopted a defensive stance that was indicative of a response to troublesome knowledge. In light of this, we suggest that the sociocritical appears particularly sensitive to the principled positions that stakeholders adopt in their efforts to influence the intent, knowledges and practices of HPE in schools.

At the end of the day, a decoupling of the words "socially" and "critical", alongside a retention of the thrust of the original proposition, was a settlement that allowed the HPE curriculum-making process to be resolved. Interestingly, many university-based researchers and teacher educators whose feedback on the perceived overplay of the sociocritical in the curriculum, are themselves undertaking highly principled, capacity-building research with marginal populations; those same populations that a critical perspective is keen to understand and strengthen. Notwithstanding the continued strength of advocacy amongst Australia's critical HPE scholars and teachers, intellectually at least, the sociocritical continues to pose a source of troublesome knowledge that unsettles the potential for transformation.

Note

1. Permission to use this qualitative data was sought and granted by Mr Robert Randall, Chief Executive Officer of ACARA in June 2017.

References

ACARA (2011) Position Paper: Health and Physical Education, Australian Government. Sydney: ACARA

Australian Curriculum, Assessment and Reporting Authority (ACARA). 2012a. *Curriculum Development Process Document v6.0*. Sydney: ACARA.

Australian Curriculum, Assessment and Reporting Authority. 2012b. *The Shape of the Australian Curriculum: Health and Physical Education*. Sydney: ACARA.

Australian Curriculum, Assessment and Reporting Authority. 2012c. *Draft Shape of the Australian Curriculum: Health and Physical Education Consultation Report*. Sydney: ACARA.

Australian Curriculum, Assessment and Reporting Authority (ACARA). 2013. *Australian Curriculum: Health and Physical Education*. Sydney: ACARA.

Australian Education Council. 1994. *A National Statement for Health and Physical Education*. Melbourne: Curriculum Corporation.

Beckett, L. 2004. Health, the body, and identity work in health and physical education. *Sport, Education and Society*, 9(2), 171–173.

Brown, D., and Evans, J. 2004. Reproducing Gender? Intergenerational links and the male PE teacher as a cultural conduit in teaching physical education. *Journal of Teaching in Physical Education*, 23, 48–70.

Cliff, K. 2012. A sociocultural perspective as a curriculum change in health and physical education. *Sport, Education and Society*, 17(3), 293–311.

Cliff, K., Wright, J., and Clarke, D. 2009. What does a 'sociocultural perspective' mean in Health and Physical Education? In M. Dinan-Thompson (Ed.), *Health and Physical Education: Issues for Curriculum in Australia and New Zealand* (pp. 165–179). South Melbourne, VIC, Australia: Oxford University Press.

Cousin, G. 2006. Threshold concepts, troublesome knowledge and emotional capital: an exploration into learning about others. In J. Meyer and R. Land (Eds.), *Overcoming Barriers to Student Understanding: Threshold Concepts and Troublesome Knowledge* (pp. 134–147). Abingdon: Routledge.

Curtner-Smith, M., and Sofo, S. 2004. Influence of a critically oriented methods course and early field experience on pre-service teachers' conceptions of teaching. *Sport, Education and Society*, 9(1), 115–142.

Dinan-Thompson, M. 2006. Why the KLA? And why now?. In R. Tinning, L. McCuaig and lisahunter (Eds.), *Teaching Health and Physical Education in Australian Schools* Sydney: Pearson Education Australia.

Donnelly, K., and K. Wiltshire. 2014. *Review of the Australian curriculum final report*. Australian Government, Canberra: Department of Education and Training.

Dowling, F. 2006. Physical education teacher educators' professional identities, continuing professional development and the issue of gender equality. *Physical Education and Sport Pedagogy*, 11(3), 247–263.

Evans, J., Davies, B., and Wright, J. (Eds.). 2004. *Body Knowledge and Control: Studies in the Sociology of Physical Education and Health*. London: Routledge.

Gard, M. and Pluim, C., 2017. Why is there so little critical physical education scholarship in the United States? The case of Fitnessgram. *Sport, Education and Society*, 22(5), 602–617.

Gard, M., and Wright, J. 2014. School and critical public health: Towards dialogue, collaboration and action. *Critical Public Health*, 24(2), 109–114.

Garrett, R., and Wrench, A. 2011. Making physical education a fairer, safer and happier place: Putting critical practices into action. *Asia-Pacific Journal of Health, Sport and Physical Education*, 2(2), 35–50.

Hargreaves, D.H. 1999. The knowledge-creating school. *British Journal of Educational Studies*, 47(2), 122–144.

Hill, J., and Azzarito, L. 2012. Researching valued bodies in PE: A visual inquiry with young people. *Physical Education and Sport Pedagogy*, 3, 263–276.

Hunter, I. 1994. *Rethinking the School: Subjectivity, Bureaucracy, Criticism*. St Leonards, NSW: Allen & Unwin.

Kirk, D. 1992. Physical education, discourse, and ideology: Bringing the hidden curriculum into view. *Quest*, 44(1), 35–56.

Kirk, D. 1996. The crisis in school physical education: An argument against the tide. *The ACHPER Healthy Lifestyles Journal*, 43(4), 25–27.

Larsson, H., and Redelius, K. 2008. Swedish physical education research questioned—current situation and future directions. *Physical Education and Sport Pedagogy*, 13(4), 381–398.

Macdonald, D. 2014. Sacred ties and fresh eyes: voicing critical public health perspectives in curriculum-making. *Critical Public Health*, 24(2), 239–247.

Macdonald, D., Hunter, L., Carlson, T., and Penney, D. 2000. Teacher knowledge and the disjunction between school curricula and teacher education. *Asia-Pacific Journal of Teacher Education*, 30(3), 259–275.

McCuaig, L., Carroll, K., and Macdonald, D. 2014. Enacting critical health literacy in the Australian secondary school curriculum: the possibilities posed by e-health. *Asia-Pacific Journal of Health, Sport and Physical Education*, 5(3), 217–231.

McCuaig, L., and Hay, P. J. 2013. Principled pursuits of 'the good citizen' in health and physical education. *Physical Education and Sport Pedagogy*, 18(3), 282–297.

McKay, J., Gore, J., and Kirk, D. 1990. Beyond the limits of technocratic physical education. *Quest*, 42(1), 52–76.

Melnychuk, N., Robinson, D. B., Lu, C., Chorney, D., and Randall, L. 2011. Physical education teacher education (PETE) in Canada. *Canadian Journal of Education/Revue canadienne de l'éducation*, 34(2), 148–168.

Meyer, J., Land, R., and Baillie, C. (Eds.). 2010. *Threshold Concepts and Transformational Learning*. Rotterdam: Sense Publishers.

Ministerial Council on Education, Employment, Training and Youth Affairs. 1989. *The Hobart Declaration on Schooling*. Retrieved December 24, 2007 from www.mceetya.edu.au/mceetya/default.asp?id=11577.

NSW Education Standards Authority (NESA). 2017. *Draft Personal Development, Health and Physical Education K-10 Syllabus*. Sydney: NESA

Penney, D., and Chandler, T. 2000. Physical education: What future (s)? *Sport, Education and Society*, 5(1), 71–87.

Philpot, R. 2015. Critical perspectives in PETE: An antipodean perspective, *Journal of Teaching in Physical Education*, 34, 316–332.

Queensland Department of Education. 1994. *Social Justice Strategy 1994–1998: A Framework for Action (Draft)*. Brisbane: Queensland Department of Education.

Queensland School Curriculum Office (QSCC). 1996. *Design Brief: Health and Physical Education Curriculum Development Project*. Brisbane: Author.

Queensland School Curriculum Council. 1999. *Health and Physical Education, Years 1–10 Syllabus.* Brisbane: Publication Services, Education Queensland.

Rovegno, I., and Kirk, D. 1995. Articulations and silences in socially critical work on Physical Education: Toward a broader agenda. *Quest*, 47, 447–474.

Shelley, K. 2018. *Shaken or Stirred? Considering the usefulness of critical pedagogy in preparing teachers to implement socio-critical health education.* Unpublished doctoral thesis, University of Queensland, Brisbane, Australia.

Swalwell, K. 2013. "With great power comes great responsibility": Privileged students' conceptions of justice-oriented citizenship. *Democracy and Education*, 21(1), Article 5. Retrieved from: http://democracyeducationjournal.org/home/vol21/iss1/5.

Tinning, R. 2004. Rethinking the preparation of Health and Physical Education teachers: Ruminations on knowledge, identity and ways of thinking. *Asia-Pacific Journal of Teacher Education*, 32(3), 241–253.

Tinning, R., and Glasby, T. 2002. Pedagogical work and the "cult of the body": Considering the role of HPE in the context of the "new public health". *Sport, Education and Society*, 17(2), 109–119.

World Health Organisation, Division of Health Promotion. 1986. Ottawa Charter of Health Promotion. Retrieved from www.ldb.org/iuhep/ottawa.htm.

Chapter 10

Socially critical PE: The influence of critical research on the social justice agenda in PETE and PE practice

Rod Philpot, Göran Gerdin and Wayne Smith

Introduction

Physical Education (PE) is often positioned as an important school subject for helping young people lay the foundation for a healthy and active lifestyle across their life-span (Hardman 2011), and promoting physical, cognitive, emotional and social development (Morgan and Bourke 2008). Drawing on our own experiences as PE and physical education teacher education (PETE) teachers and researchers in New Zealand and Sweden, we recognise the potential of PE, yet we are also cognisant that the way PE is taught does not always provide equitable or positive outcomes for all students. However, it is our belief that health equity goals can be reached when social justice and socially critical perspectives underpin PE pedagogy.

In this chapter, we examine critical research in PE and PETE. Further, the intent of the chapter is to discuss and critique the breadth of the scholarship that addresses social justice in PE and PETE before attending to our perception of the contribution this scholarship has made to social change in PE and PETE policy and pedagogical practice, while also acknowledging ongoing challenges and the need for further critical research and change.

Mapping: Critical research about social justice in PE and PETE

While practices for social justice and equity were present in PE before these concepts became part of the vernacular of education, issues of social justice in relation to PE rose in prominence in the mid-1980s with critiques of PE curricula, PETE, and PE teachers (e.g., Bain 1990, Dodds 1985, Fernández-Balboa 1995, Kirk 1986; Kirk and Tinning 1990; Tinning 1985). Through mapping the critical research in the fields of PE and PETE, we provide an overview of the issues that have been examined, the theoretical approaches used, and the knowledge that has been constructed.

In English language journals and books, the theme of social justice in PE and PETE emerged concurrently in the United States (US), United Kingdom (UK) and Australasia during the late 1980s and early 1990s. In the UK, an edited book *Physical Education, sport and schooling: Studies in the sociology of physical education* (Evans 1986) featured chapters almost exclusively from UK authors advocating for a sociological analysis of physical education to "raise questions about the origins and the purpose of physical education in contemporary British society" (Evans 1986, p. 3). The chapters in this book called for a sociological analysis of PE using "ethnographic techniques" (p. 14) and further engagement with interactionist and structural explanations of PE practice (Evans and Davies 1986). Evans (1986) explicitly positions PE as a social construct that is laden with values that serve to "condition and recondition class and power structures" and "make friends and enemies of those subjected to it" (p. 15).

In Australasia, social justice in PE and PETE can be traced back to the critical scholarship by scholars at Deakin University in Australia (Tinning 2011). 'Critical pedagogy', a term coined by Henry Giroux that prefaced educational practices for social justice based on the critical theories of the Frankfurt School and the writing of Paulo Freire, provided a theoretical basis for much of the work at Deakin. Kirk and Tinning's (1990) edited collection included work from a group of international scholars that critically examined curriculum, gender, ability and health. They framed the text as a political project written to, "open up to scrutiny the things we do, say and think about physical education" (p. 9). Kirk and Tinning identified and addressed scientific functionalism, the focus on biophysical knowledge in physical education, gender equity, motor elitism and the role of power in knowledge construction as four major issues facing PE.

Around the same period, scholars in the United States, such as Bain (1990), Dodds (1985), Fernández-Balboa (1995) and Lawson (1987) were also advocating for a social justice agenda in PE and PETE. The 'hidden curriculum', a concept taken from other educational researchers, was one of the concepts in PETE literature used to critique the "unplanned and unrecognized values taught and learned" through PE (Bain 1990, p. 92). In 1997, an edited book, *Critical postmodernism in human movement, physical education and sport* (Fernández-Balboa 1997) featuring predominantly US-based scholars, further explored how ideology principles, values and power have served to shape modern PE. Fernández-Balboa (1997) articulated a theme that continues in critical PE and PETE literature today, that was a call to "go beyond criticism and argument" and offer "valuable and viable ways for action and reflection" (p. 9).

In the ensuing decades, a growing body of literature in both PE and PETE by international scholars has investigated a broad range of social justice issues. These include edited books that focus on issues of social justice in PE and PETE such as *Gender and physical education: Contemporary issues and future directions* (Penney 2000), and more recently *Social justice in physical education* (Robinson and Randall 2016). Other scholarship that has focused on *issues* of social justice in PE includes accounts of the experiences of Muslim girls in PE (Dagkas and Benn 2016), discrimination based on sexuality (Sykes 2011), gendered bodies (Gerdin 2017), disability (Fitzgerald 2012), outsourcing of PE (Powell 2014), obesity (Burrows 2016), identity (Dowling 2006), and the influence of neoliberalism on PE and PETE (Azzarito et al. 2016), to name some.

Scholars in PETE with an interest in social justice have continued to argue the importance of educating pre-service teachers (PSTs) about sociocultural perspectives and issues (e.g., Cliff et al. 2009), critical pedagogy (e.g., Fernández-Balboa 1995, Kirk 1986, Tinning 2002), policy and curriculum (e.g., Fitzpatrick and Burrows 2017), advocacy for queer spaces in PE (e.g., lisahunter 2017), and the social construction of healthy bodies (e.g., Webb et al. 2008). Internationally, *advocacy* for pedagogies that address social justice issues in PETE include descriptions of inquiry-oriented approaches (Kirk 1986) through to more contemporary suggestions of co-constructing initial teacher education (ITE) curricula (e.g., Enright et al. 2017), critical reflection (e.g., Fernández-Balboa 1997, Hickey 2001), and negotiating assessments (e.g., Lorente and Kirk 2013).

Accounts that move beyond advocacy, that is, accounts of actual context bound critical practice are less common but growing in number. Examples include Lorente and Kirk's (2013) report on using self-assessment practices and negotiated assessment. Further accounts of pedagogical practices in PETE include Oliver (2013) and Oliver et al.'s (2015) inquiry-based practicum placements and student-centred inquiry in PETE, Legge's (2010) use of place-based pedagogies in indigenous communities, and Bruce's (2015) account of service learning where PETE students spent time working with young people who had been excluded from secondary school or young people who were from refugee and migrant backgrounds. There is an emerging quantum of research that report on the difficulties associated with requiring PETE students to reflect on their beliefs and identity (Cameron 2012, Devis-Devis and Sparkes 1999, Dowling 2006, Wrench 2017). Collectively these accounts resonate with Tinning's (2002, 2012) reminder that PETE educators much be modest in their expectations for personal change in PETE students.

Critique: A lack of understanding, pedagogy and valuing of social justice

In this section, we provide a critical commentary about the uptake of the critical agenda in PE and PETE. Commenting on teacher education more generally, Cochran-Smith (2010) argued that the pursuit of social justice in initial teacher education suffers the ignominy of being both an explicit purpose in almost every program while at the same time suffering from the claim that critical approaches are impossible (Biesta 1998). The growing body of research examining critical pedagogies in PE and PETE is instructive of the challenges including a lack of understanding, a lack of pedagogical practices, and a lack of interest in, or commitment to, social justice.

Lack of common understanding and definition
of pedagogies for social justice

In the last 20 years the terms 'critical pedagogy', 'socially-critical pedagogy', 'socio-cultural perspectives', 'inclusive physical education', 'culturally relevant pedagogy' and 'transformative pedagogy' have all become synonymous with PE pedagogies with a social justice agenda. While each expression is an articulation of social justice, PE practitioners have different understandings of the meaning and therefore the process of achieving social justice. Teachers' attempts to enact critical perspectives for social justice are further confounded as the concepts of PE and social justice are both shaped by cultural values, and the normative aspects operating in schools and cultural or traditional aspects of society.

In the field of PETE, Muros Ruiz and Fernández-Balboa (2005) found similar inconsistencies in teacher educators' understanding and practice of critical pedagogy. These authors report that, of the 17 participating teacher educators, all of whom volunteered for the study and claimed to practise a critical pedagogy, more than half did not understand the main principles of critical pedagogy. More recently, a study that investigated understandings of social justice and sociocultural perspectives of 72 PE teacher educators in the United States, UK, Australasia and Sweden (Walton-Fisette et al. 2018) found that only a very small number of the teacher educators studied, identified sociocultural issues or had an explicit understanding of the agenda of social justice pedagogies. Potentially, this uncertainty can lead to slippage to the point where teaching for social justice no longer resembles a process or a goal that has any consistency with the concept. Gerdin et al. (2018) and Philpot and Smith (2018) report that, for some PE teachers and graduating PETE students respectively, critical pedagogy had become a process of technical reflection on teaching.

Another issue for social justice advocates lies in the complex relationship between empowerment, liberation and indoctrination. Bruce (2013) argued that critical pedagogues may be guilty of channeling students' consciousness toward a destination already predetermined by the teachers. In a self-study by Dowling et al. (2015) the authors acknowledged that their own values and beliefs clouded their ability to see social justice issues beyond those they already valued stating:

> we have, in fact, been surprised by the persistence of our early private concerns, such as gender or disability, and the ways they continue to colour our engagement with education for social justice, as well as the taken-for-grantedness and often 'silent' theoretical viewpoints" (p. 1039).

In the quest for social justice based on their own positionality and their own values and beliefs, PE teachers and PETEs may be guilty of promoting critical reflexivity in others without embodying it themselves. Mordal-Moen and Green (2012) suggest that while critical reflexivity is something that teacher educators would like to believe is a consequence of teacher education, it is seldom the traditional practice of PETEs.

Lack of pedagogy for social justice

Within PETE, a growing number of scholars have stressed the need for teacher educators to develop a commitment to social justice pedagogy rather than simply to understanding social justice issues (Muros Ruiz and Fernández-Balboa 2005; Tinning 2012). Unfortunately, the increased advocacy for social justice in PE related to issues such as gender, race and (dis)ability has not been matched with examples of how PETE faculty and PE teachers could actually teach for social justice, that is, what teachers could do in their classrooms, and for whom social justice is sought (Walton-Fisette et al. 2018; Gerdin et al. 2018). More than a decade ago Curtner-Smith and Sofo (2004) suggested that little is known about critical PETE beyond why it should be enacted, with teacher educators having "little idea of the tactics, strategies, structures and organisational frameworks that PETE staff might employ" (p. 118). Similarly, Tinning (2002) reminded social justice proponents that advocacy is not the same as action, and a decade before that, O'Sullivan et al. (1992) challenged social justice proponents to move beyond criticism to action, claiming that literature on critical pedagogy in PE/PETE was "long on criticisms of existing practices in physical education. ... [and] short on descriptions of what a radical physical education would look like" (p. 275). In the ensuing decades, there appears to have been little change as there is a paucity of research in both PETE and school PE that addresses this void.

Lack of interest in, and commitment to, social justice

Studies of PETE students have highlighted that PETE students come with deeply entrenched views that privilege some and marginalise others. For many years, PE teachers and PETE students have described PE as a field focused on learning to play sport or developing fitness. Indeed, a study in Norway by Mordal-Moen and Green (2012) suggested that PETE may still privilege a traditional approach where the primary purpose of PE is to "induct student teachers into teaching and coaching sport" (p. 420). PETE has also been described as a field characterised by a resistance to changes in beliefs, thinking and practice (Rossi et al 2008). For instance, in Sweden and Norway many researchers argue that even when issues about gender, equality and social justice are raised in PETE, the students do not value this form of knowledge. PETE seems to have difficulty engaging the students in these issues and critically examining the power/knowledge relations that exist within PE (Kårhus 2004). Not surprisingly, students attracted to PETE are influenced by strong positive experiences with sport (O'Sullivan et al. 2009) and as such, graduates who are able to foreground the *physical capital* associated with the field of sports, have historically been privileged within the field (Schilling 1993). Their own positive experiences in sport and physical education have often lead to an uncritical adoption of traditional approaches to PE.

Social change: The promise of critical pedagogy in PE and PETE

The perceived lack of a practice focus is now beginning to spark the development of more practitioner approaches to critical pedagogy. Recently, Evans and Davies (2017) suggested that, *culturally*, PE has become a far kinder, nicer place for young people to be. This statement seeks to recognise that PE communities are now more aware of, and to some degree take action against, gendered practices, racial discrimination, ableism, identity, and call on pedagogies that move beyond performance. Tinning (2012) also argued that transformative successes can be seen in: 1) new curriculum and assessment policies; (2) accounts of PETE practices that enable the transformation of physical education in schools by changing how PETE students think and feel about social justice; and (3) reports of socially-critical PE practices. These successes, while limited and contextual, reflect the promise of social transformation of physical education.

The Promise of the HPE Curriculum

The promise of social change through PE is supported by changes to physical education policy documents in countries such as New Zealand and Australia where PE curricula have been replaced with health and physical education (HPE) curriculum documents that expect HPE teachers to integrate a socially-critical perspective into their pedagogy (MacDonald and Kirk 1999). As a new field of study, HPE has served to destabilise the field of PE in these countries. The field is now the field of HPE not PE (Fitzpatrick 2013).

In Australia, for example, HPE curricula changes that now span almost two decades (Queensland PE Curriculum 1999) require HPE teachers and PETE to engage with socially-critical perspectives of physical activity and health (Macdonald and Brooker 1999). Subsequent national HPE curriculums continue to represent a significant shift in thinking about the purpose of physical education in New Zealand. For example, the *National HPE Curriculum for Australia* (ACARA 2014) promotes a critical inquiry approach to HPE where students are expected to analyse, "how societal norms, stereotypes and expectations influence the way young people think about their bodies" (p. 46) and examine, "how diversity and gender are represented in the media and communities, and investigating the influence these representations have on identities" (p. 46). Similarly in New Zealand, HPE aims to "develop a sense of social justice" (Ministry of Education 2007, p. 22) and it "fosters critical thinking and action and enables students to understand the role and significance of physical activity" (p. 22). Although these curricula represent a change on a policy level, the question remains how to also further enable and facilitate such socially-critical practices in HPE classrooms that act on these curriculum approaches. However, there are more and more, yet scattered, reports on the enactment on socially-critical practices in both PETE and PE showing the promise of further social change and transformation.

The Promise of PETE

Tinning (2012) suggested that the most important determinant in adopting a socially-critical PE pedagogy is how PETE graduates *feel* about the place of social justice in PE. Further promise of social change comes from research of PETE pedagogical practices that have facilitated the examination of biographies and beliefs (Wrench 2017) and problematised the field of PE (Fernández-Balboa 1995). The authors of this chapter (Gerdin et al. 2018) recently studied the outcomes of a four-year PETE program that was allegedly underpinned by a critical orientation. Graduates of the program reported a shift in their thinking about the purpose of PE that they attributed to the program. For instance, many of the respondents stated that whilst initially their beliefs about HPE were influenced by their own sporting background and vested interests in health and fitness, that their views had changed during their time in the PETE program. The participants cited border crossing experiences and school placements in low socio-economic areas as being most influential as change agents. The pedagogies that appeared to assist students most in adopting a social justice agenda were those they attributed more to the affective domain than the cognitive, that is, they were often the experiences that engendered an emotional response to the social conditions of others.

The impact of an emotional response is also reflected in the work of others, including Dowling et al. (2015), who asserted that "nourishing pedagogical encounters" occur in "insecure pedagogical spaces" in moments where the ordinary becomes disrupted (p. 1038). Legge (2010) and Bruce (2015) also found that a healthy degree of frustration and uncertainty developed through experiences in unfamiliar contexts. Consistent with this, Philpot (2016) reported on a Freirean pedagogy used by one academic that served to agitate and infuriate PETE students, and in so doing sparked an emotional response which challenged the students to think more deeply about social justice matters. While this form of pedagogy seems to be inconsistent with Freire's (1970) descriptions of teacher–student relationships, it was based on a love for and belief in the value of equitable outcomes for all students.

The Promise of (H)PE practice

As stated earlier, the volume of advocacy for social justice in PE exceeds the accounts of 'taking action' to promote social justice and pedagogies for social justice. The following examples show promise as they provide pragmatic examples of socially critical practices being enacted in PE classrooms.

In one of the first classroom accounts, Oliver (2001) reported how she engaged grade 8 girls in a US school to critique dominant stories of the body through the use of images from popular teen magazines. In a more recent example, Oliver and Kirk (2017) identified four critical elements that they believe need to be present in order to assist girls to identify, name and negotiate barriers to their engagements with PE and participation in active lifestyles. They suggest that the development of a pedagogical model for working with girls in PE built on the four critical elements of activist research as a way of breaking the reproduction cycle and improve the current situation for girls in PE. These findings show promise and could be replicated to focus on other social justice issues.

One other example is Fitzpatrick's (2013) study of life at a high school in South Auckland, New Zealand. Using critical ethnography as an analytic, she shadowed one of the participating PE teachers, Dan, who was 'passionate about critical pedagogy' (p. 80). Dan's "classes provided a rare example of critical pedagogy in practice" (p. 99). Fitzpatrick (2013) described the key tenets of Dan's critical approach and success as; "building the environment, deconstructing power, playfulness, studying critical topics, and embodying criticality" (pp. 193–206). In our own study (Gerdin et al. 2018) we found that the seeds of critical pedagogy planted during PETE had started to develop the graduate teachers into critical HPE teachers who increasingly had "a desire to do something about social inequalities" (p. 9).

Finally, the initial findings of an ongoing research project on social justice in HPE across New Zealand, Sweden and Norway that calls on PE teacher observations and post observation critical incident interviews, has identified how broader curricular and school policy interact to facilitate the enactment of socially-critical pedagogies in HPE. These pedagogies include addressing and foregrounding cultural identity/diversity and socially-democratic principles in the everyday practices of the HPE classroom (Gerdin et al., 2018).

In the final section we offer some thoughts on how the critical and social justice project can be further reaffirmed on the research and teaching agenda in PE and PETE moving forward.

Discussion and conclusion

The uncertainty about teaching for social justice remain problematic in a time when evidence-based practice is the catch cry from politicians and many in academia. In neo-liberal times, where metrics of performance and outcomes rule, where learning outcomes and key performance indicators reign as champions of value, it is uncomfortable to suggest anything but certainty.

Even the most coherent PETE program, if it were to be focused entirely on promoting social justice, will not necessarily produce critical pedagogues (Gerdin et al. 2018). Nevertheless, is this any different from any other aspect of ITE? How are the messages of social justice enacted compared with the uptake of Games Education or Cooperative Learning, or other evidence-based PE teaching models that have been a part of PETE programs for a similar length of time? A lack of certainty of outcomes of socially critical approaches to PE and PETE should not be interpreted as failures. PETE students' attitudes toward social justice in the context of PE will continue to be filtered through their own subjectivities, histories and experiences. Beginning PE teachers will not enjoy unlimited pedagogical agency within the power relations of their school (Ovens 2017). They are not entirely 'free' to negotiate or enact curriculum based on principles of social justice. It is clear that a policy change in itself may signal an intention, but it does not necessarily result in a change in practice.

In our own work, we have reported that critical perspectives in PETE have provided a platform for PE teachers to reconsider their classroom practices. Critical pedagogies have helped them to question and plant a seed of uncertainty about the nature of PE, which was a field many students were more certain about when they entered, having entered holding the view that PE was about sport and performance improvement (Gerdin et al. 2018; Philpot and Smith 2011). However, the seeds sown require suitable conditions for germination. These conditions occur at the nexus of enabling policy, enabling institutional environments and enabling pedagogical practices (Ovens 2017). While a perfect storm of enabling conditions is not on the radar, the socially-critical PE curricula is a change in policy that represents a shift in the purpose of PE (see Penney 2010).

A critical continuum ranging from an individualistic perspective through to a focus on society provides a useful heuristic for conceptualising the aims of social justice pedagogical work in PETE. PETE should be designed to shift prospective PE teachers from wherever they sit on a continuum, towards a position where social issues become a greater focus in their decision-making including teaching content, pedagogical choices, group structure, and assessment. Inevitably, some teachers will position social justice to mean addressing individual concerns through humanistic teaching and technical reflection while others may tackle structural inequities, which requires more critical reflection based on the principles of critical theory. It strikes us that these modest changes are steps in the right direction and, as Sirna et al. (2010) suggest, position the field for further change.

To conclude, we see the need for further research that sheds light on 'good examples' of how social justice issues are addressed and acted upon across different PE teaching contexts. Good examples of social justice teaching practices from a multitude of socio-cultural contexts could help provide PE teachers with examples of practical resources and effective practices of teaching for social justice in an increasingly socio-cultural, diverse and neoliberal PE classroom (Gerdin et al., 2018). In this vein, we reiterate Fernández-Balboa (1997) call, from twenty years ago, to "go beyond criticism and argument" and to offer "valuable and viable ways for action and reflection" (p. 9) related to social justice and change in PE (O'Sullivan et al. 1992). The caveat we attach to this call for pragmatism, draws on Tinning (2017), who cautioned that a social justice and critical project agenda concerned with questions of justice, democracy and ethics in PE cannot be thought of as, yet another 'instructional model' like Sport Education, teaching games for understanding (TGfU) or Cooperative Learning that can be learned and enacted or, "a set of practices that can be reproduced (on demand as it were) irrespective of context" (Tinning 2017, p. 285). As such, the quest to strengthen and further develop the social justice and critical project agenda in PE is not about finding a 'holy grail' (Freire 1970), in terms of a pedagogical or instructional model, but rather the quest to reaffirm the need for an underpinning educational philosophy that is based on social justice, democracy and ethics in school PE.

References

Azzarito, L., Macdonald, D., Dagkas, S., and Fisette, J., 2016. Revitalizing the physical education social-justice agenda in the global era: Where do we go from here? *Quest*, 1–15. doi:10.1080/00336297.2016.1176935

Bain, L., 1990. A critical analysis of the hidden curriculum. In D. Kirk and R. Tinning, eds. *Physical education, curriculum and culture: Critical issues in the contemporary crisis.* London, UK: The Falmer Press, pp 23–42.

Biesta, G., 1998. Say you want a revolution…Suggestions for the impossibility of critical pedagogy. *Educational Theory, Fall 1998* 48(4), 499–510.

Bruce, J., 2013. Dancing on the edge: a self-study exploring postcritical possibilities in physical education, *Sport, Education and Society*, 18:6, 807–824

Bruce, J., 2015. On racism and prejudice: Exploring post-critical possibilities for service-learning within physical education teacher education. *Asia-Pacific Journal of Health, Sport and Physical Education*, 6(3), 233–244.

Burrows, L., 2016. Obesity warriors in the tertiary classroom. In E. Cameron and C. Russell, eds. *The fat pedagogy reader: Challenging weight based oppression through critical education*, pp. 101–121 New York: Peter Lang.

Cameron, E., 2012. DE/REconstructing my athlete-student-teacher self: A critical autoethnography of resistance in physical education teacher education (PETE). *PHEnex Journal*, 4(2), 1–16.

Cliff, K., Wright, J. and Clarke, D., 2009. What does a 'sociocultural perspective' mean in Health and Physical Education?, In M. Dinan-Thompson, ed. *Health and physical education*, pp. 165–169. Oxford University Press.

Cochran-Smith, M., 2010. Toward a theory of teacher education for social justice. In A. Hargreaves, A. Lieberman, M. Fullan, and D. Hopkins, eds., *Second international handbook of educational change*, pp. 445–467. London, UK: Springer Science and Business Media.

Curtner-Smith, M. and Sofo, S., 2004. Influence of a critically oriented methods course and early field experience on preservice teachers' conceptions of teaching. *Sport, Education and Society*, 9(1), 115–142.

Dagkas, S. and Benn, T., 2006. Young Muslim women's experiences of Islam and physical education in Greece and Britain: a comparative study, *Sport, Education & Society*, 11(1), 21–38.

Devis-Devis, J. and Sparkes, A., 1999. Burning the book: A biographical study of the pedagogically inspired identity crisis in physical education. *European Physical Education Review*, 5, 135–151.

Dodds, P., 1985. Are hunters of the functional curriculum seeking quarks or snarks? *Journal of Teaching in Physical Education*, 4, 91–99.

Dowling, F., 2006. Physical education teacher educators' professional identities, continuing professional development and the issue of gender equality, *Physical Education and Sport Pedagogy*, 11(3), 247–263, DOI: 10.1080/17408980600986306

Dowling, F., Fitzgerald, H. and Flintoff, A., 2015. Narratives from the road to social justice in PETE: Teacher educator perspectives. *Sport, Education and Society*, 20(8), 1029–1047.

Enright, E. Coll, L., Ní Chróinín, D. and Fitzpatrick, M., 2017. Student voice as risky praxis: democratising physical education teacher education, *Physical Education and Sport Pedagogy*, 22:5, 459–472, DOI: 10.1080/17408989.2016.1225031

Evans, J., 1986. *Physical education, sport and sociology*. London: The Falmer Press.

Evans, J. and Davies, B., 1986. Sociology, schooling and physical education. In J. Evans *Physical education, sport and sociology* (pp. 11–37). London: The Falmer Press.

Evans, J. and Davies, B., 2017. In pursuit of equity and inclusion: populism, politics and the future of educational research in physical education, health and sport. *Sport, Education and Society*, 22(5), 684–694, DOI: 10.1080/13573322.2017.1307176

Fernández-Balboa J. M., 1995. Reclaiming physical education in higher education through critical pedagogy. *Quest*, *47*, 91–114.

Fernández-Balboa, J. M., ed. 1997. *Critical postmodernism in human movement, physical education and sport.* New York: State University of New York Press.

Fitzgerald, H., 2012. 'Drawing on Disabled Students' Experiences of Physical Education and Stakeholder Responses. *Sport, Education and Society* 17(4), 443–462. DOI: 10.1080/13573322.2011.609290

Fitzpatrick, K., 2013. *Critical pedagogy, physical education and urban schooling.* New York: Peter Lang.

Fitzpatrick, K., and Burrows, L., 2017. Critical health education in Aotearoa New Zealand. *Sport, Education and Society*, 22(5), 552–568. DOI: 10.1080/13573322.2015.1131154

Freire, P., 1970. *Cultural action for freedom.* Cambridge, MA: Harvard Educational Review.

Gerdin, G., 2017. *Boys, Bodies, and Physical Education: Problematizing Identity, Schooling, and Power Relations through a Pleasure Lens.* New York: Routledge.

Gerdin, G., Philpot R., Larsson L., Schenker K., Linnér S., Mordal Moen K., Westlie K., Smith W. and Legge M., 2018. Researching social justice and health (in)equality across different school health and physical education contexts in Sweden, Norway and New Zealand. *European Physical Education Review, 1–18.* DOI: 10.1177/1356336X18783916.

Gerdin G., Philpot R. and Smith W., 2018. It is only an intervention, but it can sow very fertile seeds: graduate physical education teachers' interpretations of critical pedagogy. *Sport, Education and Society*, 23(3), 203–215.

Hardman, K., 2011. Physical Education, Movement and Physical Literacy in the 21st Century: Pupils' Competencies, Attitudes and Behaviours. In I. Prskalo and D. Novak eds. *Proceedings Book of 6th FIEP European Congress, Poreč, "Physical Education in the 21st Century-Pupils Competencies",* pp. 15–26.

Hickey, C., 2001. I feel enlightened now, but…: The limits to the pedagogical translation of critical discourses in physical education. *Journal of Teaching in Physical Education*, 20, 227–246.

Kårhus, S., 2004. Physical education teacher education and gender discourses: an analysis of Norwegian policy documents and curricula, In: P. Jørgensen & N. Vogensen, eds. *What's going on in the gym? Learning, teaching and research in physical education,* (pp. 212–221). Odense, University of Southern Denmark.

Kirk, D., 1986. A critical pedagogy for teacher education: Toward an inquiry-oriented approach. *Journal of Teaching in Physical Education*, 5, 230–246.

Kirk, D. and Tinning, R., 1990. *Physical Education, curriculum and culture: critical issues in contemporary crisis.* Bristol, PA: The Falmer Press.

Lawson, H., 1987. Teaching the body of knowledge: The neglected part of physical education. *Journal of Physical Education, Recreation and Dance*, 58(7), 70–72

Legge, M., 2010. E noho marae - Transforming learning through direct Māori cultural experience. In C. J. Jesson, V. M. Carpenter, M. McLean, M. Stephenson, and Airini eds. *University teaching reconsidered: Justice, practice, equity,* (pp. 139–149). Wellington, NZ: Dunmore Publishing Ltd.

lisahunter 2017. What a queer space is HPE, or is it yet? Queer theory, sexualities and pedagogy, *Sport, Education and Society*, DOI: 10.1080/13573322.2017.1302416

Lorente, E., and Kirk, D., 2013. Alternative democratic assessment in PETE: An action-research study exploring risks, challenges and solutions. *Sport, Education and Society*, 18(1), 77–96.

Macdonald, D., and Brooker, R., 1999. Articulating a critical pedagogy in physical education teacher education. *Journal of Sport Pedagogy*, 5(1), 51–64.

McIntyre, J., Philpot, R. and Smith, W., 2016. HPE teachers' understanding of socially critical pedagogy and the New Zealand Health and Physical Education curriculum. *The Physical Educator: Te ao Kori Aotearoa*, 49(2), 5–9.

Ministry of Education. 2007. *The New Zealand curriculum*. Wellington, New Zealand: Learning Media.

Mordal-Moen, K. and Green, K., 2012. Neither shaken nor stirring: A case of reflexivity in Norwegian physical education teacher education. *Sport, Education and Society*, 19, 415–434.

Morgan, P. and Bourke, S., 2008. Non-specialist teachers' confidence to teach PE: The nature and influence of personal school experiences in PE. *Physical Education and Sport Pedagogy*, 13(1): 1–29.

Muros Ruiz, B. and Fernández-Balboa, J. M., 2005. Physical education teacher educators' personal perspectives regarding their practice of critical pedagogy, *Journal of Teaching in Physical Education*, 24, 243–264.

Oliver, K., 2001. Images of the body from popular culture: Engaging adolescent girls in critical inquiry, *Sport, Education and Society*, 6:2, 143–164, DOI: 10.1080/13573320120084245

Oliver, K., 2013. "Beyond words: The visual as a form of student-centered inquiry of the body and physical activity." In L. Azzaritto and D. Kirk, eds. *Physical culture, pedagogies and visual methods*, pp. 15–29. New York: Routledge.

Oliver, K. and Kirk, D., 2017. Challenging body culture in physical education. In C. Ennis, ed. *The Routledge handbook of physical education pedagogies*, pp. 307–318. New York: Taylor and Francis.

Oliver, K., et al. 2015. 'The sweetness of struggle': innovation in physical education teacher education through student-centered inquiry as curriculum in a physical education methods course. *Physical Education and Sport Pedagogy*, 20:1, 97–115, DOI: 10.1080/17408989.2013.803527

O'Sullivan, M., MacPhail, A. and Tannehill, D., 2009. A career in teaching: Decisions of the heart rather than the head. *Irish Educational Studies*, 28(2), 177–191.

O'Sullivan, M., Siedentop, D. and Locke, L., 1992. Toward collegiality: Competing viewpoints among teacher educators. *Quest*, 44, 266–280.

Ovens, A., 2017. Transformative aspirations and realities in physical education teacher education (PETE). In C. Ennis, ed. *The Routledge handbook of physical education pedagogies*. New York: Taylor and Francis, pp. 295–306.

Penney, D., 2000. *Gender and physical education: Contemporary issues and future directions*. London: Routledge.

Penney, D., 2010. Health and Physical Education in Australia: A defining time? *Asia-Pacific Journal of Health, Sport and Physical Education*, 1:1, 5–12, DOI:10.1080/18377122.2010.9730320

Philpot, R., 2016. Shaking students, cages: A Freirean pedagogy that challenged PETE students' beliefs about physical education. *International Journal of Critical Pedagogy*, 7(1), 143–164.

Philpot, R. and Smith, W., 2011. Beginning and graduating teachers beliefs about physical education: A case study. *Asia-Pacific Journal of Health, Sport and Physical Education*, 2(1), 33–50.

Philpot, R. and Smith, W., 2018. Making a different difference: Physical education teacher education students' reading of critical PETE programme. *Asia-Pacific Journal of Health, Sport and Physical Education*, 9(1), 7–21.

Powell, D., 2014. Childhood obesity, corporate philanthropy and the creeping privatisation of health education. *Critical Public Health*, 24(2), 226–238. doi:10.1080/09581596.2013.846465

Queensland School Curriculum Council. 1999. *Health & physical education Years 1 to 10 syllabus*. Brisbane, Australia: Education Queensland.

Robinson, D. and Randall, L. eds., 2016. *Social justice in physical education*. Toronto CA: Canadian Scholars Press.

Rossi, T., Sirna, K., and Tinning, R., 2008. The process of becoming a health and physical education teacher: The HPE subject departmant office as a site of performance. *Teaching and Teacher Education*, 24(4), 1029–1040.

Schilling, C., 1993. *The body in social theory*. London, UK: Sage.

Sirna, K., Tinning, R. and Rossi, T., 2010. Social processes of health and physical education teachers' identity formation: Reproducing and changing culture. *British Journal of Sociology of Education*, 31(1), 71–84.

Sykes, H., 2011. *Queer bodies: Sexualities, genders, & fatness in physical education*. New York: Peter Lang.

Tinning, R., 2002. Toward a "modest pedagogy": Reflections on the problematics of critical pedagogy. *Quest*, 54, 224–240.

Tinning, R., 2011. Introduction. In R. Tinning and K. Sirna, eds. *Education, social justice and the legacy of Deakin University*, pp. xv–xxv. Rotterdam, The Netherlands: Sense Publishers.

Tinning R., 2012. A socially critical HPE (aka physical education) and the challenge for teacher education. In: B. Down and J. Smyth, eds. *Critical voices in teacher education: Teaching for social justice in conservative times*, pp. 223–238. Dordrecht, Netherlands: Springer.

Tinning, R., 2017. Transformative pedagogies and physical education. In C. Ennis, ed. *The Routledge handbook of physical education pedagogies*, pp. 281–294. New York: Routledge.

Walton-Fisette, J. et al., 2018. Implicit and Explicit Pedagogical Practices Related to Sociocultural Issues and Social Justice in Physical Education Teacher Education Programs. *Physical Education and Sport Pedagogy*. DOI:10.1080/17408989.2018.1470612

Webb, L., Quennerstedt, M., and Öhman, M., 2008. Healthy bodies: construction of the body and health in physical education, *Sport, Education and Society*, 13:4, 353–372, DOI: 10.1080/13573320802444960

Wrench, A., 2017. Spaces and physical education pre-service teachers' narrative identities. *Sport, Education and Society*, 22(7), 825–838

Critical scholarship in physical education teacher education: A journey, not a destination

Chris Hickey and Amanda Mooney

Our primary aim here is to reflect upon the ways in which critical scholarship has influenced and impacted on physical education teacher education (PETE). Initially inspired by Marxist ideology and the Frankfurt School scholars of the 'new left' (e.g., Jurgen Habermas 1972), critical theories of PE gained momentum through the 1970s and 80s as part of a wider pursuit of justice, equality, democracy and freedom as core values to drive education. At the heart of the socially critical agenda was a shared commitment to challenge conservative orthodoxies that were seen to restrict the capacity for reform and change. This involved the vigilant identification and sustained rejection of reproduction theories of education wherein technical approaches to reasoning were orientated toward known problems, with known ends generated from known means. Embedded here were pedagogical approaches that emphasised the importance of self-reflection and the potential for critique to expose regimes of domination and the reproduction of injustices in the pursuit of positive change.

By the early 1990s a new wave of critical thinkers had taken their lead from a new order of postmodern(ist) framing. The so-called postmodern turn began destabilising the previously strong normative base that critical scholarship had been built on. The epistemological foundations of enlightenment, empowerment and emancipation came under increased scrutiny on account of their over reliance on the subject and the capacity for individual self-determination. In particular, poststructural, post-colonial and feminist theorising rejected humanist ideologies that harboured grand narratives about the optimal human condition, believing that they were artefacts of some form of conservative nostalgia. At the heart of poststructural thinking was the pursuit of a more sophisticated understanding of issues of subjectivity through a deeper account of relations of power and their historical location (Foucault 1980, 2000).

Through the processes of deconstruction and reconstruction leading feminist scholars such as Patti Lather (1991, 1998) and Elizabeth Ellsworth (1989) opened up spaces for new thinking about social disadvantage, noting the limits of self-actualisation. Such commentators began to question dominant critical standpoints that positioned the process of education as a vehicle through which the empowered could empower the disempowered. Indeed, Ellsworth (1989) argued that critical pedagogy had been overwhelmingly elaborated by white male theorists and was highly abstract, utopian and hyper-rationalist. However, the rejection of humanist epistemologies as a foundation for understanding the purpose of education and schooling was not a rejection of the critical aspirations of social justice, diversity and forms of liberation. Though they were being guided by different epistemological and ontological principles, critical scholars continued to pursue a shared interest in the need for social change. Under this gaze critical scholars, from their various standpoints, have continued to reject neo-liberalist processes of schooling as part of the apparatus for maintaining and reproducing the dominant social order (Ball 2013, Smyth 2011).

Mapped into this backdrop has been a sustained engagement with critical scholarship in PETE. While some of the chapters in this book convey the differential levels of interest and engagement with the critical project across the wider physical education profession, its presence in PETE programs can be traced across three decades now (Ovens et al. 2018). During this time PETE scholars have engaged with critical sociologies of social justice and enlightenment to advance theory and practice in this sphere. Common in the endeavours that form the body of this work has been a focus on disrupting theories and applications of physical education curriculum and pedagogy that are seen to be inherently discriminatory, simultaneously privileging some while marginalising others (Tinning 1990). While their theoretical and methodological orientations can vary substantially, engagement with critical pedagogies in PETE have been orientated toward subverting the conditions and practices that serve to privilege, albeit unwittingly, individuals who project particular behaviours and dispositions, over those that do not. It is this meta perspective that has opened the way for innovative curriculum and pedagogic reforms to be implemented/trialled in PETE programs around the world.

In this chapter we draw on the tripartite framework of mapping, critiquing and changing (Markula and Silk 2011), to consider the impact of critical scholarship in PETE. Against this backdrop we explore impact as the link between theory and practice in the pursuit of a praxis of transformation. As such we acknowledge that the impact of critical scholarship can result in advances that can be theoretical, conceptual and/or practical. To this end, the value of writing and dissemination within and beyond the PETE community is incalculable. In the process of mapping impact, we discuss the preconditions that give rise to the engagement with critical scholarship within particular PETE programs. Within this we interrogate the ways in which the practices of critique are mobilised to advance critical conceptualisations of theory and practice within PETE programs. Applying the final phase of the framework we look at the translation of critical scholarship in PETE programs and the potential for critical praxis.

In the final section of the chapter we consider the contemporary warrant for critical scholarship in PETE within the wider socio-political context. In this pursuit we look at current markers of social disadvantage and how they may differ from previous/historic articulations of this condition. We track this discussion into the community spheres of sport and recreation to consider how manifestations of social disadvantage and disconnection might shape contemporary critical scholarship in PETE. In casting our lens forward we contemplate the potential for new theoretical frameworks to mobilise the next wave of critical scholarship in ways that better accommodate the complexity of a rapidly changing world. Here, we contemplate the potential for posthuman theory to provide a framework to further the critical project in a way that recognises the technological and digital advances that increasingly exist at the interface between human and non-human (Braidotti 2013).

The critical project in PETE: A 'topography' of enabling pre-conditions for criticality

As Markula and Silk (2011) explain, establishing a 'topography' or map of what is currently known about a research field or practice is an important precursor to any critique that then may follow. While our remit is to map and critique what is currently known about critical scholarship in PETE, we digress slightly for two pertinent reasons. Firstly, as others have pointed out, contributions connected with what Lather (1998) termed as the 'big tent' of critical scholarship rarely share common definitions of what the critical project is, or might be (Tinning 2016). Notwithstanding the diverse nomenclature drawn on to describe this work such as socially critical research (Devís-Devís 2006), critical pedagogy (Breuing 2009, Fernández-Balboa 1997, Tinning 2002, Wink 2011), sociocultural perspectives (Cliff et al. 2009), social justice education (Robinson and Randall 2016), and perhaps more recently transformative pedagogy[1], we also acknowledge the variable theoretical, ontological and practical orientations of this work.

Whilst critical scholarship, and critical pedagogies more specifically, cannot be considered as a homogenous set of ideas *per se*, or as constituted by only one 'narrow set of prescriptive practices' (Breuing 2011, p. 5), common to most contributions is a commitment by educators to confront their beliefs and taken-for-granted assumptions, and act against teaching practices that marginalize disadvantaged students (Garrett and Wrench 2011). Wright (2004) suggests such approaches draw on social and critical theories to help students examine and challenge the status quo, critique dominant constructions of truth/reality and the power relations that contribute to inequalities, and consider strategies for advocacy and social/community action. As others attest, the diverse ways in which the critical project manifests in PETE literature makes attempts to map this work challenging (Felis-Anaya et al. 2017, Philpot 2017), which leads us to our second point.

Laudable attempts to do this work have already been made—for example, Devís-Devís (2006) presents a comprehensive critique of knowledge produced through socially critical research in the *Handbook of Physical Education*. From an antipodean perspective (Australia and New Zeland), Philpot (2015) argues that physical education curriculum reform underpinned by socially critical perspectives has encumbered PETE programs to 'prepare teachers who are capable of engaging PE from a socially critical perspective' (p. 316). With this warrant, Philpot synthesised the collective efforts of the critical project during what others have termed the 'first generation of critical scholarship' (Felis-Anaya et al. 2017). Specifically, Philpot (2015) highlights the problematisation of knowledge, the role of critical reflection, power sharing through democratic classrooms, engaging students in critical dialogue and border-crossing experiences as significant contributions to emerge from this scholarship.

More recently, Felis-Anaya and colleagues (2017) present a systematic review of what they term, 'second generation' socio-critical research in PE, to articulate the 'influence of postmodern postulates … [on] broadening the emancipatory agenda' (p. 2). In Tinning's (2016) reflections of the critical project he acknowledges there have been positive achievements towards a transformative agenda, but tempers this observation with acknowledgement of the considerable critique levelled against it, or what he terms, 'disquiet in the tent' (p. 284). He states, 'notwithstanding these critiques of the definitional, theoretical and epistemological foundations of transformative pedagogy, there are also some very practical issues that need to be considered' (p. 285). From this perspective, we would like to draw attention to what these contributions have highlighted about the preconditions considered supportive or enabling in terms of the critical project in PETE. Drawing on Rizvi's (2011) observation that the critical project is mobilised through a disposition of *criticality*, Tinning (2016) explains that while critical scholars share an ethics of social justice, not everyone will 'do criticality' in the same way.

Whilst far from exhaustive our mapping exercise heightened our awareness of the role that biographies and habitus can play as both limiting and enabling critical dispositions in PETE. As many proponents of the PETE socialisation literature will attest, PETE students often enter initial teacher education programs with deeply entrenched views that legitimate particular ways of knowing and being in PE (at the expense of marginalised others). Compounding this, Curtner-Smith and Sofo (2004) argue that PETE students give 'little attention to political, moral, ethical, or social issues related to their teaching' (p. 116). This perspective was recently reflected by Fyall's (2017), suggestion that PETE students think of the critical project as a 'topic for discussion' (p. 223) about social disadvantage that has little to no connections 'to their own evolving epistemological beliefs and pedagogical practice' (p. 223). Indeed, PETE as an institution has routinely been implicated in reinforcing (rather than challenging) these stubbornly resistant perspectives (Larsson et al. 2016). As such, it is no surprise to read accounts of the limited influence PETE appears to have in disrupting dominant beliefs and practices (Mordal-Moen and Green 2014), particularly when the conservative micropolitics of schools during practicum appear to reaffirm them (Muros Ruiz and Fernández-Balboa 2005).

Early advocates of critical pedagogies as a means to deconstruct the pervasive influence of biographies in practices that reproduce inequalities in physical education (see for example Hickey 2001, Kirk 1986), recognised that not all PETE students respond to an invitation to criticality in the same way. There is recognition that 'who' issues this invitation is another important precondition, given that non-reflexive PETE educators are more likely to be, albeit unwittingly, complicit in reproducing inequalities (Ukpokodu 2009). As Hickey (2001) argued, if critical pedagogies are enacted naively in that these invitations are issued without consideration of the intellectual and practical resources PETE students require to 'make sense' of these sometimes confronting stories of personal complicity, we risk setting them up for failure.

Ovens and Tinning (2009) argued that the discourse community within which 'reflection as a situated practice' (p. 1125) occurs is another important precondition for the enactment of productive critical pedagogies. Institutional and cultural contexts that promote and enable student experiences of criticality (and indeed their own processes of subjectivity) in ways that recognise the fluid, contingent, temporal and personally confronting dimensions of this work are more likely to occur in a supportive discourse community like PETE classrooms, than perhaps the more conservative and performative spaces of the school practicum (Ovens and Tinning 2009). Establishing the preconditions that support criticality is important to any endeavour seeking to enact critical pedagogies in PETE, to which our attention now turns.

Critical pedagogies and the pursuit of change in PETE: An invitation to criticality

Although others have argued historically that limited research existed to examine the enactment of critical pedagogies in PETE (Curtner-Smith and Sofo 2004, Muros Ruiz and Fernández-Balboa 2005), we observe, a decade later, growing accounts of 'critical pedagogy "in action" to see if it "delivered" on its claims' (Tinning 2016, p. 282). In the critique that follows we consider the ways in which key critical endeavours have proffered alternative visions of theory and practice within PETE programs.

Problematising knowledge: Theoretical and conceptual achievements of the critical project

Whilst it is beyond the scope of this chapter to rehearse the arguments put forward in various contributions that have called for, and demonstrated the effects of, problematising knowledge/s in PETE, what we can say is the collective pursuit of the critical agenda in PETE seems to have orientated around 'conscientizing' pre-service teachers with the aim of liberating them from the shackles of ideology (Muros Ruiz and Fernández-Balboa 2005, Tinning 2002). Recognisable within this body of work has been a willingness to 'think differently' about the known and familiar through the application of different theoretical and conceptual tools. For example, Jenny Gore's (1990, 1993) early work used post-structuralist approaches to deconstruct the metanarratives of critical theory, critical pedagogy, neo-Marxism and feminism to produce an alternative reading of her practice as a PETE educator as she sought to 'present knowledge as problematic' (p. 116).

Cassidy's (2000) doctoral work examined the critical pedagogies of 'Frank', a PETE educator whose work with first year students primed to learn about the 'right-way' to teach in PE, interpreted Franks critical incursions as 'a bit esoteric' (p. 154). In a later contribution, Cassidy and Tinning (2004) elaborated on these insights to reveal the considerable 'slippage' that existed between Frank's pedagogic intentions (critical messages) and the ways the students interpreted them (messages received). This apparent lack of practical translation, combined with often 'overzealous' or forceful language drawn on by 'radicals' in their call-to-arms around the critical project, has attracted its share of critique (see O'Sullivan et al. 1992). Through praxis-orientated work, Hickey (2001) sought a 'symbiotic relationship between critical social theorizing and critical pedagogic practice' (p. 228), but like others reported that these intentions were often difficult to realise within the scope of a single university unit (Curtner-Smith 2007, Gore 1990, Philpot 2017, Philpot and Smith 2018). This critique raises questions about when and how an invitation to criticality is issued, and what systemic, pedagogic and personal resources are available to support it.

Critical praxis: Invitations to criticality in PETE

From a practical perspective there have been more recent accounts of the specific pedagogical practices PETE educators have drawn on to advocate for both personal and social change. For example, Walton-Fisette and colleagues (2018) describe the impact of 'intentional and explicit' pedagogies associated with the critical project compared with 'incidental and implicit' practices produced through 'teachable moments' in PETE. Amid calls for the need for PETE educators to turn the critical gaze inwards if critical and transformative agendas are to gain any long-term purchase in practice (Fernández-Balboa 2017), others have described the various ways in which invitations to criticality have been, albeit somewhat, successfully issued within their PETE programs. Of those who have claimed to successfully embed aspects of critical pedagogies in their PETE programmes, personal passion, knowledge and commitment to this agenda are often deemed central to the act of translation - while acknowledging its complexity (Walton-Fisette et al. 2018).

In attempting to categorise the pursuit of critical translation, we find ourselves thinking along a continuum where at one end interventions appear to be issued as 'gentle invitations' to think critically, while at the other they are unapologetically disruptive. For example, Garrett (2006), Garrett and Wrench (2011) and Dowling et al. (2015) draw on critical storytelling, reflection and narratives to 'bring to life' various issues of social justice (e.g., gender, race, somatotype) that come to bear on physical education as a curriculum practice in schools. These approaches invite students to 'respond in multiple ways as well as constructing their own knowledge around teaching and learning in physical education' (Garrett and Wrench 2011, p. 239).

In a more experiential and place-based approach to critical disruption, Legge (2010) described the impact that cultural boundary-crossing experiences had for her PETE students when they were required to participate in a situated (or immersive) learning experience in a traditional Mārae (Māori community) context. Legge (2010) explained that the approach required an embodied experience wherein dominant cultural values were confronted as students 'locate[d] their personal identity, cultural differences and understanding of the world alongside the Māori world-view' (p. 89). In somewhat different, but related, experiences others have described the ways in which participatory methodologies, namely the amplification of 'student voice' (Enright and O'Sullivan 2012), and through democratic assessment practices (Lorente-Catalán and Kirk 2014) have advanced the critical project.

At the other end of the continuum we identify some of the more explicit, confronting and disruptive approaches to advancing critical pedagogies. An example here is the use of what Shelley and McCuaig (2018) describe as the implementation of 'pedagogies of discomfort' with second and third year Health and Physical Education students. Here they describe a number of pedagogic techniques strategically designed to move students 'out of their comfort zones, to trouble, disturb or unsettle' (p. 517).

For example, students are required to construct a contemporary dance routine that conveys the ways in which gender and sexuality are socially constructed. The inital dance rehearsals require students to wear full body lycra deliberately designed 'to simulate the sense of ill-ease, exposure and self-consciousness many school students experience in HPE classes' (p. 517). Following this experience the participating students described differing degrees of 'discomfort', though most were more concerned with the act of dancing publically, rather than concern with what they were wearing. Perhaps this can be interpreted as a pedagogic attempt to invoke somatic and sociological perspectives in pursuit of deep critical engagement (Crowdes 2000, Tinning 2016). Of course, the complexity of this work remains forefront in the aspirations of critical PETE pedagogues;

> To push students to this point of dissonance is to walk a paradigmatic and pedagogical tightrope: push too far and students disavow both the message and the messenger, failure to push far enough results in the acceptance and perpetuating of existing beliefs and business as usual. (Shelley and McCuaig 2018, p. 520)

As Tinning (2016) recently argued, 'the mission of the *critical* project' remains as relevant today as it was thirty years ago 'and *criticality* is still a necessary disposition to prosecute the mission' (p. 290, original emphasis). Regardless of the ways in which an invitation to criticality is issued in PETE, we acknowledge that many of these practices remain aimed at provoking personal/ideological change and their impact has been relatively harder to track in wider professional contexts. While there has been some industrious work to create conditions that might support engagement with the critical project within PETE programmes their enduring impact on PETE students is far less secure. That said, there remains an optimism that the pursuit of critical pedagogies in PETE can 'sow fertile seeds' that hopefully cultivate the use of more productive and enabling critical pedagogies in school contexts for the purpose of social change (Gerdin et al. 2018). As we seek to progress the critical project in PETE we are reminded by Evans and Davies (2011) about the need for a certain openness to new knowledge and ways of knowing. In now turning our attention to the posthuman lens, we seek to move beyond an 'eyes wide shut' approach, to recognise 'possibilities that other pespectives and forms of theory and understanding might offer' (Evans and Davies 2011, p. 275).

Post critical theory in PETE: Towards a re-imagined future

In a rapidly changing world in which global mobilities, technological advances and digital communications are disrupting the ways we think and act in almost all aspects of our lives, we need to continually revisit the critical project in PETE to monitor its contemporality. In his book, *The Precariat*, Guy Standing (2011) characterises an emerging world wherein a new class of the vulnerable and insecure are forming around their inability to gain meaningful forms of employment or social engagement. Lacking a secure identity or pathways to personal development and satisfaction through meaningful work and lifestyle, the precariat lack self-esteem and self-worth. No longer understandable through traditional notions of social class, Standing (2011) argues that the precariat are not emerging from postcodes but are recognisable by 'a distinctive bundle of insecurities and… an equally distinctive set of demands' (p. vii). Emerging out of neo-liberal ideas about labour market flexibility, production efficiency and technological advance the emerging precariat lack a coherent occupational identity or a pathway toward one. Having no labour community from which to invoke a sense of solidarity, members of the precariat are rendered voiceless and powerless.

Standing's (2011) depiction of the precariat as an emerging class of socially and economically disadvantaged and disenfranchised is not futuristic. In the contemporary neo-liberal state in which individuals are charged with controlling their own futures and encouraged to actively pursue preferred versions of self-hood, we see young people in higher education at greater rates than ever before. This trend is forged on a social contract that connects secure futures with higher education qualifications. As we have seen through the emergence of the Occupy and Arab Spring movements (see for example Castells 2012), there exists a growing level of resentment and anger that the pathway to employment via university education is far from certain. In the shadows of the so-called global financial crisis tens of thousands of young people spilled on to the streets to voice their disapproval that the social contract they had been offered is now broken. 'Democracy is dead', they chanted. At the heart of this was their lament that the advance of neo-liberalism was disproportionately favouring the ruling elite at the expense of the majority.

Under the slogan, 'we are the 99%', the Occupy movement began in New York in September 2011 and within three weeks like protests had taken place in over 950 cities around the world. Significantly, the protest movement was made up of young people who had university degrees that had yielded significant debt but not led to employment!

During this time of profound global social, cultural, political and economic transformation there are rising concerns around youth risk, enterprise, health and well-being. It is within this context that aspirations associated with the broad suite of social justice will continue to have traction. The increasing need to counter social forces that disengage and disenfranchise (the precariat) has amplified the relevance of sport, recreation and physical activity as redemptive spaces through which to develop meaningful forms of community engagement. In this endeavour critical PETE scholars have an important role to play in fostering the aptitudes and opportunities around which individuals might develop meaningful nodes of community engagement through physical cultures.

In our contemplations of the ongoing progression of the critical project in PETE we are attracted to some of the theoretical tools being postulated around *posthumanism*. At the heart of these is the desire to disrupt agential human-centricity in the pursuit of new subject positions that invite us to think about ourselves differently. Here, the realm of posthuman thinking, such as that done by Katherine Hayles (1999), Donna Haraway (2008), Cary Wolf (2009), Stefan Herbrechter (2013) and Rosi Braidotti (2013), is opening up spaces to contest the exceptionalism of the human condition. Posthuman ethics argue for the value of life forms and practices that exist beyond the control of capitalism and its endless pursuit of profit. Embedded in this is a re-imagining of our relations with each other, and with non-human others, such as animals, machines, systems and environments, that share the planet.

To move forward here we are attracted to Braidotti's extensions of the epistemological and political foundations of post-structuralism for reimagining the human condition and the formation of subjectivity. Amid the rapid rise of bio-technologies and cybernetics wherein the human condition is uncertain, transformative and enhanced the physical condition is more adaptable than ever before. Bio-genetic manipulation, bionics and cybernetics are no longer fantasies of the future (e.g., Oscar Pistorius's participation in the 2012 Summer Olympic Games). Rather than defer to a demise of nostalgic views of the human condition, Braidotti encourages us to embrace the opportunities that lay before us. In this regard posthumanism distances itself from nihilist and apocalyptic standpoints of a technological turn in which the increasing interaction of human and machine is inherent. According to Braidotti:

> I see the posthuman turn as an amazing opportunity to decide together what and who we are capable of becoming, and a unique opportunity for humanity to reinvent itself affirmatively, through creativity and empowering ethical relations, and not only negatively through vulnerability and fear. (2013, p. 195)

Consistent across the decades of criticality in PETE has been the pursuit of contemporary theory and practice so that it can take its place in the big tent of social justice. In line with this, posthuman scholarship invites contemporary PETE scholars to engage with the conditions associated with the 'anthropocene'. Emerging from the sciences of climate change, the anthropocene has attracted increasing interest from the socio-cultural sphere as critical scholarship seeks to understand emerging global challenges (ecological, technological and political) as interconnected, networked manifestations of globalisation (Braidotti 2016). Set within a global economic regime that reveals an ever-widening gap between those that *have* (wealth, access and opportunity) and those that *have not*, the warrant for furthering the critical agenda in PETE is as powerful as ever. The posthuman lens offers new subject positions for PETE scholars from which to enable a more meaningful engagement with contemporary physical culture and the challenges and opportunities that are being ushered in amid the increased intersectionality between man and machine.

> A posthuman theory of the subject emerges, therefore, as an empirical project that aims at experimenting with what contemporary, bio-technologically mediated bodies are capable of doing. (Braidotti 2013, p. 61)

In the journey to progress critical scholarship in PETE posthumanism presents new spaces to contemplate possible futures. The promise, the hope of (re)making a more socially just world, can, we believe, no longer be invested towards the autonomous, choice making, individualized agent/subject. Structure and agency need to be re-assembled in ways that are fit for our times, and for new ways of understanding what it is to be a truly networked organism. At the heart of this is a need to recognise that technology is changing our everyday lives, including the ways we think about and enact our health and wellbeing practices. Our emergence as increasingly networked beings will usher in a range of important social, political and ethical questions. Recognising this are calls to envision new futures and new relationships with self and others (human and non-human) through new engagements with critical theory (Braidotti, 2016). It is here that a critically informed posthuman scholarship might provide:

> the launching pad for sustainable becoming or qualitative transformations of the negativity and the injustices of the present. The future is the virtual unfolding of the affirmative aspect of the present, which honours our obligations to the generations to come. (Braidotti 2016, p. 27)

Note

1. Here we follow Tinning's (2017) argument that transformative pedagogy in PETE can be considered as a 'manifestation of the critical project' (p. 281) due to its alignment with a social justice ethic and a focus on personal change.

References

Ball, S., 2013. *Foucault, Power and Education*. London: Routledge.

Braidotti, R., 2013. *The Posthuman*. Cambridge, UK: Polity Press.

Braidotti, R., 2016. Posthuman Critical Theory. In: Banerji, D. and Paranjape, M. eds. *Critical Posthumansim and Planetary Futures*. New Dehli, India: Springer, 13–32.

Breuing, M., 2009. Teaching for and about critical pedagogy in the post-secondary classroom. *Studies in Social Justice*, 3(2), 247–262.

Breuing, M., 2011. Problematizing Critical Pedagogy. *International Journal of Critical Pedagogy*, 3(3), 2–23.

Cassidy, T., 2000. *Investigating the pedagogical process in physical education teacher education*. PhD dissertation. Deakin University.

Cassidy, T. and Tinning, R., 2004. "Slippage" is not a dirty word: Considering the usefulness of Giddens' notion of knowledgeability in understanding the possibilities for teacher education. *Teaching Education*, 15(2), 175–188.

Castells, M., 2012. *Networks of outrage and hope: Social movements in the internet age*. Cambridge, UK: Polity.

Cliff, K., Wright, J. and Clarke, D., 2009. What does a sociocultural perspective mean in health and physical education? In: Dinan-Thomson, M. ed. *Health and Physical Education: Issues for curriculum in Australia and New Zealand*. Melbourne: Oxford University Press, 165–182.

Crowdes, M., 2000. Embodying sociological imagination: Pedagogical support for linking bodies to minds. *Teaching Sociology*, 28, 28–40.

Curtner-Smith, M., 2007. The impact of a critically orientated physical education teacher education course on pre-service classroom teachers. *Journal of Teaching in Physical Education*, 26(1), 35–56.

Curtner-Smith, M. and Sofo, S., 2004. Influence of a critically oriented methods course and early field experience on preservice teachers' conceptions of teaching. *Sport, Education and Society*, 9(1), 115–142.

Devís-Devís, J., 2006. Socially critical research perspectives in physical education. In: Kirk, D., Macdonald, D. and O'Sullivan, M. eds. *The handbook of physical education*. London: Sage, 37–58.

Dowling, F., Fitzgerald, H. and Flintoff, A. 2015. Narratives from the road to social justice in PETE: Teacher educator perspectives. *Sport, Education and Society*, 20(8), 1029–1047.

Ellsworth, E., 1989. Why doesn't this feel empowering?: Working through the repressive myths of critical pedagogy. *Harvard Educational Review*, 59(3), 297–324.

Evans, J. and Davies, B., 2011. New directions, new questions? Social theory, education and embodiment. *Sport, Education & Society*, 16(3), 263–278.

Felis-Anaya, M., Martos-Garcia, D. and Devís-Devís, J., 2017. Socio-critical research on teaching physical education and physical education teacher education: A systematic review. *European Physical Education Review*, doi:10.1177/1356336X17691215.

Fernández-Balboa, J. M., 1997. Physical education teacher preparation in the modern era: Toward a critical pedagogy. In: Fernández-Balboa, J. M. ed. *Critical postmodernism in human movement, physical education and sport*. Albany: State University of New York Press.

Fernández-Balboa, J. M., 2017. Imploding the boundaries of transformative/critcial pedagogy and research in physical education and sport pedagogy: Looking inward for (self) consciousness/knowledge and transformation. *Sport, Education and Society*, 22(4), 426–441.

Foucault, M., 1980. Truth and Power. *In*: Gordon, C. ed. *Power/knowledge: Selected interviews and other writings 1972–1977 by Michel Foucault*. New York: Pantheon Books, 109–133.

Foucault, M., 2000. Subjectivity and Truth. *In*: Rabinow, P. ed. *Michel Foucault Ethics, Subjectivity and Truth*. London: Penguin, 87–92.

Fyall, G., 2017. Graduating physical education student teachers perceptions of a critically oriented HPE curriculum: (Re)constructing constructivist frameworks in PETE. *Asia-Pacific Journal of Health, Sport and Physical Education*, 8(3), 211–228.

Garrett, R., 2006. Critical storytelling as a teaching strategy in physical education teacher education. *European Physical Education Review*, 12(3), 339–360.

Garrett, R. and Wrench, A., 2011. Negotiating a critical agenda in middle years physical education. *The Australian Educational Researcher*, 38(3), 239–255.

Gerdin, G., Philpot, R. and Smith, W., 2018. It is only an intervention, but it can sow very fertile seeds: graduate physical education teachers' interpretations of critical pedagogy. *Sport, Education and Society*, 23(3), 203–215.

Gore, J., 1990. Pegagogy as text in physical education teacher education: beyond the preferred reading. *In*: Kirk, D. and Tinning, R. eds. *Physical education, curriculum and culture: Critical issues in the contemporary crisis*. London: Falmer Press, 79–108.

Gore, J., 1993. *The struggle for pedagogies: Critical and feminist discourses as regimes of truth*. New York: Routledge.

Habermas, J., 1972. *Knowledge and human interests*. London: Heinemann.

Haraway, D., 2008. *When species meet*. Minneapolis: University of Minnesota Press.

Hayles, K., 1999. *How we became posthuman*. Chicago, USA: University of Chicago.

Herbrechter, S., 2013. *Posthumanism: A critical analysis*. London: Bloomsbury Publishing.

Hickey, C., 2001. "I feel enlightened now, but ...": The limits to the pedagogic translation of critical social discourses in physical education. *Journal of Teaching in Physical Education*, 20(3), 227–246.

Kirk, D. 1986., A Critical Pedagogy for Teacher Education: Toward an Inquiry-Oriented Approach. *Journal of Teaching in Physical Education*, 5(4), 230–246.

Larsson, L., Linnér, S. and Schenker, K., 2016. The doxa of physical education teacher education—set in stone? *European Physical Education Review*, 24(1), 114–130.

Lather, P., 1991. *Feminist Research in Education: Within/Against*. Geelong, Australia: Deakin University Press Monograph Series.

Lather, P., 1998. Critical pedagogy and its complicities: A praxis of stuck places. *Educational Theory*, 48(4), 487–497.

Legge, M., 2010. E noho marae: Transforming learning through direct Maori cultural experience. *In*: Jesson, J., et al. eds. *University teaching reconsidered: Justice, practice, inquiry*. Wellington, New Zealand: Dunmore Publishing, 139–149.

Lorente-Catalán, E. and Kirk, D., 2014. Making the case for democratic assessment practices within a critical pedagogy of physical education teacher education. *European Physical Education Review*, 20(1), 104–119.

Markula, P. and Silk, M., 2011. *Qualitative research for physical culture*. London, UK: Palgrave Macmillan.

Mordal-Moen, K. and Green, K., 2014. Neither shaking nor stirring: a case study of reflexivity in Norwegian physical education teacher education. *Sport, Education and Society*, 19(4), 415–434.

Muros Ruiz, B. and Fernández-Balboa, J.-M., 2005. Physical education teacher educators' personal perspectives regarding their practice of critical pedagogy. *Journal of Teaching in Physical Education*, 24(3), 243–264.

O'Sullivan, M., Siedentop, D. and Locke, L., 1992. Toward collegiality: Competing viewpoints among teacher educators. *Quest*, 44(2), 266–280.

Ovens, A., et al., 2018. How PETE comes to matter in the performance of social justice education. *Physical Education and Sport Pedagogy*, 23(5), 484–496. doi:10.1080/17408989.2018.1470614

Ovens, A. and Tinning, R., 2009. Reflection as situated practice: A memory-work study of lived experience in teacher education. *Teaching and Teacher Education*, 25(8), 1125–1131.

Philpot, R., 2015. Critical pedagogies in PETE: An antipodean perspective. *Journal of Teaching in Physical Education*, 34(2), 316–332.

Philpot, R., 2017. In search of a critical PETE programme. *European Physical Education Review*, 1–17. doi:10.1177/1356336X17703770

Philpot, R. and Smith, W., 2018. Making a different difference: physical education teacher education students' reading of critical PETE program. *Curriculum Studies in Health and Physical Education*, 9(1), 7–21.

Rizvi, F., 2011. Contesting criticality in a scholarship diaspora. *In*: Tinning, R. and Sirna, K. eds. *Education, social justice and the legacy of Deakin University: Reflections of the Deakin diaspora*. Rotterdam, The Netherlands: Sense Publishers, 145–157.

Robinson, D. and Randall, L., eds., 2016. *Social justice in physical education: Critical reflections and pedagogies for change*. Toronto: Canadian Scholars' Press.

Shelley, K. and McCuaig, L., 2018. Close encounters with critical pedagogy in socio-critically informed health education teacher education. *Physical Education and Sport Pedagogy*, 23(5), 510–523.

Smyth, J., 2011. *Critical pedagogy for social justice*. New York: Continuum International Publishing Group.

Standing, G., 2011. *The Precariat: The new dangerous class*. London: Bloomsbury Academic.

Tinning, R., 1990. *Ideology in Physical Education: Opening Pandora's Box*. Geelong, Australia: Deakin University Press.

Tinning, R., 2002. Toward a "modest pedagogy": Reflections on the problematics of critical pedagogy. *Quest*, 54(3), 224–240.

Tinning, R., 2016. Transformative pedagogies and physical education. *In*: Ennis, C. ed. *Routledge handbook of Physical Education pedagogies*. London: Routledge, 281–294.

Ukpokodu, O., 2009. The practice of transformative pedagogy. *Journal of Excellence in College Teaching*, 20(2), 32–67.

Walton-Fisette, J. L., et al., 2018. Implicit and explicit pedagogical practices related to sociocultural issues and social justice in physical education teacher education programs. *Physical Education and Sport Pedagogy*, 23(5), 497–509. doi:10.1080/17408989.2018.1470612

Wink, J., 2011. *Critical pedagogy: Notes from the real world*. Boston: Pearson.

Wolf, C., 2009. *What is posthumanism?* Minneapolis: University of Minnesota Press.

Wright, J., 2004. Critical inquiry and problem-solving in physical education. *In*: Wright, J., Macdonald, D. and Burrows, L. eds. *Critical inquiry and problem-solving in physical education*. London: Routledge, 1–16.

Chapter 12

Gender in Physical Education: A case for performative pedagogy?

Håkan Larsson

'What's going on in the gym?'

As I approach the gym, I can hear the sounds of bouncing balls and laughter. Some fifteen minutes ago, I opened up the gym, including the doors to the tool space and the music equipment, to a group of physical education student teachers. Then I left, inviting the students to take possession of the space. I have started this lesson on gender in physical education this way for many years now. The first time it was merely haphazard, since I had forgotten the student attendance list on my desk and had to go back to fetch it. However, early on I realised that this beginning suited my purpose of the lesson very well. Indeed, the next five minutes are probably the most important ones during the whole lesson.

It is now nearly twenty years ago since I decided that 'sitting-talking-seminars' in regular classrooms did not evoke the critical discussions that I was looking for. In fact, these discussions often turned into me trying to persuade the students that physical education practice was replete with gender patterns of behaviour. We rarely ever came to the point where we could discuss what these patterns meant and if they were worth challenging, let alone *how* to challenge them. The first time me and my colleague Birgitta Fagrell decided to 'go practical', back in 1999, we did not think much about what the literature said about how any particular strand of critical pedagogy could offer us insights into how the 'practical seminars' could be arranged. Again, we were pretty much driven by chance. However, since then I have engaged gradually more extensively with critical pedagogy literature (see, e.g., Giroux and McLaren 1989, Gore 1993, Kumashiro 2004, 2015) and, other mainly poststructuralist and posthumanist literature on gender (Barad 2012, Butler 1990, 1993, Foucault 1990). This has enabled me to reflect more critically on what is going on during the 'practical seminars' and how they can facilitate opportunities for discovery as well as critical reflexivity and, importantly, a way forward in terms of pedagogy.

Re-entering the gym, I immediately observe about fifteen students who are involved in a football-like game in the middle of the gym. Most of them are young men and two are young women. These students are the ones who are laughing and shouting out expressions of joy as they dribble and pass the ball between themselves. Along one of the gym's sides the rest of the class, about fifteen students, mainly female and a few male ones, are standing or sitting on the typical low gym benches. They are not entirely silent, but they talk in a regular tone of conversation. I am standing still for a while, silently imbibing the moment. Few of the students take notice of me. At least not the ones who are involved in the game. After a while I raise my voice:

- Hello everyone! Can you just stand still, please, and have a look around!

The students are looking around, some of them a bit furtively. Maybe they are the ones who would dispute that physical education is permeated by gender patterns, I conspire. Anyway, I get a strong feeling that most of the students immediately 'get' that I am looking for something special.

Interestingly, over the nearly twenty years that I have had this kind of lesson, I cannot remember one single time when it played out differently. The pattern is extremely strong. Indeed the students are hardly 'free' to do just anything, but at least they have the chance to use a range of different equipment, and they do have some possibilities to use the music equipment and, perhaps, do some dance moves. A number of records are stored beside the CD-player, and nowadays the students can easily connect their phones to the player. But, no! It is always football, which by the way is the most popular sport in Sweden, in fact both for young men and women. However, about 75 per cent of the players are male, and when played spontaneously in schools, the share of boys is even greater (see also Jonasson 2010).

- This is interesting, I remark. What does the football playing signify? Was there a deliberation about it? Were other activities considered? Or was football the given option?

I organise the class into small groups to discuss these questions. After a while I get curious, so I approach one of the groups. Apparently there was no deliberation. Football was not really 'chosen', but taken up spontaneously by those who came to the gym first. And those who arrived later silently accepted the situation. 'This is the way I have always experienced coming into gyms,' says one student, who were among the ones standing along the wall. 'It's sooo tiresome! It's always football!' This is interesting, I think, it is just as if this student never had the chance before to address the issue. The practice has become so normalised among the students, and both the football-playing students and the ones hanging out along the walls seem silently to have come to experience this situation as 'just the way it is'. I am glad that other students have the opportunity to listen to someone—who is not me—who can articulate how unfair this situation can be experienced. My silent ruminations over what is going on in the gym continue. 'That's the crux of the matter, isn't it? There are so many things happening in the gym, or during PE, which are taken to be just the way they are. Particularly when it comes to gender! One can wonder where these patterns came from. And (how) is it possible to challenge them?'

Gender in physical education

What is stated in this section is primarily about Swedish physical education. To what extent can the Swedish situation be transferable to the situation in other countries? My simple answer is, to some extent. Indeed, neither the historical development, nor the contemporary national curriculum and practice is identical to other countries. However, based on my readings of available research on the issue, my conclusion is that the situation in a range of other countries is comparatively similar (see, e.g., Berg and Lahelma 2010, Brown 2005, Kirk 1998, lisahunter 2017, Penney 2002, van Amsterdam et al. 2012). Thus, my conclusion is that the case of Sweden—and my approach based on the appraisal of the situation in this country—is to some extent transferable to other countries.

Physical education was introduced into Swedish schools during the 19th century, but until 1927 only boys were allowed into the state-run grammar schools. Beginning in 1842, however, both boys and girls were allowed into elementary schools. Even though elementary schools were for both girls and boys, in physical education the genders were separated, at least from the year they turned twelve (Lundquist Wanneberg 2004). Pia Lundquist Wanneberg (2004) shows that up until 1962, physical education in schools was about educating not only *two different genders*, but also *two different classes of people*; on the one hand workers and farmers (elementary schools), and on the other hand professionals and government officials (grammar schools). Thus, policy guidelines for physical education in schools were differentiated not only by gender, but also by class. In grammar schools, sports, which were in the main taken to foster individual character and leadership, dominated the curriculum, while in elementary schools, the curriculum was dominated by Swedish gymnastics, which was taken to foster obedient and effective bodies on a collective level (Lundquist Wanneberg 2004, see also Kirk 1998).

The abandonment of the parallel school system in the mid-1900s and the introduction of a nine-year compulsory comprehensive school followed by a three-year voluntary upper secondary school meant that the above mentioned differentiations disappeared—at least at a policy level. Co-education in physical education was not introduced until 1981, when the Swedish National School Board (1981) held that co-education was introduced "as a means to iron out gender roles" (p. 110). Later, in a school reform in 1994, schools and teachers were assigned with the task to "counteract traditional gender roles" [Swedish National Agency of Education (SNAE), 1994, p. 4; a formulation that was subsequently, in 2011, changed to "counteract traditional patterns", SNAE, 2011, p. 10]. Thus, what used to be seen as purposeful because of the differences between girls and boys, and the different roles that were assigned to girls and boys, that is, separate physical education for girls and boys, was now seen as an obstacle to gender equality. 'Why should girls be withheld a content that boys had access to?' (e.g., games and fitness training) seemed to be the underpinning question. Incidentally, however, the corresponding question—'Why should boys be withheld a content that girls had access to?' (e.g., dance and other 'aesthetic' movement activities) was unheard of. This is highly significant for what happened in the years to come.

In a series of studies, Barbro Carli (2004), myself (Larsson and colleagues 2009, 2011, 2014, SNAE 2010) and others (e.g., Lundvall 2016, Olofsson 2005, 2007) have investigated the power related effects of the introduction of co-education in Swedish physical education. This research reveals that, in essence, co-education has not in itself managed to change gender patterns and stereotypes. Sure enough, the possibilities of transgressing traditional gender boundaries have increased— and some of the students take this opportunity to queer physical education (see, e.g., Larsson et al. 2014). Overall, however, much of the traditional gender patterns, like the one in the introductory scene above, as well as ideas about boys as competitive and boisterous, and girls as calm and cautious, remain largely the same. My understanding of this situation is that while the social organisation of society has been characterised by a loosening of social gender segregation, gender difference is instead to a greater extent internalised in terms of gender identities, sometimes with reference to 'nature' (Foucault 1990, see also Braidotti 2007).

In 1991, Swedish educationalist Claes Annerstedt termed the post–World War II era—the decades between the 1950s and the 1970s—as 'the physiological phase' of Swedish physical education. This meant that physiological knowledge became one important constitutive part of the framing of physical education in schools. Becoming physical education teachers were introduced to physiological knowledge as the key pedagogical instrument when designing physical education lessons, including the idea of moderate to vigorous physical activity at least three times a week for about 40 minutes until the students become sweaty. This idea of 'physical education-as-activating students' is still very strong (Quennerstedt 2006). In addition, I have shown how this physiological knowledge, which is largely embedded in essentialist discourses on gender, simultaneously came to be one important constitutive part of how gender difference was naturalised (Larsson 2013). For instance, the propensity to construct the category male as the physiological norm (1.0), while the category female is a physiologically 'lesser version' of male has contributed to form taken for granted conceptions about 'normal' girls and boys in physical education. One consequence of this development is that present-day physical education teachers may find it difficult to make sense of the national curriculum's assignment to "counteract traditional gender patterns" (SNAE 2011, p. 8), which is embedded within constructionist discourses on gender. Some teachers, who negotiate the assignment within essentialist discourses, even take it to mean 'counteracting gender differences', which is incomprehensible. In this way assignments about equal opportunities that are formulated in policy documents that are based on constructionist ideas are obscured when introduced to a domain where essentialist reasoning dominates.

Research into physical education and sport pedagogy started in Sweden during the 1970s, but it was not until well into the 1990s and 2000s that any form of norm critical perspectives managed to achieve some sort of commonplace within physical education teacher education. And these perspectives have mainly fought their way into the area of general education within teacher education, but not, or at least not systematically, into the subject specific areas of physical education teacher education (Larsson 2009). In my understanding, this is, at least partly, because the division between general education and subject specific education is typically also imbued with a theory (= sitting, talking)/practice (= moving) divide. My own experimenting with 'practical' seminars using norm critical perspectives of physical education teaching is still an exception. But why is it so important that these perspectives are integrated into subject specific and 'practical' parts of physical education teacher education?

The challenge of changing the practice?

The decision to arrange norm critical 'practical seminars' with movement activities, was based on an experienced dissatisfaction with conventional seminars. The dissatisfaction centred around two things. Firstly, many of the students did not even acknowledge that there were any gender patterns in physical education, let alone that these patterns were problematic and could signify inequalities and exclusion. Inequality, some emphasised, was something of the past. This meant that we seldom came as far as discussing what could be done about inequalities. Secondly, after years of trial and error practise, I managed to help students become reasonably able to *analyse* physical education practice with a particular focus on gender patterns and inequalities and exclusions. However, it remained difficult for students—as well as myself—to use their insights pedagogically, as a means to change the practice in ways that it could become more inclusive and equitable. I realised that I knew a lot about 'what is' and why, and less about 'what could be'.

Poststructuralist theorising has given me valuable tools to think with. Indeed, I have long found the work of Michel Foucault (1990) and Judith Butler (1990, 1993) useful to think with when analysing and understanding physical education practice. However, sometimes they seem to have left me in a situation where there is so much focus on 'what is bad', or maybe not necessarily bad but potentially dangerous (Foucault, 1991), that it is hard to find ways forward. Thus, it was with quite some relief to discover what Sasha Roseneil (2011) writes about critical ways of theorising: "What's missing are readings that mediate between what's wrong with the world and what can be and already is counter-normative and just plain ok" (p. 129). In a sense, this focus on 'what can be and already is counter-normative and just plain ok' resembles what Foucault (1986) called *heterotopia*. Unlike utopia, which is an idealised, hypothetical and abstract situation, heterotopias exist in the real world as counter-sites, where given meanings and identities are challenged. Together with colleagues, I have used this notion in analyses of physical education practice in another publication (Larsson et al. 2014). Such analyses has offered me ways of understanding educational practice where resistance is already present. It does not necessarily have to be provoked or 'produced'. For a teacher, it is rather about becoming able to grasp the moment, acting on situations that will, inevitably, occur; situations in the gym where given meanings and identities are challenged.

Apparently, Canadian sport sociologist Pirkko Markula has grappled with similar issues. In a paper about *Affect[ing] Bodies*, Markula (2008) crafts a critical pedagogical approach to changing the current subjectivation of femininity in fitness training. She calls this approach a 'performative pedagogy'. Building up to this approach is a dissatisfaction with what norm critical perspectives have offered so far in terms of being able to facilitate change in educational practice. Markula cites physical educationalist Richard Tinning who holds that "despite 'what we know as a result of our theorising and research about how certain cultural practices contribute to limited, restricted or oppressive bodily practices, we have seen little significant systemic change in such practices'" (Tinning 2004, p. 219, cited in Markula 2008, p. 388). "Tinning concludes," Markula continues, "that while critical pedagogy provided a 'sociologically' grounded vocabulary to talk about injustice, it might have created students with socially aware minds that are, nevertheless, detached from their bodies" (p. 389).

Similarly, Markula cites Probyn (2004), who contends that critical pedagogy offers "[f]ine words, but what could they possibly mean—to students, to teachers, to the administrators of pedagogical excellence?" (Probyn 2004, p. 25, cited in Markula 2008, p. 392). This critique of a disembodied version of critical pedagogy spurred Markula to design a 'practical' fitness class for women based on a performative pedagogy of Pilates where the change potential is not only based on rational analysis 'from the side-lines', but is built in the movements and in the ways that the movements are framed narratively by the instructor. Such an approach seems to me to be based quite much on exploration and discovery, as well as on ambiguity and an openness for the uncertain, that is that the meaning of moving is never—and can never be—fixed, but has to be individually discovered and socially negotiated there and then and is always open to change. In this ambiguity lies also the change potential. The question is, however, how this approach 'fits' contemporary physical education practice?

Physical education practice: Certainty or ambiguity

Much of the literature on physical education paints a picture of a practice where focus is on control, management and certainty (see, e.g., Gard and Wright 2001, Kirk 2010). Arguably, this focus can be deduced to an ambition among physical education teachers to have the students busy, happy and good for most of the time (Placek 1983, see also Barker and Annerstedt 2016, Larsson and Redelius 2008, Öhman and Quennerstedt 2008). This is not strange considering the history of the subject as first and foremost an opportunity to build character and fitness among children and young people. This version of 'physical education-as-activating students', where physical activity is the means for assumed benefits is certainly strong in contemporary societies—perhaps even gaining in strength. However, in Sweden it is challenged by a version of 'physical education-as-embodied exploration' (Barker, Bergentoft and Nyberg 2017, see also Nyberg and Larsson 2014, Barker et al. 2017); a version that I believe is gaining in interest in Scandinavia more broadly as well as in Australia, and possibly other countries.

Physical education-as-embodied exploration emphasises what there is to explore, discover, practise and *know* in moving. Moving is not primarily seen as a means for other 'benefits'. However, participation can, of course, have such beneficial effects—but they are not to be taken for granted. Rather, moving itself is key, and embodied exploration can facilitate a greater understanding for what moving means 'to me', and what it means to be able to participate in movement culture, as well as what it takes to change the practice (Nyberg 2014, see also Barker et al. 2017). Up until now, however, the possibilities to explore cultural norms, including gender norms, has not been emphasised in this cited work. It is my contention that physical education as embodied exploration is appropriate in relation to a performative pedagogy as it is outlined by Markula (2008; although her focus is fitness training rather than physical education). Embodied exploration might be a way to conceptualise the Swedish national curriculum's assignment for elementary schools and teachers to 'counteract gender patterns'.

Embodied exploration could then be about teachers and students collaboratively exploring what gender norms are governing participation in different movement activities and situations, and how these norms—possibly—could be changed. It could also be about offering students the possibilities to suggest movements and activities that may point in other directions in relation to the majoritarian. This way of following new 'lines of flight' (Deleuze and Guattari 1987) rather than returning back to 'safe' molar lines of conventional and stable social identities such as gender, class, race, and sexuality is prominent in Pirkko Markula's attempts to fashion a *performative pedagogy*.

Physical education as performative pedagogy of embodied exploration

Markula (2008) draws extensively on the work of scholars such as Deleuze and Guattari, Probyn, and Albrecht-Crane and Daryl Slack, and in particular on their notion about *what a body can do*:

> As the body has unique ability to change the limiting molar identities, we should celebrate the actual moving body, not only to limit our praxis to theoretical constructions aimed at critical awareness. While critique is an important first step, to actually change what the body currently is, a public intellectual must actively engage with physically active bodies. (Markula 2008, p. 399)

This focus on what bodies can do is an explicit answer to the critical evaluation, offered by Tinning, Probyn and others, that a physical education teacher:

> cannot rely on writing theoretical texts in order to create critical aware-
> ness of molar lines. Instead she needs to actively think what the bodies can
> do to create change. [She] must enter into affective relationships with other
> bodies by teaching classes, giving talks, or writing. ... while most academ-
> ics, including scholars of physical activity, might consider an engagement in
> physical activity not worthy of their theoretical sophistication, I believe, it is
> necessary, particularly for scholars of physical cultural studies, not to ignore
> the powerful impact of a body's affect. As moving is what the body does, we
> should actively embrace this possibility to create change through "critical"
> movement practices. This should not mean reverting back to "all practice,"
> but should translate into theoretically informed ways to tap into the body's
> affectivity. (Markula 2008, p. 399)

In this work, Deleuze and Guattari's concept of 'lines of flight' that can mutate the molar—conventional binary categories like nature/culture, male/female and body/mind, has been of great importance. Lines of flight are deterritorialisations in the sense that they subvert binaries; a line of flight "branches out and produces multiple series and rhizomic connections" (Deleuze and Guattari 1987, p. 15). In order to potentially move physical culture studies to examine what the body can do to create social change in this way, Markula sought to identify the main molar lines, because her ambition was to "activate lines of flight, that while starting as individual desire, might create a 'quantum flow' that flees the segmentarity of the molar lines to 'decode,' deterritorialize and draw new, mutated lines" (Markula 2008, p. 403).

Practically, this approach meant a "careful focus on the content of each exer-cise session" (Markula 2008, p. 401). Markula broke down each exercise by think-ing what it 'does' (ibid.). Further, she followed Deleuze and Guattari's advice of not to use a 'sledgehammer', that is, "not to break the molar lines of identity too suddenly as that will most likely lead to rapid reterritorialization by other molar lines." Therefore, she "chose not to openly critique the molar femininity or negate the desire the participants expressed toward obtaining the ideal body shape." (Markula 2008, p. 400). In the last section of this chapter, I will try to frame my own efforts within this framework.

What's going on in the gym—now?

Having discussed the opening scene in the gym for a while, I ask the students to prepare for a round of dodgeball. Some of the students look surprised at me, while others smile a bit cleverly. There are about thirty of them, and I divide them into two teams. I have no other instructions than making sure that they know the rules. There is some deliberation over whether any parts of the body are 'free'.

The game gets going, and after maybe five minutes, one of the teams has knocked out everyone in the other team. I ask: "Was there any gender in this game?" No-one says anything. After maybe thirty seconds, one of the students gingerly says: "Nooo ...?" I quickly divide the group into three teams, ten students in each team. They play three more rounds of dodgeball, where one team is standing at the side watching the teams playing. After these rounds, the students have a lot to tell each other about who wants to knock out who, how hard the ball is thrown, what body parts are aimed at, and so on. We discuss this pattern in small groups for several minutes. It seems as if a lot of the students knew all along what the patterns were about, for instance:

- who is 'in' and who is not, i.e., who is 'worthwhile' to knock out;
- who is participating 'for real' and who is not, i.e., who is participating because they want to participate and who is participating because they must;
- who 'can take it' and who cannot, i.e., who is prepared to be hit hard by the ball, and consequently also prepared to hit someone else hard—and maybe, accidentally or not, hit someone in the head.

And all these things come up without much time for reflection. 'They can't have discovered this for the first time now', I muse. 'I'm sure they've noticed it before, but arguably there has never been room for critical deliberation until now'.

After the initial rounds of dodgeball, we do some gymnastic floor exercises, and after that some dancing. Quite early on in the process, I realised that this approach could facilitate critical reflections and discussions about the power of—mainly implicit—gender and other social norms in the gym. However, these 'practical seminars' have been somewhat mixed with success. Some groups just do not have much to discuss, which is pedagogically troublesome for me. I painstakingly refrain from telling the students what I see, or what gender patterns are 'otherwise', for instance as stated by research, permeating the practice. Because then it would not be exploration and discovery; then it would not differ much from my conventional lectures. Possibly, my sudden intervention would also work as a sledgehammer, where the molar lines of identity are broken too suddenly, which could lead to rapid reterritorialization by other molar lines (see Markula 2008, p. 400).

The selection of exercises, and how the seminar is arranged, have developed over the years. Gradually, I have realised what activities 'work' in terms of evoking affect and deliberation among the students. I have also tried to develop my way of inquiring into the students' experiences and how they view what we are doing. In this work, I have had much use of poststructuralist research about social issues (gender, class, ethnicity—and over the last ten or fifteen years or so, also intersectionality). Recently, however, and particularly since I started to engage with posthumanist literature and Markula's suggestion to "actively embrace this possibility to create change through 'critical' movement practices" (Markula 2008, p. 399), I have realised that there is still much to develop in my practical seminar.

My pedagogy is certainly based on the importance of evoking affect among the students, but at the same time this affect, as well as the careful selection of movement exercises, are still basically functioning as a basis for critical reflection and rational deliberation. There is still room for developing critical movement practices with a potential to 'immediately', as it were, create change, not as a result of rational deliberation.

In fact, in my view, one or two of the exercises may have included this potential. As a last exercise, I ask the students to pair up two and two. I put on a slow melody (typically Procul Harum's 'A Whiter Shade of Pale'), and ask the students to dance slowly to this music. Now, some of the pairs are same sex, while others are mixed, so I continue until every student has had the chance to dance both same sex and mixed sex. Without much deliberation, I ask the students to figure out how they hold their dance partner; arms over the shoulders or around the waist. I then ask them to 'do the opposite'. Interestingly, when male and female students dance with each other, there is seldom deliberation about how to hold each other. The female student typically places her arms on the male student's shoulder, while he holds his arms around her waist. Having them hold each other in the 'opposite' way creates a marvelled situation where some of the students contemplate with how to accommodate to this queer situation. Same-sex dancing, however, often includes this kind of deliberation, simply because quite a few of the students are unaccustomed to the practice.

As a final exercise, before we end the seminar, I ask the students to greet each other warmly. Most of them choose to hug each other. Some of them stroke their hands over the other person's back, while others pat the other person's back, some quite hard even. Further others, greet each other in a way where they clap'n'grab one of their hands, while simultaneously patting the other hand on the other person's back. As soon as this pattern is established, I ask the students to 'do it differently':

> If you stroke, then pat; if you pat, then stroke; if you don't usually 'just' shake hands, then do that; and if you don't usually do the clap'n'grab-pat-the-back greeting, then try it!

References

Annerstedt, C., 1991. *Idrottslärarna och idrottsämnet. utveckling, mål, kompetens: ett didaktiskt perspektiv.* PhD diss., University of Gothenburg.

Barad, K., 2012. Nature's Queer Performativity. *Kvinder, Køn og Forskning,* 1–2: 25–53.

Barker, D., Aggerholm, K., Standahl, Ø., and Larsson, H., 2017. Developing the practising model in physical education: An expository outline focusing on movement capability. *Physical Education and Sport Pedagogy,* iFirst: doi.org/10.1080/17408989.2017.1371685.

Barker, D., and Annerstedt, C., 2016. Managing physical education lessons: an interactional approach. *Sport, Education and Society,* 21(6): 924–944.

Barker, D., Nyberg, G., and Bergentoft, H., 2017. What would physical educators know about movement education? A review of literature, 2006–2016. *Quest*, iFirst: doi.org/10.1080/00336297.2016.1268180.

Berg, P., and Lahelma, E., 2010. Gendering processes in the field of Physical Education. *Gender and Education*, 22(1): 31–46.

Braidotti, R., 2007. Feminist epistemology after postmodernism: Critiquing science, technology and globalization. *Interdisciplinary Science Reviews*, 32(1): 65–74.

Brown, D., 2005. An economy of gendered practices? Learning to teach Physical Education from the perspective of Pierre Bourdieu's embodied sociology. *Sport, Education and Society*, 10(1): 3–23.

Butler, J., 1990. *Gender trouble: Feminism and the subversion of identity.* New York: Routledge.

Butler, J., 1993. *Bodies that matter. On the discursive limits of "sex".* New York: Routledge.

Carli, B., 2004. *The making and breaking of a female culture. The history of Swedish physical education "in a different voice".* PhD diss., University of Gothenburg.

Deleuze, G., and Guattari, F., 1987. *A thousand plateaus. Capitalism and schizophrenia.* Minneapolis: University of Minnesota Press.

Foucault, M., 1990. *The history of sexuality.* Vol. 1: *The will to knowledge.* Harmondsworth: Penguin.

Foucault, M., 1991. On the genealogy of ethics: An overview of work in progress', interview with Michel Foucault, in P. Rabinow, ed., *The Foucault Reader.* London: Penguin, 340–372.

Gard, M., and Wright, J., 2001. Managing uncertainty: Obesity discourses and Physical Education in a risk society. *Studies in Philosophy of Education*, 20(6): 535–549.

Giroux, H. A., and McLaren, P., 1989. *Critical pedagogy, the state and cultural struggle.* Albany: State University of New York Press.

Gore, J., 1993. *The struggle for pedagogies. Critical and feminist discourses as regimes of truth.* New York: Routledge.

Jonasson, K., 2010. *Klungan och barndomens sociala rum. Socialt gränsarbete och figurationer i rastfotbollen.* PHD. diss., Malmö University.

Kirk, D., 1998. *Schooling bodies. School practice and public discourse.* Leicester: Leicester University Press.

Kirk, D., 2010. *Physical education futures.* London: Routledge.

Kumashiro, K., 2004. Uncertain beginnings. *Theory Into Practice*, 43(2): 111–115.

Kumashiro, K., 2015. *Against common sense. Teaching and learning toward social justice.* New York: Routledge.

Larsson, H., 2013. Sport physiology research and governing gender in sport—a power–knowledge relation? *Sport, Education and Society*, 18(3): 334–348.

Larsson, H., Fagrell, B., and Redelius, K., 2009. Queering physical education: Between benevolence towards girls and a tribute to masculinity. *Physical Education and Sport Pedagogy*, 14(1): 1–17.

Larsson, H., Quennerstedt, M., and Öhman, M., 2014. Heterotopias in physical education: Towards a queer pedagogy? *Gender and Education*, 26(2): 135–150.

Larsson, H., and Redelius, K., 2008. Swedish Physical Education Research Questioned—Current situation and future directions. *Physical Education and Sport Pedagogy*, 13(4): 381–398.

Larsson, H., Redelius, K., and Fagrell, B., 2011. Moving (in) the heterosexual matrix: On heteronormativity in secondary school physical education. *Physical Education and Sport Pedagogy*, 16(1): 67–81.

Larsson, L., 2009. *Idrott—och helst lite mera idrott. Idrottslärarstudenters möte med utbildningen.* PhD diss., Stockholm University.

lisahunter, 2017. What a queer space is HPE, or is it yet? Queer theory, sexualities and pedagogy. *Sport, Education and Society*, iFirst, 10.1080/13573322.2017.1302416.

Lundquist Wanneberg, P., 2004. *Kroppens medborgarfostran. Kropp, klass och genus i skolans fysiska fostran 1919–1962.* PhD diss., Stockholm University.

Lundvall, S., 2016. Approaching a gender neutral PE-culture? An exploration of the phase of a divergent PE-culture. *Sport in Society*, 19(5): 640–652.

Markula, P., 2008. Affect[ing] Bodies. Performative Pedagogy of Pilates. *International Review of Qualitative Research*, 1(3): 381–408.

Nyberg, G., 2014. *Ways of knowing in ways of moving. A study of the meaning of capability to move.* PhD diss. Stockholm University.

Nyberg, G. and Larsson, H., 2014. Exploring 'what' to learn in physical education. *Physical Education and Sport Pedagogy*, 19(2): 123–135.

Öhman, M., and Quennerstedt, M., 2008. Feel good—be good: Subject content and governing processes in physical education. *Physical Education and Sport Pedagogy*, 13(4): 365–379.

Olofsson, E., 2005. The discursive construction of gender in physical education in Sweden, 1945–2003: Is meeting the learner's needs tantamount to meeting the market's needs? *European Physical Education Review*, 11(3): 219–238.

Olofsson, E., 2007. The Swedish sports movement and the PE teacher 1940–2003: From supporter to challenger. *Scandinavian Journal of Educational Research*, 51(2): 163–183.

Penney, D., ed., 2002. *Gender and physical education: Contemporary issues and future directions.* London: Routledge.

Placek, J., 1983. Conceptions of success in teaching: Busy, happy, and good?. In T. Templin, and J. Olson, eds. *Teaching in Physical Education*. Champaign, IL: Human Kinetics, 46–56.

Quennerstedt, M., 2006. *Att lära sig hälsa*. PhD diss., Örebro University.

Roseneil, S., 2011. Criticality, not paranoia: A generative register for feminist social research. *NORA – Nordic Journal of Feminist and Gender Research*, 19: 124–131.

SNAE, 1994. *Curriculum for the compulsory school system*. Stockholm: Swedish National Agency of Education.

SNAE, 2011. *Curriculum for the compulsory school, preschool class and the recreation centre, 2011*. Stockholm: Swedish National Agency of Education.

SNAE, 2010. *På pojkarnas planhalva. Ämnet idrott och hälsa ur ett jämställdhets-och likvärdighetsperspektiv*. Stockholm: Swedish National Agency of Education.

Swedish National School Board, 1981. *Författningssamling* (National Educational Statutes). Stockholm: Atlas.

van Amsterdam, N., et al., 2012. 'It's just the way it is …' or not? How Physical Education teachers categorise and normalise differences. *Gender and Education*, 24(7): 783–798.

Critical health examinations in education and other socio-cultural contexts

Chapter 13

Schools and health:
An argument against the tide

Carolyn Pluim and Michael Gard

Introduction

The purpose of this chapter is to problematize the state of affairs that is generally taken for granted with regard to school health policy making. By and large the idea that schools are an appropriate and efficacious place in which to prosecute health policy goals seems uncontroversial and strikingly simple. In much of the empirical literature on school health policy there tends to be a pervasive 'common-sense' or 'feel good' assumption that virtually any societal dilemma can and should be addressed and remedied in schools–obesity, drugs, smoking, violence, drinking, to name a few (Gard and Pluim 2014). At the same time, school health interventions have often become apparatuses of calculated cultural, political, financial, and ideological motivations used to shape society. A definitive and exhaustive account of why schools have and continue to be involved in public health agendas is probably impossible and beyond the scope of this chapter. Our proposition here is that we can learn a great deal by following the knowledge claims and motivations that have sustained and even undermined school-based health interventions in different places and at different times. In this chapter we focus our analysis on the policy rollout of two popular national school health interventions in American schools: anti-drug education and the Healthy Hunger-Free Kids Act (HHFKA) of 2010.

We chose these two narratives because we believe that, in their own way, they are powerfully emblematic of our central interest: the complex and problematic ways in which school health policies have been and continue to be used in schools. In the case of anti-drug education our analysis will reveal that while the 'performance' of health policy making and its enactment were often presented as convenient, in the best interest of young people, and apolitical, little attention was given to the logistics of implementation, issues of efficacy, or the ancillary personal beneficiaries of the policy. In this case it seems as though saddling schools with public health responsibilities was born less out of a careful assessment of the issue at hand, and more a matter of expediency and opportunism. Our second narrative considers the ratification, implementation, and more recent rollback of the HHFKA. This analysis reveals an analogous policy narrative and exposes the shortcomings of the current policy making environment. The narrative highlights the possibilities of establishing a more robust and democratic policy process at the same time it describes those entities that seek to undermine the construction of this. As Mintrom (2001, p. 617) suggests, "[i]n a society where market forms of organization are pervasive and democratic forms appear increasingly constrained or under threat, looking for democratic potentials in reform efforts is important, both as an exercise in meaningful theory construction and as an approach to real-world policy analysis."

Theoretically, we approach our analysis from a Foucauldian perspective. Foucault problematizes the conventional belief that knowledge is equated with power and looks for, "forms of power in how people effect knowledge to intervene in social affairs" (Popkewitz and Brennan 1998, p. 16). For Popkewitz and Brennan (pp. 16–18), Foucault's concept of power gives attention to its productive capacities, such as how power works through individual actions, institutional practices, and the "discourses of daily life." Yet all forms of power and/or knowledge are not equal. In most social contexts, particular forms of knowledge and knowledge creation will be seen as more trustworthy than others. This relationship might then confer degrees of status on different practices, people and institutions. Understood this way, knowledge is never socially neutral and so it is possible to think of knowledge and its production as a kind of economy; the power/knowledge nexus becomes a crucial engine for producing the conditions of social life and driving change. Because relations of power are by and large concealed, overt coercion is largely avoided and thus methods of provocation are often obscured (Wilson 2001). This is certainly not to think in deterministic terms but rather to propose a method for studying school policy and the practices and subjects that shape it. That is, for schools to exist and operate, highly contingent decisions about the relative value of different bodies of knowledge (and the interests they serve) must be made to inform policy. Throughout history this has often mean that schools will, for complex reasons, be the focus of both rhetoric and policies that they are often relatively powerless to resist (Gard and Pluim 2014).

Using this as our frame, we acknowledge that policy making is more complex and contested than often depicted and not a purely meritocratic struggle in which the most compelling ideas always triumph. Because of this there is value in carefully mapping the political, economic, cultural, and institutional powers that are involved in the creation of various school-based health imperatives and the value propositions that give rise to them. Such a mapping helps to shed light on the power/knowledge nexus and is consistent with Rose (1999, p. 58) when he argues for inquiry to "question and complicate, that which forms the very groundwork of the present." Or, as Troyna (1994, p. 71) has written, it is a form of inquiry driven by a "conviction that 'things', especially policy discourse, must be pulled apart" in an effort to determine whose interests they serve … and determine "'what is really going on? … and 'how come?'"

Methodologically, we drew on data collected from a range of sources such as academic commentary, media stories, government and funding body reports, press releases, policy documents, and other relevant artefacts. Our analysis of transcripts and documents attended to the existence of narratives as these are located within national contexts and discourses on the topic. Texts were analyzed for the surfacing of themes and ideas. Specifically, the following questions guided our data collection: Who and what groups proposed health programs in schools and for what purposes (stated or otherwise)? Who were the primary targets of these health reforms? Who or what groups stood to benefit from enacting various policies and practices? In answering these questions this chapter provides a contextual foreground for questioning and understanding how the present relationship between schools and public health has "come to be."

Ideological politics and the "war on drugs"

> I've always thought of September as a special month, a time when we bundle our children off to school, to the warmth of an environment in which they could fulfill the promise and hope in those restless minds. But so much has happened over these last years, so much to shake the foundations of all that we know and all that we believe in. Today, there's a drug and alcohol abuse epidemic in this country, and no one is safe from it—not you, not me, and certainly not our children, because this epidemic has their names written on it.
>
> —Nancy Reagan, September 14, 1986

Having already announced a "war on drugs" in 1982, Nancy Reagan's September 14, 1986 nationally televised speech on the subject was crucial in helping to galvanize political and media attention on the nation's drug situation (Wysong and Wright 1995). In the days following the address, President Reagan signed The Anti-Drug Abuse Act (Public Law 99-570), an omnibus bill providing $1.7 billion to fight the "war on drugs" by building new prisons, providing drug education and expanding treatment facilities. It was the most far-reaching anti-drug act ever passed by Congress and, importantly, formally launched the Drug-Free Schools and Communities program, the purpose of which was to fund and establish drug and violence education programs as "essential components of a comprehensive strategy to promote school safety and reduce the demand for and use of drugs" (Public Law 99-570, 1986). By the early 1990s the "war on drugs" had been "extended and systematized" by President Bush's "National Drug Control Strategy" (Wysong, Aniskiewicz, and Wright 1994, p. 461). In total, between the years 1985 and 1993 the federal government's annual contribution for drug treatment, law enforcement, and education rose from $2.5 billion to $13 billion (ibid.).

According to historian William Elwood (1994, p. 3) the narrative of how drug education entered schools is a complex and ideologically laden one. In his book, *Rhetoric in the War on Drugs: The Triumphs and Tragedies of Public Relations* Elwood asserted that the "war on drugs" was not about effectual policy making at all but rather a series of "rhetorical, multifaceted public relations campaigns designed to enhance the images of specific political figures" and exploit public sentiment. Essentially, there became a way of talking about the magnitude of the nation's drug problem and the appropriateness of interventions.

Considering this construction, a Foucauldian lens is particularly useful. For Foucault, discourse provides a way of generating knowledge through language. As Stuart Hall (2001) suggests, Foucault's conceptualization recognizes that all social practices, like language, have meaning and meaning influences practice, the production of knowledge, and behaviors. Thus, the Reagan administration's conceptualization and articulation of drugs as a threat to all Americans had a profound influence on the ways the public understood the 'drug problem' and the kinds of policies that were enacted in schools as a solution to the problem (Gorman 1998). Thus, while drug interventions were driven by a variety of complex political concerns, the administration's description of a national crisis of epidemic proportion garnered virtually unanimous bi-partisan and public support and thus had a magnanimous effect.

Nancy Reagan's very public involvement in the "Just Say No" (JSN) campaign can also be understood as an illustration of Elwood's claims about the symbolic value of the effort. As a number of scholars have argued, Reagan's involvement in and support for the school-based JSN campaign partially concealed more complicated political motivations (Bertram et al. 1996). According to Benze (1990, p. 792), the JSN campaign appears to have sprung, in part, out of White House concerns around Mrs. Reagan's negative public image and its effect on President Reagan's 1984 re-election chances. In response to these worries, the White House embarked on an aggressive campaign to improve Mrs. Reagan's public appeal by highlighting her anti-drug stance.

Mrs. Reagan's "just say no" catch-cry was as simplistic as it was popular. The message appealed to a moral conservative base concerned about the rise of permissive liberal humanism as well as various parent groups increasingly worried about drug use in schools (Bertram et al. 1996). Throughout the early 1980s Mrs. Reagan made dozens of media appearances and anti-drug speeches across the country. What's more, the White House's strategy seems to have worked, the press became more sympathetic towards her and in a 1985 cover story *Time* magazine concluded that: "in the last two years [Mrs. Reagan] has probably become an outright political plus, winning friends and influencing people" (Benze 1990, p. 792). In addition to bolstering her public image, Mrs. Reagan's message reached more than 25 million youth, resulting in the formation of more than 12,000 JSN Youth Clubs across the globe and, over the next ten years, helped justify the allocation of millions of dollars in federal grants to schools for adopting the JSN approach to drug prevention (Jacobsohn and Vivolo 2010).

Aside from the symbolic value of anti-drug policies in generating political and public support, the discursive effects of the JSN campaign were enduring. Consistent with the JSN approach, drug policies advocated during this era offered largely reductionistic solutions that made no "acknowledgment of the economic, social, education, and political injustices that may breed the problem or raise the issue in the first place" (Mackey-Kallis and Hahn 1991, p. 13). The campaign helped absolve the government of responsibility to address the complex structural issues associated with drug addiction and trade, even as they "claimed responsibility for resolving the drug problem by declaring war and proposing policies to ameliorate the situation" (Elwood 1994, p. 3). At the same time, the rhetorical focus on the individual fitted neatly into the broader political program of scaling back the direct role of the government and urging youth to take personal responsibility for their behaviors. In significant ways, JSN "shifted the responsibility for social problems from the arenas of politics and medicine to morality" (Mackey-Kallis and Hahn 1991, p. 13). Blaming the "hedonism and permissiveness" of individuals in the 1960s and 1970s, people who displayed a "flippant and irresponsible attitude toward drug use" also made it easier for the Reagans to frame problems and solutions in terms of self-will and restraint where schools became the reformatory of choice (Weinraub 1986). According to President Reagan, "law enforcement alone, [can] not significantly reduce drug abuse." Instead, he claimed solving the drug problem necessitated a "national crusade" directed at education (Brinkley 1986).

Speculating on the complex contextual factors that gave rise to the rapid expansion of drug policies at the local, state and federal levels described above may, in part, explain the rhetorical appeal of the JSN approach to drug prevention or why it made its way into schools. It does not however completely explain the widespread and longstanding optimism across the political spectrum about the effectiveness of school-based drug prevention. In the case of JSN, for example, support for the program had little to do with the actually efficacy of the approach in reducing risky youth behavior. Indeed, research pointing to the ineffectiveness of the JSN behavioristic approach was ignored for years during the policy's enactment (Bangert-Drowns 1988, Beck 1998, Fishbein et al. 2002, Marez 2004, Robinson and Scherle 2007). Instead, advocates of JSN suggested that in the absence of the intervention, drug use would be even more rampant among youth (Gorman 1998). Despite the time, effort and funding invested in an ineffective program such as this, the JSN program indeed had a lasting legacy. On the one hand the program reassured parents across the nation that schools were controlling substance use among students so they did not have to (Bangert-Drowns 1988). And, on the other hand it authenticated the simplistic, behavioristic, and moralistic "no use" pedagogical approach to health education that lingers in many schools to this day.

School food policy making and the HHFKA of 2010

We now turn to the issue of school food and the complex narratives that account for health policies enacted in this arena. To be sure, the economic dimensions of food in American public schools has a profound effect on the regulatory framework in which policy-making occurs. The 1946 National School Lunch Program (NSLP) has been a highly controversial piece of legislation since its inception (Levine 2010). Much of this stems from the historical context on which the merits of the program were originally proposed and debated as well as the many 'built-in' policy partners. In her historical analysis of the program Levine suggests that the commitment to offer food in schools did not at all emanate from a unified and/or enthusiastic concern for children's health, as it is often celebrated. Rather, the legislation brought together a somewhat unlikely and not always stable coalition of stakeholders with a disparate set of aspirations, ranging from the alleviation of social dilemmas to naked self-interest. Perhaps the most ongoing and unreconciled debate pertaining to school food policies—and the NSLP in particular—concerns the balance of power and authority among the policy partners.

From its inception NSLP, was never created as a stand-alone government-sponsored social policy. Rather, according to the 1945 House Committee on Agriculture—the group tasked with developing the NSLP—"The federal government has always had an active interest in providing markets for agricultural production and for maintaining agricultural production at a high level," and "any measure that will expand the domestic consumption of agricultural production, both immediately and in the future, and assure a large share of the national income to farmers, should receive support" (United States Congress, House Committee on Agriculture 1945, p. 2). Surplus agricultural commodities were also described as "price-destroying" and a national school lunch program was proposed as a way of disposing these food items (ibid). In short, a formidable strategic alliance between the US Department of Agriculture (USDA), local farmers, industry representatives, and schools emerged in support of a national lunch program, the primary purpose of which was to ensure a ready-made market during times of agricultural surplus (Levine 2010). This alliance although seemingly tactical has not always served the interests of all parties equally—particularly those of schools.

Administratively, meal programs are the responsibility of the USDA's Food and Nutrition Service's (FNS) Child Nutrition Division. This agency establishes nutrition standards, provides oversight and technical assistance to state agencies. Their authority, however, is never guaranteed and has been subject to the ever-shifting political leanings of legislators and various industry lobbies. In 1970, for example, Congress authorized the USDA to establish nutrition standards to regulate the sale of 'competitive' foods—that is, à la carte items sold in competition with the NSLP. These foods are often high-fat and high-calorie items and generate additional profits for schools as they can be sold outside the NSLP. Fearing more stringent standards would reduce these profits, a number of food companies and schools collectively protested these changes. In 1972, Congress capitulated to pressure and amended the legislation to allow schools to sell competitive foods on the condition that profits could only be used to support school organizations. At the same time, Congress relegated the entire matter to state and local agencies, a decision that effectively removed the USDA's jurisdiction on the issue. A 1977 Congressional ruling, however, restored the USDA's authority. With its reinstated authority the USDA announced a restriction on the sale of foods with minimal nutritional value, a limitation that was to be enforced from the beginning of the school day until the end of the last lunch period (Nestle 2000). In response, the National Soft Drink Association (NSDA) filed several lawsuits against the agency in an attempt to reverse the regulation (Story et al. 2000).

On November 15, 1983, the US Court of Appeals sided with the NSDA citing that the USDA had gone beyond Congressional intent in establishing time and place restrictions on school foods. For more than thirty years this ruling has effectively prevented the USDA from regulating the sale of many foods sold in schools.

Recently, due to significant pressure by public health advocates this 1983 decision was successfully challenged by the passage of the 2010 HHFKA. Amongst other stipulations the Act called for the USDA to re-establish national nutrition standards for all foods sold on campuses throughout the school day. This included foods sold as part of the federal meal programs as well as food sold outside the program, including *à la carte* items, soft drinks and foods sold in vending machines, school stores and at school fundraisers. Congress instructed the USDA to partner with the Institute of Medicine's (IOM)—an independent, nonprofit organization—to establish school food regulations that were based on scientific evidence as opposed to corporate interests.

After deliberation, a set of proposed nutrition standards and benchmarks were posted and subject to public comment. According to the USDA an "unprecedented 132,000 public comments" (USDA 2017a) were received. At the same time, various industry trade groups also voiced their perspective. The United Dairy Council, for example, protested the elimination of one percent flavored milk. The Milk Processor Education Program (MilkPeP) and the National Dairy Council partnered to run an aggressive "Raise Your Hand for Chocolate Milk" campaign. Other industry trade groups intensified their Congressional lobbying: The American Frozen Food Institute spent $543,000 in fiscal year 2011 (up from $334,000 in 2010), Schwann Food Co. spent $50,000, and ConAgra Foods Inc. spent $400,000 (Wilson and Roberts 2013). Members of Congress also rallied behind specific foods manufactured in their own states—one of the most notable was the congressional delegation led by Senator Charles Schumer (D), Senator Kirsten Gillbrand (D) and Representative Richard Hanna (R) to have Greek yogurt reinstated in schools.

After months of following the necessary legislative protocol by soliciting comments and perspectives from the public, industry, scientific, and public community, the final rules were posted. Among other things, the legislation included reductions in starchy vegetables, sodium and trans fats and increases in vegetables, fruits, and whole grain offerings. While previous standards permitted schools to serve milk of any fat content, the USDA proposed for schools to offer only unflavored one percent or fat-free flavored or unflavored milk. In the end the Act was passed with bi-partisan support and was embraced by various nonprofit organizations including the National Parent Teacher Association, National Education Association, Academy of Nutrition and Dietetics, American Medical Association, American Academy of Pediatrics and American Cancer Society.

While the new nutrition guidelines went into effect in the 2012–2013 academic year, schools were given yearly performance targets to reach to assist in transition. By 2022, schools will be asked to fully adopt all of the new food policies. Despite the staggered nature of the implementation and the overwhelming support from the public health community, there remained significant controversy about the Act.

Stakeholders working in the school food industry routinely complained about food waste among children, reduced NSLP participation, the tastefulness of meals, and cost of implementations (Sifferlin 2013). Those involved in the production and sale of school food claimed the higher nutritional standard would negatively influence their ability to turn a profit. In the face of these concerns, empirical research showed that the new standards "effectively changed the quality of foods selected by children" as they were eating more healthy foods and throwing less away (Johnson et al. 2016) and, overall the new regulations did not alter participation rates. Similar to many school food controversies in the past, the resolution to the issue increasingly became a partisan—fueled in part by the 2016 Presidential election. On September 20, 2016 when the Act came up for reauthorization, the 114th Congress failed to approve it. Absent a replacement Act, the non-renewal was a logistically moot point as it had no influence on meal funding or a school's responsibility to comply. The optics of non-renewal, however, emboldened industry representatives who long argued for less federal regulation and greater local control in school food sales—a pro-industry, Republican mainstay.

The election of President Donald Trump (R) and appointment of new Secretary of Agriculture, Sonny Purdue (R) further halted any progress in remedying the nutrition situation in schools. Following his appointment, on May 1, 2017 Purdue signed a proclamation to unilaterally rollback the HHFKA food regulations, in an effort to "make school meals great again" (USDA 2017b) In particular, Perdue removed stipulations that schools needed to comply with the Act's requirement for meals to contain more whole grains, less sodium, and fat-free milk. In justifying his decision Purdue stated, "I've got 14 grandchildren, and there is no way that I would propose something if I didn't think it was good, healthful, and the right thing to do" (Fox 2017). In other words, the decision was made absent a formal policy process to consider empirical evidence or policy effectiveness.

To be sure, the provision of food in American public schools over the last 100 years is a dauntingly convoluted story that is open to multiple interpretations. In recounting the particular intriguing sub-plot here, our purpose is to suggest how even well-meaning aspirations to promote health through schools are likely to be no match for the interconnected political struggles and complicated administrative contexts in which schools operate. Despite this, we suggest that the passage of the HHFKA represented an authentic opportunity to engage a wider constituency of stakeholders in policy making, attend to issues of efficacy and address implementation realities. Whether one agrees or disagrees with the spirit or specifics of the HHFKA we can at least point to a—albeit flawed at times—policy *process*. Public hearings were held, online discussion forums were opened, public comment periods were accommodated and the media openly reported. This is not to say that corporate entities did not influence the perspectives of public figures or the particulars of the legislation—but it is to suggest that there were 'checks' along the way that limited this influence. The recent Trump administration's bold decision to unilaterally roll-back the Act in radical ways is not just an affront to all of those who worked hard to put in place a policy that would have likely had a positive influence on children across the country, it's an affront to the expertise of educators and public health workers as well as policy making process that upholds democratic ideals.

Discussion and conclusion

We conclude by calling for a more sophisticated and democratic approach to health policy in schools. We suggest that the potential effectiveness of proposed interventions need to be assessed not only against existing historical evidence but considered against the competing roles we expect schools to play as well as the working-life realities for those charged with implementing public health policies in schools. These are inevitably questions of resources and power. However, we also think there are fundamental issues of justice about policy making as these relate to educational goals, the role of privatized entities, the motivations behind interventions, and lack of reasoned, public discourse (Trujillo 2013).

One of the purposes of this chapter has been to "distinguish the scaffolding of meanings" and motivations that have become attached to school health policy interventions and "make the politics of their construction more visible" (Dussel 2004, 85). The investigation is consistent with what Rose (1999, p. 58) argues when he called for inquiry to "question and complicate, that which forms the very groundwork of the present." While unique on their own accounts, our two narratives reveal something distinctively problematic about the school health policy making process and it outcomes. In the case the Reagans' JSN campaign we see the ways in which the rhetoric around and appearance of identifying and subsequently solving the drug problem became more important than a careful assessment of the situation at hand. Interventions were bolstered by narratives of certainty and negativity that, as Evan, Evans and Rich (2003, p. 224) write, often appear to threaten "personal, institutional, nation, global, health, and economic well-being." These discourses are marked by concerns over "immediacy and prox-imity (this is here-and-now, on-the-doorstep disease) and of risk (all may fall prey to its advances without appropriate intervention, investment and action at all levels)." Next, considering the long and complicated story of the enactment of school food policies our analysis reveals the ongoing obstacles that policy making faces in this area. The examination provides insight into how educational policies are constrained or contested and thus archetypal of the goal of having policy environments reflective of and consistent with democratic ideals.

We think our analysis raises a simple and yet pressing question: what are the limits to the role of schools in promoting health through policy? Our analysis shows that the spread of public health policy in schools is often only tangen-tially related to new and emerging health concerns and may be much more to do with wider public policy machinations. We think there is an argument for using schools to implement health programs where the reach of the program is cru-cial and the mode of implementation is straightforward. However, without the benefit of greater economic and time resources and a political commitment to an inclusive and democratic? process, school-based interventions that seek to achieve far-reaching and complex changes in children's personal behavior may continue to be just an expensive distraction. We conclude, then, by calling for a more sophisticated, reflective, and critical approach to the creation and implementation of health policies, particularly when these involve schools, teachers and students.

References

Bangert-Drowns, R. L. 1988. The effects of school-based Substance abuse education—A meta-analysis. *Journal of Drug Education* 18 (3), 243–264.

Beck, J. 1998. 100 years of "Just Say No" versus "Just Say Know" reevaluating drug education goals for the coming century. *Evaluation Review* 22 (1), 15–45.

Benze, J. 1990. Nancy Reagan china doll or dragon lady? *Presidential Studies Quarterly* 20 (4), 777–790.

Bertram, E., et al. 1996. *Drug war politics: The price of denial.* Berkeley: University of California Press.

Brinkley, J. 1986. Anti-drug law: Words, deeds, political expediency. *The New York Times*, October 27. Available from: www.nytimes.com/1986/10/27/us/anti-drug-law-words-deeds-political-expediency.html [Accessed December 2, 2017].

Dussel, I., 2004. Fashioning the schooled self through uniforms: A Foucauldian approach to contemporary school policies. In: B. K. Baker K. L. Heyning Eds., *Dangerous Coagulations.* Peter Lang: New York, 85–116.

Elwood, W. 1994. *Rhetoric in the war on drugs: The triumphs and tragedies of public relations.* Westport, CT: Greenwood.

Fishbein, M., et al. 2002. Avoiding the boomerang: Testing the relative effectiveness of antidrug public service announcements before a national campaign. *American Journal of Public Health* 92 (2), 238–245.

Fox, M. 2017. Trump administration loosens Obama school food rules. *NBC News.* Available from: www.nbcnews.com/health/health-news/trump-administration-loosens-obama-school-food-rules-n753556 [Accessed October 4, 2017].

Gard, M. and Pluim, C. 2014. *Schools and public health: Past, present, future.* Lanham, MD: Lexington Books.

Gorman, D. M. 1998. The irrelevance of evidence in the development of school-based drug prevention policy 1986–1996. *Evaluation Review* 22 (1), 118–146.

Hall, S. 2001. Foucault: Power, knowledge and discourse. In: M. Wetherell, S. Taylor, and S. Yates Eds., *Discourse, theory and practice.* London: Sage, 72–82.

Jacobsohn L. and Vivolo, A. M. Anti-drug campaigns. In: S. Hornig Priest Ed., *Encyclopedia of Science and Technology Communication.* Thousand Oaks, CA: Sage, 48–54.

Johnson, D. B., et al. 2016. Effect of the healthy hunger-free kids on the nutritional quality of meals selected by students and school lunch participation rates. *Journal of the American Medical Association Pediatrics*, 170(1), e153918–e153918.

Levine, S. 2010. *School lunch politics: The surprising history of America's favorite welfare program.* Princeton: Princeton University Press.

Mackey-Kallis, S. and Hahn, D. F. 1991. Questions of public will and private action: The power of the negative in the Reagans' "Just Say No" morality campaign. *Communication Quarterly* 39 (1), 1–17.

Marez, C. 2004. *Drug wars: The political economy of narcotics.* Minneapolis: University of Minnesota Press.

Mintrom, M. 2001. Educational governance and democratic practice. *Educational Policy*, 15, 615–643.

Nestle, M. 2000. Soft drink "pouring rights": Marketing empty calories to children. *Public Health Reports*, 115 (4), 308–319.

Popkewitz, T. S. and Brennan, M. 1998. *Foucault's challenge discourse, knowledge, and power in education*. New York: Teachers College Press.

Public Law 99-570. 1986. Anti-drug abuse act, Section 4102. Washington, DC: U.S. Government Printing Office.

Robinson, M. B. and Scherlen, R. G. 2007. *A critical analysis of claims made by the Office of National Drug Control Policy*. Albany: State University of New York Press.

Ronald Reagan Presidential Library and Museum. 1986. *Address to the nation on the campaign against drug abuse*. Available from: www.reaganlibrary.archives.gov/archives/speeches/1986/091486a.htm [Accessed December 2, 2017].

Rose, N. 1999. *Powers of freedom: Reframing political thought*. Cambridge: Cambridge University Press.

Sifferlin, A. 2013. Why some schools are saying "no thanks" to the school-lunch program. *Time*. Available from: http://healthland.time.com/2013/08/29/why-some-schools-are-saying-no-thanks-to-the-school-lunch-program/ [Accessed October 1, 2017].

Story, M., Hayes, M. and Kalina, B. 1996. Availability of foods in high schools: Is there cause for concern? *Journal of the Academy of Nutrition and Dietetics*, 96 (2), 123–126.

Troyna, B. 1994. Critical social research and education policy. *British Journal of Educational Studies*, 42 (1), 70–84.

Trujillo, T. M. 2013. The disproportionate erosion of local control: urban school boards, high-stakes accountability, and democracy. *Educational Policy*, 27 (2), 334–359.

United States Congress, House Committee on Agriculture. 1945. Report on school lunch program no. 684. *House Miscellaneous Reports*, 79, 2–3.

United States Department of Agriculture (USDA) and United States Department of Health and Human Services (HHS). 2010. *Dietary Guidelines for Americans*. Available from: www.cnpp.usda.gov/dietaryguidelines.htm [Accessed November 2, 2017].

USDA, Office of Communication. 2017a. *USDA unveils historic improvements to meals served in America's schools*. Available from: www.fns.usda.gov/pressrelease/002312 [Accessed November 14, 2017].

USDA, Office of Communication. 2017b. Ag Secretary Perdue moves to make school meals great again. Available from: www.usda.gov/media/press-releases/2017/05/01/ag-secretary-perdue-moves-make-school-meals-great-again [Accessed November 14, 2017].

Wilson, D. and Roberts, J. 2012. Special report: How Washington Went Soft on Childhood Obesity." *Reuters—US Edition*, April 27. Available from: www.reuters.com/article/2012/04/27/us-usa-foodlobby-idUSBRE83Q0ED20120427 [Accessed November 14, 2017].

Wilson, H. V. 2001. Power and partnership: A critical analysis of the surveillance discourses of child health nurses. *Journal of Advanced Nursing*, 36 (2), 294–301.

Weinraub, B. 1986. Reagan considers wider drug tests. *The New York Times*, July 31. Available from: www.nytimes.com/1986/07/31/us/reagan-considers-wider-drug-tests.html [Accessed December 2, 2017].

Wysong, E. and Wright, D. W. 1995. A decade of DARE: Efficacy, politics and drug education, *Sociological Focus*, 28 (3), 283–311.

Wysong, E., Aniskiewicz, R. and Wright, D. 1994. Truth and DARE: Tracking drug education to graduation and as symbolic politics. *Social Problems*, 41 (3), 448–472.

Chapter 14

Is asking salutogenic questions a way of being critical?

Mikael Quennerstedt and Louise McCuaig

Introduction

Globally, health has been advocated as a major objective for physical education, and despite the multiple ways that health can conceivably be interpreted, a specific health mantra seemingly dominates Western physical education contexts. Whether we are talking health in Australia, the UK, Sweden or the United States, the idea that health is linked to aerobic capacity, fitness, one's body mass index, 10,000 steps per day or what one looks like, prevails. That is, health is widely regarded as a static outcome, an end point that each citizen should strive to obtain.

Almost forty years ago however, the medical sociologist Aaron Antonovsky urged researchers and practitioners within health promotion to critically dissect this dominant, static, and quite dualistic notion of health i.e. between health and disease. Antonovsky argued that such an appraisal "leads us to face the question of whether the dichotomous approach is adequate or whether it may not be imperative to formulate a different conceptualization of health" (Antonovsky 1979, p. 39).

In this chapter, we first, as an overview, map different critical appraisals of so called pathogenically oriented notions of health within health, sport and physical education, to explore the diverse critical issues and questions that have emerged within the context of this critique. Building on these foundations, we then re-imagine these questions in relation to the salutogenic re-orientation Antonovsky proposed, where he urged research to 'move beyond post-Cartesian dualism and look to imagination, love, play, meaning, will and the social structures that foster them' (Antonovsky 1987, p. 31). Here, Antonovsky calls for a critical standpoint that asks questions about the resources people draw upon to be healthy, rather than asking about how we can understand, cure or prevent illness. As a consequence of this work, we offer 'other' salutogenically inspired questions, which we suggest further enrich the more obvious ones resulting from a critical inquiry.

These salutogenic questions and the process of their construction will be taken as a starting point to approach matters of health in relation to education, to health and physical education and to the lives of young people participating in formal schooling. Finally, a review of the recent state and national health and physical education curriculum reform in Australia will demonstrate current social change driven by a salutogenic philosophy, at least on the policy level.

Research on health in physical education—a brief salutogenic overview (mapping)

Research on health in general is massive. Typing the English word 'health' into Google scholar gives over 6 million posts, and that is just using English. The Swedish work 'hälsa' gives over 250,000 posts, and the Spanish 'salud' gives over 3 million. Adding the word sport or physical activity halves the hits, and adding physical education takes it down to about 700,000. But still it is a massive field. So, mapping the topographies of the field of health is almost impossible. Several research handbooks have done a great job in mapping aspects of health (e.g. Barton et al. 2015, Ekkekakis 2013), and in relation to physical education two extensive handbooks have been published both touching on issues of health as an aspect of physical education (Ennis 2016, Kirk et al. 2006).

In relation to physical education, ten years ago Quennerstedt (2008) wrote that there were two main lines of argument in the academic literature regarding the relation between physical education and health. Tinning (2015) recently describes these positions as a growing divide in PE research between 'interventionists' and 'educationalists'. One line of argument is founded on a critique of PE practice that focuses on sport techniques and ball-games. This position is often framed within epidemiological research and argues, instead, that public health, health-enhancing lifestyles and increased physical activity should be one of the most, if not the most, important objective of physical education (e.g. Fairclough and Stratton 2005, Trost 2004). Lately this position has more clearly been targeting obesity in young people, and thus advocating for a physical education curriculum that emphasizes an increase in moderate to vigorous physical activity (MVPA) which, as a consequence, will allegedly have important effects on the health of individuals as well as the population as a whole (e.g. Kahan and McKenzie 2015, Lonsdale et al. 2013). As Lonsdale et al. (2013) put it:

> this review indicates that interventions can increase the proportion of time students spend in MVPA during PE lessons. As most children and adolescents participate in PE, these interventions could lead to substantial public health benefits. (p. 152)

In this strand, the critical questions that are foregrounded often relate to unequal distribution of physical activity levels or physical activity opportunities regarding, for example, gender, disability or family income. However, the interest is not predominantly critical, as the concern lies in focusing on health risks and finding the best ways to deliver physical education in order to reduce sedentary time and increase MVPA for all (e.g. McKenzie and Lounsbery 2014).

In the second line of argument, public health agendas are contrasted with educational agendas according to sociocultural ideas of learning (Tinning 2015). Here, the risks associated with the adoption of an instrumental and often individualised, epidemiologically determined public health curriculum in physical education are brought to the forefront (e.g. Fitzpatrick and Russell 2015, Gard 2011, Leahy et al. 2013, Vander Schee and Gard 2014). In this vein, and as early as 2004, Evans and colleagues had already argued that one consequence of putting too much focus on public health in physical education is a problematic and limiting shift in how young people are situated as healthy or not healthy. These typically reductive notions of health are visible in many countries (e.g. Harris et al. 2016, O'Connor and Alfrey 2015, Powell and Fitzpatrick 2015, Quennerstedt, Burrows and Maivorsdotter 2010), and two interconnected themes serve to illustrate the critical literature: obesity prevention and healthy lifestyles technologies.

The critique of physical education as a site for the prevention of overweight and obesity has been quite strong over the last couple of decades (e.g. Gard and Wright 2001, Gard 2011). The focus of this critical debate is beautifully captured by Evans and colleagues who argue that obesity discourses constitute a "framework of thought, talk and action concerning the body in which 'weight' is privileged not only as a primary determinant but as a manifest index of well-being surpassing all antecedent and contingent dimensions of 'health'" (Evans et al. 2008, p. 13).

Health education as a means of obesity prevention in the population has, according to these scholars, received unparalleled attention in debates concerning the aim of health and physical education, and the critique of both the relation between health and obesity (e.g. Cliff and Wright 2010, Gard and Wright 2001, Leahy et al. 2013, Vander Schee and Gard 2014), and the practices that emerge as a consequence of obesity discourses, such as fitness testing (e.g. Cole et al. 2014). This critical literature accentuates scholars' concern that schools are increasingly being asked to engage with health in terms of obesity prevention and control instead of educating children, and this emphasis on body size and weight excludes alternate ways of doing physical education (e.g. Powell and Fitzpatrick 2015). Schools and physical education in particular, have accordingly, been identified as key sites for health surveillance and what is called biopolitical strategies (e.g. Cale, Harris and Chen 2014; Petherick 2013). Stigmatisation based on body weight and size is also emphasised in the critical literature (e.g. Cale and Harris 2013), with Sykes and McPhail (2008) for example, examining fat-phobic discourses in physical education and how these discourses are negotiated continually by students.

Lately, this critique has aligned with critical interrogations exploring the introduction of digital healthy lifestyle technologies in physical education like exergames (Öhman et al. 2014), or wearable health devices (Goodyear et al. 2017).

These devices have been positioned as effective solutions to sedentary behaviours among young people. Several critical studies point to problematic consequences of the surveillance mechanisms promoted by digital healthy lifestyle technologies (e.g. Petherick 2015, Rich and Miah 2017), and the negative impact technologies can have through a reinforcement of a narrow understanding of health equalling fitness and slenderness (e.g. Goodyear et al. 2017, Lupton 2016). Many scholars argue that the measurements of healthy lifestyle produced by the algorithms of fitness technologies, encourage people to think about health in numbers which further reinforces narrow understandings of health (Depper and Howe 2017, Lupton 2015, 2016, Öhman et al. 2014, Williamsson 2015). Included in schools, this enforced self-tracking (Pink and Fors 2017) with measurements like BMI, calorie consumption or 10.000 steps becomes embedded in the biopedagogies of education as a mirage of health (Goodyear et al. 2017, Öhman et al. 2014).

We would argue that the academic discourse within and between the two dominant positions regarding the role of health in physical education (see Tinning 2015) appears to be either for or against a public health agenda, and the many pros and cons of the various positions in health and physical education curriculum content. In these discussions, what health is, and can be, in health and physical education is often taken for granted as a condition or a state of not being diseased or overweight. However, from a salutogenic perspective these are not the only positions to take. So, the issue we seek to address in the following section is the possibility of posing critical questions to the field of health and physical education from an alternative, salutogenic, position.

Research on health in physical education—critical issues from a salutogenic perspective

So far, we have argued that what health is, and can be, in physical education is taken for granted within what can be defined as a pathogenic paradigm. Health research is then searching for or critiquing what the concept indicates, the origins (genic) of disease (pathos). In a pathogenic perspective, health promotion, health education and in consequence physical education, becomes equal to curing and preventing disease, and pathogenically guided physical education practice often disregards the social, cultural and societal aspects of health as well as of education. As a consequence, health is positioned as a human being's normal condition, and diseases and 'not-normal' behaviours are that which should be explained, explored, critiqued or promoted. Health education becomes occupied with an agenda where "social conditions allow, facilitate and encourage individuals to engage in wise, low risk behaviour" (Antonovsky 1996a, p. 13).

As an alternative to a hegemonic pathogenic paradigm in health practices like physical education, Antonovsky proposes the idea of a salutogenic perspective on health. Salutogenesis, which in ancient Latin (salus) and Greek (genesis) roughly translates to 'the origins of health', is a powerful critique against pathogenic, mainly biomedical, notions of health, but also towards morally normative perspectives. Antonovsky describes his critique as follows:

> At the core of the pathogenic paradigm, in theory and in action, is a dichotomous classification of persons as being diseased or healthy. Our linguistic apparatus, our common sense thinking, and our daily behaviour reflect this dichotomy. It is also the conceptual basis for the work of health care and disease care professionals and institutions in Western societies. (Antonovsky 1979, p. 39)

Antonovsky (1979) argues that it is imperative to advance new conceptualisations of health particularly within health promotion practices like physical education or health education. He also developed an alternative argument that health is not something we have or do not have. Instead, "we are all terminal cases. But as long as there is a breath of life in us, we are all in some measure healthy" (Antonovsky 1987, p. 50).

The consequences of Antonovsky's critical agenda (1979, 1987, 1996a, 1996b) are *first*, that we need to take a salutogenic position when asking questions, which involves focusing on why people stay healthy and what hinders health development, rather than exclusively focusing on why people become ill. According to Antonovsky, this is the actual mystery of health, not why people get disease. A strong example of this is Thedin-Jacobsson's (2014) study where, instead of looking at the obvious question of why teenage girls drop out of sport, she explores why and under what circumstances they are staying in sport.

Secondly, health is conceptualised as a continuous process of "becoming" that involves a relation between individuals and what constitutes their environment. This is captured by Antonovsky's re-configured public health metaphor of the river, where he argues that "we are all, always in the dangerous river of life. The twin questions are: How dangerous is *our* river? How well can we swim?" (Antonovsky, 1996a, p. 14). From a salutogenic perspective, health issues should accordingly always be explored as a relation between the swimmer and the river, and it is this relation that should be scrutinised 'critically'. As Antonovsky argued, in order to significantly change or develop people's health, it is probably easier to change the river, i.e. the situations and contexts that people inhabit (Quennerstedt and Öhman 2014).

Thirdly, and according to us an important contribution to the critical literature, Antonovsky urged researchers, practitioners and policymakers to ask salutogenic questions formulated in relation to the two points above, that is, as questions directed towards understanding the mystery of health and as a relation between the swimmer and the river. Examples of salutogenic questions formulated by Antonovsky are: "Why do people stay healthy?" (1979, p. 35), or "What can be done in this community—factory, geographic community, age or gender group?" (1996a, p. 16). In relation to physical education and health education in school, examples of salutogenic questions inspired by Quennerstedt and colleagues (2010) can be:

- How can we help young people today to develop their health?
- What resources do young people need to relate to and develop in order to meet the challenges of contemporary society?
- How can we facilitate opportunities for students to learn health and be healthy in any way these are construed?
- How can health and physical education help young people to grow as individuals and democratic citizens?
- How can we help young people to become critical and active transformers of society?

However, although Antonovsky was a sociologist, several reviews of research (Eriksson and Lindström 2005, 2006) have shown that the reception of a salutogenic perspective has been mainly within psychology and public health science. The reviews also reveal that salutogenically inspired research has largely put an emphasis on the swimmer, i.e., the individual aspects of the relation. What is more, despite Antonovsky's warnings that we can never take a person out of the river of life, in some research the swimmer has been removed from the water and thus regarded as disconnected from their environment. In this sense, some salutogenic research can be criticised for being individualistic and decontextualized.

Quennerstedt and Öhman (2014) maintain that in order for salutogenic questions to function as critical, it is of importance that the river metaphor is embraced in its entirety, where researchers take political, democratic and equality concerns into consideration. For example, this approach has been employed in the determination and analysis of health and physical educations' scripts of good living, drawing on Foucault's ethical fourfold for critical insight (McCuaig and Quennerstedt 2018). In this analysis, strategies that institutions (in the river) employ to incite and engage individuals (swimmers) to live a good life are explored according to ethical fourfold questions such as: how would you define a good life?, what resources do you use in order to live a good life?, what factors motivate you to engage in particular practices in your life? or, what kind of life do you want to lead? In this sense, health resources, as McCuaig and Quennerstedt (2018) argue, can be seen as "different ways in which people from different backgrounds and in diverse contexts draw upon different resources to live a good life" (p. 119).

Others have explored disability according to the salutogenic question of: "why do many people with serious and persistent disabilities report that they experience a good or excellent quality of life when to most external observers these individuals seem to live an undesirable daily existence?" (Albrecht and Devlieger 1999, p. 977). More recently, Eriksson and colleagues (2017) investigated the health resources drawn upon by older women who continued resistance training five years after a physical activity intervention, and Thorburn and Horrell (2014) looked at reflective wisdom, life-satisfaction and welfare using comparable theories from both moral philosophy and positive psychology. These studies all ask well-founded, critical salutogenic questions.

Recent scholarship, not necessarily defining themselves as salutogenic, also shares much of the same agenda, for example, considering the potential of positive pedagogies in coaching (Light and Harvey 2017), and appreciative inquiry (Enright et al. 2014), using what we would consider salutogenic questions to inquire about different resources and how they support swimmers' capacity to negotiate the river of life. Another interesting example is the critical scholarship of Fox and Ward (2008a, 2008b). In their quest to understand health identities, these scholars drew on the theories of Deleuze and Guattari to devise (salutogenic) questions such as: 'What can a body do?', and 'What else can a body do?'.

All these scholars share Antonovsky's concern about dualistic, instrumental and individualised notions of health and try to move beyond the hegemonic grip that pathogenic theories have in regards to health. They also share a commitment to asking critical questions of health, physical education and sport practices, where the relation between the swimmer and the river is in focus, and where unjust practices can be scrutinized without necessarily accepting the pathogenic position.

In discussing the swimmer in the river, Antonovsky (1996b) likewise reminds us that different forms of particularism, such as undemocratic societies, fundamentalism, patriarchies or other limiting patterns of the river, of course can potentially lead to good health, but only for those who have power (Antonovsky 1996b). Antonovsky instead promoted societies, institutions and practices building on pluralism, equity and democratic participation as routes to making the river, and thus the possibility for better health for all, more forthcoming.

Social change: Journey of salutogenic theory in the Australian Curriculum HPE

While much of the reviewed salutogenic scholarship and action has remained within research oriented communities, there is growing evidence that salutogenic questions and the process of their construction are informing health perspectives and practices in relation to the schooling of young people. As an example of this translation, we provide a review of recent Australian Health and Physical Education (HPE) curriculum reform to demonstrate current social change driven by a salutogenic philosophy, at least on the policy level. We suggest that curriculum reform offers a site through which social change can be, if not secured, then pursued as, "the crucible in which subject disciplines are formed shape our future possibilities as social agents" (McLaren 1993, p. 176). An appreciation of salutogenic theory's potential for Australian HPE programs emerged within the context of Swedish-Australian research collaborations. As indicated previously, scholars involved in this exchange were wrestling with the challenge of an increasing emphasis on interventionist, deficit, fix-it approaches to young people's engagement in sport and school HPE (see Quennerstedt 2008, Thedin-Jakobsson et al. 2012). Given their role as leaders and advisors in the national reform of core HPE programs, the Australian scholars were afforded a unique opportunity to embed a salutogenic orientation to the study of HPE in Australian schools.

The Australian Curriculum, Assessment and Reporting Authority (ACARA), established in 2008, was responsible for the development of Australia's second attempt at a national curriculum (ACARA 2012a). Importantly, ACARA had been charged with making "clear to teachers what has to be taught" and "what achievement standards are expected of them", while teachers were considered best placed to "make decisions about the pedagogical approach that will give the best learning outcomes" (NCB 2009, p. 15). As such, ACARA was mandated to address curriculum and assessment matters, but pedagogical practice was to be left to schools and teachers. ACARA adopted an extensive and collaborative curriculum development process that involved four phases of activity: shaping, writing, implementation, monitoring and evaluation (ACARA 2012a). In the shaping phase, a broad outline of the Foundation to Year 12 (F–12) curriculum for a learning area or subject was developed and disseminated through the Shape of the Australian Curriculum: Health and Physical Education (AC:HPE) document (ACARA 2012b).

According to the AC:HPE Shape position statement (ACARA 2012b), salutogenic theory and questions informed the resulting strengths-based approach, which sat alongside four other "big ideas" that included: a focus on educative outcomes; value learning in, about and through movement; developing health literacy; and critical inquiry approach. As the lead writer of the HPE Shape paper, Macdonald (2013) advocated a strengths-based approach to Australian HPE that employed the affirmative orientation underpinning positive youth psychology and salutogenic perspectives of healthy living. More specifically for our purposes here, Macdonald (2013) states that the salutogenic model of health "supports a critical view of health education with a focus on the learner embedded within a community's structural facilitators, assets and constraints" (p. 100).

Extensive feedback from the profession following the release of the draft Shape of the Australian HPE document supported the inclusion of a strengths-based approach. As McCuaig and colleagues (2013) argued, a salutogenically informed strengths-based approach encouraged teachers of the AC:HPE to:

- focus more on the promotion of health rather than on preventing illness,
- view healthy living as multi-dimensional and encompasses physical as well as social, mental, spiritual, environmental, and community dimensions,
- consider health as something dynamic, always in the process of becoming,
- view health as something more and also something else than the absence of disease,
- acknowledge humans as active agents, living in relation to their contexts, and
- that health is not regarded as an end goal in itself, but rather as an important prerequisite for living a good life.

As with the implementation of any new curriculum, the release of the AC:HPE resulted in a burgeoning body of learning and teacher professional development resources. Initially, those who had been closely involved with the construction of the AC:HPE were authors or contributors to the content of these materials. Consequently, the sociological and critical orientation of the strengths-based approach was to maintain its integrity. For example, Wright (2014) points teachers to curriculum descriptors that capture how a strengths-based approach and critical inquiry together produce an educative focus as follows:

- Examine the benefits to individuals and communities of valuing diversity and promoting inclusivity (e.g. Investigating how respecting diversity and challenging racism, sexism, disability discrimination and homophobia influence individual and community health) (Years 7 and 8)
- Plan, implement and critique strategies to enhance the health, safety and wellbeing of their communities (e.g. Creating and evaluating visual and multimodal health campaigns in print-based and digital environments to promote health and wellbeing in their community) (Years 8 and 9).

Nonetheless, this integrity was to be relatively short lived, as the various education authorities undertook the translation of the national curriculum into state-based iterations that reflected local political, economic and social agendas and policies. Evidence of the re-orientation towards an individualistic, deficit-risk interpretation of a strengths-based philosophy has been provided by Australian researchers exploring the role of external providers in shaping school mental health and physical activity programs (McCuaig et al. 2016). Data gathered within the context of this study revealed how school-based positive psychology and mental health programs were encouraging teachers and their students to: push past or cope with their circumstances; have the confidence to be themselves; be more reflective and self-aware; control thoughts; walk-the-talk; and, consider their own self-talk. Given the enactment of these programs followed the release of the AC:HPE, it was disheartening to report the privileging of a focus on the "the swimmer", with little reference to the sociocultural resources or factors of "the river". In fact, there was a notable absence of reference to the AC:HPE in much of the gathered data, an absence that underscored the interventionist, as opposed to educative, orientation of the mental health programs provided by external providers in school settings.

Notwithstanding this 'wash out' of the critical components of a salutogenically oriented curriculum, a subsequent reform of Queensland's high stakes, elective senior Health Education curriculum offers greater hope for sustainable social change. In response to renewed enthusiasm for national cohesion of schooling, a review of current practice in the final phase of schooling across the country was undertaken. In the state of Queensland, this review led to the introduction of external assessment and high definition syllabuses for all subjects that determined students' subsequent entrance into tertiary studies (Australian Council for Educational Research 2014). One of the imperatives for the curriculum designers involved in this senior schooling reform, was to ensure that new courses of study aligned with the underpinning principles of the Australian years F-10 curriculum. In the resulting new Senior Health subject, the salutogenic model of health has been established as the conceptual foundations for the course's Health Inquiry model (see Queensland Curriculum and Assessment Authority 2018).

As stated in the syllabus, "health literacy and social justice, alongside barriers and enablers, influence an individual's access to and use of personal, social and community resources" (Queensland Curriculum and Assessment Authority 2018, p. 10). Unlike the AC:HPE, the Senior Health inquiry model mandates a pedagogical approach that scaffolds the purposeful investigation of resources, barriers and enablers that influence the dynamic ever-present relation between the swimmer and the river. As such, this curriculum acknowledges that a salutogenic orientation is as much about *how* we teach in terms of "problem solving, democratic participation, and a critical stance towards individualistic and moralistic perceptions of health" (McCuaig, Quennerstedt and Macdonald 2013, p. 122), as it is about what we teach. In this sense, student-centred pedagogical approaches that support student's capacities to grow as individuals and democratic citizens, encourage teachers to respect and develop children's rights and help young people to become critical and active transformers of society are of utmost importance.

Conclusion

So, is asking salutogenic questions a way of being critical? Well it of course depends on what we mean by being critical. Using the three aims of critical research used in this book—*mapping, critiquing and social change*—a salutogenic perspective can serve as one way to widen the notion of health and thus map issues of health differently. Such mapping involves health issues in the river, of the swimmer and in the relation between the swimmer and the river (see McCuaig and Quennerstedt 2016, Mittelmark et al. 2017). In its most basic sense, a salutogenic perspective on health also offers a powerful critique of the dualistic notion of health that dominates health research and health practices in many contexts. A salutogenic perspective thus offers a position from where research can critically scrutinize problematic scientific or moral norms affecting health education and physical education practices that take the swimmer, the river and the relations between them into account. The Australian experience however, confirms Quennerstedt and Öhman's (2014) concerns that the operationalisation of a salutogenic approach is vulnerable to the danger of overemphasising the individual aspects of health and students' agency. Students' lack of individual strengths or action are positioned as the problem and victim-blaming approaches can be inadvertently re-invigorated. Notwithstanding this caveat, a salutogenic perspective can, and has, informed the design and philosophical orientations of curriculum policy as illustrated on a national level, revealing the potential for social change by shifting teachers' and students' attention towards those personal, social and community resources that underpin a good life, rather than simply focussing on the risks and disease that compromise healthy living.

References

Australian Council for Educational Research (ACER), 2014. *Re-designing the secondary-tertiary interface. Queensland Review of Senior Assessment and Tertiary Entrance.* Brisbane: ACER.

Australian Curriculum, Assessment and Reporting Authority (ACARA), 2012a). *Curriculum development process. Version 6.* Sydney: ACARA.

Australian Curriculum, Assessment and Reporting Authority, (2012b). *The shape of the Australian Curriculum: Health and Physical Education.* Sydney: ACARA.

Australian Curriculum, Assessment and Reporting Authority, (2013). *Australian Curriculum: Health and Physical Education.* Sydney: ACARA.

Albrecht, G. L., and Devlieger, P. J., 1999. The disability paradox: High quality of life against all odds. *Social Science and Medicine,* 48(8), 977–988.

Antonovsky, A., 1979. *Health, stress and coping.* San Francisco: Jossey-Bass.

Antonovsky, A., 1987. *Unraveling the mystery of health.* San Francisco: Jossey-Bass.

Antonovsky, A., 1996a. The salutogenic model as a theory to guide health promotion. *Health Promotion International,* 11(1), 11–18.

Antonovsky, A., 1996b. Aaron Antonovsky's last article. The sense of coherence—an historical and future perspective. *Israeli Journal of Medical Science,* 32(3–4), 170–178.

Barton, H., et al. (Eds.), 2015. *The Routledge handbook of planning for health and well-being: Shaping a sustainable and healthy future.* London: Routledge.

Cale, L., and Harris, J., 2013. 'Every child (of every size) matters' in physical education! Physical education's role in childhood obesity. *Sport, Education and Society,* 18(4), 433–452.

Cale, L., Harris, J., and Chen, M. H., 2014. Monitoring health, activity and fitness in physical education: its current and future state of health. *Sport, Education and Society,* 19(4), 376–397.

Cliff, K., and Wright, J., 2010. Confusing and contradictory: Considering obesity discourse and eating disorders as they shape body pedagogies in HPE. *Sport, Education and Society,* 15(2), 221–233.

Depper, A., and Howe, P. D. 2017. Are we fit yet? English adolescent girls' experiences of health and fitness apps. *Health Sociology Review,* 26(1), 98–112.

Ekkekakis, P. (Ed.), (2013). *Routledge handbook of physical activity and mental health.* London: Routledge.

Ennis, C. D. (Ed.), 2016. *Routledge handbook of physical education pedagogies.* London: Routledge.

Enright, E., et al., 2014. Looking beyond what's broken: towards an appreciative research agenda for physical education and sport pedagogy. *Sport, Education and Society,* 1(7), 912–926.

Ericson, H., et al., 2017. Health resources, ageing and physical activity: a study of physically active women aged 69–75 years. *Qualitative Research in Sport, Exercise and Health,* 1–17.

Eriksson, M., and Lindström, B., 2005. Validity of Antonovsky's sense of coherence scale: A systematic review. *Journal of Epidemiology and Community Health,* 59(6), 460–466.

Eriksson, M., and Lindström, B., 2006. Antonovsky's sense of coherence scale and the relation with health: A systematic review. *Journal of Epidemiology and Community Health,* 60(5), 376–381.

Evans, J., et al., 2008. *Education, disordered eating and obesity discourse: Fat fabrications*. London: Routledge.

Fairclough, S., and Stratton, G., 2005 'Physical education makes you fit and healthy'. Physical education's contribution to young people's physical activity levels. *Health Education Research*, 20(1), 14–23.

Fitzpatrick, K., and Russell, D., 2015. On being critical in health and physical education. *Physical Education and Sport Pedagogy*, 20(2), 159–173.

Fitzpatrick, K., and Burrows, L., 2017. Critical health education in Aotearoa New Zealand. *Sport, Education and Society*, 22(5), 552–568.

Fox, K., Cooper, A. and McKenna, J., 2004. The school and the promotion of children's health-enhancing physical activity: Perspectives from the United Kingdom, *Journal of Teaching in Physical Education*, 23, 338–357.

Fox, N. J., and Ward, K. J., 2008a. What are health identities and how may we study them? *Sociology of Health and Illness*, 30(7), 1007–1021.

Fox, N. J., and Ward, K. J., 2008b. You are what you eat? Vegetarianism, health and identity. *Social Science and Medicine*, 66(12), 2585–2595.

Gard, M., 2011. Truth, belief and the cultural politics of obesity scholarship and public health policy. *Critical Public Health*, 21(1), 37–48.

Gard, M., and Wright, J., 2001. Managing uncertainty: Obesity discourses and physical education in a risk society. *Studies in philosophy and education*, 20(6), 535–549.

Goodyear, V. A., Kerner, C., and Quennerstedt, M., 2017. Young people's uses of wearable healthy lifestyle technologies; surveillance, self-surveillance and resistance. *Sport, Education and Society*, 1–14.

Harris, J., et al., 2016. Young people's knowledge and understanding of health, fitness and physical activity: Issues, divides and dilemmas. *Sport, Education and Society*, 1–4.

Kahan, D., and McKenzie, T. L., 2015. The potential and reality of physical education in controlling overweight and obesity. *American Journal of Public Health*, 105(4), 653–659.

Kirk, D., MacDonald, D., and O'Sullivan, M. (Eds.), 2006. *Handbook of physical education*. London: Sage.

Leahy, D., O'Flynn, G., and Wright, J., 2013. A critical 'critical inquiry' proposition in health and physical education. *Asia-Pacific Journal of Health, Sport and Physical Education*, 4(2), 175–187.

Light, R. L., and Harvey, S., 2017. Positive pedagogy for sport coaching. *Sport, Education and Society*, 22(2), 271–287.

Lonsdale, C., et al., 2013. A systematic review and meta-analysis of interventions designed to increase moderate-to-vigorous physical activity in school physical education lessons. *Preventive Medicine*, 56(2), 152–161.

Lupton, D., 2015. Quantified sex: a critical analysis of sexual and reproductive self-tracking using apps. *Culture, Health & Sexuality*, 17(4), 440–453.

Lupton, D., 2016. The diverse domains of quantified selves: Self-tracking modes and dataveillance. *Economy and Society*, 45(1), 101–122.

Macdonald, D., 2013. The new Australian health and physical education curriculum: A case of/for gradualism in curriculum reform?. *Asia-Pacific Journal of Health, Sport and Physical Education*, 4(2), 95–108.

McCuaig, L., Quennerstedt, M., and Macdonald, D., 2013. A salutogenic, strengths-based approach as a theory to guide HPE curriculum change. *Asia-Pacific Journal of Health, Sport and Physical Education*, 4(2), 109–125.

McCuaig, L., et al., 2016. An eroding social justice agenda: The case of Physical Education and Health Edu-business in schools. *Research Quarterly for Exercise and Sport*, 87(2), 151–164.

McCuaig, L., and Quennerstedt, M., 2018. Health by stealth—exploring the sociocultural dimensions of salutogenesis for sport, health and physical education research. *Sport, Education and Society*, 23(2), 111–122.

McKenzie, T. L., and Lounsbery, M. A., 2014. The pill not taken: Revisiting physical education teacher effectiveness in a public health context. *Research Quarterly for Exercise and Sport*, 85(3), 287–292.

McLaren, P., 1993. Book reviews. *Qualitative Studies in Education*, 6(2), 171–182.

Mittelmark, M. B., et al., 2017. *The handbook of salutogenesis*. Springer.

National Curriculum Board, 2008. *National curriculum development paper*. Melbourne: National Curriculum Board.

Öhman, M., et al., 2014. Competing for ideal bodies: a study of exergames used as teaching aids in schools. *Critical Public Health*, 24(2), 196–209.

O'Connor, J., and Alfrey, L., 2015. Activating the curriculum: a socio-ecological action research frame for health and physical education. *Sport, Education and Society*, 20(6), 691–709.

Petherick, L., 2013. Producing the young biocitizen: secondary school students' negotiation of learning in physical education. *Sport, Education and Society*, 18, 711–730.

Petherick, L., 2015. Shaping the child as a healthy child: Health surveillance, schools, and biopedagogies. *Cultural Studies Critical Methodologies*, 15(5), 361–370.

Pink, S., and Fors, V., 2017. Self-tracking and mobile media: New digital materialities. *Mobile Media & Communication*, 5(3), 219–238.

Powell, D. and Fitzpatrick, K., 2015. 'Getting fit basically just means, like, nonfat': Childrens lessons in fitness and fatness. *Sport, Education and Society*, 20(4), 463–484.

Queensland Curriculum and Assessment Authority, 2018. *Health 2019 v1.1*. Brisbane: Author. Available at www.qcaa.qld.edu.au/downloads/portal/syllabuses/snr_health_19_syll.pdf.

Quennerstedt, M., 2008. Exploring the relation between physical activity and health—a salutogenic approach to physical education. *Sport, Education and Society*, 13(3), 267–283.

Quennerstedt, M., Burrows, L., and Maivorsdotter, N., 2010. From teaching young people to be healthy to learning health. *Utbildning och Demokrati*, 19(2), 97–112.

Quennerstedt, M., and Öhman, M., 2014. Salutogenic approaches to health and the body. In Fitzpatrick, K., and Tinning, R., *Health Education: Critical perspectives*, 190–203. London: Routledge.

Rich, E., and Miah, A., 2017. Mobile, wearable and ingestible health technologies: Towards a critical research agenda. *Health Sociology Review*, 26(1), 84–97.

Sykes, H. and McPhail, D., 2008. Unbearable lessons: Contesting fat phobia in physical education. *Sociology of Sport Journal*, 25, 66–96.

Thedin-Jakobsson, B., 2014. What makes teenagers continue? A salutogenic approach to understanding youth participation in Swedish club sports. *Physical Education and Sport Pedagogy*, 19(3), 239–252.

Thedin-Jakobsson, B., et al., 2012. Almost all start but who continue? A longitudinal study of youth participation in Swedish club sports. *European Physical Education Review*, 18(1), 3–18.

Thorburn, M., and Horrell, A., 2014. Grand designs! Analysing the conceptual tensions associated with new physical education and health and well-being curriculum. *Sport, Education and Society*, 19(5), 621–636.

Tinning, R., 2015. 'I don't read fiction': academic discourse and the relationship between health and physical education. *Sport, Education and Society*, 20(6), 710–721.

Trost, S., 2004. School physical education in the post-report era: An analysis from public health, *Journal of Teaching in Physical Education*, 23, 318–337.

Vander Schee, C., and Gard, M., 2014. Healthy, happy and ready to teach, or why kids can't learn from fat teachers: The discursive politics of school reform and teacher health. *Critical Public Health*, 24(2), 210–225.

Williamson, B., 2015. Algorithmic skin: health-tracking technologies, personal analytics and the biopedagogies of digitized health and physical education. *Sport, Education and Society*, 20(1), 133–151.

Wright, J., 2014. The role of the five propositions in the Australian curriculum: Health and Physical Education. *Active + Healthy Magazine*, 21(4), 1–6.

Chapter 15

Cruel optimism? Socially critical perspectives on the obesity assemblage

Lisette Burrows, Deana Leahy and Jan Wright

Introduction

Childhood overweight and obesity concerns are relentlessly shaping what goes on in the name of Health and Physical Education globally (Burrows, 2010; Leahy and Pike, 2015). For example in the United States, Canada, Sweden, UK, Australia, New Zealand and Singapore both government and nongovernment organisations as well as health promotion agencies point to schools as key sites that can effectively address the assumed 'obesity epidemic' through the incorporation of knowledge and pedagogies intended to change behavior in relation to healthy eating (eating less) and increasing physical activity.

On the one hand, one could apply Berlant's (2011) notion of 'cruel optimism' to this endeavour, that is, those who place their hopes in health and physical education as the resolution to the problem of obesity, are firstly focusing on a utopia that is unachievable, and secondly, following Rasmussen (2015), are pursuing a utopia that distracts attention from important ethical, social and political questions such as health inequalities and the determinants of obesity (Leahy et al., 2016). We would also argue that while such efforts might not make a difference in reducing obesity or changing students' behaviours in the ways intended, they leave a damaging legacy, which cannot be ignored (e.g. weight-based oppression, victim blaming, discrimination, body hating, stigmatization, weight bias and so on).

In other spaces, the notion of 'cruel optimism' has been applied to the endeavours of critical health educators to bring about change (see Leahy et al., 2016). As a general point, the idea that a critical approach to health education can overturn the juggernaut of the anti-obesity proponents, in the face of a culture that 'pathologises, insults and oppresses difference and fatness' (Aphramor, 2005, p. 334), might also seem to be a form of cruel optimism? However, in this chapter we argue that it is both possible and necessary to take a stand, to engage in actions which counter/challenge obesity discourse and its associated practices. We argue that rather than distracting from important ethical, social and political questions, such questions need to be placed at the centre of our pedagogy as a means to redirect or upend the usual pedagogical forces that the obesity epidemic generates within HPE spaces (Burrows, 2016; Burrows and Wright, 2004; Leahy, 2014;

Pringle and Pringle, 2012). We want to suggest that to *not* take a position is to ignore the damage that obesity discourse does and the political and moral circumstances in which it prevails.

To do this we look to Butler's (1993) notions of performativity alongside Deleuze and Guattari's concept of (de-)territorialisation. We are particularly interested in how such insights help us to disrupt the 'normal'/the taken for granted. We argue that through [small] repetitive events/practices, the constant recitation of an alternative discourse, we may be able de-territorialise the hold of "obesity" science/discourse in the political arena but also in everyday lives, in those places where obesity discourse takes hold and does damage. Through the re-citation of an alternative, we can and have influenced health educators and health practitioners' practice by making visible the operation and effects of the discourse and making alternative ways of thinking possible. We want to suggest that such counter practices are important. Following Youdell (2011) we agree that schools also, and in our case, HPE spaces provide us with a significant spaces for the establishment of a counter politics (Leahy et al., 2016; Youdell, 2011).

We acknowledge the scepticism that has been levelled at such attempts to do critical work in the area of health education and obesity science. Indeed it has become something of a (necessary) trend in education and, for our purposes health and physical education, to interrogate the very notion of critique to ask: what constitutes a critical health education/physical education; does it do the work it purports to do; is it successful or, as Gard (2016) suggests, are critical obesity scholars generating a backlash and resistance through their advocacy of their own (often passionately held) position? This has prompted, we would argue, a healthy level of reflexivity, that hopefully addresses the simple 'us' and 'them' of the David and Goliath binary described by Gard (2011) in *The End of the Obesity Epidemic*. In addition to encouraging critical obesity scholars to 'make the limits of their political and moral motivations more transparent to themselves', Gard (2016, p. 248) argues for a pedagogical solution that emphasises the process of working with students—by 'offering resources for understanding' that demonstrate how 'truths' are uncertain and shifting and need to be interrogated.

In the following section we share two brief efforts to counter practices inspired by obesity knowledge and comment more specifically on other ways of dealing with 'the obesity assemblage' in the context of HPE. We do not regard any of our examples as exceptional, nor definitive examples of practices that will always facilitate alternate understandings. Rather, we are hopeful as Biesta (2005) is, that these efforts remind us that things can be different, that there are alternative ways of knowing and thinking about bodies, health and weight and that micro counter-practices can show 'that the way things were was only one limited possibility' (p. 155).

Every-body counts

Lisette was involved in a two year collaborative teaching and learning project where, with two colleagues (see Petrie et al., 2014), she sought to re-imagine possibilities for a primary school health and physical education that engaged diversely positioned children in a more inclusive and celebratory way. Four primary school teachers and three academics collaborated in this project that served to facilitate substantive shifts in both what was taught in HPE programs and how students learned (Ministry of Education, 2013). Below we briefly document what and who interrupted normative thinking throughout this project, signaling the critical moments or 'tipping points' that functioned to illuminate the effects of obesity discourse and provoke a desire to do and think in alternative ways.

For the teachers, it was the voices of children (some as young as 5 years of age), prompted by a series of individual and focus group interviews and a range of classroom activities as part of an 'environmental audit' that sowed seeds of doubt in relation to their existing practices. Hearing what their students believed about health and physical activity, why and from where they drew their current understandings, prompted personal reflections on the degree to which they had contributed to the entrenchment of oft-times narrow understandings of health, fitness and bodies. It also prompted cognizance of the ways outside matters (television advertisements, public health agendas, family proclivities and mass media campaigns) shape young people's sense of who they are and who they can become?

The teachers were relatively unaware of the extent to which their students equated 'health' with particular body types (slim ones) and particular practices (eating the right foods and exercising a lot). They were similarly baffled by the almost exclusive equation of good health with matters of the body, despite their efforts to teach holistically and embrace the broader multi-faceted notion of health evident in the New Zealand Curriculum (Ministry of Education, 2007). Questions like, "what am I/we doing that might contribute to my children thinking about being healthy and unhealthy in such narrow ways?", "what might it be like to be a child in my class/our school who doesn't really 'fit' these views of being healthy?", and "what could we do differently in HPE?", were raised in collective think-tank sessions.

For one of the teachers, questions like these prompted "a complete mind shift", a rethink of ideas and priorities she had previously held dear. For another, questioning common-sense orthodoxies provoked a keen awareness of how food and body messages were played out in friends' and families' homes and in the stories his own students told at sharing time. He recalled one 5-year-old telling her teacher that she loved dancing and danced for hours at home. Her mother had told her she should keep on dancing as this would help her lose weight. These poignant moments coalesced to produce a shared understanding that as teachers, parents, friends, and siblings, we each contribute to how children make sense of food, bodies and health. The words we use in everyday conversations, the activities we choose to privilege and our willingness to simply accept the 'truth' of health messages that contour the lives of children were understood as all influencing how children might come to think of their own and others' health and physicality.

For the project teachers and the academics, this recognition of the ubiquity of health messages fuelled a desire to critically interrogate orthodoxies and to find ways to enable students to also question what they were seeing and hearing about health and physical activity via new media, families, friends and public health messages. It also afforded a tipping point for reimagining what HPE could look and feel like in classrooms. After much discussion the research group came up with an 'ethos'—a series of 'touchstones' that reflected revised aspirations for Health and Physical Education in schools. In brief, this comprised the following principles. Children will:

- Know when, why and how to use knowledge in different contexts
- Understand notions of wellbeing that are holistic, multidimensional and interrelated
- Articulate, question and share multiple perspectives about being well
- Celebrate diversity
- Think critically about their world and accepted 'norms'. (Petrie et al., 2014)

Despite the resonance of the aforementioned tenets with the New Zealand Health and Physical Education in the New Zealand Curriculum, the project team realised that Health and Physical Education signals to many (both students and teachers) a fairly predictable suite of activities and ideas. Sports, fitness, healthy eating and fundamental motor skills, are just a few of the words both researchers and the 'public' associate with HPE (Tinning, 2010). Changing the name, we thought, might facilitate a change in ethos. If children did not think they were 'doing HPE' they and their teachers may be more open to different ways of thinking about what the learning area is all about. EBC—every-body counts—worked as a label that captured the cornerstones of our ethos, emphasising our desire to create a version of HPE that was potentially inclusive of all, that is, all body types, all dispositions, all backgrounds, cultural affiliations, genders and proclivities.

While space does not permit a discussion of the pedagogies enacted en route to progressing this ethos, suffice to say that the voices of children, together with attentiveness to language and what this sediments were the pivotal resources needed to interrupt HPE 'as normal'. The recitation of an alternative name (EBC versus HPE); the repetitive use of a different language to describe bodies, weight and wellbeing within and outside of classrooms; the openness to and commitment to changing curricula priorities and pedagogical norms upon recognition that old ways may be contributing to behaviours and dispositions in children that teachers found abhorrent, was enough to prompt a seismic change in the teachers positionings.

Perhaps it is primary teachers' positioning as people who 'care' for the wellbeing of children (Noddings, 2012), their unmitigated passion for ensuring teaching and learning meets the interests and needs of students, that permitted this somewhat dramatic shift in philosophical position and enacted pedagogy. As Tinning (2002) suggests, often HPE teachers regard themselves as saviours of young people in relation to obesity concerns, imagining themselves as obesity warriors (Burrows, 2016) who can and must endeavour to make students fitter and thinner via their pedagogies. In the case described above, the discomfort created by reflecting on what their students knew and how they came to know it, escalated the teachers' desire to 'save', but not from the perils of obesity. Rather, the teachers mobilised their discomfort, or, in Lather's (2006) terms, their 'distress' to re-build their own and their students' understandings about what matters in terms of health and wellbeing. The very relation of care and respect that prompted their initial engagement with obesity discourses drove their ongoing attempts to challenge the latter.

One of the issues with these kinds of projects is what happens when the funding dries up and researchers move back to their swivel chairs, on to new projects, potentially leaving the teachers in the lurch with their newly formed insights but bereft of resources to continue their change work with young people. In this case, as signalled above, the seismic shift in teacher understandings, their willingness to share it with colleagues and significant support from primary school managers created an opportunity to continue working with an EBC framework. It is the relationships between and across teachers within schools, their commitment to exchanging their experience and knowledge with others that fuels ongoing experiments with re-envisioning what Health and Physical Education might look and feel like in primary school classes.

Poststructuralist interventions every day

In a shift from school based pedagogical examples, we want also to include what might be loosely called serendipitous public pedagogical moments which point to the importance of the developing body of critical obesity scholarship as a resource to both expose and prise apart the various fractures and fissures that are an inherent part of any governmental assemblage (see Leahy, 2012; Youdell, 2011). Drawing on the poststructuralist notion that seemingly insignificant moments, micro claims and practices can do productive work in altering thinking about bodies and weight, we describe two pedagogical encounters with medics that we would argue from our experience (and the Fat Studies literature) are not isolated but represent an attempt by individuals directly impacted by obesity discourse to push back.

A prevalent theme across research studies and anecdotal reports is the phenomenon of doctors seizing opportunities (Gay, 2017; Phelan et al., 2015), no matter what the context, to lecture patients about weight-based matters. For example, one of us has a colleague who went to an eye specialist. Instead of gleaning information about her eyes, she was quizzed about how much she exercised and her daily eating habits. While one response might have been to acquiesce to her doctor's expertise, in this instance she re-positioned this distressing encounter as a pedagogical opportunity to educate her doctor. She challenged the doctor's assumptions that her body size and shape revealed anything about her lifestyle, queried the links drawn between weight and eye health, produced scholarly articles (including some of our own) for the doctor to read and engaged in ongoing discussion about the discursive resources available to specialists when having clinical consultations with clients and the assumptions that drive deficit medical perceptions. An apology from the doctor, a commitment to reading, thinking and practice otherwise and reflection on the affect generated in such encounters ensued.

In another example, another of us received a 'thank you email' describing an experience with her doctor from whom she was seeking diagnostic advice about her weight and fat distribution. While space prohibits reproducing the entire email exchange here, with Mary's permission, we share a little of this encounter as it speaks directly to the capacity of weight-based discourse to shape medics' interactions with clients, but more importantly, the profound impact speaking back to this discourse (by drawing on critical obesity literature) can have in shifting sedimented perceptions. Her initial email reads:

> Yes I have had another run in with a doctor. It is funny how if you are fat they seem to think you feel no pain or have no brain. But this encounter was really weird because up until now this doctor has treated me with respect heavens we even discussed literature. ... I have delivered the letter to the doctor's surgery and booked an appointment for next Tuesday. I will also be taking information of both your books to him. I hope this leads to a new understanding and a fresh start.
>
> Mary D

A section of the letter Mary sent is below:

> Dear Dr ****,
> I don't want to offend you but I need you to understand how I feel. If I seemed confused on Tuesday and had trouble expressing myself it was because I was trying to avoid tears. I am very sensitive to the subject of obesity as experience has taught me that the moment a doctor mentions my weight and goes straight to diet he/she no longer sees past my size meaning serious illness might go unnoticed or untreated. The fight or flight reaction kicked in and I became more stressed as the feelings of rejection increased. Ironically, having come to trust and respect you I had made the appointment specifically to discuss my weight and the unusual structure of the fat, on my abdomen and between my shoulders, which is possibly not entirely attributable to Lymphodema (sic) but I didn't have that opportunity.
>
> It seemed to me that you did not believe me when I tried to outline my regular diet. To clear up any confusion: my diet mainly consists of lean meat, grilled fish, smoked salmon or six oysters, eggs (yolk removed after first egg) and various salad leaves (the dressing of which are sugar free and no fat, or plain lemon juice, or Balsamic vinegar) and seasonal vegetables steamed or stir fried in olive oil (mainly English spinach, fresh asparagus, capsicum, aubergine, microwaved mushrooms, spring onions, broccoli, celery etc).

When you pulled up <http://www.sugarstacks.com/blog/> I felt it as an act of infantalization, as you had formerly treated me as an intelligent and cultured woman. No part of the picture blog, with its demonstration pile of white sugar cubes, applied to me. I do not consume fizzy drinks, fast food or processed foods nor do I eat pizza and would never darken the door of McDonalds or Kentucky fried because surprise, surprise, I am a very good cook and when I was slim and wealthy mostly dined at the finest restaurants in many parts of the world. I was staggered when you said I should replace fruit with a carrot. I eat one small serving of fresh fruit maybe once a day (raspberries, strawberries, red grapefruit, passionfruit etc and tomato) all of which are not much above the carrot in sugar content. I do not have bread, milk, sweets, cake or biscuits in the house. Items like the repellant tins of John West tuna, sardines or baked beans you suggested are quite foreign to my eating experience.

... I really felt that stress on the way home when I recalled you saying to me "If you keep going this way you might be one of those people who have eventually to be removed from their house by a forklift truck (sic)" and tears started to roll down my face. Overcome by embarrassment, I fled to the shopping centre in a blur wanting to be comforted, I bought things I have not bought for years. For dinner on Tuesday night I fought against sorrow with two dozen oysters, an entire bottle of decent wine and a whole bar of chocolate. Bring on the forklift truck!

... I know more about weight and diet than most health workers because I live it. What I need is a doctor - I need you, Dr ****, I need the cultured man who reads books and I had come to respect. The doctor who treated me as an intelligent woman who was once a top flight journalist and award winning screenwriter, not merely a cretinous fat blob. Dr ****, I need you as a diagnostician, and it is there that you excel.

I will make another appointment. Do you think we could start again?

Mary D

The response from Mary's doctor reads:

Thanks for letting me know how badly I misjudged things with my attempted advice to you last week.

I fear I did not detect the cues that I was upsetting you.

I do remain worried about the medical effects of your build and the difficulties with hernia, heart disease etc but I will leave the subject alone unless there is a particular issue you want to raise.

I am very happy to continue with your general medical care if you wish. I would do my best but I can't promise always to get it right.

The above pedagogical encounter scarcely needs analysis. Mary has done it herself. She succinctly conveys the affect her doctor produced. She helps him see how his weight-based paradigm impacts her subjectivity, her sense of herself as intelligent, creative, viable human. The visceral effects of his language are keenly realised in Mary's letter. The doctor's response signals at least, a recognition of this, and at most a promise to do and perhaps think differently with Mary and perhaps with other clients.

Both of the pedagogical encounters discussed above are discomforting ones –for the professional and client involved. Both involve the client drawing on socio-logical critiques of obesity to educate professionals and doing so from an initial position of vulnerability. Both women are educated in the traditional sense, hold prestigious positions in their chosen fields and have the intellectual resources, access to critical perspectives and resilience to challenge the hold of obesity sci-ence despite an initial desire to flee rather than stay. Clearly, these are not cir-cumstances, nor resources that all would have access to. Nevertheless, harking back to our introductory comments, the recitation of an alternative discourse would seem to have de-territorialised, at least for a moment, the hold of obesity science in these two doctors' practice and thought. While Gard (2016) suggests asking uncomfortable questions as a key strategy in challenging obesity discourse, perhaps responding to uncomfortable questions is also a promising tactic for elic-iting alternative ways of thinking.

Discussion

Despite the promises detailed in the encounters above, neither of the two exam-ples above take on the obesity discourse head on as part of health knowledge within the HPE curriculum. In Australia and New Zealand, there are curriculum spaces that would allow educators to move beyond a 'health education' fuelled solely by public health obesity prevention discourses and practices (see for exam-ple the new Australian Curriculum: Health and Physical Education). The focus on an 'educative' purpose of health education and on critical inquiry, we would argue, makes it possible to disrupt/de-territorialise the hold of medicalised health promotion messages about obesity that are re-cited in school health education. The focus on an educative purpose makes it possible to pose the question: what might be possible if obesity became our object of critical study? In asking this question we follow Metzl's lead (2010) to think about the capacity of our class-rooms to engage in a process that unpacks the concept of obesity from inter-disciplinary perspectives and explore its assumptions, reliances and effects with our students. Within this space we could explore, for example, what particular meanings of obesity and associated practices impact people's lives, their bodies and their health. Such an approach requires 'deliberate interruptions' or what Evans et al. (2011, p. 339) refers to as 'throwing a monkey wrench into a system of knowledge that perpetuates' the familiar and troubling practices of HPE'.

We recognise that there are limits to these possibilities both in schools and in teacher education. Recent research with HPE teacher education students, for example, suggests that despite their considerable enthusiasm to assist their students live healthier lives, this continues to be in the narrowest of terms, associated with risk-based approaches focusing on individual responsibility and behaviour change, despite health and physical education subjects which examine health from a critical perspective (Wright, O'Flynn and Welch, 2017). We would also argue that in Australia at least, health and physical education teachers are often ill-prepared to teach outside the status quo, that is to teach *about* obesity as a socio-cultural phenomenon. The coupling of health and physical education means that those preparing to teach these subjects in secondary schools are required to take foundational subjects in anatomy and physiology and other science based subjects but not in the social sciences or humanities (see Leahy and McCuaig, 2014; Wright et al., 2017). Yet the health knowledge they draw on and are expected to teach in an educative fashion, can best be understood, we argue, with some grounding in sociology and/or cultural studies. Such a grounding provides the tools to examine knowledge, including health knowledge as contingent, as shaped by social and historical circumstances, and with particular consequences for how people make sense of their bodies and their lives and those of others.

Given the substantial body of literature that points to the challenges of dealing critically with obesity knowledge in the context of schools and teacher education (Alfrey, O'Connor and Jeanes, 2016; Burrows, 2016), we argue that there are other productive ways to disrupt the cultural assumptions associated with the multiplicity of interrelated knowledges and practices that comprise the 'obesity assemblage'. These include critical perspectives about obesity that reach the general public through public pedagogies in the form of museum based exhibitions, community arts based projects and performance poetry to name a few. For example, the Wellcome Collection in London, has curated an exhibition entitled *Medicine Now*. One of the issues covered in the exhibition is obesity'. The Wellcome Collection, and indeed this particular exhibition attempts to attend to interdisciplinary perspectives. With reference to the obesity section of the exhibition, visitors are invited to engage with a varying range of installations that explicitly adopt more than 'medicalised' obesity knowledges. As you walk into the room for example a John Isaacs sculpture of an oversized obese, pink and fleshy body dominates the room. It immediately draws the visitors' attention. The sculpture is called 'I can't help the way I feel' and, according to the artist, is an attempt to enlist the visitor into feeling

> [the] emotional landscape of someone who might glance in the mirror and see themselves in a certain way when in reality they look nothing of the sort. So it's a piece about obesity, but it's equally a piece about anorexia and about body dysmorphia; it's about the personal implications of a society obsessed with an 'obesity epidemic' and with body image. (Morgan and Dornan, 2014)

In addition to the sculpture, there are various photographs, medical paraphernalia related to bariatric surgery in a glass case, nutrition advice, and an installation that includes a full ceiling to floor bookcase loaded with diet books. While the critical potential of the exhibition itself is the focus of ongoing research by Leahy, we want to highlight the possibilities that exhibition learning in general offers as a way to critically engage publics (including pre service teachers and school students) with interdisciplinary approaches that take us outside the usual medicalized orbits we often find ourselves in. While the 'usual suspects' dominated the exhibition, that is biomedical approaches, there were attempts to open up other spaces for thinking 'otherwise'. For example, the sheer volume of diet books sitting on the enormous bookshelf evoked a visceral response in relation to the overwhelming profusion of advice that was on offer for a 'dieter' to feast upon. Picking up a phone to listen to fat activists and artists talk about fat and the body differently necessarily took the listener on a very different journey, outside and away from biomedical and public health discourses—if only for a moment. Despite our excitement and optimism about the potential of exhibitions as critical spaces, our enthusiasm about the potential of this particular exhibition is mixed given the dominance of biomedical approaches. We also read Charlotte Cooper's (2016) blog post about her reaction to the Obesity exhibit. Her post entitled 'How to killjoy an obesity display one #bodyspectacular at a time' reveals that she loathes the obesity display, and has done ever since it was installed in 2007. She writes that the exhibition,

> that consists of a sculpture, weight loss technology, diet books, audio recordings of anti-obesity proponents and a token fat woman, and objects implying that people have become less active and over-reliant on labour-saving devices is a pitch perfect depiction of the dominant medicalized rhetoric that circulates around the Obesity Epidemic.

She goes on to add that she experiences the exhibition as a hate zone. Given this, we necessarily find ourselves back at the drawing board, trying to think through the various critical opportunities this exhibition, and others, might offer us pedagogically. And while we want to suggest that much more needs to be done in this particular exhibition space in the name of criticality, we do think, following Ellsworth (2007) that exhibition spaces can offer some new ways to think about how we might engage students in thinking about the body, fat, medicine, health, shame, disgust to name but a few. One of the ways to try to ensure that the exhibition might have a better chance of realizing its critical promises is to ensure that the initial brief explicitly sets up the exhibition to tend to critical perspectives.

In addition to exhibitions, there is growing recognition of the potential of the arts, including theatre, performance and poetry to engage publics in questions related to how fat and obesity is portrayed, represented and culturally read (Mobely, 2014)[1]. For example the performance poetry of English radical dietician and poet Lucy Aphramor. Aphramor (2016) tells us, in an overview of her work on her blog that:

> Spoken word poems reach people in viscerally, pivotally different ways than any lecture or workshop ever could. Poems can hold stories that will always be too big, too rich, too unwieldy for an article. I use them to disturb the

routine view on health that pretends there is no such thing as society. To disrupt the rules on what counts and whose voices matter. To share facts that have not had their soul ripped out with statistics. They do not assume a single, static, sorted, standpoint, but—in short, they shake things up and this is the starting point for change.

Her performances engage the audience members in a process that critically identifies and purposefully disrupts deeply held beliefs that serve to maintain the obesity assemblage (see Aphramor, Gingras and Morley, 2012). While critical pedagogues have for some time utilized these methods to gain critical leverage (see for example Goldstein, 2013; Huye, 2015), these forms are relatively new in the critical study of obesity in the HPE space (as an exception, see Fitzpatrick, 2018; Welch, 2013, 2017). Given the above though we want to suggest that the potential exists and that such approaches may help us forge new directions. If obesity discourses, and the constellation of affects that accompany obesity prevention, are so intractable, perhaps recruiting new ways of working critically that make explicit attempts to work viscerally might help get us to a different place.

Note

1. Additionally the journal *Fat Studies* has a special themed special issue in production at the time of writing this chapter entitled "Fat in Theatre Performance."

References

Alfrey, L., O'Connor, J., and Jeanes, R. (2017). Teachers as policy actors: co-creating and enacting critical inquiry in secondary health and physical education. *Physical Education and Sport Pedagogy*, 22(2), 107–120.

Aphramor, L. (2005). Is a weight-centred health framework salutogenic? Some thoughts on unhinging certain dietary ideologies, *Social Theory & Health*, (3), 315–340.

Aphramor, L. (2016). Poet Lucy: Spoken Word Poet (Blog). Retrieved from http://lucyaphramor.com/poet/about/

Aphramor, L., Gingras, J., and Morley, C. (2012). Coming in from the Edgelands: Artist dietitians speak. 2nd Annual Critical Dietetics Conference, Sydney Australia.

Berlant, L. (2010). Risky bigness: On obesity, eating and the ambiguity of health. In Johnathon Metzl and Anna Krikland (Eds.), *Against health: How health became the new morality* (pp. 26–39). New York: New York University Press.

Berlant, L. (2011). *Cruel optimism*. Durham, NC: Duke University Press.

Burrows, L. (2010). Kiwi kids are Weetabix kids: Body matters in childhood. *Sport, Education and Society*, 15(2), 235–251.

Burrows, L. (2016). "Obesity" warriors in the tertiary classroom. In Erin Cameron and Constance Russell (Eds.), *The fat pedagogy reader: Challenging weight-based oppression through critical education* (pp. 101–112) New York: Peter Lang.

Burrows, L. and Wright, J. (2004). The good life: New Zealand children's perspectives of health and self. *Sport, Education and Society*, 9(2), 193–205.

Butler, J. (1993). *Bodies that matter: On the discursive limits of 'sex'*. New York and London: Routledge.

Cooper, C. (2016). How to killjoy an obesity display one #bodyspectacular at a time. Retrievedfromhttps://obesitytimebomb.blogspot.com.au/2016/10/how-to-killjoy-obesity-display-one.html

Fitzpatrick, K. (2018). Poetry in motion: in search of the poetic in health and physical education. *Sport, Education and Society*, 23, 123–134.

Gard, M. (2011). *The end of the obesity epidemic*. Abingdon, Oxon, UK: Routledge.

Gard, M. (2016). Navigating morality, politics and reason: Towards scientifically literate and intellectually ethical fat pedagogies. In Erin Cameron and Constance Russell (Eds.), *The fat pedagogy reader: Challenging weight-based oppression through critical education* (pp. 241–250). New York: Peter Lang.

Gay, T. (2017). *Hunger: A memoir of (my) body*. New York: HarperCollins.

Goldstein, T. (2013). *Zero Tolerance and other plays: Disrupting racism, xenophobia and homophobia in school*. Rotterdam, The Netherlands: Sense Publishers.

Huye, H. (2015). Using poetry and art analysis to evoke critical thinking and challenging reflection in senior-level nutrition students. *Journal of Nutrition Education and Behavior*, 47(3), 283–285.

Lather, P. (2006). Paradigm proliferation as a good thing to think with: Teaching research in education as a wild profusion. *International Journal of Qualitative Studies in Education*, 19(1), 35–57.

Leahy, D. 2014. Assembling a health[y] subject: Risky and shameful pedagogies in health education. *Critical Public Health*, 24(2), 171–181.

Leahy, D., and McCuaig, L. (2014). Disrupting the field: Teacher education in health education. In K. Fitzpatrick and R. Tinning (Eds.). *Health education: Critical perspectives* (pp. 220–232) London: Routledge.

Leahy, D., Burrows, L., McCuaig, L., Wright, J., and Penney, D. (2016). *School health education in changing times: Policies, pedagogies and partnerships*. London: Routledge.

Metzl, J. (2010). Introduction: Why against health? In: J Metzl and A. Kirkland (Eds.), *Against health: How health became the new morality* (pp. 1–11). New York: New York University Press.

Ministry of Education. (2007). *The New Zealand Curriculum*. Wellington: Learning Media.

Mobely, J. (2014). *Female bodies on the American stage: Enter fat actress*. New York: Palgrave Macmillan.

Morgan, C., and Dornan, R. (2014). Perspectives: I can't help the way I feel. Retrieved from https://wellcomecollection.org/articles/perspectives-i-cant-help-the-way-i-feel/

Noddings, N. (2012). The language of care ethics. *Knowledge Quest*, 40(5), 52–56.

Petrie, K., Burrows, L., and Cosgriff, M. (2013). *Every-body counts? Reimagining Health and Physical Education in primary schools*. Final Report. Wellington: Teaching and Learning Research Initiative.

Petrie, K., Burrows, L., and Cosgriff, M. (2014). Building a community of collaborative inquiry: A pathway to re-imagining practice in health and physical education. *Australian Journal of Teacher Education* 39(2). DOI: 10.14221/ajte.2014v39n2.3.

Phelan, S. M. Burgess, D. J., Yeazel, M. W., Hellerstedt, W. L., Griffin, J. M., and van Ryn, M. (2015). Impact of weight bias and stigma on quality of care and outcomes for patients with obesity. *Obesity Reviews*, 16(4), 319–326.

Rasmussen, M. L. (2015). Cruel optimism and contemporary Australian critical theory in educational research. *Educational Philosophy and Theory*, 47(2), 192–206.

Tinning, R. (2010). *Pedagogy and human movement: Theory, practice, research.* London: Routledge.

Welch, R. (2013). Tracing contemporary healthscapes: Pre-service primary teachers' subjectivities in relation to health and the body. PhD dissertation, University of Wollongong, NSW, Australia. http://ro.uow.edu.au/cgi/viewcontent.cgi?article=4791&context=theses

Welch, R. (2017). Within and against each other: Comparative poetic vignettes as an analytic and educative tool in school health education. Paper presented at the *(Un)Making Europe: Capitalism, Solidarities, Subjectivities European Sociological Association (ESA) Conference*, Athens. https://www.conftool.pro/esa2017/index.php?page=browseSessions&form_session=1487

Wright, J., O'Flynn, G., and Welch, R. (2017) In search of the socially critical in health education: Exploring the views of health and physical education preservice teachers in Australia. *Health Education.* 118 (2), 117–130.

Youdell, D. (2011). *School trouble: Identity, power and politics in education.* New York: Routledge.

Chapter 16

Critical research in exercise and fitness

Pirkko Markula

Introduction

Although fitness and exercise are often located within the domains of exercise physiology and exercise psychology, they entered into socio-cultural research on sport in the 1980s, primarily in the wake of aerobics, a group fitness class created for women by women. Judi Sheppart-Missett and Jackie Sorensen are credited as the founders of the first commercialized aerobics programs in the late 1970s that were then further popularized by Jane Fonda in the 1980s (Markula 1993). Considering the origin of commercialized fitness as women's activity, it is hardly surprising that the early research stemmed from feminist traditions. Despite the popularity of aerobics among women, the feminist scholars, however, were unconvinced of its positive qualities. Critical feminists, particularly, condemned aerobics as 'a feminized' activity that supported patriarchal hegemony and thus, women's oppression (Kagan and Morse 1988, Lenskyj 1986, Theberge 1987). It was at this conjuncture that I entered the field that we now characterize as socio-cultural research of fitness.

Following the trends of the time, I investigated aerobics and its meanings to women participants. As an instructor myself, I had ready access to its latest variations, its participants, and its location, 'the gym.' Although aerobics is now almost extinct, the gym, commercial or communal, continues to exist as the space to exercise in the Westernized world.[1]

As the fitness industry has developed into a globally popular enterprise, the interest in studying exercise as a social, cultural, and political issue has increased. To illustrate its current diversity, I first map how socio-cultural study of fitness and exercise has evolved, theoretically and methodologically, since the early 1990s. Acknowledging the multiplicity of research approaches, I then highlight how theory, particularly, has advanced how we know about and practice fitness. Finally, I compare and contrast the impact of critical research with poststructuralist research to assess how different knowledges might produce social change through exercise and fitness.

The Mapping the socio-cultural exercise and fitness research

Socio-cultural research in exercise and fitness has evolved around two large, yet overlapping, themes: critiques of the fit body ideal in the popular media and accounts of exercisers' lived experiences with 'working out.' I detail each theme separately to illustrate their significance to the existing analysis of exercise and fitness.

Reading popular media images

The earliest socio-cultural studies focused on images of fitness videotapes, innovative and popular at the time, that promoted a singular, heterosexually attractive, fit, feminine body (Kagan and Morse 1988, MacNeill 1998). Several feminist researchers continued this early critique with an expanded focus on various fitness magazines (e.g., Duncan 1994, Dworkin and Wachs 2009, Eskes, Duncan and Miller 1998, Jette 2006, Lloyd 1996, Markula 2001). This critical research, mainly from a Foucauldian perspective, conceptualized the popular fitness magazines as parts of a modern-day Panopticon where an invisible power continually controlled individuals' behavior through self-surveillance of the ideal body shape. In addition to critiquing the body ideal, feminist fitness researchers observed a close intertwining with health: In the (fitness) media women's health was, and continues to be, culturally expressed in aesthetic terms as a thin, healthy looking body (e.g., Markula and Kennedy 2011). While the focus has been, largely, on women's fit body ideal, there is emerging socio-cultural research on men's fitness media, particularly the internationally circulated men's lifestyle magazines *Men's Fitness* and *Men's Health*.

Similar to women's fitness magazines, men's fitness is promoted through an ideal heterosexual, lean, and muscular body shape to be obtained by disciplinary self-work. Such an image acts as a counterpart to the fit, feminine body to reproduce hegemonic masculinity through visible dominance of white male bodies (e.g., Alexander 2003, Crawshaw 2007, Labre 2005, Lawrence 2016, Ricciardelli, Clow, and White 2010). While the fitness magazines continue to sell exercise as a tool to shape the body towards the ideal looks, the rapidly changing media scape now provides other avenues to market the fit body.

Although the Internet is steaming with exercise and fitness sites, there is not much research on its textual or image world. Some exceptions are Meredith Nash's (2016) critical feminist examination of the Australian Lorna Jane internet fitness wear retail website, Stephanie Jong and Jon Drummond's (2016) study of young women's use of social networking sites to obtain information on fitness and health, and Brad Millington's (2014, 2017) work on Nintendo Wii Plus Fit exercise videogame and new fitness technologies. This research overwhelmingly assigns the new media as arbitrators of biopedagogies that facilitate the entrance of the biopolitics of healthism and self-surveillance in more expansive ways into individual, private lives.

The various socio-cultural analyses of diverse fitness media sources have quite unanimously condemned the gendered images of fitness as oppressive. Following such strong critique, another strand of researchers has found that an emphasis on the media texts ignores the lived, possibly positive experiences of fitness. After all, fitness is popular activity with potentially multiple meanings to its diverse participants.

Understanding lived experiences of fitness

To counterbalance the analyses of popular fitness media images, there is an established body of research on exercisers' lived experiences in diverse settings. Using such methods as ethnography and interviews, the socio-cultural researchers of fitness have investigated 'embodied' experiences of 'working out' in Japan (Spielvogel 2002, 2003), Europe (e.g., Crossley 2006, Lewis 2008, Maguire and Mansfield 1998, Markula 2004, Parviainen 2011, Sassatelli 2010), and the United States (e.g., Dworkin 2003, Gimlin 2002, Markula 1995, 2003, Smith Maguire 2007). With the expansion of the fitness industry, this research now examines diverse forms of exercise such as CrossFit (Dawson 2017, Knapp 2015, Washington and Economides 2016), Les Mills (Parviainen 2011), pole dancing (Holland 2010), yoga (Lewis 2008), or Zumba (Nieri and Hughes 2016). There is less research on the meanings exercisers assign to individualized exercise forms such as resistance training or cardio-vascular workouts on treadmills or exercise bikes (e.g., Dworkin 2003).

Employing multiple theoretical perspectives, these examinations indicate that lived exercise experiences are constructed parallel to the fitness media images: Body shape dominates exercise practices and the participants gain self-confidence when they look good. In addition, individual exercisers seem to accept that it is their personal responsibility to improve their body shapes. This research reveals further opportunities to negotiate understandings of the body that, while indeed dominated by the ideologies structuring the fitness field, are also increasingly nuanced and varied.

Interpretive researches drawing from Goffman's sociology or phenomenology have demonstrated that women can actively build a self that, while influenced by the aesthetics of the feminine body, is not entirely suppressed by it (e.g., Gimlin 2002, Lewis 2008, McDermott 2000, Pike 2011, Sassatelli 1999). Critical feminist research expands on this theme to interrogate the resistant, liberating potential of women's exercise. Although aware of the ideological construction of the feminized fitness, many women participate in fitness for additional reasons such as physical health (Malin 2010), strength (Dworkin 2003), belonging to a community (Malin 2010, Markula 2003, Wray 2003), or simply to have fun (Nieri and Hughes 2016). Many exercising women also question the young, thin, and toned media ideal (Craig and Liberty 2007, Haravon Collins 2002, Markula 1995, 2003). Some researchers have further exposed the dominance of westernized values of women's health and well-being (McDermott 2000, Wray 2003) by including

South Asian women's (George and Rail 2006), muslin women's (Wray 2002, 2011), older women's (Pike 2011), and large women's (Synne Groven, Nyheim Solbraekke and Engelsrud 2011) experiences in their investigations.

In addition to participants' involvement, the fitness instructors' and personal trainers' role in the construction of the gendered world of the fitness industry have interested fitness scholars. These fitness professionals can shape their participants' views significantly through the content of the exercise programs and group fitness classes. According to several researchers, personal trainers (PTs) (Frew and McGilligvray 2005, Phillips and Drummond 2001, Smith Maguire 2007, 2001) reinforce the clients' personal responsibility to adopt a healthy lifestyle. Wiest, Andrews, and Giardina (2015) added that PTs often judged their clients' state of health by surveying their clients' 'looks.' Consequently, these fitness professionals commonly accepted the perfect, healthy looking body as an essential part of fitness culture and prescribed exercise to combat the clients' undesired fat and flab that they, unquestionably, expected consumers to want to work on. The PTs worked hard to maintain their own bodies, which they believed was an indication of their dedication to fitness.

Group fitness instructors operate in a very similar environment. Like the PTs, they tended to emphasize building the healthy looking, fit body as each participant's personal responsibility (Berman et al. 2005, D'Abundo 2009, Dworkin and Wachs 2009, Mansfield 2011, Petersson McIntyre 2011, Wray 2011). Like the PTs, the instructors believed that they act as role models for their clients and thus, needed to maintain a fit looking body (e.g., Markula and Chikinda 2016). Nevertheless, they wanted to provide a comfortable, safe, and supportive learning environment for diverse participants (D'Abundo 2009, Petersson McIntyre 2011). Markula (2004) indicated that the mindful instructors in her study were reluctant to use the improved body shape as a selling point preferring to promote such exercise benefits as relaxation and improved body alignment. Yet, they found building a fit looking body appealing to their clientele and thus, continued to construct these types of bodies through their practices. Therefore, although aware of the problems associated with the ideal fit body, the instructors lacked knowledge to design alternative practices. Similarly, Wiest, Andrews, and Giardina (2015) found PTs unquestioningly promoted health without locating their training practices in the larger cultural and commercial context of the fitness industry. This research concludes, thus, that neoliberal healthism intertwined with the aesthetics of the ideal body continues to permeate the lived world of fitness. This context, then, shapes the fitness professionals' and their participants' meanings about exercise and the fit body.

Critical issues: Problems with the construction of inequities

While there has been a steady growth of critical research in exercise and fitness over the decades, the central concerns have not varied to great extent. They remain remarkably identical in research around the globe; a finding that reflects the nature of commercial fitness industry demand of clientele with the means and inclination to buy their services in the countries with sufficient level of commercial development. Nevertheless, three main critical issues emerge from the previous literature. First, socio-cultural study of fitness and exercise is a research area with a central focus on women and the construction of the fit, feminine body. Second, the fit feminine body is generally condemned as oppressive, particularly as it is represented in the media. Third, women exercisers live in contradiction between compliance to continual body shaping and an acknowledgement of its narrowness and impossibility. These findings are supported with several interlinked binaries that provide the foundation for much of the critical exercise and fitness literature: the feminine—masculine identity; the mediated fitness images—lived experiences of fitness; and oppression—liberation. While these binaries provide tools to effectively critique the oppressive nature of the commercial fitness industry/media nexus, they also result in a stalemate in terms moving from critique to social change. To further illustrate my argument, I discuss each of the main binaries underlying the critical exercise and fitness research in more detail.

The feminine—masculine identity

The majority of critical exercise and fitness research analyses the construction of the fit feminine body through a critical feminist lens: The fit feminine body is ideologically constructed as the polar opposite to the masculine body that constitutes the dominant end of the binary. This ideological dominance is sustained by the hegemonic groups (of white men) who control, for example, the media industry. According to this theoretical viewpoint, women's fitness is marketed and enacted to support traditional feminine characteristics such as the emphasis on appearance rather than skill and strength, emphasis on thinness and tone rather than muscularity, and emphasis on dance, fun, and group fitness rather than 'serious' pursuit of individual, high intensity resistance and cardio-vascular training. The fitness industry as a locus of neoliberal control and healthism further supports this identity construction: Exercising women (and men) are to take individual responsibility for their health that is closely intertwined with the aesthetics of the fit body. Even 'new' trends such as the currently popular CrossFit that markets itself to women with such slogan as 'strong is the new sexy' (e.g., Dawson 2017), is built around obtaining the sleek feminine body. Washington and Economides (2016, p. 143) describe the CrossFit images: "the markers of femininity such as tight clothing, perfectly styled hair, and makeup contrast against traditional markers of masculinity such as well-defined muscles, weightlifting accoutrements, and strength." Although preoccupied with the construction of a feminine body through fitness, some exercise and fitness researchers now focus on intersectional identity construction aligned with the neoliberal initiatives to build a healthy, fat free aging body, ethnic body, or obese body through exercise. While this research, indeed, has effectively critiqued the oppressive nature of the fit heteronormative, white, and young feminine identity, it typically does not offer suggestions for changing the social orientation to women's fitness.

The mediated fitness versus lived experiences of fitness

If some critical exercise and fitness researchers have condemned the fitness industry as oppressive, others have pointed out that such judgement is based largely on reading the media representations of fitness. Such media images, these researchers argue, do not reflect the lived experiences of fitness and as such, the magazines' glossy image world has little to do with embodied ways of 'working out' (e.g., Crossley 2006, Malin 2010). In this research, the idea of 'embodiment' as a source for active agency is juxtaposed with the dominance of textual representation. The embodiment/textuality binary introduces another dichotomy between the interpretive researchers who look for authentic fitness experiences and the critical (feminist) researchers who focus on the ideological construction of the fit, feminine identity.[2] Although accused of exclusively focusing on textuality, several critical researchers, nevertheless, have analyzed individual exercisers' agentic resistance to the hegemony of masculine, heteronormative, healthist, and ageist ideologies. I locate the efforts to identify individual resistance further under oppression/resistance binary.

Oppression versus resistance

The oppression/resistance binary characterizes particularly the critical feminist analyses of exercise and fitness. To expand the strong focus on oppressive media readings, the analyses of lived, every day, embodied experiences search for women's resistant agency or what I label here as embodied subjectivity. There are two main theoretical paths to analyze embodied subjectivity. The first draws from critical theory to investigate how individual women use their active agency as a way to liberate themselves from shaping the ideal, fit, feminine body. The agency does not require a conscious engagement in resistance to an ideology, but rather, the researcher assigns and detects certain acts as signs of resistance against a theoretical reading of oppressive femininity. For example, exercise forms such as weight lifting, bodybuilding, or CrossFit that are designed to create a muscular body theoretically constitute resistance to the production of the current feminine ideal. Despite their potential for resistance, the researchers note, many women continue to carefully negotiate their muscularity and deep down, work relentlessly toward the toned, feminine ideal. In addition to critical feminism, Foucault's insights have been applied to examine embodied subjectivity as active agency.

The application of Foucault's work to building an embodied subjectivity within the fitness industry combines his concepts of governmentality and the technologies of the self to assume a 'self-governing' individual who acts upon others as well as one's self (Markula 2014c). The embodied subjectivity, deriving from exercise experiences in the micro context of everyday life, is read to counteract the oppression of neoliberal healthism. Despite slightly different concepts, this type of Foucauldian work aligns closely with the premise of critical theory to reinforce the individual's agency to counteract ideological oppression[3] and further polarizes exercising identities as oppressive or resistant.

While women continue to negotiate their contradictory exercise experiences, the mediated image of the fit feminine body as well as the fitness industry offerings, with slight modifications, have remained unchanged. Thus, there has not been a remarkable change into the inequalities characterizing the fitness industry as a result of the critical focus on binary-based identity politics.

Social change?

When theoretical analysis oscillates between the binary of oppressive/resistant identity, it is possible to critique the social construction of dominance, but not to enact significant structural change. In addition, the media and the fitness industries effectively appropriate these critiques to sustain the existing power structures by offering more nuanced marketing campaigns that advertise for (women's) empowerment within the existing framework of femininity. Such campaigns emphasize women's choice: Individual women can now choose to be sexualized that is then celebrated as a sign of liberation and freedom. For example, pole fitness that openly draws from women's sexual exploitation by the sex industry, is now credited as empowering women to be strong and sensual. Several feminist writers characterize this as an era of post-feminism where "hyper-culture of commercial sexuality" is celebrated (McRobbie 2004, p. 259), but that cleverly gives an impression of "engaging in a well-informed and even well-intended response to feminism" (p. 255). What is the role of theory in this contradictory world where critique is manipulated for commercial profit and continued coercion?

Some scholars might see themselves primarily as social critics whose role is to issue poignant critique of the oppressive nature of the fit, feminine body ideal, not to act as active agents for social change. What if, however, a researcher was interested in going beyond critique? If the focus on socially constructed oppression through binary identity construction offers limited force towards change, what is the role of theory and scholarship in creating social change in the neoliberal times of individualized fitness, health, and exercise responsibility? I argue that theory is fundamental in any attempt to enact social change that, nevertheless, cannot take place, constructively, without a critique of the existing conditions. As substantial critique of the fitness industry and its exercise practices already exists, it is timely to consider conditions for transformation. Because of the limitations of binary-based social constructionism, I offer poststructuralist theorizing as an attempt to move beyond bipolarized identity politics to examine, more broadly, how we have become to know ourselves, and act, through binaries. More importantly, however, I employ poststructuralist insights to suggest some ways to break out from the limitations of identity politics. Using theoretical insights by Foucault and Deleuze to broaden the theoretical horizon to account for social change, some fitness and exercise researchers have shifted their focus from the social construction of identity to consider, more comprehensively, the multiple knowledges that currently structure exercise and fitness.

Fitness knowledges

To transcend the binary identity construction and the following debate about oppressive and resistance practices, it is important to consider how we began to know about fitness in a specific manner. Here I draw from Foucault's (1970, 1972, see also Deleuze 1988) insight that all knowledge is constructed as a part of power relations and the following practices, then, are shaped based on specific ways of knowing. Foucault's conception of knowledge—all individuals participate in its production—clearly departs from the notion of 'ideology' (a belief system endorsed by the dominant groups). From this perspective, excavating the types of knowledges that shape fitness in the contemporary society, including both the popular media representations of the fit body and the individual experiences of working out, will provide space for social change. Because scholars, among others, play an active role in knowledge production, they can also shape these knowledges towards more ethical fitness practices. Several existing studies have analyzed a variety of fitness texts using Foucault's notion of power/knowledge nexus. Smith Maguire (2007, p. 125), for example, discovered how psychological conceptualization of motivation underlines exercise manual information to "individualize the question of physical fitness." In this context, exercise practice is presented to require continuous self-discipline, clear timetabling, body measurement, and motivational techniques for successful completion. In their research, Markula and Pringle (2006) added that medicine and exercise physiology operate together to construct an idea of 'health-related fitness' to further endorse disciplinary, individualized exercise practices. In my reading of the *Yoga Journal* covers (Markula 2014b), I conceptualized them as 'discursive formations' that shaped how yoga became, over the years, to be understood by constructing a preferred self through popular psychological knowledge; a lithe, flexible, and healthy body through medical knowledge; and a socially aware citizen through ecological, religious, and nationalist discourses. With a colleague (Markula and Clark in press), I continued this project with an analysis of the knowledges defining the currently popular Barre exercise workouts available on the internet. It was perhaps not surprising that these classes primarily promised to develop the appearance of the long legged, lean, and light ballerina. While such an analysis does not necessarily effect social change directly, it reveals the dominant knowledges that structure exercise and fitness practices. If we determine that these knowledges fabricate limiting, disciplinary practices, we can then offer alternative, more ethical ways to know about fitness. As knowledge producers, socio-cultural scholars operate directly in the force field of fitness and have an opportunity to push for knowledges with alternative effects to the current neoliberal forces. Our task is to actively strategize what socio-cultural knowledge has the capacity to transform the existing power/knowledge nexus in fitness. It is evident that mere critique is insufficient in creating social change.

Another poststructuralist insight, for me, has been Foucault's (1978) observation of power relations operating at the micro level of society. While power hierarchies exist, all individuals are producers of power relations. Some individuals or groups, nevertheless, are more equipped to problematize the workings of power. Following this schema, exercisers are in lesser position to change fitness practices as they do not have broad knowledge base or skills to design exercise regimes, the gym equipment, or the class offerings. The fitness instructors and PTs, on the other hand, have more professional knowledge and thus, direct influence on the content of exercise programs. According to previous research, however, they generally do not problematize the powerful physiological/medical knowledge that dominates their training or the aesthetics of the healthy-looking body that dominates the commercial fitness industry (Markula and Chikinda 2016, Smith Maguire 2007). For example, I, together with a colleague Joy Chikinda, conducted a study of women fitness instructors' 'fitness knowledges.' It was clear that while wanting to promote health broadly in their classes, these instructors relied on narrow, medical and physiological knowledge to design their classes. In addition, they struggled with the strong pressure from their clients (and the industry) to adhere to practices toward the aesthetics of the healthy-looking body. Furthermore, the instructors were unable to make a connection between the actual exercises taught in their classes and the 'knowledges' that framed certain exercises as suitable for a class. This finding aligned with my previous study (Markula 2004) on the UK 'Hybrid' instructors who did not want to promote the body beautiful in their classes, but lacked knowledge to redesign their exercise vocabulary to promote other ways to know the fit body. This disconnect between the practice and the ways the instructors 'knew' about fitness, health, and body at a more 'theoretical' level struck me forcibly. It became evident that power, indeed, operates effectively through fitness practices that, unlike exercise identity, are seldom problematized in critical analyses of fitness and exercise.

The studio and fitness center owners are in a more powerful position to challenge the premise of biopower of health promotion or anatomopolitical power of commercialized aesthetics of the healthy-looking body.[4] No doubt, there are studios defying the commercial realities of running a successful fitness business, but modest critical research on the management level of fitness industry. This gap offers fertile ground for further research.

It is clear that initiating change in the fitness industry requires moving from the critical focus on socially constructed exercise identity to poststructuralist reading of how fitness knowledge and practice are intertwined to produce power relations. We as academics, however, are in a very strong position to problematize the currently dominant ways of knowing fitness to advocate for more diverse and ethical practices. These poststructuralist insights have inspired my most recent attempts to enact social change by engaging in fitness practices directly (Markula 2009, 2011, 2014a).

Fitness practices

While it is crucial to conduct research that problematizes the existing dominant fitness and exercise knowledges, poststructuralism also lends itself to research projects with more direct advocacy against inequity. Poststructuralist scholars have several further options to more directly impact the fitness industry operation. The first option is to offer university courses that sensitize students to the limitations of current ways of knowing about the fit bodies, but also offer opportunities to find more ethical ways to operate within it. Over several years, I have developed an undergraduate kinesiology course that is structured based on the dominant fitness knowledges (e.g., health, aesthetics of fit body, mindfulness, functionality), their limitations and potentials to create ethical exercise practices for diverse individuals. When I ask my students what should be done to make the fitness industry better, they invariably suggest more courses that help problematize the current practice and apply more ethical ways of practicing exercise. Further research that investigates the impact of such courses to the students' professional fitness practice is, nevertheless, required.

The second option is to exert direct impact on fitness instructor and PT training certifications through an input on their course materials or continuing education workshops. The diversity of the certifying bodies, however, complicates such research projects. In North America, for example, the commercially offered fitness industry qualifications are not regulated or credited, unlike other health professions, by official, governmental bodies and thus, can be of hugely varied quality. While governmental control can be based on singular knowledge base, it provides a minimum skill set requirement for a professional. Currently, for example, anyone can establish an internet fitness/exercise advice business without any qualifications. Therefore, more research projects that problematize the complexities of fitness industry certification process and then include alternative knowledges into the certification courses and continuing education courses are necessary for changing the industry operations.

The third option is to attempt to change fitness industry practice directly. As a certified Pilates instructor, I have sought, with various level of success, to teach classes with a different premise (everyday functionality) from the usual illness prevention or the aesthetics of healthy looking body (Markula 2009, 2011, 2014a). These research experiments have illuminated the difficulty of enacting social change when constrained by the pressures from the clients and the industry to sustain commercially viable practices. Although adhering to the participants' expectation of thinning and toning is tempting, it is, nevertheless, possible to impact on their fitness and exercise preferences. This, however, requires more than usual effort to design an exercise class with social consciousness in addition to including balanced and safe exercise vocabulary. Such design, however, marks a research project that intertwines poststructuralist theory to create alternative practices to reach beyond unproblematized community service or professional practice.

To further affect social change beyond the field of socio-cultural exercise and fitness research, poststructuralist scholars should consider alternative ways of disseminating their research. Strategies to reach general audience can include using the new media outlets, conducting community workshops, or providing public talks.

Conclusion

There is a significant body of feminist fitness and exercise research that critiques the construction of oppressive heteronormative femininity by the media. To complement these critiques, a second strand of research focuses on the exercisers' contradictory experiences within coinciding oppression and resistance within the industry. Both strands, nevertheless, concentrate on the social construction of binary identity categories in fitness. While the oppressiveness of such categorization should be challenged, this critique has not significantly transformed the ways commercial fitness and exercise is constructed and practiced. Poststructuralist theory can help identify how different knowledges work in tandem to reproduce the identity based politics. Poststructuralist standpoint, therefore, does not mean ignoring the oppression resulting from the binary identity categories that continue to have very real effect in the neoliberal cultural economy. To my reading, fitness research drawing from poststructuralist works can offer constructive ways to enact social change by problematizing the dominant knowledge construction of fitness practices (the popular aesthetics of the ideal, healthy looking body and the medical and exercise science discourse of exercise as illness prevention) and considering alternative knowledges designed to change the neoliberal contention of individualized, body shaping regimes.

Equally important to knowledge production is to analyze the actual fitness practices. From poststructuralist perspectives, new practices that derive from currently marginalized knowledges or employ the dominant knowledges toward more ethical goals can result in larger social change of how the fit bodies are constructed.

As the same time, it is important to problematize the premise that simply changing exercise practices will self-evidently produce social change. The fitness industry repeatedly transforms itself masterfully: New fads constantly emerge only to disappear a year or two later. These types of changes, however, remain superficial as they do not challenge the dominant fitness knowledge base and thus, the dominant power relations. Attempts for social change need to be grounded in social theory that problematizes the power/knowledge nexus to initiate more ethical exercise practices. It is crucial, nevertheless, to encourage both thinking and moving differently if we are to create change that transcends mere adjustments to individual behavior. This type of social change is, necessarily, embedded in social theory.

Notes

1. In this context, I limit my discussion to the fitness industry excluding, thus, governmental physical activity campaigns that are based on individuals increasing their physical activity levels on their own. While exercise denotes a very specific form of physical activity to improve one of the components of health related fitness (e.g., cardio-vascular fitness, muscle strength and endurance, flexibility, body composition), I use it, following most socio-cultural researchers, in its more generic form to include different types of group exercise forms.

2. While embodiment is seldom defined, it can be considered broadly to refer to bodily experiences of exercise that are considered primordial and thus, unshaped by social, ideological constructions of fitness, and thus, more true 'representations' of what exercise is about. From this perspective, the idea is to disengage with social to reach to a world more authentic and less polluted by social problems. Helping exercisers to reach embodied experiences will thus aid, eventually, in operating differently in the world in interactions with others, but is not directly engaged in changing or critiquing the current construction of fitness.

3. Throughout his work, Foucault critiqued of the top-down understanding of power in critical theory (e.g., Foucault 1978). Thus, Foucault (1980) himself might see conceptual modifications such as 'embodied subjectivity'—whose autonomous, agentic self is awakened by everyday body experiences to resist ideological, governmental dominance—as a convincing 'strategic elaboration' of a dominant, critical theory conceptualization of hegemony/agency interaction.

4. Foucault understood power operation through two main functions: bio-power and anatomo-political power. Bio-politics refers to a function of power through "administering and controlling life in a particular multiplicity, provided the multiplicity is large (a population) and the space spread out or open" (Deleuze 1988, 61). Current governmental campaigns for active, healthy lifestyle, are aimed at increased longevity and illness prevention in a population. Such campaigns are often supported by bio-medical or exercise science research that have provided scientific evidence to link increased physical fitness and thinness with absence of illness.

   Anatomo-politics (Deleuze 1988) refers to use of power that typically employs the technologies of discipline on a multiplicity of individuals. By analyzing this type of power, Foucault (1991) illustrated how power operates through techniques of discipline that normalize individuals into useful, docile bodies. Exercise can also be understood as a form of disciplinary technique that creates docile bodies.

References

Alexander, S., 2003. Stylish hard bodies: Branded masculinity in *Men's Health* magazine. *Sociological Perspectives*, 46(4), 535–554.

Berman, E. and de Souza, M. J., 2005. A qualitative examination of weight concerns, eating and exercise behaviors in recreational exercisers. *Women in Sport and Physical Activity Journal*, 14(1), 24–38.

Crawshaw, K.W., 2007. Governing the healthy male citizen: men, masculinity and popular health in *Men's Health* magazine. *Social Science & Medicine*, 65(8), 1606–1618.

Craig, M. L. and Liberty, R., 2007. "Cause that's what girls do": The making of a feminized gym. *Gender & Society* 21(5), 676–699.

D'Abundo, M. L., 2009. Issues of health, appearance and physical activity in aerobic classes for women. *Sport, Education and Society*, 14(3), 301–319.

Dawson, M., 2017. CrossFit: Fitness cult or reinventive institution. *International Review for the Sociology of Sport*, 52(3), 36–379.

Deleuze, G., 1988. *Foucault*. London: Continuum.

Duncan, M. C., 1994. The politics of women's body images and practices: Foucault, and Panopticon and *Shape* magazine. *Journal of Sport & Social Issues*, 18(1), 48–65.

Dworkin, S. L., 2003. A woman's place is in the … cardiovascular room? Gender relations, the body, and the gym. In: A. Bolin and J. Granskog, eds. *Athletic intruders: Ethnographic research on women, culture, and exercise*. Albany: State University of New York Press, 131–158.

Dworkin, S. L. and Wachs, F. L., 2009. *Body panic: Gender, health, and the selling of fitness*. New York: New York University Press.

Eskes, T. B., Duncan, M. C., and Miller, E. M., 1998. The discourse of empowerment: Foucault, Marcuse, and women's fitness texts. *Journal of Sport and Social Issues*, 22(3), 317–344.

Foucault, M., 1970. *The order of things: An archaeology of the human sciences*. London: Tavistock.

Foucault, M., 1972. *The archaeology of knowledge and discourse on language*. New York: Pantheon Books.

Foucault, M., 1978. *The history of sexuality*, Volume 1: *An introduction*. London: Penguin Books.

Foucault, M., 1980. Power and strategies. In: C. Gordon ed. *Power/Knowledge: Selected interviews and other writings 1972–1977*. Harlow, UK: Harvester, 134–145.

Foucault, M., 1991. *Discipline and punish: The birth of the prison*. London: Penguin Books.

George, T. and Rail, G., 2006. Barbie meets the Bindi: Constructions of health among second generation South Asian Canadian women. *Journal of Women's Health and Urban Life*, 4(2), 45–67.

Gill, R., 2007. Postfeminist media culture: Elements of a sensibility. *European Journal of Cultural Studies*, 10(2), 47–166.

Gimlin, D., 2002. *Body work: Beauty and self-Image in American culture*. Berkeley: University of California Press.

Haravon Collins, L., 2002. Working out contradictions: Feminism and aerobics. *Journal of Sport & Social Issues*, 26(1), 85–109.

Holland, S., 2010. *Pole dancing, empowerment and embodiment*. Springer.

Jette, S., 2006. Fit for two? A critical discourse analysis of *Oxygen Fitness Magazine*. *Sociology of Sport Journal*, 23(4), 331–351.

Jong, S. T. and Drummond, M. J., 2016. Exploring online fitness culture and young females. *Leisure Studies*, 35(6), 758–770.

Kagan, E. and Morse, M., 1988. The body electronic: Aerobic exercise on video. *The Drama Review*, 32(4), 164–180.

Knapp, B. A., 2015. Rx'd and shirtless: An examination of gender in a CrossFit box. *Women in Sport and Physical Activity*, 23(1), 42–53.

Labre, M. P., 2005. Burn fat, build muscle: A content analysis of *Men's Health* and *Men's Fitness*. *International Journal of Men's Health*, 4(2), 187–200.

Lawrence, S., 2016. Racialising the 'great man': A critical race study of idealized male athletic bodies in *Men's Health* magazine. *International Review for the Sociology of Sport*, 51(7), 777–799.

Lenskyj, H., 1986. *Out of bounds: Women, sport and sexuality*. Toronto: Women's Press.

Lewis, C. S., 2008. Life chances and wellness: Meaning and motion in the 'yoga market.' *Sport in Society*, 11(5), 535–545.

Lloyd, M., 1996. Feminism, aerobics and the politics of the body. *Body & Society*, 2(2), 79–98.

MacNeill, M., 1998. Sex, lies, and videotape: The political and cultural economies of celebrity fitness videos. In: G. Rail, ed. *Sport and postmodern times*. Albany: State University of New York Press, 163–184.

Maguire, J. and Mansfield, L., 1998. "No-body is perfect": Women, aerobics, and the body beautiful. *Sociology of Sport Journal*, 15(2), 109–137.

Malin, J., 2010. *My life at the gym: Feminist perspectives on community through the body*. Albany: State University of New York Press.

Markula, P., 1993. *Total-body-tone-up: Paradox and women's realities in aerobics*. Ph.D. Dissertation. University of Illinois at Urbana-Champaign.

Markula, P., 1995. Firm but shapely, fit but sexy, strong but thin: The postmodern aerobicizing female bodies. *Sociology of Sport Journal*, 12(4), 424–453.

Markula, P., 2001. Beyond the perfect body: Women's body image distortion in fitness magazine discourse. *Journal of Sport & Social Issues*, 25(2), 158–179.

Markula, P., 2003. Postmodern aerobics: Contradiction and resistance. In: A. Bolin and J. Granskog, eds., *Athletic intruders: Ethnographic research on women, culture, and exercise*. Albany: State University of New York Press, 53–78.

Markula, P., 2004. "Tuning into one's self": Foucault's technologies of the self and mindful fitness. *Sociology of Sport Journal*, 21(3), 302–321.

Markula, P., 2009. Affect[ing] bodies: Performative pedagogy of Pilates. *International Review of Qualitative Research*, 3, 381–408.

Markula, P., 2014a. The moving body and social change. *Cultural Studies—Critical Methodologies*, 14(5), 471–482.

Markula, P., 2014b. Reading yoga: Changing discourses of postural yoga on the *Yoga Journal* Covers. *Communication & Sport*, 2(2), 143–171.

Markula, P., 2014c. Embodied subjectivities: Intersections of discursive and critical psychology with socio-cultural exercise research. *Sociology of Sport Journal*, 31(2), 139–161.

Markula, P. and Chikinda, J., 2016. Group fitness instructors as local level health promoters: A Foucauldian analysis of the politics of health/fitness dynamic, *International Journal of Sport Policy and Politics*, 8(4), 625–646.

Markula, P. and Clark, M., 2018. Ballet inspired workouts: Intersections of ballet and fitness. In: P. Markula and M. Clark, eds. *The evolving feminine ballet body*. Edmonton, AB: University of Alberta Press, 49–74.

Markula, P. and Kennedy, E., 2011. Introduction: Beyond binaries: Contemporary approaches to women fitness. In: E. Kennedy and P. Markula, eds. *Women and exercise: The body, health and consumerism*. New York: Routledge, 1–26.

Markula, P. and Pringle, R., 2006. *Foucault, sport and exercise: Power, knowledge and transforming the self*. London: Routledge.

McDermott, L., 2000. A qualitative assessment of the significance of body perception to women's physical activity experiences: Revisiting discussions of physicalities. *Sociology of Sport Journal*, 17(4), 331–363.

McRobbie, A., 2004. Post-feminism and popular culture. *Feminist Media Studies*, 4(3), 255–264.

Millington, B., 2014. Amusing ourselves to life: Fitness consumerism and the birth of bio-games. *Journal of Sport and Social Issues*, 38(6), 491–508.

Millington, B., 2017. *Fitness, technology and society: Amusing ourselves to life*. Abingdon, UK: Routledge.

Nash, M., 2016. Selling health and fitness to sporty sisters: A critical feminist multi-modal discourse analysis of the Lorna Jane retain website. *Sociology of Sport Journal*, 33(3), 219–229.

Nieri, T. and Hughes, E., 2016. All about having fun: Women's experiences of Zumba fitness. *Sociology of Sport Journal*, 33(2), 135–145.

Parviainen, J., 2011. The standardization process of movement in the fitness industry. *European Journal of Cultural Studies*, 14(5), 526–541.

Petersson McIntyre, M., 2011. Keep your clothes on! Fit and sexy through strip tease aerobics. In: E. Kennedy and P. Markula, eds. *Women and exercise: The body, health and consumerism*. New York: Routledge, 247–265.

Phillips, J. N. and Drummond, M. J. N., 2001. An investigation into the body image perception, body satisfaction and exercise expectations of male fitness leaders: Implications for professional practice. *Leisure Studies*, 20(2), 95–105.

Pike, E. C. J., 2011. Growing old (dis)gracefully? Gender/aging/exercise nexus. In: E. Kennedy and P. Markula, eds. *Women and exercise: The body, health and consumerism*. New York: Routledge, 180–196.

Ricciardelli, R., Clow, K., and White, P., 2010. Investigating hegemonic masculinity: Portrayals of masculinity in men's lifestyle magazines. *Sex Roles*, 63(1–2), 64–88.

Sassatelli, R., 1999. Interaction order and beyond: A field analysis of body culture Within fitness gyms. *Body & Society*, 5(2-3), 227–248.

Sassatelli, R., 2010. *Fitness culture: Gyms and the commercialisation of discipline and fun*. Basingstoke, UK: Palgrave.

Smith Maguire, J., 2001. Fit and flexible: The fitness industry, personal trainers and emotional service labor. *Sociology of Sport Journal*, 18(4), 379–402.

Smith Maguire, J., 2007. *Fit for consumption: Sociology and the business of fitness*. London: Routledge.

Spielvogel, L. G., 2002. The discipline of space in a Japanese fitness club. *Sociology of Sport Journal*, 19(2), 189–205.

Spielvogel, L. G., 2003. *Working out in Japan: Shaping the female body in Tokyo fitness clubs*. Durham: Duke University Press.

Synne Groven, K., Nyheim Solbaekke, L., and Engelsrud, G., 2011. Large women's experiences of exercise. In: E. Kennedy and P. Markula, eds. *Women and exercise: The body, health and consumerism*. New York: Routledge, 121–137.

Theberge, N., 1987. Sport and women's empowerment. *Women's Studies International Forum*, 10(4), 387–393.

Washington, M. S. and Economides, M., 2016. Strong is the new sexy: Women's CrossFit and the new postfeminist ideal. *Journal of Sport and Social Issues*, 40(2), 143–161.

Wiest, A. L., Andrews, D. L., and Giardina, M. D., 2015. Training the body for healthism: Reifying vitality in and through the clinical gaze of the neoliberal fitness club. *Review of Education, Pedagogy, and Cultural Studies*, 37(1), 21–40.

Wray, S., 2011. The significance of Western health promotion discourse for older women in diverse ethnic backgrounds. In: E. Kennedy and P. Markula, eds. *Women and exercise: The body, health and consumerism*. New York: Routledge, 161–179.

Chapter 17

Un-charting the course: Critical indigenous research into Sport, Health and Physical Education

Brendan Hokowhitu

'Mapping' (Markula and Silk, 2011) is an unfortunate metaphor for critical research in relation to Indigenous peoples. Indeed, it demonstrates that, sub-consciously or not, there remains in the ways we choose to construct and frame research Endeavours[1] a will towards universal knowledge as underpinned by the European Enlightenment project. Originally at least the myth of universal knowledge obscured local Indigenous knowledges giving rise to a postcolonial society ill at ease; a society of the *dis*-eased and *invalid*. The Indigenous peoples etched by death and disease who, nonetheless, have survived their predicted evo-lutionary demise. And the unsettlers[2], unwilling to comprehend the beauty and horror that surrounds them rendering their ontological dominance by invalidat-ing that other world. Here, the autopsy of a cancerous victim, reveals besieged cells ravaged by tension, emanating from confusion between mind and body, native and alien whilst the underlying truth of unworldly Indigenous epistemol-ogies remains ordinary, unspoken, uninvestigated, but present; the monsters of these lands remain to haunt, to whisper the possibilities of ordinary lives, at ease.

Thus, in the context of this Chapter, we must question whether any focus on physicality as a 'critical' (read modernistic) proposition leading to the promised land, is simply another form of neo-colonialism? I question on what metaphysical grounds can current conceptions of sport, health and physical education move towards deeply challenging colonization's 'relentless constitution' of indigeneity? Far from being the beacon of Indigenous advancement that many purport, the increasing focus on Indigenous health, and the integration of Indigenous peoples into society through sport and physical education resembles the continued produc-tion of discourses centred on savagery. We need tread carefully, therefore, for no better reason as it was the naturalization of biological racism through the scientific age, which gave credence to the atrocities of colonisation and imperialism. Indeed, the compartmentalisation of the 'physical' within the present collection suggests mere tinkering at the edges of a metaphysical Indigenous epistemology and, as a consequence, the coinage of 'critical physical research' is oxymoronic. As we have learnt from Fanon's (1963) decolonial recourse to violence, for instance, an existential 'decolonization' without the materiality of violent revolution to affect an *epistemological* 'break' from the subjugation of colonialism is deemed pointless.

Mapping the indigenous body[3]

> About 999 out of 1000 could not bear the strain of higher education. In com-
> merce Maori could not hope to compete with the Pakeha. In the trades the
> Maoris were splendid copyists, but not originators. As carpenters they would
> cope under a capable supervisor but not otherwise. Agriculture was the one
> calling suitable for Maoris ... it was therefore necessary to teach them the
> nobility of labour.
> —Rev. Butterfield [headmaster of a Māori boarding school] speech to the
> Young Māori Party in 1910, cited Barrington 1988: 49

Any critical research into indigeneity and sport, health and physical education
(hereafter referred to as 'critical physical research') must be cognisant of the subjugation of 'local knowledges' that I discuss in more depth below. Yet, the more
typical narrative of dispossession, death, oppression and violent synthesis is also
important, especially when focused in on the roles that sport health, and physical education have played in the production of Indigenous bodies within colonial biopolitical landscapes. In *The History of Sexuality: Volume I* (1978) Foucault
argues that the biopolitical regulation of a population operates beyond the conscious production and control of knowledge. That is, crucial to biopower is internalisation; the profound molecular imposition of regulatory mechanisms so that
the material, the corporeal and ethos function in unison. In the context of the
present chapter then, it could be argued that the conditioning of the Indigenous
body throughout colonisation has not only a symbolic genealogy but a material
existence. Here, the etiological importance of the word 'genealogy' should not
be underestimated, for it does not merely mean a textual genealogy. Foucault's
nomenclature is literally referring to the material and biological descent of corporeality, where the body is "totally imprinted by history" (Foucault, 1991, 83).

If savagery is understood from the perspective of enlightenment rationalism,
then it is apparent that it portends a state of un-enlightenment, where reason
is ruled by physical impulses and/or superstition. What Foucault refers to as the
invisible 'breath' that inhabits discontinuous discourses, even as they mutate,
I conceive of as 'physicality' with reference to the colonised Indigenous savage.
As a sub-theme of the primitive/modern dialectic, physicality describes a complex of interconnecting discourses that enables unitary discursive knowledge to
develop around the colonised Indigenous subject. The thematic of Indigenous
physicality in the colonial state was "capable of linking, and animating a group
of discourses, like an organism with its own needs, its own internal force and its
own capacity for survival" (Foucault, 2002, 39). Darwin's evolutionary theory, for
instance, "directed research from afar" acting as "a preposition rather than named,
regrouped, and explained ... a theme that always presupposed more than one was
aware of ... forcibly transformed into discursive knowledge" (Foucault, 2002, 39).
Such discursive knowledge underpinned Indigenous 'savagery' and was transcribed into physical terms, onto the Indigenous body and about Indigenous

bodily practices. Physicality, thus, is one of those 'dense transfer points'[4] that enabled the production of the Indigenous body as a discursive formation; a lynchpin that strategically enables the imprint of history upon the Indigenous body.

Foucault's notion of biopower provides a useful frame for critical physical research because it understands the body as a material site where discursive formations are fleshed out; where discourse, as a "border concept", operates between ethereal knowledge and material conditions. Biopower, thus, refers to, "a power whose task is to take charge of life" requiring "continuous regulatory and corrective mechanisms" (Foucault, cited in Rabinow, 1984, p. 20). Michael Hardt and Antonio Negri (2009) similarly define biopower as "the power over life—or, really, the power to administer and produce life—that functions through the government of populations, managing their health, reproductive capacities and so forth" (p. 57). Importantly, Hardt and Negri (2009) recognize the "productive" (as opposed to suppressive) nature of biopower, which is a fundamental concern of my own work in that I find the standard hierarchical and oppressive analytic of power largely unhelpful in explaining the productive nature of colonialism. That is, how do Indigenous peoples continue within a neocolonial condition without the desire to kill the colonizer?

The production of the coloniser/Indigenous, Self/Other dialectic has functioned through the bodily enactment of that dialectic. What it means/meant to be an authentic and tradition abiding Indigenous subject was materialised and reified by the bodily enactments of authentically Indigenous bodily practices. In relation to critical physical research, what it meant to be a bone fide Indigenous person became intertwined with institutional discourses that located indigeneity within the physical realm, which in-turn disciplined through limiting and employing the Indigenous body in physical labour. Sites of work, leisure, sport, home-life, schools and practices such as eating, cleaning, and exercising have disciplined the Indigenous body throughout colonisation. The majority of Indigenous people of my grandparents and parents' generation, for example, acquired relations with their bodies conditioned by the labour of modernity and influenced by notions of tradition. A necessary effect of a physically intensive life meant that in many Indigenous communities, sub-cultures developed based on relationships with a physically labouring body that, in turn, came to symbolise an ontologically authentic indigeneity (Hokowhitu, 2004, 2013).

This traditionalised ontology was/is unmistakably a by-product of savage discourses premised on a Cartesian assessment of the cerebral European and the emotive/physical savage. If savagery is understood from the perspective of enlightenment rationalism, then it is apparent that it portends a state of un-enlightenment, where reason is ruled by physical impulses and/or superstition. What Foucault refers to as the invisible 'breath' that inhabits discontinuous discourses, even as they mutate, I conceive of as 'physicality' with reference to the colonised Indigenous savage. As a sub-theme of the primitive/modern dialectic, physicality describes a complex of interconnecting discourses that enables unitary discursive knowledge to develop around the colonised Indigenous subject.

The thematic of Indigenous physicality in the colonial state was "capable of linking, and animating a group of discourses, like an organism with its own needs, its own internal force and its own capacity for survival" (Foucault, 2002, 39). Darwin's evolutionary theory, for instance, "directed research from afar" acting as "a preposition rather than named, regrouped, and explained ... a theme that always presupposed more than one was aware of ... forcibly transformed into discursive knowledge" (Foucault, 2002, 39). Such discursive knowledge underpinned Indigenous 'savagery' and was transcribed into physical terms, onto the Indigenous body and about Indigenous bodily practices. Physicality, thus, is one of those 'dense transfer points' that enabled the production of the Indigenous body as a discursive formation; a lynchpin that strategically enables the imprint of history upon the Indigenous body.

One of the fallouts being Indigenous populations being offered limited curricula in the emerging native schools, being assumed to be unintelligent, and eventually assuming ontologies that reflected the Cartesian discourses proffered generations prior. Indeed, such was the internalisation process that a western educated Indigenous person could be at times rebuked by some in their own communities as inauthentic and even as an interloper made foreign; an agent of the colonial State. In Aotearoa, 'plastic Māori' was a common term used for educated Maori in the 1970s and 1980s. An emerging criticism of postcolonial Indigenous subjectivities is, therefore, that the forms of indigeneity produced, far from challenging the settler colonial narrative, have in fact reified it.

The link between discourses of savagery, the unintelligent Indigenous trope and today's woeful Indigenous health indices is clear. In direct relation to health research, access to Indigenous communities validated upon pathologising Indigenous peoples as unhealthy and, consequently, in demand of medical intervention has a long genealogy in colonial history. Underpinning the "ethics" of colonialism was "the white-man's-burden" to civilise the world and, furthermore, inherent to the civilisation project were the merciless languages of medicine and morality that pathologised Indigenous peoples as savaged by disease and uncleanliness. A pathology that has its roots in Social Darwinism, where by mere contact with the stronger, more evolved European, the frailties (both physical and moral) are exposed, leading to degradation and extinction.

A Foucauldian analysis would suggest such pathologising functions not to oppress, but rather to produce. Health research, in the New Zealand context at least, thus is the most prominent of all research fields focused on Māori and produced by both Māori and non-Māori scholars. A number of Māori health models, for instance, have sprung up in the last 30 years in particular. Mason Durie's (1998) 'Whare Tapa Wha' (four-sided house) model reflects a holistic health model including *tinana* (physical), *hinengaro* (mental), *whānau* (relationships) and *wairua* (spiritual). While Durie's model is popular and often cited, the reason for this is possibly because the four cornerstones merely reflect western holistic models of health and thus simplistic translations of *wairua* to spirituality, for example, allow for conceptual assimilation. In reality, none of these concepts are translatable to western frameworks, especially *wairua*, which is akin to a sub-atomic global essence that pervades all things, both living and inanimate. The point being that, although Durie's health configuration begins with Indigenous concepts, its production within the broader medical discourse soon disfigures, disassembles and reconfigures it to fit a western medical taxonomy.

Un-mapping the Order of Things: Meta-physical possibilities

In Foucault's well-known preface to *The Order of Things* (1970) he makes reference to 'a certain Chinese encyclopaedia' which although fictitious nonetheless refers to an unworldly taxonomy: "In the wonderment of this taxonomy, the thing we apprehend in one great leap, the thing that, by means of the fable, is demonstrated as the exotic charm of another system of thought, is the limitation of our own, the stark impossibility of thinking *that*" (xv). The presence of an alternative metaphysical reality in Indigenous cultures signalled an allegorical monster in relation to western rationalism. Indigenous cultures were not the monster per se, rather those aspects of them that were inexplicability reached beyond the depths of the rational European mind that demanded empiricism. The determination of 'savagery' helped veil what the Enlightenment project failed to comprehend via a western scientific taxonomy. The allegorical side-product of such certainty was the construction of 'Other' cultures as immoral, monstrous and mythical:

> The native is declared insensible to ethics; he represents not only the absence of values, but also the negation of values. He is, let us dare to admit, the enemy of values, and in this sense he is the absolute evil … All values, in fact, are irrevocably poisoned and *diseased* as soon as they are allowed in contact with the colonized race. The customs of the colonized people, their traditions, their myths—above all, their myths—are the very sign of that poverty of spirit and of their constitutional depravity. (Fanon, 1963, pp. 41–42, emphasis added)

The Enlightenment's desire for universal knowledge insisted upon a fundamental investment in coding alterity within the realms of rationality, in disavowing the monsters of the unfathomable; to make what is irrational, rational and what is incomprehensible disappear. From the universal mind-set, the inability to contain the irrational, the unfathomable to the boundaries of a universal epistemology leads to cancerous tension; *dis*-ease.

Key to Enlightenment rationalism and its reliance on reason to know and to authenticate the objective world was its faith in the mind/body dichotomy orated by Plato and canonised by Descartes. Indigenous cultures as unenlightened were, from an occipital logic, inherently more 'physical', ruled by their passions, and less intelligent than their civilised brethren. The apparent lack of division between the indigene's mind, body, spirit and the external world only served to augment the belief of European colonisers' that they were indeed encountering savage races, with 'minds like children'. Moreover, Enlightenment philosophers avoided questions of inconsistency in equality and autonomy arising from colonial subjugation by locating the Indigenous being in the realm of the physical and irrational, so as to deny full humanity and, accordingly, access to the same privileges bestowed upon the European.

This has obvious implications for how we begin to frame critical physical research in relation to Indigenous peoples today. Firstly, it is critical to establish that the collision of supposedly embodied Indigenous epistemologies with disembodied Enlightenment rationalism left an inauthentic void that European settlers, at least, desired to chart through authenticating disciplines such as anthropology and archaeology. If we are to conceive of critical physical research in relation to Indigenous peoples, then we must first comprehend the unnatural Cartesian compartmentalisation of the physical. Without wanting to be essentialist, it is clear that key to the success of the colonial project was the deconstruction of interwoven epistemic knowledge based on fleshy metaphysical cognition or, in the parlance of our times, 'mind/body/spirit'. The first principle of colonising the Indigenous body, then, was to bring the philosophical underpinnings of the savage under the logic of the coloniser. Through my research (see, for instance, Hokowhitu, 2003) I began to understand the enormity for Indigenous peoples of what I describe here as the 'Cartesian compartmentalisation of the physical', which provoked a profound feeling of loss as I came to grasp the depths of colonization; the implication of the Indigenous body in all of this; the implication of my own body; the bodies of my children; my father. The everydayness of the metaphysical had left us.

Secondly, critical physical research should comprehend that the colonial synthesis of Indigenous practices and the inevitable epistemological transformation that Indigenous people must have undergone (i.e., as they began to see the world differently) implies that what survived the onslaught of colonisation has been fundamentally altered and, indeed, it could be argued that any semblance of pre-colonial thought has been lost to most. This is not to suggest harkening back to days of yore. Indeed, quite the opposite in that Critical Indigenous Studies must reject the desire to reconfigure the disassembled pre-Indigenous self. Foucault's conception of biopower, where individuals become unconsciously aware of themselves and their place in the world through the disciplined nature of their own body, speaks to the material depth of colonisation and the forlorn nature of a decolonial project. That is, to a large degree Indigenous people cannot deny the embodiment of colonisation. Many try, and many delude themselves into thinking this is possible, whilst developing a schizophrenic envisioning of an authentic Indigenous self, divorced from a 'self' located in the here and now and even their material genealogical reality.

Inevitably, such schizophrenia detracts from an Indigenous existentialism that embraces the present. Yet, I must believe in the possibility for insurrection. I freely admit I have been colonized; or rather I have failed to be decolonised. As a consequence, the feeling of 'being postcolonial' resembles a state of anxiety, a state of tension, a state of dis-ease that Indigenous people ingest in the pursuit of an unrealizable dream, that of decolonisation. Being postcolonial is thus the realization that decolonisation will not return Indigenous people to an imagined pre-colonial purity and living within the tension of the coloniser/colonised binary. Hopefully, it also acknowledges at least the existential possibility of freedom beyond disciplinary constraint. As Foucault states, people "are much freer than they feel, that people accept as truth, as evidence, some themes which have built up at a certain moment during history, and this so-called evidence can be criticized and destroyed" (1988, 9).

Lastly, Indigenous critical physical research requires a genealogical approach that comprehends the 'breath of physicality', which inhabits the discourses surrounding Indigenous people. This genealogical grounding signifies that the potentiality of Indigenous critical physical research to encourage social transformation is necessarily epistemological:

> [Genealogy] is a way of playing local, discontinuous, disqualified, or non-legitimized knowledges off against the unitary theoretical instance that claims to be able to filter them, organize them into a hierarchy, organize them in the name of a true body of knowledge, in the name of the rights of a science that is in the hands of the few. Genealogies are therefore not positivistic returns to a form of science that is more attentive or more accurate. Genealogies are quite specifically, antisciences ... the *insurrections of knowledges* ... an insurrection against the centralizing power-effects that are bound up with the institutionalization and workings of any scientific discourse. (Foucault 2003: 9)

Admittedly the enormity of such a project in relation to research praxis is daunting, but also speaks to why so many 'social justice' oriented research projects centred on Indigenous peoples at least largely fail.

Yet, I must hold the view that the discursive formation of the Indigenous body need not necessarily be conceived of as terminally oppressive; I look to Fanon for inspiration:

> The dialectic that brings necessity into the foundation of my freedom drives me out of myself. It shatters my unreflected position. Still in terms of consciousness, black consciousness is immanent in its own eyes. I am not a potentiality of something, I am wholly what I am. I do not have to look for the universal. No probability has any place inside me. My Negro consciousness does not hold itself out as a lack. It is. It is its own follower. (1967, 103)

Thus, I conceive the nexus 'critical' AND 'Indigenous' to mean that form of knowledge unintelligible to the western academy; that knowledge which refuses western classification via its lexicon and taxonomic cataloguing. I seek a form of 'critical' AND 'Indigenous' that strikes bedridden the imperative to be 'part of the same'. How does critical/Indigenous move beyond the confines of western rationalism, to produce socially transformative research where Indigenous meta-physicality is presented in a form without having to be translated into dominant codes of understanding?

In turning to Foucault's genealogical method, I seek material practices that uncover how local knowledge is ordered within generalizing scientific knowl-edge, and that reinstate local knowledge systems. It is important to note here that Foucault does not merely see this project as an abstract one, rather he argues genealogies are 'insurrections of knowledge'. Read alongside the conception of biopolitics, insurrections of knowledge can be viewed as intelligence that propa-gates resistance through bodies to produce dissenting subjectivities. In unsettler/colonial states, the potential for insurrections of knowledge and the production of dissenting subjectivities remains (for both Indigenous and non-Indigenous peo-ples) in the largely subjugated (i.e., hidden or disfigured and re-woven within a western taxonomy) Indigenous intelligence that haunts postcolonial lands. I refer to such Indigenous intelligence as 'monstrous'; a hyperbolic device to force atten-tion to the peril unintelligible knowledge poses to the universalization project of the western academy; the monster that lurks in the metaphysical landscapes coded as 'resources', epistemologies coded as 'myth', cultures coded as 'traditions', and peoples coded as 'Other'.

Indigenous Studies, as with Feminist Cultural Studies, is best to position itself outside the western, white masculine intellectual tradition of mind/body dualism: "an approach which refuses to privilege mind over body ... and which assumes that the body cannot be transcended, is one which ... emphasises contingency, locatedness, the irreducibility of difference, the passage of emotions and desire, and the worldliness of being" (Ahmed and Stacey, 2001, p. 3). Such a positioning is double-edged, however, as the colo-nial project "limited the identity of the colonised to the materiality of their bodies" (Featherstone, 2005, 65–66) and thus the analysis must be at once deconstructory and existential. Meaning, it is dangerous ground not to firstly problematise Indigenous theorisation stemming from the body, prior to fore-grounding the body as a realm of study from where Indigenous knowledge insurrections can consecrate.

Ironically and dangerously, then, it is the *immediacy* of the Indigenous body, which must take centre-stage within critical physical research as insurrection. In the condition of postcoloniality it is difficult to disengage with a mind/body duality, but it is at this fundamental level where theorizing towards critical research must begin; the thinking body; the conceptualization of the body as a material producer of thought; the body as a holistic notion where physiology and the interplay between history, present and future interact to flesh-out social meaning. This will demand an epistemological leap. Of course, and as already stressed, the epistemological mind/body dualism of the Enlightenment must be exhumed prior to conceptualising such an insurrection. Indeed, the first step to analysing the existential and metaphysical possibilities of the Indigenous body is to activate (de-pacify) its materiality beyond binary oppositions such as traditional/non-traditional, authentic/inauthentic, civilised/non-civilised and Self/Other.

While many Indigenous scholars have challenged the mind/body dichotomy by describing holistic Indigenous epistemologies that typically include the physical, spiritual, mental and material truth of place, almost without fail such holistic theorising seeks to authenticate an Indigenous tradition. Thus, the Indigenous body has remained a traditional spectre in the academy at least while lacking any material immediacy. Accordingly, a preface to critical physical research as insurrection is an analysis of how the spectre of tradition remains written upon the Indigenous body. How, for instance, the location of indigeneity in the primitive past marks the Indigenous body in tourist sites and voyeuristic cultural performances of Indigenous culture, whilst determining 'culture' as that which existed prior to now. To use Māori as an example, when 'culture' is employed in relation to research it typically refers to either customary concepts or practices. Seldom do researchers mobilise 'Māori culture' to refer to everyday practices, and never does it coincide with those colonial cultural practices welcomed by Māori, which now hold a great degree of meaning within everyday or 'ordinary' Māori *culture* such as sporting teams. The 'everyday' in research on Indigenous peoples, for example, is either positioned in terms of Indigenous political struggles, especially in regard to jurisprudence, or in terms of 'victim-hood' conceived of as the genealogical descendant of the trauma of colonisation. Research that looks at contemporary cultural formations is, thus, typically deficit oriented and focused on social ills such as poor health, gangs, suicide and violence. Such scholarship is necessarily reactionary as opposed to existential.

In contrast, Indigenous critical physical research as insurrection needs attention to the past, future and, most significant to this paper, the *immediacy* of the here and now; the everyday; the ordinary. The idealism Indigenous people locate in the pure-past limits how we conceive of ourselves through the *immediacy* of experience. From my own context, insurrections of Māori knowledge reveal spiritual immediacy. That is, metaphysical practices ingrained within the immediacy of the *everyday*. From this epistemological understanding, there is no genealogical distance between nature, corporeality and knowledge. There is no distance between the ordinary and supra-culture; between the superstructure and the material. Elsewhere (Hokowhitu, 2014) I introduced the notion of 'body-logic', as an insurrection of Indigenous intelligence that disrupts the physical/metaphysical binary and mind/body duality. I define body-logic as that corporeal intelligence willingly residing beyond rational thought; willingly producing subjectivities able to live beyond the taxonomies ascribed by colonization; willingly fleshing out and unravelling the madness that overlays the postcolonial world. Such an analysis, I argue,

> should be driven towards an Indigenous existentialism that confronts and theorizes the everyday materialism of the Indigenous body, whilst encouraging an epistemological leap where a body-logic is made possible. Here, then, body-logic refers to what culture 'feels like' as opposed to the production of Indigenous culture to be viewed, or Indigenous knowledge to be 'preserved'. (2014, 44)

Within this framework of what culture 'feels like', we might begin to think of an Indigenous critical physical insurrection consecrated by an 'ordinary metaphysicality'; the propagation of an everyday Indigenous metaphysicality as part of a broader desire for Indigenous sovereignty. Here, Indigenous sovereignty, is defined as the determination of Indigenous peoples to live their knowledge beyond western taxonomies and the violent will to synthesise.

So much focus in the Indigenous social movement and Indigenous scholarship has been on juridical and political forms of struggle, which has of course been necessary, yet we have forgotten that Indigenous peoples live their lives. The notion of 'ordinary' is important to understanding the *immediacy* of the Indigenous body because it locates the body outside the disciplinary complex. It acknowledges at least the existential possibility of freedom beyond disciplinary constraint. As Foucault states, people "are much freer than they feel, that people accept as truth, as evidence, some themes which have built up at a certain moment during history, and this so-called evidence can be criticized and destroyed" (1988, 9). This idea speaks to a variant philosophical imperative that counters the rational and utilitarian foundations that pervade desires to 'fix the Indian problem'. Rather, the philosophical imperative is determined by a *metaphysical economy* invested in the desire of Indigenous peoples to live ordinary lives underpinned by their own epistemology and unencumbered by the neo-colonial state's desire to assimilate.

Indigenous life is an everyday experience, and it is possibly at this level that Indigenous sovereignty might most effectively occur. An everyday sovereignty that flies under the radar of the neo-colonial state unwilling to imagine nations within nations, and yet unimaginative enough to notice the biopolitics of an 'ordinary' revolution. Here, then, I want to reread Fanon:

> This struggle for freedom does not give back to the national culture its former values and shapes; this struggle which aims at a fundamentally different set of relations between men cannot leave intact either the form or the content of the people's culture. After the conflict there is not only the disappearance of colonialism but also the disappearance of the colonized man. (2010, 496)

Undoubtedly Fanon is referring here to the existential and decolonial possibilities of violent struggle, yet is it also possible an 'ordinary metaphysical revolution' might achieve the disappearance of colonial taxonomic order?

Conclusion

> Maori play a particular type of rugby. It's spontaneous and exuberant. In rugby we celebrate the joy of living. So, we're prepared to take risks and to do things just for the hell of it. In our day it wasn't whether we won or lost but the way we played the game. I don't know whether that's being coached out of our players. And I don't know whether New Zealand rugby has room now for our philosophy.
> —Ex-Māori All Black, Tutekawa 'Tu' Wylie cited in Shortland, 1993, p. 47

The first step for an Indigenous critical physical research as insurrection begins by taking on the full-weight of Homi Bhabha's analysis, where he suggests European Rationalism preserves "the boundaries of sense" (1983, 24). Indigenous theorizing cannot fully develop without the possibility for existential agency and ordinary lives, where Indigenous bodies are infused by metaphysical comprehension. I do not want to believe that the atrocities of colonisation were the defining point where the Indigenous body remains scarred indeterminately, and metaphysical presences remain as whispers. The physical endurance of pain may not be a choice, but Indigenous people can choose to live beyond the genealogical scarring inflicted by colonisation. Ordinary Indigenous live must materialize beyond such embodied and genealogical pain; we can choose to live our lives.

Insurrection is written into Māori lore itself, as embodied by the demi-god Māui-tikitiki-a-Taranga (Māui), the Nietzschean-like Übermensch figure common to many Polynesian cultures, whose knowledge transgressions necessitated change. Although a *pōtiki* (youngest child)[5] Māui's tenacity, creativity and desire to go beyond the limits of truth established his leadership qualities. Although Māori narratives, which were meant to inform the everyday, have been mythologised, Māui's metaphysical presence suggests the possibility of insurrection in the present. Ironically enough then, Indigenous critical physical research begins with recoding metaphysical culture as 'everyday'. That is, without the unnatural divide between transcendent forces and the body, where the everyday becomes enchanted. The project of Indigenous critical physical research as insurrection, therefore, must be at once deconstructory and existential.

Notes

1. Reference to Captain James Cook's First Voyage aboard HMS *Endeavour*.
2. The term 'settler' has always sat uncomfortably with me and is clearly derived from a European colonial centric positionality. For Indigenous people there was absolutely nothing 'settling' about colonisation. Unequivocally, colonisation unsettled and unravelled the ways by which Indigenous peoples ordered their lives. Thus, from an Indigenous perspective, colonisers are 'unsettlers'.
3. 'Indigenous Body' here reflects the will of the Enlightenment project to create a knowable universal Indigenous subject, rather than believing such a construct is true.

4. In *The History of Sexuality* Foucault refers to sexuality in similar fashion, where sexuality is "an especially dense transfer point for relations of power ... sexuality is not the most intractable element in power relations, but rather one of those endowed with the greatest instrumentality: useful for the greatest number of manoeuvres and capable of serving as a point of support, as a lynchpin, for the most varied strategies" (1978: 103).
5. In the system of genealogical power, the last-born is typically accorded a lower rank in relation to older siblings. Both pre- and post-colonial Māori social structures suggest an oligarchy based on genealogy, where certain genealogical branches were deemed more noble and, therefore, held more *mana* (prestige) than others and passed this aristocratic *mana* from one generation to the next and especially the *mātāmua* or first-born child, who if on a chiefly lineage of first-borns would be granted *Ariki* (high-chief) status.

References

Ahmed, S., and Stacey, J. (eds.). (2001). *Thinking through skin: Transformations: Thinking through feminism*. New York: Routledge.

Barrington, J. M. (1988). 'Learning the "dignity of labour": Secondary education policy for Maoris'. *New Zealand Journal of Educational Studies 23*(1), pp. 45–58.

Bhabha, H. (1983). 'The other question'. *Screen 24*(6), pp. 18–36.

Durie, M. (1998). *Whaiora: Māori health development* (2nd ed.). Auckland, NZ: Oxford University Press.

Fanon, F. (1963). *The wretched of the earth* (C. Farrington, Trans.). New York: Grove Press.

Fanon, F. (1967). *Black skin, white masks*. New York: Grove Press.

Fanon, F. (2010). 'On national culture'. In Grinker R., Lubkemann, S., Steiner, C. (eds.), *Perspectives on Africa: A reader in culture, history and representation* (2nd ed.). Oxford, UK: Blackwell.

Featherstone, S. (2005). *Postcolonial cultures*. Jackson: University Press of Mississippi.

Foucault, M. (1970). *The order of things: An archaeology of the human sciences*. New York: Pantheon.

Foucault, M. (1978). *The history of sexuality: Volume 1*. Harmondsworth, UK: Penguin.

Foucault, M. (1988). 'Truth, power, self: An interview with Michel Foucault—October 25th, 1982'. In Martin, L. H., Gutman, H., and Hutton, P. H. (eds.), *Technologies of the self: A seminar with Michel Foucault*. London, UK: Tavistock.

Foucault, M. (1991). 'Nietzsche, genealogy, history'. In Rabinow, P. (ed.), *The Foucault reader*. London: Penguin.

Foucault, M. (2002). *The archaeology of knowledge* (A. M. Sheridan Smith, Trans.). London: Routledge.

Foucault, M. (2003). *Society must be defended: Lectures at the Collège de France 1975–1976* (D. Macey, Trans.). New York: Picador.

Hardt, M., and Negri, A. (2009). *Commonwealth*. Cambridge, MA: Harvard University Press.

Hokowhitu, B. (2003). 'Māori physicality: Stereotypes, Sport and the "Physical Education" of New Zealand Māori'. *Culture, Sport, Society, 6*(2), pp. 192–218.

Hokowhitu, B. (2004). 'Tackling Māori Masculinity: A Colonial Genealogy of Savagery and Sport'. *The Contemporary Pacific, 15*(2), pp. 259–284.

Hokowhitu, B. (2012). 'Educating Jake: A genealogy of Māori masculinity'. In Bowl, M., Tobias, R. Leahy, J., and Gage, J. (eds.), *Gender, masculinities and lifelong learning*. London: Routledge Education, pp. 47–57.

Hokowhitu, B. (2014). 'If you are not healthy, then what are you: Healthism, colonial disease and body-logic'. In Katie Fitzpatrick and Richard Tinning (eds.), *Health education: Critical perspectives*. New York: Routledge, pp. 31–47.

Markula, P., and Silk, M. L. (2011). *Qualitative research for physical culture*. London: Palgrave Macmillan.

Rabinow, P. (Ed.). (1984). *The Foucault reader*. New York: Pantheon Books.

Shortland, W. (1993). 'Paradise lost'. *Mana Magazine*, January–February, pp. 46–47.

Chapter 18

"What do we want? When do we want it? Now!": Some concluding observations

Richard Pringle, Håkan Larsson and Göran Gerdin

We were motivated, in part, to co-edit this text as we had each felt an element of disappointment or frustration with respect to the social influence of our critical research endeavours. A frustration which broadly recognised that although social change was evident, the pace of change felt unjustifiably slow and there was minimal evidence of shifts in dominant sets of power relations across a range of fields: hence, the necessity to keep the same social justice issues on the research agenda year after year. In hindsight, we can trace our frustrations back to a degree of naive optimism (see Lisette Burrows, Deana Leahy and Jan Wright's chapter fifteen) and the desire for change 'now' as the protest chants typically implore. Through on-going reflection on the complex rhizomatic linkages between diverse sets of knowledge/power/material assemblages we are now more accepting of the limitations of orchestrating widespread change in a timely manner via research outputs. Yet we still aspire to make a difference and we retain a sense of optimism about the value of undertaking critical research. Indeed, this co-edited book project has reinvigorated our belief in the value of critical research. Moreover, we recognise that our initial feelings of discontent were not entirely negative—we did not become exhausted cynics—but drew on these feelings as productive sources of inspiration to strategise about how our research endeavours could make more of a difference. This co-edited text is a pragmatic outcome of some of those earlier frustrations.

Through inviting leading global scholars within the critical study of sport, physical education and health to contribute chapters to this text, we have been able to gain a broader sense of what a diverse set of critical researchers do and with what influence. Through reading each of our contributors' chapters it is overwhelmingly clear that a variety of social justice concerns have impelled the authors to strive to make a difference in teaching, researching and via an assortment of public pedagogical strategies. Despite what looks to us, as an array of impressive 'emancipatory' aspirations and forms of *praxis* (which we understand as a commitment to comprehend social realities and then using the findings or knowledges to make a difference), we note that many of our authors have similarly revealed a degree of frustration about their critical influence.

Richard Tinning (chapter seven), as an example, via reflection on his stellar career in critical HPE studies revealed mixed emotions about the broader influence of critical research:

> I am also bothered by the fact that perhaps the main beneficiaries of our work have been 'we the critical scholars'. ... I have managed to keep motivated over my years as a critical scholar, despite the lack of obvious signs of influence, because I remain committed to the ideal of a more just, equitable and peaceful world. There are, however, ever-present dangers that the ideals of equity that drive critical scholarship become mere bureaucratic rhetorical devices that limit the possibilities of change.

We note that Tinning is not alone in having mixed feelings about one's critical research endeavours. Indeed, a palpable sense of frustration emanates throughout the text. Jim Denison and Joe Mills (chapter six), for example, reflected on their efforts towards encouraging sport coaches to adopt a Foucauldian stance, by paraphrasing Foucault and rhetorically questioning: "do you think we have really been working as hard as we have the last decade problematizing what coaches say and do just to be annoying or a nuisance?" Whereas, Roy McCree's (chapter four) narrative on his efforts to be a public sociologist and desire to confront FIFA's corrupt vice president (Jack Warner) reveals a variety of tensions and difficulties, as reflected in the chapter's sub-title "Engagement, disengagement and despair". Within other chapters the frustration with making a critical research difference pales in relation to the anger felt towards particular sources of social injustices. Brendan Hokowhitu's (chapter seventeen) sense of vile exasperation is clearly evident in his deliberately disruptive chapter concerning colonisation and indigenous 'health'. He notes:

> I freely admit I have been colonised; or rather I have failed to be decolonised. As a consequence, the feeling of 'being postcolonial' resembles a state of anxiety, a state of tension, a state of *dis*-ease that Indigenous people ingest in the pursuit of an unrealizable dream, that of decolonisation.

Billy Hawkins's (chapter five) critique of contemporary race relations in the United States similarly reveals the sickening effects of life in a racist (and sexist) country: "The disease of white supremacy and unobstructed white male privilege continues to undergird the social institutions of this nation and sport is not inoculated against the associated psychosocial damage". Despite Hawkins's acknowledgement and mapping of the recent growth of sporting research underpinned by critical race theory and the resurgence of athletic activism (e.g. Colin Kaepernick's brave and inspiring efforts in taking a knee during the national anthem), he draws a melancholic conclusion with the suggestion that the future of race relations in the United States currently appears somewhat "hopeless".

Although we have acknowledged that the feelings of research frustration and anger can be conceptualised as productive, given that they inspire transformative actions, we also note that, at times, they appear to delimit a sense of productive achievements. This is evident in several of the chapters, as the following two examples attest. In chapter nine, Louise McCuaig, Janice Atkin and Doune Macdonald discussed the construction and reception of a new critically oriented health and physical education (HPE) curriculum in Australia. The focus of the chapter was not on the victory of gaining the first ever national curriculum in Australia and, more specifically, a curriculum that is underpinned by a socio-critical perspective and a strength-based approach. In contrast, the focus was on the political difficulties of the curriculum making process and the problems of powerful voices from the biophysical sciences. The critical examination of political processes is undoubtedly important to share amongst those who aim to make a difference, as they provide illustrative evidence of how power is exercised in bureaucratic processes. This knowledge can then be drawn upon in future political negotiations.

Yet within the realm of critical research, where victories are not always readily apparent, we believe that the production of a new curriculum, with an underpinning axis of socio-critical concern, is worthy of celebration. Within this celebration we should also recognise the work of an array of critical scholars whose cumulative efforts over several decades have helped pave the way for the production of this socio-critical curriculum (e.g. Linda Bain, Patt Dodds, Miguel Fernández-Balboa, David Kirk, Chris Hickey, Ian Culpan, Doune Macdonald Richard Tinning, Sheila Scraton and Jan Wright to name but a few). Moreover, we recognise that the delivery of this curriculum within HPE settings offers further possibilities for challenging social injustices. At the least, as Richard Tinning (chapter seven) observes, this broad critical shift in research interests has encouraged recognition of the "needs of many kids who were previously alienated and/or marginalized by participation in PE classes".

In chapter three, Jayne Caudwell and Graham Spacey similarly reveal successful achievement worthy of celebration but the chapter is still tinged with a sense of frustration. They detail an intervention project, via a unique performative pedagogy, to challenge heteronormativity in UK football (soccer). The project correspondingly reflects the research trend that Cooky (2017) identified, with a shift from studying inequality to greater public engagement. Within their chapter, Caudwell and Spacey document how the project raised awareness and contributed to making a difference for those involved. Moreover, they note that the intervention project has been successfully organised each year since its inception in 2012 and its success has been dependent on university student volunteers. Despite identifying these successes, Caudwell and Spacey's last sentence reads: "it is impossible to conclude that this performative pedagogy subverts the obdurate structures of heteronormativity".

We agree that a small-scale intervention cannot subvert broadly entrenched sets of power relations, yet we also see this project as a micro-victory and therefore worthy of celebration in the face of 'obdurate structures'. As Burrows, Leahy and Wright (chapter fifteen) illustrate, social change can take place through small and repetitive actions that reveal and allow alternative ways of thinking and being. In the following sections, we reflect on several of the critical projects presented in this text and take a more positive stance to reveal how they are working to make a difference.

The value of critique

Critical research and the act of repetitive public critique can contribute to making a difference. A disparaging analysis of critical research is, however, that it is often big on critique but short on actual strategies for political intervention (see O'Sullivan, Siedentop and Locke, 1992). In other words, the value of critique, without action, is underestimated. Yet such a position fails to recognise that transformative efforts evolve through processes of critical analysis. Although Foucault's (1978) text, *The history of sexuality, volume 1*, was not a manifesto for sexual reform, Halperin (1995) asserted that it has been the "single most important intellectual source of political inspiration for contemporary AIDS activists" (p. 15). In similar respect, we suggest a 'line of flight' could be traced between Foucault's critique of sexualities, the growth of feminist poststructuralism and queer studies, and contemporary forms of activism such as the recent protests surrounding Trump's rescinding of transgender toilet protocols.

Within this text the value of critique has not been underestimated. Indeed, signs of hope, and recognition of the challenges, associated with critical analysis and critique are evident. Carolyn Pluim and Michael Gard's chapter (thirteen), as an example, makes the familiar strange by providing two critical case studies that illustrate why it is problematic to uncritically accept that schools are ideal places to prosecute public health policy. Their critical warning offers a message moving forward with respect to the need to interrogate the politics that inspired the initial 'health' interventions and the efficacy of their implementations. Pluim and Gard correspondingly offer a novel conceptual framework for reconsidering health policy implementation in schools.

Simon C. Darnell (chapter two) similarly offers ways forward for future research into the usage of sport for development and peace (SDP) objectives. Darnell cautiously concludes that the dominant manner within which SDP programs have been implemented tend not to focus on pursuing socio-cultural change but on equipping individuals to merely cope with the challenges of their existing social realities. Drawing from this critical observation, Darnell encourages SDP researchers to develop a political vision and to work with participants, partners and stakeholders, through participatory action research approaches with desire to pursue or create social change.

In a similar manner Rod Philpot, Göran Gerdin and Wayne Smith (chapter ten) offer three interacting critiques to illustrate factors that have limited the realities of a social justice agenda working effectively in PE. Through this process of critical analysis, they offer possible ways forward through identifying policies/ curricula and practices in physical education teacher education (PETE) and PE across different contexts that foreground and enact socially critical perspectives: thus, highlighting the promise of social change taking place as a result of critical research. Philpot, Gerdin and Smith conclude by stating that the strengthening of the social justice agenda in PE should not be about constructing a universal teaching model but about reaffirming an underpinning educational philosophy built on social justice, democracy and ethics.

Finally, Burrows, Leahy and Wright (chapter fifteen) provide examples of what they call 'serendipitous public pedagogical moments'. These moments, they detail, stem from the circulation of critique (e.g. fat studies literature) and how this critique allows for seemingly insignificant moments of resistance and transformation. Their pertinent example of how a 'patient' challenged a medical doctor's biomedical knowledge (and the associated power relationship between doctor/patient) to promote the promise of a more humane dialogue moving forward. Although only a singular example, it provides confirmation of how critique can filter through the webs of power that we are all enmeshed within to make a difference.

Social theory and strategies for social change

Social theory plays an integral role in the research process and in developing critique and forging critical analysis. Karl Marx (1843/2005) prophetically asserted that theory can act as a weapon for transformation as once it has "gripped the masses" it can become a "material force" that can be used to overthrow opposing material forces. More recently, Judith Butler expressed the idea that "theory is itself transformative" (2004, p. 204) as it "presupposes a vision of the world, of what is right, of what is just, of what is abhorrent, of what human action is and can be" (ibid., p. 205). In this respect, Butler positioned theory as underpinning all overt political actions. Stuart Hall (1992) acknowledged, nevertheless, that given theory is constructed in a particular socio-historic context for particular problems, there is need to reflect on the value of theoretical tools: a process that he referred to as "wrestling with the angels" (p. 280). Hall explained this phrase by suggesting that, at times, when social contexts or realities change and theory is no longer apposite, researchers need to question the semi-sacred ideas of the esteemed theoreticians. We correspondingly acknowledge:

> researchers should constantly reflect upon the theoretical tools that they adopt: do they work? Do they help produce new insights? Or do they reaffirm what is already known? In this respect, researchers need to challenge their theoretical lens, test it in new contexts and if it is found wanting be prepared to modify or search for alternative theoretical tools. (Pringle and Thorpe, 2017, p. 35)

Within this co-edited text, the critical transformative work of a number of the contributing authors has been to advocate for new theoretical directions and/or to promote or challenge thinking around existing theory. Jim Denison and Joe Mills' chapter (six) is a key example, within which they adopt a Foucauldian lens to problematize existing coach practices and challenge coaches to question their normal ways of being and doing. Their chapter highlights the benefits of thinking through a different theoretical lens.

Pirkko Markula (chapter sixteen), as a further example of the transformative power of theory, acknowledged that although there has been a growth in critical research concerning health and fitness that the central concerns and associated critiques have remained essentially the same. Moreover, she illustrated that these critiques, which have focused on the social construction of dominance within three binary sets, have not had any significant influence in the ways that commercial fitness and exercise has been constructed and practiced. To move past this "stalemate" and produce critique that enables social change, Markula advocated for greater adoption of poststructuralist theory:

> Attempts for social change need to be grounded in social theory that problematizes the power/knowledge nexus to initiate more ethical exercise practices. It is crucial, nevertheless, to encourage both thinking and moving differently if we are to create change that transcends mere adjustments to individual behavior. This type of social change is, necessarily, embedded in social theory.

In a similar manner to Markula, Chris Hickey and Amanda Mooney (chapter eleven) identified research issues within existing PETE literature and advocated for greater adoption of posthumanist theorising. Their prime concern for the recommendation of alternative ways of theorizing related to their recognition of new social problems, such as: sustainability issues in the Anthropocene, the entrenchment of neoliberalism and the associated growth of the precariat class. In relation to these problems, Hickey and Mooney specifically endorsed Rosi Braidotti's theorising with the hope that it would enable PETE scholars to create "more meaningful engagement with contemporary physical culture and the challenges and opportunities that are being ushered in amid the increased intersectionality between man and machine".

Brendan Hokowhitu (chapter seventeen) similarly drew on 'post' theorising as a tool for enacting change, yet he combined poststructural and postcolonial thought with the insights from Māori ways of knowing, to develop a unique form of indigenous theorizing. His prime aim was to gain theoretical insight into how to move forward with an intractable social issue: the scarring from colonisation. His theoretical contribution offers hope, not necessarily with challenging pervasive discourses of prejudice, but with how indigenous peoples can understand the social terrain (or comprehend their metaphysical condition) in order to have the freedom to choose to live the lives they want.

Concerning strategies for social change, the relatively sparse success for critical pedagogical approaches among physical education teachers and teacher students may relate to everyday interpretations of the term 'critical'. Being critical is often taken to be 'negative' and perhaps even hostile towards a certain practice, such as PE. Further, Håkan Larsson (chapter twelve) has experienced that school teachers are concerned about the fact that researchers typically only observe fractions of their work. Arguably, the imminent issue is that researchers will be able to see 'the whole picture'. The tension is added by the fact that researchers are often also seen as representatives of 'expertise' on their research subjects. In relation to this situation, we anticipate that the position of a *critical friend* could be a useful way forward to attract practitioners' attention to the need for critical considerations that can spearhead change. According to Costa and Kallick (1993) a critical friend is:

> a trusted person who asks provocative questions, provides data to be examined through another lens, and offers critiques of a person's work as a friend. A critical friend takes the time to fully understand the context of the work presented and the outcomes that the person or group is working toward. The friend is an advocate for the success of that work. (p. 50)

Thus, a critical friend falls between the extremes of either an 'adverse observer' and an 'uncritical admirer'. Such a position could be included in an action research approach, where teachers themselves, possibly in collaboration with researchers, become knowledge producers and change agents, rather than objects of research and receivers of answers (cf. Casey and Larsson, 2018). Critique could then be offered within "a professional relationship based on mutual regard and the willingness to question and challenge" (Creasy et al., 2004, 63).

Combining research actions with social and political interventions

Social theory can be understood as the inspiration for all politically inspired transformative actions given its capacity to operate as a heuristic device, illuminate and direct critical attention (Butler, 2004). Yet this does not mean that one can simply rest on the promotion of theory to ensure change. Moreover, we recognise that theory can illuminate but it can also obscure. In other words, as much as theory can focus our attention on select issues it has a corresponding propensity to obscure our ability to see other issues. Postcolonial scholar, Edward Said (2004), even warned that theory has propensity to obfuscate so that there is a danger that the humanities could become a "whole factory of word-spinning ... that in their jargon and special pleading address only like-minded people, acolytes, and other academics" (p. 14). Said was concerned, therefore, about the so-called fetishisation of theory and its ability to detour academics away from "the critical investigation of values, history and freedom" (p. 14).

It is in this light that we concur with Pierre Bourdieu and Loïc Wacquant (1992) who promoted the importance of a dialogue between theory and research, as they explained: "research without theory is blind, and theory without research is empty" (p. 16). In other words, the importance of testing theory in the field via empirical research and the reciprocal and circular importance of drawing upon theory to undertake research. Yet we draw from Judith Butler to acknowledge that *something* besides theory and research must also take place if we want theory/research to be more directly transformative. Butler (2004) recognised theory as underpinning all transformation yet she also emphasised the need for "interventions at social and political levels that involve actions, sustained labor, and institutionalized practice, which are not quite the same as the exercise of theory" (Butler, 2004, pp. 204–205). In other words, to strive for social transformation, Butler stressed the importance of productive connections between theory, research and political labour.

Jayne Caudwell and Graham Spacey's chapter (three), as already discussed, provides an exemplary overview of the links between theory, practice and political intervention. Mikael Quennerstedt and Louise McCuaig's chapter (fourteen) also provides a pertinent example. As inspired by the theoretical work of Aaron Antonovsky and through involvement in various research projects exploring salutogenic philosophy within HPE, they detail the political labour necessary to see the inclusion of a salutogenic model of health within Queensland's Health Education curriculum. More broadly, Quennerstedt and McCuaig emphasise that the adoption of Antonovsky's model of health within the curriculum has the capacity for producing social change "by shifting teachers' and students' attention towards those personal, social and community resources that underpin a good life, rather than simply focusing on the risks and disease that compromise healthy living".

Håkan Larsson's chapter (twelve) is also a pertinent example of working the connections between theory, research and pragmatic implementations (i.e. political labour). Through reflecting on gender issues in PE and the challenge of how to change teaching practice he devised a performative pedagogy, inspired by Markula's (2008) work on pilates, to transform understandings of gender. In designing his performative pedagogy, he drew closely from poststructural and posthumanist theorists to develop a teaching style that was designed to evoke student affect through a series of critical movement practices. Larsson has found that through dance classes that encourage queer situations, students are not told what to think but can move in a manner that allows for possibilities of lines of flight.

David Kirk (chapter eight) provides a voice of optimism through offering his critique of the history of critical pedagogy within PE. He correspondingly calls for a critical pedagogy which is more acutely focused to the issues prevalent in specific contexts with particular reference to precarity. Kirk then suggests three priorities for moving forward: these priorities focus on activist pedagogies that recognize the importance of affect (e.g. with recognition of mental health issues), professional learning for teachers that focus on specialized skills to work with young people, and networked learning communities. Through focusing on the specific problems of youth and with specific strategies to manage these issues, Kirk highlights that critical pedagogy may not solve the broader power relation problems *but* such teaching strategies can aid the relevance of PE for students and make a difference in their lives. In our view, Kirk's message is clear—do what you can in your local environment with respect to issues of social justice and you are making a worthwhile (critical) difference.

It is in this light, that we can gain an appreciation for the variety of critical projects discussed in this book, the associated forms of praxis and the difference that this research makes. Although we acknowledge that the broader sets of power relations have been slow to change and may even appear obdurate, there is a need to not despair, but retain a sense of optimism (as similar to what fueled Richard Tinning over his career). This is why we believe it is important to keep our enthusiasm for critical research, since each micro victory also creates a new set of problems to be made aware of and act on. Critical research in our view is therefore a continuing endeavor to keep the critical spirit alive and ask the question: what now needs to be addressed in the name of social justice, democracy and ethics?

Ways to move forward

If you are reading this concluding section with expectation of being provided with an erudite and novel 'research recipe' on how to make the world a better place then you will be let down: likewise, if you are looking for new revolutionary ideas on how to make a critical difference via public protest. Yet we suggest that such confessions should not be disheartening, as they indirectly indicate that what critical researchers in our fields have been doing *have* been contributing to matters of concern and social justice, *albeit slowly*. Relatedly, if one is so passionate about making a critical difference in a more expedient manner then the pathway of being a fulltime activist is likely attractive. Yet the role of critical researcher within public protest is still important. Indeed, Foucault (1991) believed that the role of critical researchers was to reveal the strengths and weaknesses of the workings of power within specific social contexts so that those who are more intimately involved in political action "could be better informed in their design of strategies and actions" (Markula and Pringle, 2006, p. 18).

In this light, and with a recognised tinge of irony, we now call for *more* of the same research in order to make a difference. More of the same, however, means: more innovation; more exploration of alternative ways of knowing; more challenging of the methodologies we employ (e.g. by asking difficult questions such as 'should quantitative research continue to be marginalised via critical researchers?'); more focus on topics of political importance; more interaction in the public sphere (e.g. as activist/scholars and circulating critique via public forums); more research in local communities as critical friends; the continued resurrection of marginalised and indigenous knowledges; the ongoing critical evaluation of our theoretical tools; the continued forging of interdisciplinary connections between the humanities and the sciences—with desire to bring a critical edge to the sciences; on-going critiques of neoliberalism within and outside of universities; and, the critical reflection of our own academic privileges while also challenging the diminution of the liberal arts/social sciences in universities. In essence, more research that aims to make more of a difference in matters of social importance.

The need for critical scholarship and public researchers is clearly warranted in today's turbulent times. Yet as Denzin and Giardina (2018) stated, there are now so many problematic political issues that it is even difficult to know what to focus on or where to begin. As evidence, they cite a range of current crises circulating in the news:

> Donald Trump. Brexit. Acts of terrorism in Europe. Syrian civil war. Gun violence and mass shootings in the United States. Horrifying hurricane damage in Florida, Puerto Rico, and the Virgin Islands. Nuclear threats by North Korea. The ongoing denial of climate change. (p. 1)

Denzin and Giardina are nevertheless at pains to point out that very real issues also challenge the existence of critical qualitative research within universities: issues related to the continued squeeze on the humanities and arts, the pressure for securing external 'research dollars', the associated push for randomised control studies (see also Saiani, 2018), the continued casualization of academia, and the ongoing marketization of universities. While, at the same time, Denzin and Giardina recognise that attacks on research knowledge, such as climate change evidence, are occurring for political purposes. In this broad respect, they implore academics to turn their critical eyes to the politics of knowledge production within their own tertiary institutes. Indeed, if we are going to strive to make a difference in broader matters of public concern, then we need to engage with our own institutional challenges to secure our ability to do so.

In the lead-up to co-editing this book we had observed how the same critical research topics were routinely re/presented at annual conferences and how these presentations tended to draw similar conclusions. Yet if we look back over a larger time scale, say the last 50 years, we can see that critical change has occurred with respect to select issues associated, as examples, with genders, sexualities, ethnicities and environmental sensibilities within sport and HPE contexts. We recognise that the pace and extent of change is never entirely satisfying, *and*, we accept that critical examination of topics of concern within sport and HPE contexts will not provide answers to the diverse set of problems that plague our globalised world. Yet, through undertaking this book project we have been reassured, to a certain extent, that our efforts can and do make differences. Indeed, the lesson we have learned, is that addressing local problems—via mapping, critique and social change interventions (see Markula and Silk, 2011)—can make a difference. And, even if these differences are small they are worth pursuing.

References

Bourdieu, P., and Wacquant, L. J. D., 1992. *An invitation to reflexive sociology*. Cambridge: Polity Press.

Butler, J., 2004. *Undoing Gender*. New York: Routledge.

Casey, A., and Larsson, H., 2018. "It's groundhog day": Foucault's governmentality and crisis discourses in physical education. *Quest*, iFirst, doi: 10.1080/00336297.2018.1451347.

Cooky, C., 2017. "We cannot stand idly by": A necessary call for a public sociology of sport. *Sociology of Sport Journal*, 34(1), 1–11.

Costa, A., and Kallick, B., 1993. Through the Lens of a Critical Friend. *Educational Leadership*, 51(2), 49–51.

Creasy, J., Smith, P., West-Burnham, J., and Barnes, I., 2004. *Meeting the Challenge: Growing Tomorrow's School Leaders*. Nottingham: National College for School Leadership.

Denzin, N. K., and Giardina, M., 2018. Introduction. In N. K. Denzin and M. Giardina, eds., *Qualitative inquiry in the public sphere* (1-15). New York: Routledge.

Foucault, M., 1978. *The history of sexuality*, Volume 1. Harmondsworth: Penguin.

Foucault, M., 1991. *Remarks on Marx: Conversations with Duccio Trombadori*. New York: semiotext(e).

Halperin, D., 1995. *Saint Foucault: Towards a gay hagiography*. New York: Oxford University Press.

Hall, S., 1992. Cultural studies and its theoretical legacies. In: L. Grossberg, C. Nelson, and P. Treichler (Eds), *Cultural studies*, 277–294. London: Routledge.

Markula, P., and Silk, M. L., 2011. *Qualitative research for physical culture*. Basingstoke: Palgrave Macmillan.

Marx, K., 1843/2005. A contribution to the critique of Hegel's philosophy of right: introduction. Available at: www.marxists.org/archive/marx/works/1843/critique-hpr/intro.htm. (Accessed: June 5, 2018).

Pringle, R., and Markula, P., 2006. *Foucault, sport and exercise: Power, knowledge and transforming the self*. London: Routledge.

Pringle, R., and Thorpe, H., 2017. Theory and reflexivity. In: M. Silk, D. Andrews & H. Thorpe (Eds.), *Routledge handbook of physical cultural studies* (32–41). Routledge: Oxford.

O'Sullivan, M., Siedentop, D., and Locke, L. F., 1992. Toward collegiality: Competing viewpoints among teacher educators. *Quest*, 44(2), 266–280.

Said, E., 2004. *Humanism and democratic criticism*. Basingstoke, UK: Palgrave Macmillan.

Saiani, P. P., 2018. Doing sociology in the age of 'evidence-based research': Scientific epistemology versus political dominance. *The American Sociologist*, 49(1), 80–97.

Index